THE ENIGMA OF ETHNICITY

The enigma of ethnicity

ANOTHER AMERICAN DILEMMA

WILBUR ZELINSKY

UNIVERSITY OF IOWA PRESS Ψ IOWA CITY

University of Iowa Press,
Iowa City 52242
Copyright © 2001 by the
University of Iowa Press

Printed in the United States
of America
Design by Richard Hendel
http://www.uiowa.edu/~uipress

The publication of this book was
generously supported by the University
of Iowa Foundation.

Printed on acid-free paper

Library of Congress
Cataloging-in-Publication Data
Zelinsky, Wilbur, 1921–
The enigma of ethnicity: another
American dilemma / by Wilbur Zelinsky.
  p.   cm.
Includes bibliographical references and
index.
ISBN 0-87745-749-2 (cloth) —
ISBN 0-87745-750-6 (pbk.)
1. United States—Ethnic relations.
2. Ethnicity—United States.
3. Pluralism (Social sciences)—United
States.   I. Title.

E184.AI Z45   2001
305.8'00973—dc21

                    00-051157

01 02 03 04 05 C
5 4 3 2 1

01 02 03 04 05 P
5 4 3 2 1

An earlier version of chapter 3, written
in collaboration with Barrett A. Lee,
appeared as "Heterolocalism: An
Alternative Model of the Sociospatial
Behaviour of Immigrant Ethnic
Communities," in the *International
Journal of Population Geography* 4
(1998): 1–18. A different version of
chapter 4 appears under the title "The
World and Its Identity Crisis," in Karen
Till, Steven Hoelscher, and Paul Adams,
eds., *Textures of Place* (Minneapolis:
University of Minnesota Press,
forthcoming, 2001).

For Gladys, now and forever

CONTENTS

In recent years ethnic issues have commanded an inordinate amount of interest in both scholarly and public discourse in the United States and many other parts of the world. The result has been a vast outpouring of literature — more, it seems, than any single individual could digest and master. It might also seem that the topic has been examined exhaustively, that we have run out of meaningful questions to ask, so that no real gaps remain in our understanding. As Abner Cohen has put it, "Ethnicity has already become the subject of such an extensive literature that there can hardly be any conceptual formulation about it not made by someone before" (1981: 307). I do not concur. If I did, I would be committing an unpardonable act of redundancy by offering in the extended essay that follows a product that would waste the knowledgeable reader's time and mine. When, several years ago, I began this study — one that has proved to be a sequel of sorts to *Nation into State* (Zelinsky 1988a) — I was motivated only by a vague, generalized curiosity, the urge to educate myself about a subject that could not be ignored by a geographer or anyone else intent upon grasping the realities of contemporary America. But as I plowed through many hundreds of books and articles, consulted with colleagues, dipped into recollections of my earlier years, and peered at landscapes in a variety of places, the realization gradually grew that something crucial has been lacking in our hefty corpus of ethnic writings, or, rather, two closely related somethings.

First, we have been afflicted with an unspoken consensus, a quite convenient one for certain analytical purposes, to the effect that ethnicity is eternal and changeless, that this primordial quiddity has always characterized virtually all complex societies. But the actuality, as I have learned to perceive it, and will emphasize relentlessly through-

out this work, is that ethnicity is a recent, time-dependent development to be found only in particular periods and places. Such a notion
may not be completely original, but other authors seem at best only
dimly cognizant of such temporality, and none has showcased it as I
have striven to do.

Then what is truly surprising is that, apart from some rare, unde-
servedly obscure exceptions, no one has paused to examine the essential character of ethnicity, to define the concept in critical fashion,
and then to explore the larger significance of this taken-for-granted
notion. The three or four scholars who have taken up the challenge
after a fashion are given their due in the final chapter. However, their
ideas and findings have suffered from an apparently complete lack of
notice in the academy, so that, in a sense, my agenda here is to con-
summate their mission, to stir up greater interest in what I consider
to be a powerfully provocative way of looking at our present-day
scene. I wish, then, as biographer and critic of ethnicity, to essay the
task by retrieving, fitting together, and bringing into sharp, original
focus a wide array of data and ideas. If I succeed, I shall have made
explicit and whole an immanent reality only hinted at previously
when we stumbled across some of its scattered fragments.

Further, by way of preface, I would like to comment on the
uniqueness of our current phase of ethnic awareness. It is always
tempting to believe that history can repeat itself. But in truth it never
can, it only seems to. The current American excitement over ethnic
issues is a case in point. There are indeed some superficial parallels
between the American experience from the 1880s through the 1920s,
when nativist passions raged fiercely in the face of major influxes of
exotic immigrants, and what has gone on since the 1950s with a great
new wave of newcomers even more "alien" in traits and appearance.
Quite predictably, we have witnessed a certain resurgence of xenophobia — drives to limit ingress, to curtail social benefits and legal
protection for the newer arrivals and their offspring, and campaigns
to make English the only permissible language. But the qualitative
differences between the two eras are deep and several.

In the first place, the flow of immigrants that crested in the early
twentieth century proved to be finite in character. It may not have

seemed possible at the time but the influx did cease abruptly with the outbreak of World War I. There then ensued a virtual moratorium with the passage of restrictive legislation in the 1920s and a relaxation of the "push factor" in the European countries that had supplied the vast bulk of the immigrants, not to mention the effects of the Great Depression and World War II. Today, in contrast, we have a greatly altered set of national and international circumstances. Barring some major, unpredictable economic or political convulsion, immigrants, refugees, and asylum-seekers will continue to enter the United States from overwhelmingly non-European sources in substantial numbers far into an indefinite future. Furthermore, what might have seemed highly unlikely a few generations ago has occurred. Uncouth and unassimilable as the strangers from eastern and southern Europe may have seemed at first, these Judeo-Christian Caucasians, or at least their children and grandchildren, did undergo intensive acculturation, ultimately becoming almost indistinguishable outwardly from old-stock citizenry. Indeed, by the 1930s, to all appearances the melting pot had worked its magic. Over most of the land — that is, all those great stretches of territory where there was little evidence of African American, Latino, or Native American minorities — it was possible to envision a perfected, socially and culturally unified nation. Thus, for the great majority of Americans, the Other had ceased to be a concern. Today, instead, it appears highly problematic whether our newest Americans, often so nontraditional in religion and general cultural heritage and so non-Caucasian in bodily aspect, will ever be accepted as full, equal partners in the national community. The fact that substantial acculturation has been going on among the Asian, Latino, Caribbean, Middle Eastern, and African newcomers fails to alleviate the difficulty in any decisive way.

Another striking distinction between past and present is that the American situation circa 1900 was a singular one. The United States was the only settler country where the absorption of unfamiliar types of immigrants posed a major policy issue. Because of exclusionary practices, it was a nonissue in Australia and New Zealand and evidently of only minimal salience in Brazil, Argentina, South Africa, and Canada. (The seemingly perpetual ethnic and communal difficulties in such areas as the Balkans, India, and Southwest Asia present a qualitatively different set of challenges.) At the present time, however, the United States is far from being alone. The Australians, Canadians, and most European countries, among others, must cope with strangers in their midst and have initiated debates not unlike those being articulated by Americans.

The growing universality of the physical juxtaposition of ethnic groups once widely separated parallels a rather less tangible development. As is happening in the United States and elsewhere, not only do we find greater territorial dispersion of the Other within the national borders but, whether in professional or menial roles or something betwixt, they have also invaded the general consciousness as never before. Images of distant, alien places and peoples permeate movies, television, popular culture, and all manner of publications on a worldwide basis. The same is true of a great range of commodities, whether authentic samples or reasonable facsimiles, that speak to us of the exotic. Moreover, increasing throngs of middle- and working-class individuals have encountered foreign destinations as tourists and have had at least superficial contact with unfamiliar ways of life. The material and mental confrontation of diverse worlds at a global scale, this ever-growing interpenetration of people, things, and perceptions, is a unique, unprecedented feature of contemporary life.

But the most remarkable divergence from earlier American practices regarding the Other is attitudinal. If dread, disdain, and marginal tolerance, the "political correctness" of yore, were once the accepted mode of dealing with the alien hordes, something approaching a total turnabout has since taken place. The official line, one widely voiced in schools and nearly all public forums, is to laud ethnic heritage, to cherish and celebrate diversity. It boggles the mind to imagine William McKinley or Woodrow Wilson touting the virtues of interracial or interethnic brotherhood and harmony, but that is exactly what we heard from Bill Clinton's bully pulpit and the mouths of countless community leaders. And this latter-day contagion of feel-good fraternity, whether mere lip service or a genuine change of heart, is not confined to the United States.

What does ethnicity have to do with all this? Quite a bit, as it turns out. The perception of ethnicity as a Good Thing is an integral part of the remarkable transformation just described. On the surface it would appear that such an enshrinement of cultural entities is an unalloyed blessing. However, closer examination of the concept of ethnicity — a central mission of this study — will leave us with a more equivocal, less cheerful judgment. But I must not anticipate a rather complex argument, and ask that the reader bear with me as I lay the groundwork for an unsettling conclusion.

The argument that follows is divided into five chapters. I am tempted to apologize for the first, which may initially strike too many readers as an arid, pedantic exercise in lexicography and casuistic quibbling as I grope for a rigorous definition of *ethnic group* and, later, *Ethnicity* (the reason for upper-case exaltation will emerge later). But please persevere; greener pastures lie beyond. As it turns out, this search for definitional precision yields rich, complex, and unexpected rewards.

The central three chapters are essentially empirical in character, each being devoted to exploring the positioning of American ethnic phenomena within one of three varieties of space. These essays may not directly address the issue of Ethnicity, but they furnish the background material needed to put it into proper context. Chapter 2 deals with the ways the attributes of ethnic/racial groups are expressed and perceived in cultural space. It does so from three perspectives: the survival or attrition of indigenous and immigrant traits under Anglo-American conditions; then, the consideration and treatment of the cultures of various "minorities" by the dominant majority; and, finally, the self-conscious assertion, the proud, outward projection of their special characteristics, by all manner of older and newer communities.

Chapter 3, perhaps the most original or innovative, is an excursion into what might be described as geographic-cum-social space. After reviewing the standard theories of assimilationism (or the "ecological model") and pluralism and finding both seriously wanting with respect to the current American scene, I propose a new model named *heterolocalism*, one that describes the geographic and social behavior of certain recent immigrant groups. That proposal is linked with another recent development: the emergence of *transnationalism* and *transnationals* as millions of migrants have begun shaping a novel form of action-space whereby ethnic groups can inhabit two or more countries simultaneously. Such behavior has begun to redefine the meaning of ethnic identity.

Chapter 4 takes us far afield in social space and through much history and prehistory as it discusses the world's recent pandemic identity crisis (Who am I? What are we?) and reviews various alternatives for assuaging the malaise. The major finding is that ethnic identity is the most consequential of all possible palliatives but falls well short of really solving our personal and collective dilemmas. Furthermore, even if everyone were encased in a solid ethnic identity, we would have made little progress in coping with the perplexities of a multi-ethnic society.

All of the preceding material prepares the reader for an assault in the closing chapter on the ultimate objective: understanding the multiple natures of multiculturalism, that most divisive and fateful of current social controversies, and its relationship to Ethnicity, and the possible ways of dealing with the challenges posed by these phenomena. For the hurried or impatient, this is the chapter I would most urgently recommend, but the prudent reader should proceed sequentially from the beginning. Any possible revelations are cumulative in character, building on what has gone before.

In creating this work, I have not associated myself with any of the recent ideologies that are de rigueur today in the more rarefied and fashionable of academic circles. Instead, my strategy has been naively inductive, to gather as much data and opinion as is practical, then to digest and brood over the material for an extended period, awaiting whatever fresh patterns, insights, and questions might emerge. I have not sought to champion, attack, test, verify, or falsify any of the isms du jour. If this be idiosyncrasy, I plead guilty, but ask merely that the reader approach my findings with the same dispassionate naiveté I have tried to employ. As far as language is concerned, I endeavor to avoid the turgidity and deadliness of too much of the prose I have been obliged to read.

The design of this inquiry and the deficiencies of this investigator are such that some interesting topics, for example, ethnic politics, are touched upon lightly or not at all. I particularly regret being able to say so little about the important issue of class. In some instances a topic is relevant, but the lacuna in treatment simply indicates a dearth of information, a cue for launching serious study. Among the items that have received ample attention by others, but are slighted here, the most conspicuous may be the economics of the ethnic enclave. The subject happens to be tangential to this study (quite apart from my lack of competence in this area), but the interested reader would do well to consult D. O. Lee (1992, 1995), Light and Bhachu (1993), Min (1988), Portes and Jensen (1987), Portes and Manning (1991), Sakong (1990), Waldinger (1996), Waldinger and Aldrich (1990), Waldinger et al. (1990), and Zhou (1992).

Although the topic is obviously germane, I say little directly about immigration (or emigration) for the simple reason that so many authors have dealt with it so thoroughly and expertly that I have nothing of value to add. Within a rich literature, the following publications are especially commendable: Bodnar (1985), Chiswick and Sullivan (1995), Daniels (1990), Dinnerstein and Reimers (1988), Higham (1984, 1990), Isbister (1996), Jacobson (1996), Jasso and Rosenzweig (1990), Kivisto (1990), Massey (1995), Millman (1997), Morawska (1990), Muller (1993), Pedraza-Bailey (1990), Portes and Rumbaut (1990), Reimers (1992), Rumbaut (1991, 1994), Takaki (1989), Ungar (1995), and Warren and Kraly (1985).

Any attempt to discuss the general ethnic phenomenon in its larger dimensions would have produced an outsized volume. In any event, the feat has already been performed admirably in Mann (1979) and Nash (1989), while there is much useful information in D. Bell (1975a), Jordan-Bychko and Domosh (1998), Ware (1931), Yinger (1985), and several articles in Thernstrom (1980).

The most glaring shortcoming in this study, its relatively parochial orientation, is intentional, but it troubles me greatly nonetheless. Quite properly, William Petersen has fumed over the issue.

There has been a flood of American writings about race and ethnicity in books, scholarly journals, and popular magazines, and it continues with no sign of abatement. Most of these works have pertained to the United States. . . . Whether excellent or poor by other criteria, most of these books and articles are parochial in the sense that no comparison is made or implied with any other real society. (1997:1)

I can muster three arguments in self-defense. It is inevitable that the United States should inspire so much of the ethnic oeuvre in light of the fact that no other country has received nearly as many immigrants or nearly so varied a mixture thereof. Secondly, even if the raw materials — detailed, penetrating accounts of the ethnic situation in all relevant lands — were available, and they are not, achieving an adequate international analysis would be a truly monumental, perhaps lifelong task and one far beyond my feeble grasp. And, finally, whenever the opportunity presents itself, I suggest the value of international and cross-cultural comparisons. Perhaps others will take the hint.

Among the items portraying the American ethnic scene in its totality, some of the most praiseworthy are Allen and Turner (1996), Buenker and Ratner (1992), Lieberson and Waters (1988), Raitz (1978, 1979), Steinberg (1989), Thernstrom (1980), and Vecoli (1970, 1985). The coverage of specific metropolises and regions is certainly spotty, but there is still much to be gained by consulting the following: for New York City, Binder and Reimers (1995), Foner (1987), Mollenkopf (1993), Salvo and Ortiz (1992), and Waldinger (1996); for Los Angeles, Allen and Turner (1997), Kelley (1993), Pearlstone (1990), and Waldinger and Bozorgmehr (1996); for Chicago, Holli and Jones (1995), Pacyga and Skerrett (1986), and Suttles (1968); for Washington, Cary (1996) and Manning (1994a); for Atlanta, Pillsbury et al. (1993) and Waldrop (1993); for Miami, Portes and Stepick (1993); for Philadelphia, Golab (1977); and for San Francisco, Godfrey (1988).

At the state level we have, for Kansas, Carman (1962); North Dakota, Sherman (1983); Texas, Murdock and Ellis (1991); and Wisconsin, Zaniewski and Rosen (1998). I must also note that, in the listing of references toward the end of this volume, I have flagged, by means of asterisks, a number of items of particular interest and importance.

How could I ever forgive myself if I failed to acknowledge gratefully the assistance rendered (sometimes unbeknownst to them) by the following persons: James Allen, Daniel Arreola, Calvin Beale, James Blaut, Irene Blevins, June Rachuy Brindel, Robert Bruegmann, Stanley Brunn, Anne Buttimer, Olivia Cadaval, George Carney, Francine Cary, Kathleen Conzen, Michael Conzen, James Curtis, Irving Cutler, Drew Dedrick, Lorraine Dowler, Gary Dunbar, Gabriel Escobar, Peter Friedman, Joel Garreau, Caroline Golab, Linda Gordon, Robert Janiskee, Terry Jordan-Bychkov, Young-Key Kim-Renaud, Michael Lacey, Barry Lee, Robert Manning, Ed Marciniak, Stephen Matthews, Donald Meinig, Ines Miyares, Carla Mulford, Timothy Oakes, Si Young Park, Jeffrey Passel, William Peterman, Marie Price, Curtis Roseman, Helen Sclair, Roberto Suro, Rick Swartz, Joseph Velikonja, Dan Walden, Morton Winsberg, Larry Wolf, Denis Wood, Joseph Wood, and two anonymous reviewers.

And now, off to the chase!

THE ENIGMA OF ETHNICITY

I COMING TO TERMS

What exactly is ethnicity? And just what do we mean when we talk about ethnic groups? Basic questions? Obviously. But we find the answers are far from obvious when we give these questions the hard look they deserve. The most productive strategy is to begin with the notion of the ethnic group.

Before setting forth on our definitional expedition, it might be helpful to acknowledge the unspoken assumptions that operate when we think, write, or utter the word "ethnic." It is something that seldom comes to the lips of the modal American gazing into a mirror, even though, as I hope to demonstrate, the term does apply, whatever his/her ancestry might be. Taken for granted is the chasm between Us and Them when we scrutinize ethnic groups and their members, rather like zoological specimens on a laboratory table. Condescension and distancing are implicit in the discreetly pejorative term *ethnic*, and, depending upon the temper of the times, *ethnics* strike us as either quaint and amusing or vaguely threatening. *Ethnic* is a word to be handled with care.

DEFINING THE ETHNIC GROUP

An awkward problem in dealing with *ethnic group* is the term itself. Of relatively recent origin or usage, it is a cumbersome academic expression and certainly forms no part of the ordinary citizen's everyday vocabulary. "There is as yet no acceptable single word in English for the phrase 'ethnic group,' no word equivalent to 'class,' 'caste,' or 'family,' to describe a group self-consciously united around particular cultural traditions" (De Vos 1975:9). This gap in our vernacular lexicon leads one to suspect, correctly as it turns out, the modernity of the concept. For lack of a suitable alternative, we are stuck with the term.

None of the possible synonyms in English or other languages — people, tribe, clan, *Volk*, society, minority, nation, nationality, brotherhood, community, cultural unit, or *ethnie* — comes close to conveying whatever meaning we apprehend, however fuzzily, upon encountering *ethnic group*.

A number of scholars have tried defining ethnic groups or have critically reviewed previous attempts (e.g., Isajiw 1974, 1975; Nash 1989:1–20; Petersen 1997:31–49; Royce 1982:17–33), so that it is hardly necessary here to replicate the efforts of the cited authors. What might be more rewarding is a close examination of the central assumptions, spoken and unspoken, that seem to undergird all the definitions. Suffice it to say that the following three randomly selected quotations represent a safe consensus, the core attributes of the ethnic group as commonly accepted by the scholarly community.

> An ethnic group is a self-perceived group of people who hold in common a set of traditions not shared by others with whom they are in contact. Such traditions typically include "folk" religious beliefs and practices, language, a sense of historical continuity, and common ancestry or place of origin. (De Vos 1975:9)

> In brief, the ethnic identity of a group of people consists of their subjective symbolic or emblematic use of any aspect of culture, in order to differentiate themselves from other groups. These emblems can be imposed from outside or embraced from within. (De Vos 1975:16)

> An ethnic group has been operationally defined by Abner Cohen as a collectivity of people who share some patterns of normative behavior and form part of a larger population, interacting with people from other collectivities within the framework of a social system. (Saran 1985:5)

Reasonable though such statements may seem at first, we find, after careful reflection, that some of their assertions, along with some omissions or unspoken implications, are subject to debate. Left unstated, for example, is the issue of magnitude. Is there some numerical threshold to be crossed before a given social entity can qualify as an ethnic group? How many hundreds or thousands of persons? And, turning to the other extreme, how many millions of heads are to be counted before a social community ceases to be an ethnic group and turns into something else? Anticipating my later, more detailed discussion, I claim that size does matter.

The definitions given above and all other similar attempts of which I am aware are silent on the often salient, sometimes urgent topics of territory and location. A glance around the contemporary world reveals many instances in which duly recognized ethnic groups identify their existence or soul in terms of some actual or hoped-for attachment to a specific parcel of the earth's surface. At the same time, however, there are other equally valid claimants for status as ethnic groups who display little or no interest in inhabiting any sort of homeland. That is certainly the case in settler countries in general and the United States in particular, where surviving aboriginal societies agitate for confirmation or reclamation of title to an ancestral patch of ground. Then there is the related question of whether a putative ethnic group must reside in concentrated fashion within a specific area or whether it is feasible for the members thereof to be scattered among many localities and still keep intact their peculiar peoplehood. The foregoing observations oblige us to ask whether a single simple geographical formula can be found that will help in defining all ethnic groups in every corner of the world and in all historical periods. The answer must be that the conventional definitions are correct in omitting territorial consideration as essential to the characterization of ethnic groups.

A more perplexing question arises when we regard the ethnic group "as a collectivity of people who . . . form part of a larger population." Such a perception is certainly widespread in the United States. We have become accustomed to equating ethnic groups (formerly designated, *inter alia*, as "nationalities" or "races") as "minorities." But this practice leads to some anomalies.[1] If, as is commonly done, we classify the millions of Mexicans or Mexican Americans residing in the United States as an ethnic group, what label do we apply to those people of Mexico who periodically commute between the two countries? The same query could be posed for Cubans in

Florida, Israelis in New York City, Iranians in Los Angeles, or any number of other ethnic groups. Is the ethnic label contingent upon what might be temporary location?

We confront the same sort of riddle even when the population in question remains in situ. When the Bengali, or Bengladeshis, formed part of British India or the initial Pakistan, few would have hesitated to categorize them as an ethnic group. But what is the proper term now that the community has attained sovereign statehood? Similarly, we have the Slovaks, recently one of several distinct ethnic groups housed within the former Czechoslovakia but now citizens of a newborn nation-state, transformed overnight from "ethnics" to what? Comparable quandaries may occur if and when such entities as the Chechens, Kurds, Sikhs, and other aspirants to fuller autonomy or outright independence were to realize their political dreams — or if the Confederacy had managed to win the American Civil War.

The preceding examples drive us toward the realization of how hard it is to draw a meaningful distinction between ethnic group (or *ethnie*) and nation except on the dubious basis of political status. The relationships between the two concepts have been close and complex as they have developed historically (Calhoun 1993). Incidentally, the terms *ethnie* and *nation* are etymologically parallel, however much they may have diverged in ordinary usage, the one derived from the Greek, the other from Latin. We can slice this definitional Gordian knot by simply confessing to the absence of any genuine inherent difference between the more or less perfected nation-state and the ethnic group. Indeed several of the more advanced and successful modern states have deliberately set about fabricating a synthetic national identity, a set of cultural norms coincident with their territory, and submerging any antecedent local particularities into a standardized ethnic unity where none had previously existed.

Thus, although none of these projects has ever been totally consummated, we can speak seriously today of virtually the entire native-born population of France as comprising a French ethnic group and advance similar claims for Great Britain, Germany, Italy, Sweden, Japan, Israel, and, perhaps less confidently, for Mexico, Brazil, or Iran. But the most spectacular example, despite its improbable genesis, has been the United States, a country that has invented itself out of a medley of old and new ingredients (Zelinsky 1988a). The American national, that is ethnic, character is unique, internally pervasive, and instantly recognizable by all outsiders. People, ethos, and territory are one. But, of course, we must also acknowledge the fact that ethnic entities can inhabit a multilayered conceptual space. Below the transcendent all-American ethnic essence, within a hierarchy of identities, there dwell lower levels of "hyphenated" groups. Indeed, were this not so, there could be no excuse for this study.

The same program, namely, the knitting together of a sovereign state with some distinctive ethnic group, has also operated in reverse. In the immediate aftermath of both world wars, the Wilsonian doctrine of reshaping international boundaries so as to conform with presumed ethnic realities dominated the minds and actions of decision makers. That, at least, was the practice followed in Europe and in certain Asian examples. The severing of Pakistan and the dismemberment of Yugoslavia are in accord with this doctrine, while the recent disintegration of the Soviet Union and Czechoslovakia also echoes the Wilsonian ideal, though with less bloodshed. But, whichever the direction of policy, all too frequently the results of trying to effect a partnering of political state with ethnic group have been disappointing. Thus, for example, we have witnessed the flawed efforts of Canada, Indonesia, India, the Philippines, Sri Lanka, Guatemala, Guyana, and China.

In summary, then, the generalized claim that an ethnic group must necessarily form part, presumably a minority, of a grander population is unacceptable. Although it may apply in a majority of situations, in others the ethnic group is itself the larger population, or even virtually the totality of all inhabitants, however that outcome may have come to pass. But however interesting such observations may be, we still find ourselves far from a definitive definition of the ethnic group.

Left unstated in the standard definitions is the intersection, in a number of instances, of social caste with ethnic group (Glazer 1983: 239–240). Although India far outdistances all other countries in the complexity of its caste system, few of the vast array of its caste communities clearly qualify as ethnic groups. But a quite different situation has prevailed in South Africa with its Cape Coloured and Black populations, in the African American community of the United States, or the dual, caste-ridden societies and ethnic cultures of New Zealand, Mexico, Guatemala, Peru, and Ecuador, or the triune societies of Trinidad, Guyana, and Malaysia (and perhaps the emergent German-Turkish or French–North African situations in Europe). The barriers between groups and the subsequent intensification of ethnic peculiarities are based primarily on perceived racial identities. However, perceived racial heterogeneity does not inevitably result in well-defined castes or ethnic groups. Brazil is the most outstanding of exceptions. In any case, the conclusion must be that, again, as with political status, the existence of caste or racial categories is neither a necessary nor a sufficient element in working up a robust definition of ethnic groupdom.

So much has been written on the relevance of language to ethnic identity that citations would be superfluous. Little can be added here except to note that linguistic affiliation, like the preceding items, fails to serve as *the* universal criterion for defining ethnic groups. However, it does perform admirably in too many instances to enumerate fully. Thus, in such examples as Hungary, Lithuania, Malta, Iceland, Armenia, Korea, Japan, Greece, Finland, and the Malagasy Republic, for all practical purposes state, ethnic group, and language are coextensive and interchangeable (despite whatever emigration may occur). Similarly, in such cases as those of the stateless Basques, Kurds, Catalans, and Boers, language and ethnic affiliation are synonymous. Something of the same situation also prevails within India, where a number of linguistic communities, some of which control the republic's constituent states, are fiercely aware of their ethnic distinctiveness.

Also to be noted are instances where dialects of multinational languages are markers of group identity. Thus the local spoken versions of English enable one to recognize readily enough members of the Australian community (speakers of "strine"), or the Irish, Scottish, Jamaican, and, sometimes, African American. In like fashion, the two distinctly different French patois prevalent in Quebec and Haiti are emphatic indicators of the ethnic individuality of the two communities. National variants of Castilian Spanish permit the canny listener to decide who is native to Mexico as opposed to Argentina or to Puerto Rico rather than Chile. But all the same, it is obvious that, critical though it may be in many cases, language cannot function as a universal criterion for specifying ethnic groups. The Barbadian in London with complete command of the queen's English cannot automatically shed her ethnic label, nor can the college-educated Cherokee who happens to be monolingual in American English.

Religion is another attribute that operates powerfully to set apart an interesting minority of ethnic groups. Coming readily to mind are such examples as the Druze and Maronites of Lebanon, the Tibetans with their special brand of Buddhism, Armenians, Georgians, Sikhs, the Moros of Mindanao, and, if we admit their ethnic status, the Mormons of Utah. Note also how a particular form of Roman Catholicism helps make the Irish Irish. The most widely cited case, of course, is that of the Jews, past or present, in eastern Europe, Russia, North Africa, and elsewhere. But, again, we must conclude that, just as with language, religion is not always available as a marker of ethnic identity.

Language and religion are not the only cultural attributes conducive to ethnic cohesion, though they certainly rank high in occurrence. It is also possible to exploit dress, music, foodways, literature, and real or imagined history as the adhesive that binds together candidates for ethnic fraternity. But there is another, more problematic though scarcely ubiquitous, criterion that has been invoked all too often: race. All the cultural elements noted above are patently aspects of learned behavior, ways of doing and thinking that we acquire individually or collectively within a social setting. In contrast, in the case of race, we have suffered from two common misperceptions that, taken together, effectively eliminate the elements of choice and nurture: first, that there exist a certain number of biologically distinct, separate races within the human species, groups defined by descent, that can be identified and characterized with scientific exactitude;

and, second, that there is a meaningful correlation between racial identity and mental — and thus ultimately cultural — attributes.

The first of these notions was widely accepted by scholars and laypersons alike until rather recently, indeed ever since the idea of the racial division of humankind "was fully conceptualized and became deeply imbedded in our understandings and explanations of the world" roughly three hundred years ago (Hannaford 1996:6). Built into most of these formulations, explicitly or otherwise, is a hierarchical arrangement of racial types, a rank ordering in terms of mental, moral, and other qualities presumed to originate from the vagaries of biological evolution, environmental conditioning, or divine will.

After decades of effort during which many classificatory schemes were proposed, then rejected, physical anthropologists have finally admitted defeat. It has proved impossible to arrive at a set of quantifiable morphological and physiological features whereby we can unequivocally compartmentalize all human beings into a small array of discrete races or subspecies (Shipman 1994). The truth is that *Homo sapiens* is a thoroughly intermixed species, and becoming more so with each passing day. The only possible exceptions — and they are literally marginal and probably facing extinction — are communities that have been physically and socially isolated for many generations, groups such as the Ainu, Inuit, Lapps (Sami), or the San of southwest Africa. If some may argue for at least a superficial appearance of physical distinctiveness in the case of the relatively isolated Japanese, Koreans, or Polynesians, all the evidence suggests that they too, like nearly all of us, are products of hybridization.

Perhaps the best way to summarize the current status of racial theory among knowledgeable scientists is with the following quotation:

New discoveries have so fundamentally challenged the superstructure, substructure, and terminology of biological science that any scientific analysis which includes raciation must be flawed because it arises — like Georg Stahl's phlogiston theory, Johann Blumenbach's formative force, and August Weismann's germ-plasm theory — from *a priori* assumptions. Such analysis is much more concerned with maintaining the postulates of past classifications and nomenclatures than with pursuing scientific explanations of the awful chaos of human variability. (Hannaford 1996:7)

But whatever the new scientific consensus may be, the belief that races of human beings really do exist and exhibit vital differences remains alive and vigorous among a clear majority of the world's inhabitants today. In terms of practical consequences, race as something collectively perceived, as a social construct, far outweighs its dubious validity as a biological hypothesis. In popular parlance the term has often been bandied about carelessly in such usages as "French race" or "Russian race," but without visible harm to anyone. But the situation can become ugly when dominant segments of a population attribute some genuine biological causation to the alterity of suspect communities, when there is a conflation of ethnic and racial identities. It was not too long ago that many Britons and Americans truly believed the Irish were a race apart or that immigrants into the United States from southern Europe were not regarded as authentic Caucasians (Omi and Winant 1986:64–65; Pavalko 1980). The most notorious example is that of the Jews, whom many persons to this day characterize as a specific race, as well as a religious or ethnic community.

We have already touched briefly on the racial aspects of castes that happen to be distinct ethnic entities within complex societies. But there are also instances of casteless nations that are perceived by themselves to be both racially and ethnically a cut above all foreigners.[2] Such a matching of ethnic character and belief in racial excellence can detected among the Vietnamese and high-caste Hindus. The Anglo-Saxon delusion among the English and WASPs and the credulity among some Germans as to the nobility of their Nordic ancestry have had powerful political and social consequences.

The interconnections between socially constructed racial and ethnic identities are immensely important in the United States (not to mention other multiethnic countries), where we "recognize the racial dimension present in *every* identity, institution, and social practice" (Omi and Winant 1986:68; Winant 1995); and we shall delve deeper into these bondings at a later point. For the present, suffice it to note that, until quite recently, there were vehement, overt expressions of dread and hatred on the part of Anglo-Americans toward all "alien" racial/ethnic communities, most viciously toward African Americans but certainly not sparing Native Americans, Latinos, and the various Asian groups (Wu 1982).

The preceding discussion generally ratifies, with some reservations, that portion of the standard definition that stresses the salience of "religious beliefs and practices, language, a sense of historical continuity, and common ancestry or place of origin." But we dare not overlook a crucial distinction between race and any of the several cultural elements that can contribute to defining the ethnic group. Specifically, none of those attributes is subject to anything so virulent and ineradicable as racism (Shohat and Stam 1994:18–25). Briefly defined, racism may be considered to be a strongly held belief in the biological (and hence cultural) superiority (or inferiority) of one's "racial" group and thus the devaluation of lesser "breeds" as questionably human or even subhuman.[3] But a more comprehensive definition, one with far-reaching implications, is this:

> By "racism" is meant ideas, systems of thought, institutional practices, and all behavior that deterministically ascribe fixed roles and negatively evaluated group characteristics (moral, intellectual, cultural) to peoples on the basis of selected physical attributes, whereby their oppression and exploitation are legitimized and perpetuated. (San Juan 1992:2–3)

Racism must not be confused with xenophobia or ethnocentrism (a quite recent coinage, incidentally).[4] In any event, nonracial antagonisms are potentially curable, even though the process may entail much time, agony, and luck. Who could have foreseen the current level of cordiality between such formerly bitter antagonists as the French and Germans, Americans and Japanese, or Irish Americans and WASPs? Religious bigotry, intense and murderous though it may become, exists on a different plane from racism. Conversion of individuals or groups is always an option, and reconciliation between contesting creeds has been known to happen. Linguistic chauvinism is another troublesome phenomenon, and tempers do flare over language disputes, but people can learn foreign tongues or how to tolerate them, and, taking the long view, whatever crises may arise are transient. But racism is not a transient thing. Its superficial symptoms may be papered over or cosmeticized, yet its essence penetrates so deeply into conscious and subconscious thought, into the core emotions of modern societies, that prospects for eradication are remote. In the final chapter we will examine some of the implications of this stubborn reality as they impinge upon the evolving ethnic dimensions of American life.

Ethnic Identification

By viewing ethnic/racial groups, as we have just done, on a rather academic level, adopting the perspectives of cultural anthropologists and geographers, we may have inched closer toward the truly meaningful definition being sought in this chapter. However, a more penetrating shaft of light might be directed at the matter by looking at the practicalities of ethnic and racial identification as they are played out in the theater of the real-life world. In our late modern and possibly postmodern societies, governmental agencies, other corporate entities, and single human beings find it necessary or convenient to recognize or contrive ethnic and racial categories and then match communities and individuals to such concepts. By seeing just how this is done, we push closer to the heart of our definitional quandary and begin to glimpse its possible resolution. If the following discussion focuses largely on the United States, the questions at hand certainly bedevil many other countries.

The classification of populations into presumably meaningful ethnic and racial categories by official data-gathering bodies is a relatively late development.[5] The earliest national censuses in such European states as Great Britain, France, and Sweden avoided the problem by simply assuming a homogeneous citizenry. The American situation was different, initially because of a constitutional mandate and later because of the increasing diversity of the population. Race has been the primary issue. When, after bitter debate, the 1787 Constitutional Convention reached the excruciatingly Solomonic decision that a Negro slave should be counted as only three-fifths of a person for purposes of congressional representation, the enumeration of such fractional human beings became a political necessity. Consequently, the slave population was duly enumerated every ten years from 1790 through 1860. In addition, although it was not as politically urgent, "Free Negroes" comprised another statistical category for which heads were counted — an illustration of how unbridgeable the divide between whites and blacks has been for at least the past two hundred years.

Before and for several decades after Emancipation, racial classifications were made by the enumerator. The formula of "one drop of blood" was almost invariably adopted. That is, anyone known to the enumerator or community to have an African ancestor, however remote, would automatically be designated as a Negro. (The fact that the population so distinguished from the Euro-American might also be considered to be an ethnic group was not clearly perceived in earlier times.) The Census Office devised some rather bizarre subcategories for the African American population over the years, reaching a climax in 1890 when statistical tables included the number of blacks, mulattos, quadroons, and octoroons. But however dark or light the complexion, individuals socially recognized as being wholly or partially African in descent comprised a distinct caste as well as a statistical entity. During the early years of the republic, Native Americans languished in a censual limbo. Enumerators made no effort to track down and count the "tribal" groups or even to recognize those "civilized" persons who had undergone some degree of assimilation.

As the apparent ethnic/racial diversity of the American population kept growing markedly from the 1840s onward and, rather recently, as the political and material, as well as psychological, rewards of official designation as a racial group have expanded substantially, decision makers dealing with such matters within the federal bureaucracy have confronted insuperable quandaries (Anderson and Fienberg 1995; Edmonston and Schultze 1995; Evinger 1995; S. M. Lee 1993; Wright 1994).[6] Because of changing perceptions, conflicting claims, and differential success in lobbying efforts, the racial classifications appearing on census forms have varied significantly from one decennial enumeration to the next since the late nineteenth century.

One generalization does emerge. There has been profound, hopeless confusion between the two concepts of race and ethnic identity. In the words of Sharon Lee (1993),

> it is apparent that the racial classifications offered on census schedules are not classifications of race, defined sociologically. Instead, we observe a medley (indeed we might emphasize that it is a motley medley) of racial and ethnic terms. (86). . . . Census classifications are a taxonomic nightmare, where racial and ethnic categories are mixed together. This represents more clearly than anything else the political and ideological negotiations that underlie the decision-making process by which groups come to be defined as races or ethnic groups, and which groups get listed in census schedules. (91)[7]

Many of the so-called racial categories arrived at through these negotiations are highly questionable and sometimes downright absurd, anthropologically. Thus Hindus were classified as a race in 1930 and 1940, while a recent census would have us believe that Filipinos constitute a valid morphological division of humankind and that there are meaningful racial distinctions to be made among Samoans, Tongans, and Hawaiians, or among all the officially recognized Native American "tribes."

But the ultimate in perplexity is reached in handling the second largest of American "minorities," those persons labeled, *inter alia*, as Hispanics or Latinos. For some time, the census has not been able to settle definitively upon the racial identity of Puerto Ricans or Mexicans. And what to do currently with all those millions of actually quite diverse residents not only from Mexico but from Central America, South America, the Spanish Caribbean, and Iberia (Cresce et al. 1992 : 18–30; Farley 1990)? Are we to classify them as a linguistic community, a racial or ethnic entity, or as belonging to a geographic category, that is, by country of origin? The temporizing solution as of 1990, one that pleases no one and irritates many, has been to create a unique classificatory pigeonhole: "persons of Hispanic origin." Within that umbrella term, the persons counted are parceled out into some five racial categories and also distinguished by country of origin.

In contrast to the tortuous history of official racial designations in the United States, the federal establishment has never essayed any direct taxonomy of ethnic groups, although it has generated much relevant information while flirting with the notion. The first six of the decennial censuses collected no data on nationality or place of birth. By 1850, however, with a massive, ongoing influx of Irish, German, and other immigrants and the annexation of much of northern Mexico and its non-Anglo inhabitants, the wisdom of gathering information for characterizing a polyglot population seemed obvious. Beginning in that year and consistently thereafter, the census has sought to ascertain the nativity of Americans by country of origin and, frequently, of their parents as well. Such a rough-and-ready approach to ethnic ascription may work well enough for persons arriving from such countries as Norway, Portugal, or the Netherlands, but it has proved most unsatisfactory for former residents of the multiethnic Russian empire, Austria-Hungary, Belgium, and Canada.

A variety of ethnically relevant questions concerning mother tongue and language usage has also appeared on census schedules, but, because of a politically timid interpretation of the First Amendment, the decennial census has never quizzed the populace about its religious affiliations or practices.[8] This abstention has resulted most notably in the lack of any official data on the numbers or attributes of Jews, but also in a dearth of information on the religious/ethnic identity of immigrants from Lebanon, India, Ireland, Yugoslavia, and other religiously heterogeneous lands.

As ethnic issues have become increasingly prominent in political and public discourse in recent years, the Bureau of the Census has striven to improve the range and reliability of the relevant data. Given the existence of a fearfully complex reality, however, the task is more than merely challenging; it is, in the final analysis, impossible.[9] One can only aspire to useful approximations (Goldscheider 1992; McKenney and Cresce 1992). "Unfortunately, the Bureau does not know how to conduct a scientific ethnic census. That should not be surprising, because social science has yet to offer validated methodological instruction" (Lowry 1982:42).

The expedient adopted by the bureau in 1980, 1990, and 2000 has been to ask individuals to identify their ancestry and that of their family members, with options available for those who do not select a single answer. The rationale for this strategy is that

> ethnic identity cannot be established by objective criteria. We therefore accept that an individual's ethnicity is whatever he [*sic*] says it is. The Bureau's job is to elicit self-identification and then to group the responses into recognizable categories that (a) are mandated for federal civil rights enforcement, (b) satisfy the more vocal ethnic lobbies, and (c) provide enough continuity with past census statistics to satisfy social scientists engaged in longitudinal analysis. (Lowry 1982)[10]

The introduction of the ancestry question has only partially solved the difficulties faced by the bureau and by American society in general in coping with ethnic issues, although it has certainly served up a cornucopia of useful and interesting material.[11] A persistent problem results from the fact that, despite heroic efforts by census professionals, the wording of instructions and the specific examples given regarding the items on race, Hispanic identity, and ancestry all too often confuse or mislead respondents. Perhaps the most flagrant example is that of Brazilians and other Portuguese-speaking communities, including the Portuguese, Cape Verdeans, and Azoreans, who discovered upon encountering the ancestry question in 1990 that the only box they could possibly check was "other Spanish/Hispanic," a choice that made little sense to people who do not speak Spanish (Margolis 1994:252–257). As a result,

> the 1990 census counted 94,023 foreign-born Brazilians living in the United States, with 37,817 living in the Northeast. This is almost certainly a significant undercount. . . . Even the most conservative estimates of the Brazilian population in various regions of the Northeast and in the United States as a whole suggest an undercount ranging from 33 percent to over 80 percent. (Margolis 1994:256)

But greatly overshadowing the Brazilian debacle is the perennial mystery of how many Native Americans reside in the United States.

Continuing a trend that had emerged some years earlier, the increase in numbers reported by the census — from 1,479,000 in 1980 to 2,056,000 in 1990, a gain of 44 percent — far exceeds what is demographically credible. In any event, "depending on how American Indians are defined [and how growth in ethnic pride emboldens candidates for such status] population estimates can range from less than 1.0 million to nearly 7.0 million" (Snipp 1986:237; also see Quinn 1990 and Sutton et al. 1993).

A great many conscientious Americans whose mixed European ancestry extends back several generations were genuinely baffled by the ancestry question and responded with "unknown" or the vague term "American." "We may now be in an era of optional ethnicity, in which no simple census question will distinguish those who identify strongly with a specific European group from those who report symbolic or imagined ethnicity" (Farley 1991:411). Euro-American partners in a "mixed" marriage might be able to characterize themselves, but "we are also reasonably confident that part of the increase in the 'unknown' category reflects genuine social change such that parents have no sense of what to label their children even if they can describe themselves in ethnic terms" (Lieberson and Waters 1993:443; see also Lieberson and Waters 1986:79).

Of course not everyone has been eager to greet the census enumerator. The undercounting of ethnic and racial minorities, especially in the inner city, despite zealous exertions by the bureau, remains a persistent, worrisome problem with obvious political and social implications (Whitford 1993). Especially troublesome has been the understandable reluctance to be tallied on the part of illegal, undocumented immigrants or sojourners (including many Europeans and Asians, in addition to the higher-profile Latin Americans), despite the bureau's ironclad pledge of confidentiality. We can only speculate how greatly such avoidance distorts official figures or our understanding of the ethnic geography and sociology of the nation. But some insight into the magnitude of the problem is available from the fieldwork of Sarah Mahler (1996), who observed, interviewed, and quite actively involved herself in the lives of Latinos, primarily Salvadorans but also Peruvians and other South Americans, in a certain

Long Island neighborhood. "An alternative enumeration of Salvadorans I performed on Long Island . . . found that the Bureau of the Census had undercounted the Salvadorans in my neighborhood by over 50 percent" (17).

Even if we assume complete and accurate responses to the ancestry and related questions, some serious pitfalls may still be encountered in their interpretation and eventual publication. Thus we have in an article provocatively entitled "Are the Armenians Really Russians?" a detailed, not entirely laudatory, critique of how the bureau categorized 1980 ancestries for persons of European origin (Magocsi 1987). Even more of a conundrum is the problem of classifying the (seriously undercounted) racially ambiguous Cape Verdeans (Machado 1981). Given their mixed European and African ancestry, are they merely to be thrust into the African American category, or do they merit membership in a separate ethnic slot within the broader class — of which, African or European? — or as a subgroup under the heading of Portuguese?

Assuming again, for the sake of argument, perfect responsiveness on the part of the population, as well as unassailable anthropological logic and sensitivity among those in the bureau who process and publish information on racial and ethnic identity, would we really be much further along in the pursuit of definitional closure? Could we then specify genuine social groups and parcel out our 275 million or so Americans into compartments that are more than conceptual abstractions? Probably not. The recent self-assignment by individuals to ethnic/racial categories of their own choosing or of bureaucratic devising tells us precious little about the strength of affiliation, or lack thereof, and even less about their possible involvement in the life and activities of what may or may not be a functioning ethnic community.

By the late twentieth century the phenomenon of ethnic/racial identification had become quite different from what it was not many years before. The transition was from an era of "compulsory ethnicity" to the contemporary practice of "ethnicity by consent" (Lal 1983). Previously there was seldom much doubt about the cultural classification of individuals and families. The community at large would inform the undecided in no uncertain terms, by word or deed, of their proper station in society. If you were not a regular American, then you were unquestionably labeled a German, Irishman, Swede, Dago, or Bohunk (regardless of what you might consider yourself to be in the Old Country) or a "darky," heathen Chinee, Mexican, savage redskin, or some other instantly recognizable type of creature by virtue of appearance and behavior. And claiming "half-breed" status would not help much.

Nowadays, following some remarkable shifts in personal and collective sensibilities, not to mention the deeper, fundamental restructuring of society and economy, selecting or retaining an ethnic identity is increasingly a matter of individual choice or of optimizing benefits. Recently quite a few scholars have come to the realization that

> whereas the *old* ethnicity in America represented localism and the lack of knowledge of choice, the *new* ethnicity presupposes both self-consciousness and choice. Ethnicity, in fact, serves as a buffer, frequently self-proclaimed, between the individual and the impersonal city or nation-state. As a check on the depersonalization process of modern metropolitan life, people collect eccentricities, of which ethnicity is one of the most acceptable today. (Schuchat 1981:93)

Or, in the same vein,

> to one degree or another, everyone [now!] has many identities; all persons are peripheral to several cultures and subcultures; in some respects, each of us is a marginal man. Persons with a particular attribute that marks them as units in a statistical aggregate have more than one identity, so that the presumed unity is only partial. Yet the process of defining an ethnos is often ignored by those who collect or use ethnic data. (Petersen 1997:273)[12]

A postethnic perspective challenges the right of one's grandfather or grandmother to determine primary identity. Individuals should be allowed to affiliate or disaffiliate with their own communities of descent to an extent that they choose, while affiliating with whatever nondescent communities are available and appealing to them. (Hollinger 1995:116)

Under such circumstances, as suggested by these authors and others, not only is a man or woman free to engage in identity shopping, but the choice need not be immutable. Whatever ethnic role is adopted may be contingent upon place, social milieu, or even whim. Indeed rapid, frequent changes in identity — "altercasting," to use Aubrey Bonnett's (1990) promising neologism — can be virtually automatic in a manner analogous to language switching among persons fluent in multiple languages or dialects. But one need not subscribe to extreme doctrines concerning fluidity and ephemerality of identities espoused by the more doctrinaire postmodernists. Altercasting can result from the confluence of external forces and personal agendas. Perhaps no group better exemplifies this transactional, contingent situation than does that of the black Haitians, whose affiliations depend upon the constituency to which they are relating (Laguerre 1984:157–158). Thus

some West Indian professionals, finding themselves cast in the black role, may attempt to employ the more profitable universal human being identity, or extremely talented meritocrat, doctor, actor, lawyer, etc. . . . These are the ethnics who would avoid at all costs living in ethnic suburban or urban areas and utilizing ethnic cues. And there are others, those who may assume the ethnic West Indian identity before a partisan West Indian audience, a black identity when addressing Afro-Americans, and the larger universal identity (all god's people, human beings, one of humankind, Americans) when facing members of the dominant group. (Bonnett 1990:157)

There are many other good examples, but an especially intriguing one is that of the families of male Punjabi farmworkers in the Imperial Valley who have married non-Punjabi (usually Mexican) women; the members thereof exhibit plasticity in ethnic self-definition, once again depending upon the immediate social or legal situation (Leonard 1992).

Another aspect of ethnic self-definition, one that has received less attention from investigators than it merits, is one's placement within a hierarchical framework of nested segments, the vertical dimension, so to speak, as illustrated in the following examples. This placement differs from horizontal siting – for example, Québecois versus Anglo-Canadian, Albanian versus Greek. "The nested segments that make up ethnic consciousness need not exclude one another and typically do not. For example, a person's ethnic identity simultaneously encompasses being European, Italian, Tuscan, and paisano, although one of them normally predominates in a given role" (Light 1981:71). Or, as a geographer writing in Great Britain has noted, "it is the ethnicity of others that makes us aware of our own. Because ethnicity is many layered and because the ethnicity of others is many layered, the degree to which ethnicity is displayed depends in part on the other actors. I may be Welsh in England, British in Germany, and European in Thailand" (Peach 1983:123).

In searching for a truly rigorous definition of the ethnic group we have seen that the externally imposed official criteria — often quite artificial, arbitrary, or politically motivated — are of limited value. Resorting to the individual level, to the choices either transmitted from kith and kin or arrived at by exercising free will, is a rather more fruitful strategy. But, again, there are severe limitations. It appears that today's ethnic group is a porous entity that can have multiple strata of meaning, that persons can cross and recross its boundaries frequently and with impunity, so that we are still left in the dark as to just what it is that they are affiliating with or disaffiliating from.

Intermarriage and Its Sequelae

An already vexed situation becomes even more muddled when we begin to consider the ever more insistent phenomenon of intermarriage involving ethnically or racially identifiable individuals.[13] Concerning its growing importance there can be no dispute (Fuchs 1990:327–331), although sociologists tended to ignore its significance in the past (Hirschman 1991:4).

> Intermarriage was extensive for descendants of all major European ancestry groups. . . . It was so common in the postwar era

that by 1980 the vast majority of Americans had relatives, through birth or their own marriage, from at least two different ethnic backgrounds. Only one-fifth of husbands and wives born in 1950 came from the same single ethnic ancestry (outside of the South, only 15 percent). (Fuchs 1990:327)

As a historical generalization, the incidence of "interracial" marriages has always lagged well behind the virtual panmixia that has developed within the greater Euro-American/Judeo-Christian community. But although firm statistics will forever elude us, it is obvious that there has always been a significant amount of mating among persons of different "races" in the United States without benefit of clergy, in the form of temporary liaisons, concubinage, and even violence. Recently, however, we see many signs of a persistent upward, probably accelerating trend involving Asian-Caucasian, Hispanic–non-Hispanic, and black-nonblack pairings and all other possible permutations (Lopez and Espiritu 1990:219; Posadas 1981; Sandefur and McKinnell 1986; Shinagawa and Pang 1988; Sung 1990; Tinker 1973; D. W. S. Wong 1998a, 1998b).[14] Thus, for example, by 1980, 31.5 percent of all Chinese marriages involved a Caucasian spouse (M. G. Wong 1989:87). Quite predictably, it has been shown that rates of intermarriage are negatively correlated with degree of residential segregation and distance between potential partners (Peach 1980), but positively related to socioeconomic status, level of acculturation, and, at least for the Chinese, recency of arrival (M. G. Wong 1989).

It would be reasonable to expect that such cross-ethnic/racial marriages might well lead to the dilution and eventual extinction of certain groups (or, as noted below, the creation of some utterly novel social entities). And indeed that is a culmination clearly within sight for the progeny of the Caucasian immigrants arriving before the mid 1920s as they fuse into a single Euro-American mass (Ibson 1981; Lieberson and Waters 1988; Warner and Srole 1945). As for the impact of intermarriage on more recent, largely non-European stock, we must wait and see.

But there are at least two ethnic groups for whom recent and prospective developments may defy expectations: Japanese Americans and Jewish Americans. The incidence of exogamy for both communities has been high, accounting for more than half of Japanese marriages recently (Kikumura and Kitano 1973; Mass 1992; Tinker 1973). The steadily mounting percentage has occasioned much vocal anguish as to whether Japanese cultural (and religious) integrity can be maintained. But, surprisingly enough, mixed marriages do not necessarily signal loss of Japaneseness or Jewishness among the offspring. "The level of involvement in the ethnic community of the intermarried [Japanese Americans] still far exceeds that of third-generation European ethnic group members" (Fugita and O'Brien 1991:13). "How the offspring will define themselves remains to be seen. However, one clue is offered in that some, now entering universities, rather than trying to 'pass,' seem to be taking pride in their dual heritage and showing particular interest in things Japanese" (P. I. Rose 1985:193).

A parallel situation has been discerned in studies of Jewish-gentile marriages. Thus one investigator notes that such unions frequently result in the conversion of the gentile spouse and a revitalization of Judaism or Jewish identity (Toll 1991:156, 161–162). Another scholar, reporting on her work on the Denver Jewish community, claims that "despite the barriers the Jewish community has erected to inhibit the entrance of others, more than a fourth of the [mixed] couples in this study persist in their efforts to raise their children Jewish" (Judd 1990:264).

Such unusual detours from the standard path of assimilation for the offspring of such unions — and it is difficult to think of other examples — might be ascribed to the social history of the groups in question. "A critical difference between European ethnic groups that have failed to retain ethnic community solidarity and those groups, such as the Jews and Japanese, that have maintained a high degree of solidarity is that, in contrast to the cultural orientation of peasant village life, the latter came to the United States with a strong sense of peoplehood" (Fugita and O'Brien 1991:36).

The confluence of two important trends — a substantial influx of non-European immigrants and the growing incidence of interethnic and "interracial" matings — engendered a phenomenon that caught social scientists, government, and the general public off guard in the

1990s. We now have a young population of mixed ancestry too large to be ignored, one that cannot be stowed away conveniently within preexisting categories. It is truly a situation without precedent. There have been cases of modern hybrid populations that have realized their own sort of coherence and social solidarity by virtue of spatial and/or social segregation and governmental policy, instances such as Canada's Métis and South Africa's Cape Coloured. In the American past, all persons of black-white, black-Indian, or black-white-Indian derivation were routinely designated as Negroes. Other combinations, including Asian-Caucasian, aboriginal-Caucasian, Hispanic–non-Hispanic, or "triracial isolates" (Daniel 1992) were too small in magnitude or too inconspicuous to cause much social or political anxiety.

The challenge today is the existence of a not inconsiderable, increasingly vocal, if ill-defined, company of persons who style themselves as being of "mixed race" while not joining ranks with any aggregation of their forebears. The racial/ethnic blends in question are of every conceivable variety, but none has coagulated out of this confusion into a sharp, recognizable entity, nor does there seem to be much inclination to move in that direction. Neither does a merger with the dominant Euro-American community seem likely in the foreseeable future. The nation seems unprepared for this unprecedented social reality, while the members of this novel variegated minority have only just begun to assert themselves.

In the last decade, a movement has begun among people of multiracial and multiethnic descent, defining and asserting themselves through political and social activists, through scholarship and education, and through self-expression in the arts. In doing this, multiracial people are challenging what this country has traditionally seen as being "race" and "ethnicity," "culture" and "community." By insisting that they exist and that they are what they are, multiracial and multiethnic people have blurred the boundaries between groups. Of course, this upsets a lot of people who depend on group boundaries for privilege or political or economic interest or sense of self, and it worries those who have static, undynamic ways of defining cultural and group pride and preservation. (Nakashima 1992:177–178)

The growing presence of this baffling mélange of the unclassifiable has belatedly given rise to a miniexplosion of scholarly literature (Root 1992; Spickard 1989; Zack 1992). It is still too early to expect any consensus or paradigmatic thrust to emerge from these pioneering efforts. However, one promising notion has been propounded, namely, that Hawaii, which happens to be the most ethnically aberrant of the fifty states, may serve as the model, the most advanced precursor of a multiracial-ethnic mixed population for the twenty-first-century mainland (Johnson 1992).

By most accounts the cultural, social, and political climate of North America remains regressive and oppressive toward racially mixed individuals. No attempt has been made to include mixed-race populations by any designation in formal census accounts, and there is no informal non-pejorative language for referring to such individuals. In the Hawaiian Islands, where White racial mixes are now recognized largely without stigma as *hapa haole* (half White) or simply *hapa*, the attitude of acceptance toward racial mixing likely resulted from the eventual proliferation of mixed-race marriages and relationships. In North America, there is no comparable attitude of acceptance, nor is there a similarly accepted semantic acknowledgment of mixed-race peoples. (Bradshaw 1992:87)

Whether the Hawaiian pattern of tolerance toward ethnic/racial ambiguity can be transplanted and eventually take root in the mainland United States is beyond anyone's powers of prediction. More immediately, it is not clear which of two paths the individuals in question will follow. One is simply to alternate among two or more ethnic roles as circumstances dictate, in keeping with the findings in a study of "mixed-heritage" Japanese American and Hispanic college students in Hawaii and New Mexico.

Contrary to the hypothesis of both assimilationists and pluralists, mixed-heritage people have multiple identities. . . . The finding that no respondent in either sample consistently used a single mixed-heritage identity suggests that mixed-heritage identities are less stable or more sensitive to situational variation than is single-heritage identity. (Stephan and Stephan 1989:514–515)

On the other hand, as indicated above, we are witnessing an incipient awareness that a novel sort of social community is being formed, one that both acknowledges and takes pride in its anomalous status. Such sentiments have practical consequences, most notably in the consternation generated among census officials and special-interest groups over the question of providing an acceptable category in the 2000 census for persons unwilling to identify with any of the more-or-less standard "races" (Sandor 1994; Wright 1994). A compromise seems to have been reached by the Office of Management and Budget in July 1997, whereby individuals may claim two or more "racial" ancestries if they wish (O'Hare 1998). This decision does not cause rejoicing among all the constituencies involved, and some thorny technical questions involving data tabulation still await resolution.

In any event, the only conclusion to be drawn after considering the option of having ethnic groups defined by their actual or prospective members is that this strategy compounds confusion and uncertainty among all concerned. And, most particularly, when we introduce the phenomenon of an expanding mixed-heritage population, an already murky definitional puzzle becomes even more problematic.

The Ethnic Group as Social Construct

In light of the preceding discussion, the title for this section is more than slightly redundant, or overdue. By this point any alert reader should be willing to entertain the notion that many contemporary ethnic groups are indeed social artifacts, the products of the internal actions and beliefs of their members and/or the external pressures and decisions on the part of the larger community (K. N. Conzen et al. 1990). But I have been working my way toward an even bolder generalization: that *all* ethnic groups, without exception, are socially constructed and — a closely related thesis — that they are all of recent origin. (Logically, then, the title of this section should read "The Ethnic Group as a Modern Social Construct.")

The claim of recency, that the formation of what we recognize as ethnic groups is conceivable only in modern times, derives from one portion of the standard definition beyond challenge: that it is "a self-perceived group of people." We could reduce ethnic groups to the trivial case of populations confined to a single village or small cluster of villages, situations where every person comes into face-to-face contact with everyone else on a fairly regular basis. But such a contraction would eliminate all the more populous entities, those "imagined communities," to use Benedict Anderson's (1983) felicitous term, whose ranks number anywhere from the tens of thousands up to the many millions. In such grander agglomerations, direct personal interaction is limited to a small fraction of one's putative community even over the course of a long lifetime. Any possibility of self-perception as a unique collection of human beings under such circumstances is realizable only with the aid of near-universal literacy, printed matter, photography, standardized school curricula, and various modern modes of transportation and mass communication, plus all the other devices in the armamentarium of cultural persuasion.

A vitally important corollary accompanies the claim that all full-fledged ethnic groups are modern in origin. If such recency is a valid notion, then it seems unreasonable to expect such social artifacts of a particular era to remain unchanged, to languish as static primordial entities (Upton 1996). A more plausible assumption is that these groups are necessarily dynamic collectivities subject to all manner of alteration over time. And, as we shall see, recent developments do lend some credibility to this idea.

Another key aspect of the life of the ethnic group is maintenance of boundaries against other groups, as asserted by the oft-cited Fredrik Barth (1969) and his followers (e.g., Jenkins 1994; See and Wilson 1988).[15] And assuredly such an essential category of behavior in the life of an ethnic community implies shared awareness not only of the cherished particularities of one's own group but also of those less savory attributes of alien neighbors as well, however flawed or incomplete the information may be. Once again, such forms of consciousness are simply not feasible for populations of *substantial* magnitude in the absence of modern modes of travel, communication, and indoctrination — again eliminating the examples of small, pre-modern "tribal" societies. What is observable, then, is another critical component of a more meaningful definition of the ethnic group: latent or active resistance to incursions — territorial, political, cultural — by the Other.[16]

The modernity of the ethnic group is one of those propositions that seem to violate common sense. We are all by nature "presentists" in our mental makeup. We assume, casually but incorrectly that, obvious technological innovations aside, all the really important, familiar aspects of our collective lives have existed virtually forever, originating in the mists of prehistoric times. Thus we assume the antiquity of such concepts and creations as adolescence, police forces, organized charity, asylums for the insane, and romantic love, to take some nonethnic examples. Critical scrutiny of the historical evidence often results in rude awakenings (Hobsbawm 1983). And so it is with the ethnic group.

Scholars who have actively hunted for traces of premodern ethnic groups, for example, Armstrong (1982), have failed to make a convincing case and admit the ambiguity of their findings. The most thorough of such investigations, by Anthony Smith (1987), does offer certain signs and portents of the phenomenon and demonstrates the possibility that proto-, pre-, sub-, hypo-, quasi-ethnic entities may have come close to existing in the classical Mediterranean world and other times and places. Such premodern societies as the Hebrew, Gypsy, Aztec, Phoenician, and Norse may have possessed some of the ingredients for fabricating a genuine ethnic group, but the process was never fully consummated.

The characterization of the ethnic group as a primordial phenomenon, as a complex of cultural traits and practices passed along intact from remote ancestors over many centuries or even millennia, is an article of faith among some scholars. It also seems to be part of the conventional, if usually unarticulated, wisdom of the general public. Perhaps no one has promoted the idea more eloquently than Harold Isaacs (1975). He has certainly shown how various, presumably traditional social elements, such as language, mythical progenitors, religion, foodways, and historical events, can be mobilized in the service of present-day ethnic causes. However, critical examination of his thesis has found it to be more a reflection of late twentieth-century sociopolitical agendas than a straightforward rendering of cultural realities (Eller and Coughlan 1993; McKay 1982; Scott 1990; Thompson 1989:67; Yancey et al. 1976:400). The venerability of some major resources in the ethnic arsenal is hardly proof of their continuous salience. We have too many instances of latter-day exhumation or manipulation of moribund, defunct, or forgotten cultural assets — or even outright forgery of them — to admit at face value any claims for the primordial authenticity of any twenty-first-century ethnic group.

The fact that certain ancient civilizations and political states have enjoyed great longevity without fatal interruption scarcely validates the primordiality of their ethnic character. The prolonged existence of the Japanese, Chinese, Ethiopian, French, British, Iranian, Thai, Vietnamese, and other such durable polities may merit congratulation, but they are political, not ethnic, continuities.[17] In fact, the fashioning of genuine ethnic solidarity is still a work in progress in some of the cited cases, and is always uncertain as to outcome.

Ethnogenesis

"Something new has appeared" (Glazer and Moynihan 1988:2). And that innovation is the ethnic group, a development which, like the nation-state, industrial capitalism, the idea of race, mass tourism, and popular culture, could see the light of day only at a certain stage in the process of modernization.[18] The emergence of ethnic groups, or perhaps the belated recognition of their presence, struck many observers as a counterintuitive development. The conventional view before the 1970s had been that "modernization will bring about a decrease in the importance of ethnic distinctions. . . . The diffusion-erasure model implies that the salience of ethnicity should decrease as modernization diffuses over a culturally heterogeneous population" (Nielsen 1985:133). But the reality was quite different, in fact just the opposite, and had been for some time before the 1970s.

Ethnogenesis, a term that first appears in print in 1966 (Nagel 1996:16), is the construction, or at least the dawning awareness, of an ethnic group, an entity that had not previously existed. It has followed two distinctly different, not entirely synchronous paths. As far back as the seventeenth century, as Europeans began to colonize overseas territories, the settlers, quite unwittingly, set about creating cultural communities that were imperfect replicas of what they had left behind in the homelands (Fischer 1989; Meinig 1986). The task of nation building, of forging an ethnic body coincident with the young nation-state, had barely begun in the 1600s and 1700s, even in such countries as Great Britain and France. The results of transplantation were first noticeable in the Americas, specifically along the British Atlantic Seaboard and in Quebec and Mexico. Subsequently, parallel developments materialized among the Boers of South Africa, the Chinese groups in Southeast Asia, and, at the national scale, in Brazil, Argentina, and Australia. Then, as later waves of immigrants from sources other than those of the founding nation entered the settler lands, another stage of ethnogenesis ensued, more exuberantly in the United States than anywhere else.

A second process, the assertion of ethnic identity by indigenous populations at the subnational level — again in apparent defiance of the logic of modernization — has been relatively recent, beginning in Europe in the nineteenth century, then spreading to Asia, Africa, and Latin America. "As a political idea, as a mobilizing principle, ethnicity in our time has spread round the world with the curious consequence of sameness and difference that is encountered with other such phenomena. A common rhetoric attaches to widely disparate conditions, with luxuriantly varied results" (Glazer and Moynihan 1988: 20). In sharp contrast to transient emigrants, the people in the old homelands have been literally grounded in specific patches of land, presumably over many generations. More often than not they have nurtured a passionate attachment to their sacred soil, however contentious the bounds thereof may be. The many claims and disputes arising from this brand of ethnogenesis have spawned an extensive literature, but little of it relevant to the United States.

Few American ethnic groups are place-bound, their possible ranks including only some Native American communities, the Cajuns, Mormons, and perhaps the Chicanos of New Mexico and thereabouts.[19] Much more widespread and theoretically challenging has been the experience of all the relatively mobile immigrants and their offspring. Although the claim by Frederick Buell that "America has been ideologically exceptionalist as the country where a world-significant ethnogenesis is always still under way, not one where it has been wrapped up and finally institutionalized" (1994:146) may be a trifle inflated, no other land has witnessed so large, varied, and provocative a set of ethnogenetic projects, past, present, and prospective.

Although the public at large tacitly adheres to the primordialist view of ethnic identity in the United States, a majority of interested scholars have eventually come around to the conclusion that "the facts . . . demonstrate that ethnic ties developed only on American soil" (Sarna 1978:370; also see Mann 1979:155–156 and Nelli 1970: 5).[20] One of the earliest authors to grasp the actualities of ethnogenesis in both Europe and America was the influential Oscar Handlin.

> It was no easy matter then to define the nature of such groupings. Much later, in deceptive retrospect, a man might tell his children, Why, we were Poles and stayed that way — or Italians, or Irish or Germans or Czechoslovaks. The memories were in error. These people had arrived in the New World with no such identification. The terms referred to national states not yet in existence or just come into being. The immigrants defined themselves rather by the place of their birth, the village, or else by the provincial region that shared dialect and custom; they were Masurians or Corkonians or Apulians or Bohemians or Bavarians. The parents back across the Atlantic, troubled by a son's too quick abandonment of the old ways, begged that he keep in himself the feeling of a Pozniak. (They did not say Pole.) (1951:186)

At the risk of bludgeoning the reader into numbness with too many examples, the following array of specific cases should confirm the universal validity of Handlin's claim.[21]

The two earliest of the major immigrant influxes into republican America, indeed among the largest to date, were the German and the Irish. Although Anglo-Americans may have perceived the former as a monolithic mass, in reality the persons called German were a remarkably miscellaneous lot, being split along lines of religion, dialect, province, folklore, class, and political leanings. Their relative homogenization into German Americans during the latter two-thirds of the nineteenth century, even as a nominally unified Reich was being born, was a heroic achievement and a tale expertly narrated and analyzed by Kathleen Conzen (1985). In similar fashion, Irish American peoplehood came into full bloom in the United States concurrently with the upsurge of nationalism in the homeland (Miller 1990).

We may be accustomed to regarding all Swedish immigrants as instant Swedish Americans, but the image does not coincide with fact. In a study of members of the Augustana Synod, Dag Blanck discovered that

> most students at the school Augustana College [*sic*] had come to America without any real sense of a national Swedish identity. Instead, their loyalties tended to be local and regional, tied to a particular province or district in Sweden, and it was not until they came to Augustana that they were exposed to the national Swedish heritage. The same was of course true for the second-generation Swedish-American students. (1989:138–139)

Much the same story line applies to Norwegian immigrants. In a detailed account of the 1925 Norse-American Centennial celebration in Minneapolis, April Schultz (1994) has shown how a unified Norwegian American collectivity was not fully fleshed out until that year.

Much more varied than anything observable in Scandinavia were the cultural particularities, including dialect, foodways, costume, vernacular buildings, and much else, within the Kingdom of Italy, whence streamed so many immigrants and sojourners from the 1880s onward. It was not simply a matter of an obvious disconformity between the northern and southern halves of the country but of sharp differences within individual provinces and districts.[22]

At the height of immigration, the *campanilismo* of southern Italy had been recreated in

> the checkered settlement of the ghetto, whereby immigrants settled near others from the same village and province. In this period, immigrants regarded themselves not as Italians but as resi-

dents of a particular *paese*. These identifications were reflected, among other places, in immigrant mutual-aid societies, which were formed and named on the basis of village and provincial ties. But as the period of settlement wore on, the focus of identity enlarged to take in the rest of the Italian peninsula. "Italian" or "Italian-American," as a self-identification, increasingly replaced such labels as Neapolitan or Catanian. This identification with the entire group may not have affected so much the immigrant generation, whose self-identification was well-developed and stable, as it did the second. Identification with a village they had never seen was obviously not easy for the American-born; and, in any event, other Americans did not recognize these place distinctions, but treated, or more usually mistreated, all those of Italian background as "Italians." (Alba 1985a : 74–75)[23]

The genesis of an American Polonia followed a similar scenario. "The Poles seem not to have learned of their larger 'Polishness' until after their arrival in America; it was here they confronted the counter-realities of an Anglo-American macro-culture and a multiplicity of nationalities" (Golab 1977 : 155). And in his study of Polish American church architecture, Gyrisco (1997) reached the same conclusion. Then, at a higher level of ethnogenesis, persons of Lithuanian, Polish, Czech, Slovak, Ruthenian, and other eastern European origins seem to have attained a temporary supraethnic identity before arriving at the final condition of "unhyphenated" Euro-Americans (Gedmintas 1989 : 146).

Although the gentile community habitually regards Jewish Americans as always having formed a seamless, solid ethnic front, the historical record diverges sharply from popular perception. It took more than a single generation for any sort of mutual accommodation to materialize among Jews of Sephardic extraction, a relatively elite German contingent, and the eastern European masses, who were, in turn, diversified in terms of provincial origin. The recent advent of Soviet Jews and Israelis has added further unpredictable complications to the ongoing process of ethnogenesis (Mittelberg and Waters 1992 : 424).

But if we look at the largest Jewish group ever to gravitate to America, we learn that,

in 1890, the entity "East European Jew" did not exist save in the minds of people outside both Judaism and Eastern Europe. Instead there were Litvaks and Galitsianers and Ukrainian Jews. They had a sense of commonality with other Jewish immigrants, but in their personal lives they identified themselves as natives of their region or *shtetl*. They joined pan-Jewish synagogues, but their strongest ties were with the *landsmanshaftn*, benevolent associations organized by geographical origin. (Spickard 1989 : 215)

If any immigrant community has gained a reputation for cohesiveness and awareness of a unified homeland, it is the Japanese American. But, once again, appearances are deceiving.

The Japanese immigrants had a subnational sense of ethnic identity. They regarded themselves first as inhabitants of their respective villages and prefectures, and only secondarily as members of the Japanese nation. . . . The much-touted, all-consuming Japanese nationalism, the emperor worship, was a product of a later period — the 1930s — long after the Issei had left for America. (Spickard 1989 : 104)

Different generations of immigrants may arrive with quite dissimilar ethnic stories, a case in point being the Portuguese experience.[24]

While their forefathers frequently thought of themselves as being from a particular village or island first, followed by the Azores and lastly, as Portuguese, the perspective is almost the reverse now. A sense of being Portuguese permeates these newcomers. . . . This sense of nationalism is a fairly recent phenomenon and is a result, in part, of the nature of the prolonged colonial wars in Africa and the Portuguese government's efforts to generate patriotic support for an unpopular war. (J. R. Williams 1982 : 116 – 117)

In other instances, when the countries of origin are still struggling to achieve some semblance of cultural unity at the national scale, it is

not surprising to find their natives bearing with them only an embry-
onic sense of ethnic togetherness on the voyage to America. Thus, in
a 1973 study of the Filipino community in Salinas, California, a Filipino American participant-observer found that

> although the labor camps were usually run by Filipino labor con-
> tractors who employed Filipino cooks to serve cheap Filipino
> dishes, there was hardly any development of a sense of a Filipino
> *communitas* except on a regional level. The Ilocanos talked and
> went out with the Ilocanos, the Tagalogs with the Tagalogs and
> the Cebuanos with Cebuanos. (Almirol 1985:54; also see Pido
> 1986:17)

There may be no finer example of the congealing of a totally novel
ethnic identity in the American crucible than that of the Lao Hmong.
As refugees in border camps drawn from many isolated localities,
then later resettled in the United States, they have just begun to realize a sense of common peoplehood unknown in a homeland that has
yet to emerge from its premodern status (Lynch 1995:265–266).

All the reshapings of identities discussed, except for the diasporic
Jews, have to do with immigrants drawn from a specific country, one
which may or may not have become a fully consummated nation-
state or reasonable facsimile thereof. Falling into an utterly different
category is another hugely consequential ethnogenetic phenomenon: the creation of the African American community. The slaves
who were shipped to North America, many via the West Indies, were
assembled from over the greater part of a vast continent during a
period preceding most European conquests and colony formation
and long before any independent African states (aside from Liberia)
came into existence. In terms of cultural patterns prevalent among
the various African nations or "tribes," the disparities were at least on
the same order as those within Europe, while the cross-cultural contacts and mutual knowledge among these peoples were probably less
extensive than in Eurasia.

Much remains to be learned about how such a heterogeneous
mass of captives with so little in common came to be fused into a de-

cidedly homogeneous ethnic group in the United States.[25] Some of the blame can be assigned to the slave dealers and plantation owners who, for obvious security reasons, scrambled together groups of slaves from scattered localities, persons who spoke mutually unintelligible languages. Fostered thereby, and quite inadvertently on the part of the masters, was an impromptu activation and sharing of whatever ur- or pan-African cultural traits these immigrants could dredge out of the primeval stratum of their pre–New World past. Another notable phase of the process was, of course, the forced acquisition of a great deal of Euro-American culture. (The reverse flow of influences was hardly trivial, but that is another story.)

We must also consider African Americans' rather widespread intermixing with aboriginal groups, as well as with Caucasians, and a consequent interchange of cultural items. In addition, there was a certain degree of mobility and mixing among slaves sold by, or migrating with, their proprietors, as well as the movements of freed and fugitive blacks. But whatever mechanisms may have operated over nearly four centuries of New World experience, the outcome has been a durable, cohesive ethnic group of some thirty million or thereabouts, distributed over most of the United States, a cultural community qualitatively distinct from, though related to, both its African antecedents and its Caucasian neighbors.

Currently, a good many generations after the initial African American ethnogenesis, the process may have reached a new, rather different stage as black immigrants from the Caribbean and Africa have begun entering the United States in significant numbers (Apraku 1991). Members of the first generation of these newcomers are acutely aware of their cultural incompatibility with earlier and much larger African American communities and have labored diligently to keep their social and cultural distance from them, evidently to little avail, as far as the second and later generations are concerned. In a study of Haitians in the Chicago area, Woldemikael's "most important . . . finding is the transformation of identity between the first- and second-generation Haitians. . . . American-born children of Haitian parentage become more like their Afro-American peers than like their

Haitian parents" (1989:166; also see Stafford 1987).[26] And in research among adolescent West Indians and Haitians in New York
City, Mary Waters (1994) reached an identical conclusion.

It will be interesting to see whether this scenario plays out among
the recently arrived Ethiopians and Somalis who fall phenotypically
between the Negroid and Caucasoid categories. Even more problematic is the destiny of perhaps some three hundred thousand Afri-
can-appearing, Portuguese-speaking, Roman Catholic Cape Verdeans now residing in the Northeast. Because of sharp differences in
language, religion, and other cultural attributes, which happen to be
sustained by vigorous to-and-froing between the home islands and
the United States, they have striven to isolate themselves from African Americans (Halter 1993).

Left for last in this account is what may well be the most unusual
episode of ethnogenesis the modern world has ever beheld: the
abrupt emergence of the Euro-American community or, if we embrace all the marginal affiliates of this vast cultural entity, the American nation. After a 170-year colonial prelude, thirteen of the British
colonies in eastern North America rather improbably gained their independence, then set about, with amazing speed and success, to develop a novel cultural as well as political personality. The ancestral
linkages with Great Britain were, and are, obvious enough, but the
cultural alchemy involved not just the English, Welsh, Cornish, Protestant Irish, Scots, and Scots-Irish but also crucial infusions of others.
Thus there were dealings by the progeny of the British Isles with Germans, Dutch, Scandinavians, and French Huguenots, *inter alia*, along
with significant contact with aborigines and encounters with distinctly non-European, but not totally alien, physical environments.

All this made for a quite original cultural system in addition to the
revolutionary character of the new governmental arrangements. We
can find certain parallels in other European offshoots, in the likes of
British Canada, Quebec, South Africa, Australia, New Zealand, and
the various Latin American and Caribbean republics. All of them have
moved more slowly and imperfectly toward whatever uniqueness
they might claim today. Nowhere else was genesis so sudden and divergence from antecedents so dramatic as in the United States.[27]

Attempts to shape a politically defined community into a relatively uniform ethnic group were going on simultaneously in western Europe with varied degrees of success, and subsequently in southern and eastern Europe and eventually in Asia and Africa. But what sets the American case apart from the others is not only how swiftly and passionately the national character evolved but also its special ideological cast. Readily apparent was an active disdain for the past (any pretense of primordiality would have been absurd), the championing of the noblest aspirations of the Enlightenment, and, truly uniquely, that implicit compact with the world to offer a democratic welcome and all manner of freedoms to potential (albeit preferably Caucasian) Americans from the far corners of the world.[28]

I am oversimplifying, of course. The professed ideals of the young republic were not strictly adhered to. Many of the newcomers encountered a rather rough reception, and the long list of misdeeds tucked into the dark underside of American history is difficult to conceal.[29] Nonetheless the distinctive ethnic amalgam of the early nineteenth century has continued to evolve, to become more richly and complexly American. What was initially a predominantly Anglo complex has gradually turned into a Euro-American compound of "unhyphenated whites," a population merging ingredients from throughout Europe and elsewhere, and a work still very much in progress (Alba 1990; Lieberson 1985; Lieberson and Waters 1988; Waters 1990).

As external onlookers, Americans can readily discern the match between polity and citizenry, the existence of an ethnic identity almost ideally corresponding with the state in such instances as Ukraine, Korea, Japan, Turkey (sans Kurds), Hungary, Ireland, the Netherlands, and Finland, among others. Seeing such a relationship from within national borders is a bit trickier. Americans are constantly aware of the United States as a looming, quite special political presence and as an economic or military power, but are generally oblivious to its ethnic particularity. But the actuality becomes vivid enough when traveling abroad or observing American behavior in foreign settings, such as settled groups of expatriates, in some Mexican locales or in military posts in Germany and elsewhere. It also becomes more palpable during periods of social angst, as happened a hundred years ago when so many nativists were worried that the flood of exotic immigrants was imperiling the integrity of the American way of life — or the present period of renewed disquiet over immigrant and language issues.[30]

Defining virtually the entire population of the United States and certain other countries as genuine ethnic groups may seem at first like too extravagant a stretching of the concept of ethnogenesis. But, as previously argued, consider recent and prospective history. If the Ibos had been victorious in the Nigerian civil war of 1967–70 and had established a Biafran republic, would they automatically have ceased being an ethnic group? When an independent Tibet was absorbed into the People's Republic of China in 1950, were Tibetans suddenly demoted to the rank of a mere subnational ethnic group — or had they been such all along? It is not unimaginable that the Québecois and even the Scots might some day create sovereign states. Would such a turn of events cancel their eligibility as ethnic groups?

When the nation-state approaches coincidence with an ethnic group, as is the case with the United States, such a collectivity stands at the top of a multitiered hierarchy. We have already encountered some of the subnational components of this layered system, but there remains a further, quite distinctive type of ethnic entity, namely, panethnicity.

Panethnicity

This term applies to the situation when several ethnic groups — perceived by themselves or, more generally, by the larger society, to share some degree of cultural and/or racial kinship — are labeled with some broad designation *and* proceed to form umbrella organizations and act in unison on certain occasions. It is important to note that, whether or not the supraethnic entity operates effectively, the component groups retain their identity, unlike the cases of African American and Jewish American ethnogenesis. We have here, then, an additional stratum within our layered hierarchy. In its fully developed form, the phenomenon does not seem to predate the 1950s, becoming significant only since the 1960s (Lopez and Espiritu 1990:210).

Panethnicity seems to have made more progress in the United States than anywhere else, but there are parallel cases in Canada and Australia with the activation of panethnic movements among their "First Nations" and aboriginal groups, respectively, and in the United Kingdom with its Caribbean communities (Sutton and Makiesky-Barrow 1987).

Perhaps the most searching account of panethnicity in the United States is that by Lopez and Espiritu (1990), in which they contend that the question of race is fundamental. In the course of their study, they also advance the bold claim that "today [panethnicity] may well be supplanting both assimilation and ethnic particularism as the direction of change for racial/ethnic minorities" (1990:198). However, they add the reservation that "the central question to ask of panethnic developments is the degree to which they represent genuine generalization of ethnic solidarity and identity, as opposed to alliances of convenience" (1990:200).

And, indeed, political expedience has been the driving force behind panethnicity more often than has disinterested ethnic passion. In this connection it is well to recall that the initial impulse for creating the macrocategory in question may derive from the U.S. Bureau of the Census or other governmental agencies. But artificiality does not exclude the possibility of acquiescence by the parties being classified. "The influence of official labels on social processes can already be detected in the many individuals of Asian backgrounds who have begun to refer to themselves using the pan-ethnic term 'Asian American'" (S. M. Lee 1993:85).

Lopez and Espiritu identify and discuss four large panethnic groups: Asian Americans; Latinos; Native Americans; and Indo-Americans, that is, Asian Indians. The last group can be just as readily categorized as ethnogenetic, whether in the homeland or the United States, or as a panethnic entity. The decision depends upon one's perspective.

There is a fifth candidate for panethnic status in the United States, one not treated by Lopez and Espiritu: the Caribbean.[31] Although the immigrant communities recently arrived from Haiti, the Bahamas, Jamaica, Guyana, and the Lesser Antilles are keenly aware of, and energetically perpetuate, their insular particularities, a larger regional sensibility has begun to emerge (Kasinitz 1992; Kasinitz and Freidenberg-Herbstein 1987:388; Sutton 1992; Sutton and Makiesky-Barrow 1987), as documented via content analysis of an ethnic newspaper in Washington, D.C., where the investigators found a "tendency to identify more with the Caribbean community as a whole than with their specific islands" (Regis and Lashley 1992:387). This new pan-Caribbean spirit is also publicly manifested in lively fashion during the annual Labor Day carnival in Brooklyn (Kasinitz 1992: 133–159). As already noted, there is a serious question as to whether the children of black Caribbean immigrants can resist absorption into an African American melting pot. But as long as immigration and frequent visits and other contacts with the home islands persist at something close to their present levels, the continuity of some sort of pan-Caribbean community seems assured.

The oldest and in many ways most complex of American panethnic groups is the Native American. Indeed at contact time there was probably a greater degree of cultural diversity (and possibly also wider differentials in levels of social and technological development) among aboriginal American societies than prevailed within any of our other panethnic groups — or within all of Europe, for that matter. When Europeans first encountered these peoples, they found them so utterly alien, so absolutely un-European, that they tended to overlook their many dissimilarities and acquired the habit of lumping all the indigenous communities into a single racial category. This perception was readily translated into governmental policy.

At this point I can do no better in explicating the panethnic process for the population in question than to quote Lopez and Espiritu at length.

> Linguistically, religiously, and geographically diverse, Native Americans do not generally see themselves as a single people. Like Asian Americans and Indo-Americans, Native Americans lack a single cultural heritage to draw upon in the formation of panethnicity. For the most part, Native Americans still maintain their tribal identities. The U.S. government recognizes approximately

five hundred tribal entities, over three hundred of which still function as quasi-sovereign nations under treaty status.

The case of Native Americans is unique because their ethnic organization is largely determined by federal Indian policies. The government appears to pursue a two-pronged strategy. On the one hand, they recognize tribes as geopolitical units and the foci of various government programmes and legislation. To avail themselves of the special "privileges" of being Native American, Indians must prove membership with their particular tribe. As such, tribal organizations continue to be essential and inescapable for them. On the other hand, the government insists that Indianness is the relevant ethnic distinction for political policy purposes, thus making pan-Indian organization necessary.

Unwittingly, some government policies fostered pan-Indianism by facilitating inter-tribal contact and communication. In particular, federal Indian education policies required all Indians to learn English, thus providing the linguistically diverse tribes with a common language for inter-tribal communication. In addition, the boarding schools established in the early twentieth century provided an opportunity for American Indians to interact with members of different tribes. (1990:216)

The panethnic impulse that federal authorities may have inadvertently energized has acquired a life of its own. This new sociopolitical entity has pursued a number of varied strategies, including the strident Red Power movement (Clifton 1990; Hertzberg 1971; Jarvenpa 1985; Nagel 1996; Trotter 1981). Quite recently, there has even been some international, cross-cultural outreach to aboriginal groups in other countries. Despite being the only one of our American panethnic groups not to be constantly reinforced through immigration, and despite a high rate of intermarriage with other "racial" groups, an exceptionally high rate of natural increase and the material advantages of claiming Native American status seem certain to guarantee the viability of both individual tribes and panethnic activity well into the future.

The panethnic Latinos are not only the largest of such aggregations in the United States, but they are also projected to become the largest so-called "minority" at some point in the early twenty-first century, when they will surpass African Americans in number. As has been the case with other such groups, however, any sense of commonality or unity of purpose has begun to materialize only recently. Despite such superficial attributes as a shared language and other cultural features ultimately traceable to Iberia, and the predominance, but not total monopoly, of at least nominal Roman Catholicism, there have been major historical, political, and socioeconomic differences among populations drawn from a varied set of Middle American, West Indian, South American, and European sources. Moreover, their clearly various "racial" traits have given the Bureau of the Census some serious classificatory headaches. But whatever obstacles still persist, conditions of life in the United States have nurtured coalescence, the formation of a "Hispanic nation" within this country (Fox 1996). Observations derived from research on Mexicans and Puerto Ricans in Chicago have nationwide applicability. "The kind of Latino ethnic identity and consciousness described in this study may have relatively little to do with Latin America. It seems clear that this group identification is largely a phenomenon of American urban life . . . by the encounter of the Spanish-speaking with systems of racism and inequality in this society" (Padilla 1985:144).

The most improbable of the panethnic contrivances is the Asian American. Given both the stark cultural gaps among the various homelands, venomous antagonisms between certain pairs of them — hostilities that have sometimes festered for centuries — forging a collective identity in the United States would appear to be a messy proposition. The crucial factor may well be the proclivity of so many Euro-Americans to regard all persons from eastern and southeastern Asia as members of a single undifferentiated mass.[32] The principal components of this mass have been the Chinese, Japanese, Koreans, Taiwanese, Vietnamese, Cambodians, Laotians, Thai, and, by virtue of location, the Filipinos, who have been categorized as occupying the cusp between Latino and Asian identities (Espiritu 1992:172). The marked cultural differences among them are as great as, or greater than, anything observable among the nations of Europe.

Once again, the census has reflected popular myopia by devising the curious portmanteau racial category "Asians and Pacific Islanders" (Shinagawa 1993). But however potent the forces dividing the ethnic groups in question, they are being overcome gradually by their common plight as they face discrimination and misunderstanding on the part of the dominant society. The panethnic process is, predictably enough, especially visible in California, the home of such a large plurality of Asian Americans. The resulting alliances may be ad hoc in character, but even if the occasional united political or cultural front may be ephemeral, there is little question that an underlying sense of being Asian American is beginning to take hold, complementing and perhaps overriding less comprehensive or more specific identities (Espiritu 1992; Lowe 1991; Wei 1993).

As has been happening with Latino Americans, the special circumstances of American life are such that connections with ancestral cultures are becoming less urgent than innovative arrangements that enable the groups to integrate partially and with minimal discomfort into the larger American ethnos along something approximating their own terms. In any event, there is every reason to anticipate that, despite its fictive genesis, the panethnic Asian American constituency will become an ever more assertive and noticeable part of the American scene. And, as is equally true for the other panethnic entities, it is likely, if history is any guide, that their perceived "racial" distinctiveness will inhibit any complete merger with the larger Euro-American population at any point in the foreseeable future. Indeed "no non-white ethnic group has ever fully assimilated into American society" (Lopez and Espiritu 1990:220).

A Definition at Last

After this lengthy, somewhat circuitous disquisition, we have finally arrived at the point where it is feasible to offer a pair of definitions of the ethnic group. For those who prefer a sound-byte that can be readily memorized, the following stripped-down version has a certain validity. It simply states: *The ethnic group is any substantial aggregation of persons who are perceived by themselves and/or others to share a unique set of cultural and historical commonalities.*

But, rather apologetically, I must also tender to the intellectually demanding a much longer, more complex and meaningful definition, as follows: *The ethnic group is a modern social construct, one undergoing constant change, an imagined community too large for intimate contact among its members, persons who are perceived by themselves and/or others to share a unique set of cultural and historical commonalities, which may be real or imagined. It comes into being by reasons of its relationships with other social entities, usually by experiencing some degree of friction with other groups that adjoin it in physical or social space. Levels of awareness of its existence can vary considerably over time and in accordance with circumstances. Ethnic groups can exist within a hierarchy that ranges from the smallest aggregation meeting the stated criteria to a politically sovereign national community or even beyond to entities transcending international boundaries.[33] For individuals, affiliation with the ethnic group may be either mandatory or a matter of personal option, one susceptible to change and contingent upon political and social circumstances.*

It may be prudent to add two codicils. First, as noted previously, and important though it may be for many groups, association with a specific territory is *not* essential for defining the generality of ethnic groups. It is also worth pointing out again that, in a significant number of cases, the cultural commonalities believed to define the group are regarded as being racial in origin. The fact that there is no anthropological basis for such a belief is irrelevant. Perception is what counts.

WHAT IS ETHNICITY?

Thus far I have carefully refrained from using the term *ethnicity* except, unavoidably, in quotations and in the neologistic compound *panethnicity*. This is not a matter of personal perversity but rather the result of an ever-deepening conviction that ethnicity is a novel, special concept, one obviously related to, but distinct from, *ethnic group, ethnic identity, ethnicism,* and a cluster of other terms, old and new, festooned upon the *ethnos* root.

It may come as a surprise to many readers to learn that *ethnicity*, a word indeed so ubiquitous today, did not materialize until the mid-twentieth century. As late as the 1970s, Gunnar Myrdal complained that he was unable to locate it in his dictionary (1974 : 28). Curiously enough, only a handful of authors have noticed this late arrival or have dwelt upon the significance thereof. As Glazer and Moynihan have realized, "ethnicity seems to be a new term. In the sense in which we use it — the character or quality of an ethnic group — it does not appear in the 1933 edition of the *Oxford English Dictionary* (*OED*) but it makes its appearance in the 1972 *Supplement* where the first usage recorded is that of David Riesman in 1953" (1988 : 1).

Werner Sollors has been more diligent in tracing the history of the term:

> In 1977 Riesman reacted with surprise to the suggestion that he invented "ethnicity." After an elaborate search for the origins of the word — an appropriate enterprise in the ethnic field that inspires so many people to turn to origins in ancestor-hunting — I found the apparently first occurrences of "ethnicity" in W. Lloyd Warner's *Yankee City Series*, the well-known five-volume community study of Newburyport, Massachusetts, which began to appear in 1941. (1986 : 23) [34]

Such an investigation is not mere pedantry. Words embody concepts, and new words convey new concepts, major and minor. Ethnicity most decidedly belongs in the major category. Nancy Fraser and Linda Gordon, authors of a brilliant biography of the term *dependency*, offer a viewpoint I endorse. They credit their approach, in part, to Raymond Williams, English cultural-materialist critic:

> Following Williams and others, we assume that the terms that are used to describe social life are also active forces shaping it. A crucial element of politics, then, is the struggle to define social reality and to interpret people's inchoate aspirations and needs. Particular words and expressions often become focal in such struggles, functioning as keywords, sites at which the meaning of social experience is negotiated and contested. Keywords typically carry unspoken assumptions and connotations that can powerfully influence the discourses they permeate — in part by constituting a body of *doxa*, or taken-for-granted common-sense belief that escapes critical scrutiny. (Fraser and Gordon 1992 : 78)

TABLE 1. The Term "Ethnicity" in Titles of Articles
Listed in the *Social Sciences Citation Index*, 1956–1998

Year	No.	Per Annum	Year	No.	Per Annum
1956–65	29	2.9	1992	476	476
1966–70	115	23	1993	624	624
1971–75	488	97.6	1994	646	646
1976–80	1,264	252.8	1995	779	779
1981–85	1,466	293.2	1996	872	872
1986–90	1,838	367.6	1997	913	913
1991	587	587	1998	794	794

As startling as the tardiness of its arrival is the extraordinary surge in popularity of the term *ethnicity* in both scholarly and popular discourse over the past four decades or so. Thus in 1978 Ronald Cohen could write: "Quite suddenly, with little comment or ceremony, ethnicity is a ubiquitous presence" (1978:379). Its incidence in the titles of articles in social science journals has been documented in the *Social Sciences Citation Index* ever since that publication began tracking such information in 1956 (table 1). Whether, or how long, the proliferation of such titles will continue its remarkable upward trajectory — and presumably also in social science books and monographs — is, of course, a matter for conjecture. It seems safe to assume a similar explosion of items concerned with ethnicity in the humanistic literature. Interestingly, the very first, if belated, entry under the heading "Ethnicity" in the *Reader's Guide to Periodical Literature* refers to an article appearing in May 1976.

How, then, do we define a term that has gained such strong currency in so short a span of years? Unfortunately, *ethnicity* is not among the keywords that Raymond Williams chose for critical examination. When we turn to recent standard lexicons of the English language, the results are vague, uninformative, and even misleading.

The 1969 *World Book Dictionary* offers "ethnic status, quality, or character." In its 1976 New College Edition, the *American Heritage Dictionary* defines *ethnicity* as "1. The condition of belonging to a particular ethnic group. 2. Ethnic pride." Arrayed alongside forty-seven other *ethn*-entries, we find our term characterized as "ethnic character or peculiarity" in the *Oxford English Dictionary. Webster's Third New*

International Dictionary (1986) says nothing more than "ethnic quality or affiliation." In *Chambers Twentieth-Century Dictionary* (1983), *ethnicity* appears along with twenty subentries but without a definition and is identified only as an adjective! Finally, in its 1987 edition, the *Random House Dictionary* comes up with "ethnic traits, background, allegiance, or association." Evidently lexicographers either are bewildered or have not given the question a great deal of thought.

In keeping with the notion expressed by Glazer and Moynihan that "a new word reflects a new reality and a new usage reflects a change in that reality" (1988:5), we shall have to search for that new reality — and its further evolution. What is obvious is that the concept of ethnicity has something to do with attitudes toward the Other on the part of all or a major portion of a national population. But let us also be clear as to what it is not. Human communities have always regarded alien groups with suspicion, distrust, or outright hostility, but until quite recently they have never discerned any generic commonality about them aside from their strangeness and questionable human status.

In the case of settler countries, unfamiliar immigrants were lumped together (often ethnogenetically, as we have seen) into nationalities, even when no such collective identities had been realized previously. They were looked down upon by the dominant society as inferior beings, while the least desirable were considered disgusting and even dangerous. Some such scornful epithet as "barbarians" or, in Yiddish parlance, "goyim" might cover the entire array of strangers. But whatever noun came into play, there was nothing appealing about them, no pervasive qualities to be admired. Particular groups may have been viewed, correctly or otherwise, as sharing a special cultural complex. In the popular mind, then, not too long ago, there may have been vague perceptions of Irishness, Polishness, and the like, but no one, except for the occasional eccentric scholar or dilettante, would have thought it worthwhile to pay much attention to the cultural traits in question, much less consider cherishing them or trying to abstract whatever commonalities might be shared among all the various groups.

Now, in a sharp break with past attitudes and with astonishing rapidity, we have come to recognize a quintessential quality called Ethnicity (capitalized hereinafter to distinguish my definition from more casual usage) that pervades all cultural communities — excepting perhaps our dominant own — a quality that may be defined with merciful succinctness as *the generic condition of being ethnic*, no matter what interchangeable species of ethnic may be under consideration.[35] I cannot overemphasize the criticality of the term *generic*. Ethnicity is not the special property of any single group; it is shared by all. Ethnicity transcends the particular while presumably distilling the innate wonderfulness imbedded within mere Greekness, Koreanness, Turkishness, or whatever, to become a radiantly delectable sublimation, a near-mystical good.

I freely admit that the definition offered here has a certain oxymoronic ring to it. At one level, it is equivalent to claiming the absurd: that Ethnicity means remaining our own special cultural selves but also being just like everyone else. But on another level, more meaningful, I believe, it suggests that we are all imbued with a universal humor (if I may resurrect that medieval, but still useful, concept) that elevates us above our superficial differences.

Although ethnicism, or ethnocentrism, can be malignant, and the clashes between antagonistic groups are heartily deplored by all right-thinking individuals, Ethnicity dwells upon an ethereal plane beyond cavil or reproach. The exaltation of this quintessence of being ethnic seems most advanced in the United States but can also be discerned in other countries.[36] This unprecedented phenomenon we call Ethnicity is something to be sought after, celebrated, revered, preserved, taught, enhanced — the interethnic strife of yore replaced by mutual admiration — and it is also eminently merchandisable.

As it undergoes commodification, a sublimated, fungible Ethnicity is detached from its local roots. Consequently, in the fabrication of ethnic goods for the extraethnic trade, we encounter interchangeable sets of actors in a globalized fiesta of Ethnicity. Thus

American importers who purchase weavings in a number of places around the Third World are cross-fertilizing designs and materials between ethnic groups in an effort to reach new market niches in the United States. Several importers commented that while Mexican rugs are cheaper than Navajo, Pakistani, and Afghan rugs in the United States market, Dhuri rugs produced in India of cotton/wool blends are cheaper and compete with Zapotec rugs at the lower end of the United States carpet market. These importers acknowledged that they have contacted Indian weavers to produce "Zapotec" rugs made of cotton and cotton/wool blends. (Stephen 1993:47)

The mind boggles at the number of such incongruities that already exist or are about to be created by imaginative entrepreneurs.

In apotheosizing Ethnicity we must overcome a pair of serious intellectual difficulties. First, the concept is seldom, if ever, applied to seriously assimilated Euro-Americans or to the bearers of the ancestral English culture.[37] Somehow such folks stand apart and above the exotic Others. Why so?

And then consider the following ethnic communities among a good many others resident in the United States, each with its own specific cultural heritage and history: Samoans, Portuguese, Armenians, Koreans, Thai, Puerto Ricans, Yemeni, Gypsies, Senegalese, Iraqis, Latvians, Menominees, Japanese, Dominicans, Inuit. What possible innate quiddity is common to all? I am not aware of any, except perhaps their alterity, their not being properly Anglo-American. In reality, each cultural complex, each sense of peoplehood is reasonably distinct — though also fluid in composition and time-dependent — bounded and separated from the others. Thus the word Ethnicity, conveying a fictitious commonality, blurs and demeans whatever genuine individuality inheres in these communities, makes problematic their seat in the grand banquet hall of peoples.

The timing of the burgeoning of Ethnicity is not fortuitous. Indeed it is impossible to envision any significant social innovation or shift in public attitude as occurring in a historical vacuum. As Manning Nash has so cogently remarked,

The study of ethnicity needs to be rooted in a definite time period, with an eye to the malleability of the combination of elements that go into its construction at different times and places, all this with a sensitivity to the continuum of cultural-political-natural which also has a dynamic shaped by history, circumstance, politics, and economics. (1989:6–7)[38]

This is a research strategy to be implemented at a later point in this study, as we probe the question of why the sudden need for a new term when we had been getting along so well for so many years without it. (But to anticipate a key finding, we will discover that Ethnicity is a sublimated form of assimilationism and the smothering of genuine diversity.) But, in the meantime, it may be instructive to muse upon the quasi-dialectical relationship between Ethnicity and racism. Although their origins may be out of sync temporally and the attitudes in question are in near-polar opposition, these phenomena share a common process: the fabrication of a pervasive generalization, a generic quiddity based upon the perceived attributes, real or imagined, of many and varied social groups.

Ethnic Identity in Recent Historical Perspective

Another more immediately useful, if relatively narrow, approach to understanding the advent of Ethnicity is to view it as the culmination of a series of evolutionary stages in the behavior of American (and perhaps other) ethnics and the perception thereof by the wider public. The conventional wisdom found formal expression in Milton Gordon's highly influential *Assimilation in American Life* (1964). This volume postulates that the immigrant generation and its descendants pass through a series of stages of accommodation and assimilation until terminal structural absorption into the larger society is realized.

Consequently, both scholars and the general public were more than slightly taken aback by the abrupt appearance of a so-called ethnic revival in the United States in the 1970s (TeSelle 1974; Vigilante 1972; Weed 1973). It was a movement spearheaded by European "ethnics," that is non-British European immigrants and their progeny, and abrasively enunciated in Michael Novak's scriptural manifesto *The Rise of the Unmeltable Ethnics* (1972) and in other of his writings (e.g., Novak 1974). Claims by Novak and his supporters gave rise to a considerable polemical literature, more often than not unsympathetic (e.g., Alter 1972; Aversa 1978; Mann 1979 : 19– 45; Myrdal 1974; A. D. Smith 1981; Stein and Hill 1977; Steinberg 1989; Yinger 1981 : 257–260). In any case, public expression of revitalized ethnic pride was lively among groups of eastern and southern European origin, most rambunctiously perhaps among Italian Americans (Pileggi 1979; J. A. Williams 1989).[39]

Looked at narrowly, the pronouncements of the Euro-American ethnic revivalists might be considered to be a backlash — the politics of resentment — against the Black Pride movement that had ignited a few years earlier and a concurrent ethnic assertiveness among Native Americans, Chicanos, and Cajuns (Gold 1979 : 277), as well as the product of a more general social malaise. From such a perspective,

> in retrospect we can see that the white-ethnic revival was part of the multi-crisis that mushroomed in the late sixties. It fed into, and was fed by, the divisiveness issuing from war, prejudice, poverty, warfare, crime, pornography, pollution, the counter culture, the breakdown of authority, inflation, and everything else that called into question the legitimacy of American society. (Mann 1979 : 18)

But even such a broad view is too constricted. Something larger was happening, a phenomenon on a much grander geographic scale. Even as some American ethnic communities were feeling their oats, some long-simmering, low-level ethnic/regional campaigns in western Europe, Canada, and elsewhere began to exhibit a new urgency (Petersen 1980; A. D. Smith 1981). Interestingly, the protagonists included not only such self-conscious entities as Basques, Bretons, Corsicans, Québecois, Catalans, Welsh, Scots, and some aboriginal groups in Australia and New Zealand, but also other submerged, hitherto silent constituencies. Rather ironically, it was in France and Great Britain, the earliest, most nearly ideal textbook examples of the perfected nation-state, that we observe efforts to breathe life into such things as Cornish and Provençal identities and a variety of other moribund regional cultures.

Almost as abruptly as it had surfaced, the agitation among the unmeltable Euro-American ethnics melted away by the 1980s, leaving minimal residue on the social scene, while the "racially" defined causes of African Americans, Latinos, Native Americans, Middle Easterners, and Asians continued to gain visibility and force. "The lack of an autonomist, let alone separatist, nationalistic component in the ideology of 'neo-ethnicity' underlines its difference from the norm of 'ethnic revival' and transformation, which we find elsewhere" (A. D. Smith 1981:156).

Symbolic Ethnicity

Although the short-lived ethnic revival received much adverse criticism, the net effect of all the fuss was to focus attention on Ethnicity and ultimately to brighten its image. Taking the broadest of views, the ethnic revival of the 1970s was an ephemeral side channel flowing parallel to the mainstream of sociocultural development on whose current one and all among assimilated Euro-Americans were being borne into the realm of *symbolic ethnicity*. It was Herbert Gans (1979) who first set forth clearly and convincingly the advent of this final stage of any sort of distinctive ethnic identity among nth-generation members of Caucasian immigrant stock. Persons who indulge in symbolic ethnicity do so both optionally and part-time (Kellogg 1990; Waters 1990).[40] While they may be indistinguishable from "ordinary" Americans in their quotidian activities, they may choose to remember, cherish and honor the ancestral culture (or two or more such heritages if they are of mixed background) by consuming certain foods and beverages on certain occasions, using a few pungent words or phrases from an otherwise forgotten language, simulating traditional practices during culturally resonant holidays, festivals, and ceremonies, attending rites of passage, and occasionally visiting ethnic churches, cemeteries, or residual ethnic neighborhoods and shops. "If people no longer perceive a threat to their individual life chances from ethnic discrimination, their ethnic identity can be used at will and discarded when its psychological or social purpose is fulfilled" (Waters 1990:7).

The reductio ad absurdum of symbolic ethnicity may be seen in the performances of some politicos campaigning for the electoral support of ethnic constituencies. There is something surrealistic in the spectacle of an office seeker noshing on a half-dozen different ethnic delicacies in as many different neighborhoods in the course of a day, while also possibly wearing the proper hats, sashes, buttons, or whatever and mispronouncing various foreign catchphrases.

Anny Bakalian's (1993) findings in a study of Armenian Americans apply to any number of other groups of Greater European origin, including Italians (Tricarico 1984), Serbs (Padgett 1980, 1981), and the more "successful" Hispanics (Nelson and Tienda 1985).

> The study emphasizes the symbolic component of symbolic Armenianness, making a case for increased situational, individualistic forms of expression and the importance of convenience in its application. Most frequently, Armenianness is manifested during one's leisure time. Armenian identity for later generations is no longer exclusive, all-engulfing, but tangential to people's lives and daily preoccupations. Consequently, its liability is also limited, making it easier to be a symbolic Armenian. . . . With continued assimilation and upward mobility, if Armenianness is to survive in the United States among large proportions of men and women of Armenian descent, it can only do so in its symbolic form. (Bakalian 1993 : 7–8)

As we contemplate symbolic ethnicity, it is obvious we are standing on the threshold of Ethnicity as previously defined. It is a short step from sentimental obeisance toward a single receding heritage to the apotheosis of all heritages that is Ethnicity, to that commingling of the alluring essences of all the world's cultures that purports to express their common, radiant meaning.

2 EXPRESSIONS

We have seen that ethnic identity is a time-dependent phenomenon with multiple meanings, that it exists in various forms between countries and over quite a range of spatial and social scales, and that, for many flexible individuals, there may be two or more choices as to ethnic affiliation. But all such considerations would have little more than theoretical interest if such identities could not be perceived, however realistically or otherwise, by the individuals and groups in question and by those outsiders who observe and judge them.

It is essential, then, to examine the various modes of ethnic expression as they have been manifested in the United States with special attention to the ways they have evolved over time. In doing so, we can also learn much about the eventual genesis and changing character of Ethnicity itself and about shifts in the attitudes of the larger society. The most useful strategy for treating the topic may be to take each of three perspectives in rough chronological turn: (1) the residual, observable, basically unselfconscious cultural attributes retained by immigrants and their progeny, whether temporarily or over protracted periods; (2) the images of particular ethnic/racial groups maintained by the Anglo-American host population; and (3) the images created and projected outward to the world at large, more or less deliberately, by the various ethnic communities. It is important to note again that Ethnicity, as I have defined it, does not appear on the scene until quite late in the narrative. Consequently, we shall have no occasion to refer to it at all until we reach the third and final perspective.

CULTURAL RESIDUE

We have on hand an enormous literature covering the history of immigration into the United States in its entirety and also in terms of specific groups and periods. Also quite massive in volume are the publications dealing with the economic, ecological, political, and sociological adjustments experienced by tens of millions of newcomers over more than two centuries of international reshuffling. More modest in number and scope are the studies that have looked into the transmission and survival of cultural elements from alien lands before and after the formation of a distinctly American culture (K. N. Conzen 1991). The missing empirical material would be welcome not only for its own sake but also for its theoretical implications.

The evidence to date suggests only one valid generalization concerning the levels at which traditional attributes survive after transplantation, namely, that no generalization holds for all groups and periods. If we focus on the specific group, the degree to which it is capable of preserving its customary ways of life — and thus being readily perceived as ethnically distinct by so-called "ordinary" Americans — depends on several factors. They include the volume of the immigrant influx; its timing; width of the cultural gap between the immigrants and the founding Anglo society; extent of deliberate social isolation; maintenance of links with the originating society, or lack thereof; the severity of the environmental shock in unfamiliar physical surroundings; and, perhaps most germane of all, just where the newcomers decide to settle and how accessible such localities happen to be. All these variables help determine the continued vitality, or demise, of ancestral traits.

In the case of the Cajuns, as with many New Mexican Chicanos whose arrival predates the Anglo occupation, with the Sea Island blacks, the Hutterites, and certain Native American groups (most famously the Hopi and Seminole), sheer physical apartness has greatly retarded the forces of acculturation. A combination of geographic and social remoteness has also helped ensure the viability of an archipelago of scattered triracial isolates (Daniel 1992). In other instances, most notably the Amish of Pennsylvania, Indiana, and elsewhere and the Hasidim of the New York metro area, spatial proximity to large host populations has been effectively neutralized by social abstention. It is interesting to note, incidentally, that in at least three cases — those of the Amish, Cajuns, and Hopi — the appeal of the exotic has spawned a thriving tourist trade (Clifton 1990:16).

The timing of two or more waves of immigrants from a given

country can have important consequences. Because cultural systems and other conditions in every single homeland in question have undergone serious, accelerated change in recent decades, the package of attributes imported by our potential citizens is time-dependent. Thus the social chemistry between successive cohorts of compatriots resettled in the United States can be less than ideal. And, because of the ever-changing American milieu, the various generations of immigrants can interact in different ways with the host population and offer different sets of cultural traits for possible adoption. Such diachronic disparities are touched on in incidental fashion in the case of the Chinese (Takaki 1989:432; B. Wong 1992), Japanese (Osako 1995:436); Asian Indians (Leonard 1992:185–196), Jews (Markowitz 1993; Orleck 1987; Shokeid 1988:5), Koreans (I. Kim 1981:23), Lithuanians (Gedmintas 1989:48–49; Van Reenan 1990:182–185), Serbs and Croats (Bennett 1981:84; Kornblum 1974:24; Padgett 1981), Hungarians (Schuchat 1981), and Poles (Ungar 1995:218–221).

If we adhere to orthodox assimilationist doctrine, then we must believe that, after three or four generations, and perhaps a good deal of intermarriage, virtually all traces of foreignness will have vanished among the descendants of immigrants. Only the more sentimental among them will sporadically engage in some sort of symbolic ethnicity. Thus the celebrated melting pot will have done its work, while the non–Anglo-American contributions to the mixture are usually deemed too slight to merit serious notice. Life, however, is not that simple.

Some groups may indeed have become totally submerged and erased. Where, for example, do we find the Flemish residue in our contemporary cultural amalgam? But others remain detectable though not strikingly "ethnic" in the current colloquial sense. A strong case has been made for the initial and persistent presence of Celtic (i.e., Scots Irish, Scots, Welsh, and Irish) cultural mores in the United States (Evans 1965; Clark 1986), and especially in the South, where it may have been a significant component in the molding of that region's culture (McWhiney 1987). The partial acculturation of Mexican and Central American Latinos (and who could be more "ethnic"?) in California and the Southwest is apparent to even the most casual of observers, and is readily explained by the ease of constant contact with the communities of origin. A parallel, if less arresting, situation seems to prevail among French Canadians in some localities in the Northeast. Turning to a more recent influx, it is likely that West Indian immigrants and sojourners can succeed in retaining their distinctly non–Euro-American cultural personalities indefinitely, thanks again to the intensity of movement and communication between origins and destinations.

The Native American story is, of course, much more complicated (Steele 1982). A good many groups are now either biologically or culturally extinct, or both, while, through intermarriage and acculturation, many of the numerous individuals currently claiming Indian identity are not readily distinguishable from their Caucasian neighbors in looks or behavior. On the other hand, a number of other "tribes," especially in the western states, have kept intact enough of their cultural complex to attract the tourist gaze. When it comes to such tourist traps as a Cherokee complex in western North Carolina, Tahlequah, Oklahoma, or a Seminole Village in south Florida, we are dealing with an entirely different mode of ethnic expression (one discussed later in this chapter), and we are entitled to doubts about authenticity. In fact, these and similar Native American enterprises usually purvey a generic pan-Indian set of objects and performances rather than any based on the local community (Curtis 1997).

The most interesting case of cultural survival among a transplanted population and arguably the one with the greatest ideological implications is that of African Americans. For many years, the conventional wisdom was that, after enduring the horrors of the Middle Passage and the deliberate scrambling of different ethnic groups by slave dealers and owners, the millions of slaves shipped to North America had lost all vestiges of their African culture. They were assumed to have been reduced instead to being bearers of a debased caricature of Anglo-American culture.

This standard view was first challenged by Melville Herskovits's *Myth of the Negro Past* (1941), a volume setting forth evidence of a wide range of African survivals that could be detected by diligent, open-minded investigators. He made the general case that these items formed a significant component of the community's identity. Since that path-breaking publication, other scholars have confirmed and extended Herskovits's thesis within a wide range of cultural phenomena, including language (Mufwene et al. 1998) and the built landscape (Vlach 1976). Now that a dismissive attitude toward African American culture is no longer possible in scholarly circles, an even bolder claim has come to the fore. Among others, William Piersen (1993) and Shelley Fisher Fishkin (1995) have argued that African Americans have played a significant role in molding American culture, at the national as well as regional scale.

There is still a great deal to be learned about how non-English elements introduced by both immigrant and indigenous peoples have figured in shaping American ways of life. Thus, in addition to the apparently substantial African and Celtic heritages, there were many significant transfers of Native American items (Axtell 1985; Hallowell 1959). Transfers from all the varied non-British sources could occur even when the total cultural package had disintegrated in the course of assimilation. Identifying the specific individual traits contributed by Hispanic, Jewish, Italian, and German immigrants, for example, as well as others, should prove rewarding, but such a strategy would take us beyond the mission of this study.[1]

Language

It should be clear by now that the extent and pace at which non-Anglo peoples and cultures are absorbed into the dominant system vary considerably, depending upon the specific group, place, and period in question. For further insights into the persistence and significance of residual nonmainstream cultures in America it is useful to look at particular phases of those cultures.

The scholarly consensus is that the most critical of these, the one element most often decisive in forging a sense of ethnic unity, is language. Furthermore, this subject has enjoyed ample attention, so that confident generalizations are available. Thanks to the definitive work of Joshua Fishman and his associates (1966; 1980; 1985 : 129–156), we have robust documentation of the steady decline and, frequently, total loss of the ancestral tongue among second and later generations of non-Anglophone immigrant stock.[2] The exceptions are to be found, as might be expected, in the more isolated communities. Thus, ignoring for the moment our recent immigrants, *some* Native Americans still speak their own languages, a dwindling number of Pennsylvania Germans converse in their special dialect, a version of French remains current in some southern Louisiana localities, and Spanish is alive, well, and relatively unthreatened in some older, relatively sequestered, as well as newer, Chicano populations.

Whatever their eventual fate, immigrant languages have certainly been vital aspects of the new life in America for at least the first generation of newcomers and usually for their children as well, regardless of how quickly or slowly they picked up American English. In addition to regular use of the native tongue within the family and other social groups, the neighborhood, church, shops, and, quite often, the workplace, an enormous number of ethnic newspapers and other periodicals sprang up (Wynar and Wynar 1976; Wynar 1988), then gradually faded away as linguistic acculturation took hold. A number of ethnic communities were also able to create lively theatrical productions, which, like the newspapers and magazines, were directed solely to coethnics. These had at least one notable linguistic consequence, one also nurtured by the print media and film. More often than not, the immigrants had been fluent only in the local dialect of their native district, but "ethnic theatre introduced immigrants who spoke regional dialects to the 'standard' vocabulary and pronunciation of their native languages" (Seller 1983 : 6–7).

Currently, radio and television are having something of the same effect on the Spanish language as it flourishes in the United States.

> The media . . . do not preserve the language unchanged. Two powerful forces are at work, altering and reshaping the Spanish used in the media. One is the mutual influence of professionals with twenty or more different accents working in the same newsroom or story conference. Eventually, they all begin to sound alike. The other force is the constant input from the surrounding English-language culture, tending to make their Spanish more and more

like English in word order, grammar, and vocabulary and less like what was spoken in the home country. (Fox 1996:58–59)

The Spanish language (and Spanglish) may be a special ethno-genetic case by reason of the sheer size of the community in question and its continuous replenishment through immigration and intense transactions with the homelands. However, the notion that all non-English tongues have been destined for obliteration in America, one that seems to apply particularly well to pre–World War II examples, may be outliving its usefulness. The New Americans arriving since the 1960s may be less eager to turn into monolingual Anglophones. "The significant new ingredient brought about by contemporary immigration is . . . the presence of a sizable minority of educated newcomers who are able both to understand the advantages of fluent bilingualism and to maintain it" (Portes and Rumbaut 1990:220).[3]

But the feasibility of indefinite linguistic survival, along with a peculiar case of bilingualism, is most forcefully presented by the largest of all our ethnic minorities, the African American. Although none of the ancestral African tongues seem to have remained intact after the Atlantic crossing, many individual words, phonological features, and grammatical constructions did manage to linger on and to contribute to the formation of that highly controversial dialect or language called Black English (Mufwene et al. 1998). As an integral part of the lifestyle of millions of individuals, most of whom are capable of switching back and forth between Standard and Black English as prompted by the social context, there is no prospect that the latter will vanish in any predictable future.

As already suggested, the chances for retaining original languages among recent immigrant ethnic groups may be brighter today than was the case for pre–World War II communities, thanks to newer technologies and modes of social and spatial behavior. If local foreign-language radio broadcasts did little to retard language loss among the latter, the advent of the culturally more potent media of television, tape cassettes, and satellite telecasts (Kadaba 1998), along with the ease of lively intranational and international exchanges, has created a new array of linguistic landscapes. The most conspicuous example is, again, that of the Spanish-speaking population:

> No other minority now or in the history of the United States has had as extensive an apparatus for maintaining its language and propagating its myths . . . . Only in Spanish is there a nationwide system of television, broadcasting most hours of the day every day and producing and reproducing similar images to all speakers of the language. And this makes all the difference, creating a common set of images that influence even the non-TV media. (Fox 1996:40–41)

A comparable claim might be advanced for the African American community, which also has its national networks, in addition to local stations. It would be surprising if Black English were not spoken more than occasionally in these broadcasts. But other smaller communities have also availed themselves of these technological opportunities. Thus Iranian Americans based in Los Angeles have produced, syndicated, and broadcast via satellite a substantial volume of programs in Farsi throughout Iranian America, and have even managed to transmit a good deal back to the homeland (Naficy 1993: 6, 68–69).

It must be noted again that all such television items, tapes, and films, whether imported or domestic, along with traditional books, magazines, recordings, and newspapers using the immigrant tongues, all of which are thriving currently, are directed inwardly to the particular community. But seldom, if ever, is there any effort to shut out nonmembers. Any outsider inclined to do so can tap into these intramural expressions of cultural/linguistic togetherness, but rare is the gentile individual who actually enters these alien language worlds. For most native-stock Anglophone persons, the contacts are casual, accidental, and unimportant.

One such contact has to do with names, both personal and geographic. In the case of many immigrants from beyond the British Isles, their strange-sounding surnames and given names were often partially or completely Anglicized or shortened, or underwent a spelling change. Not infrequently, such changes took place immediately at the port of entry, at the suggestion or insistence of an immigration officer. But the revisions often came about later, perhaps delayed until the second or later generation. Nonetheless, for those millions of residents bearing some semblance of Irish, Swedish, Greek, Jewish, Korean, Armenian, or other decidedly non-British names, that most intimate part of one's vocabulary offers strangers an instant whiff of ethnic distinctiveness.

When it comes to placenames, the situation is murkier. The first wave of settlers and town founders generally drew terms from their own lexicons or natal regions in labeling physical and humanmade features. The majority of choices were English in character, but other groups have left their onomastic mark upon the landscape.[4] Thus, to take a random example, a casual look at the map of Minnesota discloses the presence, *inter alia*, of Hamburg, Heidelberg, Kilkenny, Luxemburg, New Germany, New Munich, New Ulm, New Prague, Norseland, Stockholm, Sveadahl, and Upsala.

But by far the largest, most widespread set of non-English placenames strewn across the American map is aboriginal in origin. Unlike the toponyms arriving from other lands, the spelling and pronunciation of these many thousands of items have usually been woefully corrupted, and the etymologies are obscure or unfathomable. In any event, these and other placenames from exotic sources have become semantically opaque. How often do residents of Nebraska, Kankakee, or Seattle pause to consider the history of those names? But even when the genesis of their town names is quite transparent, as in De Kalb, Des Moines, Eldorado, Marathon, or Troy, how aware are the locals of the original meanings? The conclusion must be that, as conservators of ethnic identity, placenames are weak vessels.

However long or meaningfully languages other than English may linger on the lips of Americans, they do have a sort of afterlife, not just on maps but in the speech patterns of presumably assimilated immigrant stock. Italian, Irish, Jewish, Polish, Norwegian American and other accents remain detectable a generation or more after the ancestral tongue has been abandoned. Indeed such accents most assuredly contribute to the distinctiveness of certain metropolitan and regional dialects of American English.

Religion

It is generally acknowledged that religion is the only other component within a cultural system rivaling the criticality of language in defining that system's essence. Furthermore, with few exceptions, church, language, and cultural survival are all intimately interconnected as immigrant, African American, and Native American communities confront the challenges of American life. More than any other institution, the church, synagogue, temple, or mosque provides the social, cultural, and perhaps economic and political, as well as spiritual, core of collective survival (Warner 1998). The examples are endless. Among the more familiar, we have the divers ethnic parishes established by the Roman Catholic Church in a good number of metropolitan areas and the dominant role of orthodox synagogues and parochial schools in the Jewish neighborhoods of such cities as New York, Chicago, and Philadelphia.

But perhaps the most striking case is that of the recently burgeoning Korean American population. In terms of the enthusiasm with which they have founded so many (predominantly Protestant) congregations and focused their communal life upon these institutions, they may have no peer. Indeed "the Korean group seems to show a higher level of affiliation with ethnic churches than any other ethnic group in the United States" (Min 1992:1376). Selecting other communities at random, we have a study of how the Methodist chapel has been the mainstay of ethnic and linguistic, as well as religious, identity among the Welsh of rural Wisconsin (Knowles 1997) and another of the pivotal function of the church in preserving Ukrainian culture in a Chicago neighborhood (Creuzinger 1987). Without exception, it would seem, it is the house of worship where the native language endures longest and in purest form in both liturgical and social usage, even as it is imperiled or extinguished in profane settings.

But, however conservative the ways of the church and its congregants, ultimately they cannot prevail against the acculturative forces of the larger American world. Although it is still too early to detect any such trend among adherents of Islam in the United States, the Americanization of Roman Catholicism and Judaism is obvious even to the casual onlooker. Such "naturalization" was also the experience of the Protestant denominations arriving from northwestern Europe in colonial times. Thus, if Presbyterianism was once closely associated with the Scots Irish or the Quaker faith with the British, nowadays that alliance is greatly attenuated. Similarly, some churches of Germanic or Dutch origin have attracted many parishioners from outside their initial ethnic bounds, while a reverse osmosis has also gone on. Indeed the extent and frequency of switching among denominations by individuals and families has been quite notable. Such comparison-shopping parallels the withering away of the bitter doctrinal disputes that formerly inflamed so many churchgoers. This phenomenon may be linked to another development that appears to have little precedent. It is no longer unusual to find a single church structure used sequentially by two or more different congregations or housing an ethnically mixed flock (Fuchs 1990:311–312). More often than not, the entities in question cater to recent immigrants. The ecumenical tolerance displayed in Chinese sections of the New York borough of Queens is not unique. "Because of the influx of new immigrants, multiethnic churches have become common here, with different schedules for two or more different language services in the same church" (Chen 1992:39).

What is increasingly obvious among all but the most reclusive of the various Judeo-Christian faiths is not only the Americanization, but also the cultural convergence of the various denominations. If one could apply a quantitative measure to the current differences in behavior, social function, and perhaps even architecture among churches in the United States, they might well be less than those between them and their counterparts in the countries of origin. The same statement is becoming valid for religions beyond the Judeo-Christian fold. "As generations pass, the [Asian] Indian religions transplanted into American cultural soil should look more and more like uniquely American variants of the parenting religious tradition" (Fenton 1988:x). "Asian Indians are in the United States, not South

Asia, so the long-term process to observe will be the formation of an American Hinduism and an American Islam with a new American character. Because of the selectivity of immigration laws and the peculiar ethos of American culture, these new national forms will be unique" (R. B. Williams 1988 : 281).

But there are some possible exceptions to the trends generally prevailing among white Christians, Jews, Hindus, and, possibly, Moslems: the African American and Native American faiths. Unlike the situations in Brazil and the Caribbean, the African slaves in North America were unable to retain intact any of their original creeds, but it is clear that a good many elements thereof did endure and were incorporated into the syncretic religions that emerged during their period of captivity (as also happened in the realms of music and dance). Syncretism has also characterized the post-contact religious history of some Native American communities. For both groups, full convergence with mainstream religious practices is not an immediate prospect.

Foodways

Pierre van den Berghe may be correct in claiming that "along with language, the food complex becomes a basic badge of ethnicity" (1984a : 392). But, under the conditions of immigrant accommodation to the American environment, foodways do not seem to compare favorably with the obstinacy of either language or religion as a rallying point for ethnic survival.[5] At least that would seem to have been the experience of European immigrants up through the early twentieth century, as far as one can judge from a fragmentary literature. The Americanization of diet within, but especially outside, the home proceeded rapidly, almost as rapidly as did integration into the larger economy, even though a few traditional items may have remained on the menu. However, the symbolic power of the ancestral diet would be manifest during observances of major holidays and in wedding feasts and other meals marking rites of passage (Waters 1990 : 118–121).

Initially there was little transfer of food or drink from the tables or ethnic grocery shops of the foreign newcomers to the kitchens and dining rooms of mainstream Americans. Indeed, the latter regarded the comestibles of people from eastern and southern Europe with suspicion or outright dread, and the sampling of non-European foods was virtually unthinkable.

Eventually the barriers between nativistic and imported foodways began to crumble before the latter had completely vanished. The outstanding example is that of the Italian Americans, although it is paralleled to some extent by the Jewish and Chinese stories.

> Among the outward manifestations of culture, cuisine is probably unique in the sense that its weakening among Italians and its acceptability in the wider society brings about a convergence, in which acculturation occurs as a two-way process of interaction between ethnic group and host society rather than as a one-way imposition of it by host culture on the new group. (Alba 1985a: 133–134)

It is too early for confident judgment as to how tenaciously the post-1965 wave of immigrants will adhere to their traditional foodways. Preliminary observation suggests, however, that despite some inevitable indulgence in standard American fare, recent arrivals from Latin America, the Caribbean, Africa, China, and other Asian lands are displaying as much, or greater, loyalty to the dietary regimes of their forebears than did earlier immigrants. And, of course, most African Americans and Latinos in the United States show few signs of abandoning the core culinary practices of their ancestors. Simultaneously, native-born Americans are now not just willing but eager for nutritional adventurism, for experimentation with unfamiliar food and drink.

Music and Dance

These rank among the more readily observable features whereby we can characterize a given culture (Stokes 1994:1–27). Their fate among immigrants coming to America has been rather similar to that of foodways. In many instances, steady attrition has resulted in these inherited modes of expression being demoted to the realm of symbolic ethnicity, items resuscitated for holidays, festivals, and other celebrations. But there are exceptions. No one can deny the ongoing vitality of African American music and dance in both church and secular venues. Similarly, there are Hispanic Americans who not only generate or listen to their distinctive music every day but also exploit it as a key device for anchoring and asserting ethnic identity (Fox 1996 : 186–187). Old-stock Americans learned to savor unfamiliar music and dance some years before they deigned to taste nonstandard cuisines. Thus there was ecumenical acceptance of certain varieties of ethnic and folk dance by the population at large as early as the 1920s (Greene 1990 : 19–20) at the very time the polka and other types of Slavic and German popular music were beginning to win general approval (Greene 1990 : 148–158).

Social Practices

As crucial as any other phase of life in maintaining transported or conquered social systems is that large, diverse set of activities falling under the umbrella term "social behavior." We encounter here many poorly known phenomena among immigrant and "minority" populations that cry out for scholarly exploration. We are especially ignorant about the role of ethnic organizations and associations in sustaining older modes of feeling and behavior.

Although it may be impractical to draw a sharp boundary between two halves of the spectrum occupied by these social entities, the effort is worthwhile. Toward the more formal, durable pole of the spectrum we find corporate bodies with offices and salaried officers, whose mission is to promote the interests of a given ethnic/racial group at the metropolitan, state, regional, national, or even international level. Over the past hundred years or more, they have been particularly active in advancing the political and social welfare of their constituencies, often operating social service agencies, insurance plans, hospitals, retirement homes, and various publication programs. Some, like the Knights of Columbus, may be church affiliated. The explicit preservation and nurturing of traditional culture is usually a somewhat less urgent item on their agendas. For some notion of the abundance and range of these organizations, one can consult a national directory such as Wynar (1975).

In contrast to such relatively visible outfits, there has been at least as numerous a set of smaller, less formal, narrowly defined, group-specific social clubs whose members are drawn, usually by dint of chain migration, from an intimate locality in the homeland. Perhaps *verein* is the most suitable generic term for them. As I can attest from personal experience,[6] the periodic meetings of such *vereins* work splendidly to feed and freshen memories, language, oratory, food-ways, music, dance, folklore, ancient and modern grievances, indeed the whole panoply of ethnic experience — at least for the immigrant generation.

No one has attempted to trace the full history of the phenomenon, but I conjecture it may have first blossomed with the massive influx of Germans beginning in the 1840s and 1850s, then continued and intensified as great numbers of New Americans arrived from eastern and southern Europe. Unless membership was steadily replenished by further immigration, the *verein* would generally fade away, then vanish as the foreign-born participants aged and passed on. Their offspring seldom harbored that burning emotional hunger essential for keeping *vereins* alive and well.[7]

If the older, Europe-based *vereins* are now largely things of the past, the institution flourishes today as vigorously as ever, but with new sets of actors. These latter-day ethnic clubs, once again the result of chain migration, seem to be especially abundant in New York City with its recent, sustained infusion of Latino and Caribbean immigrants and sojourners. Apparently the only groups to have enjoyed serious academic scrutiny are the Dominicans and Colombians (Georges 1987; Sassen-Koob 1987), but there are many others to be observed. Casually mentioned in the literature are a host of Mexican clubs in California, the Southwest, and elsewhere whose clienteles are limited to narrowly focused areas at both source and destination (Kearney 1995b; Nagengast and Kearney 1990). We also have reports of such activities among Asian Indians (Saran 1985:14) and Japanese (Kendis 1989: 123–137). The latter prove to be the exception to the general rule inasmuch as third- and later-generation Japanese Americans in Orange County maintain an intense sort of interconnectivity despite being spread across broad suburban expanses.

More casual than any variety of social club but equally useful in bolstering the vitality of ethnic tradition are the bars, coffee shops, dance halls, and the like patronized by particular sets of coethnics. Although the importance of the Irish American saloon and the Greek American coffeehouse has long been taken for granted, there are parallel instances among other groups about which the social science literature has been mute.

The club or bar may provide the genesis or focal point for still another activity whereby the spontaneous expression of ethnic spirit is feasible: competitive sport (Eisen and Wiggins 1994). This was largely a twentieth-century development and, in the great majority of cases, something outside the traditional culture, originating in the United States but still a highly effective way of cementing ethnic self-consciousness. Although some nineteenth-century Irish, German, and Czech immigrants may have engaged in intragroup field sports and gymnastics, until recently most newcomers had little if any athletic heritage and precious little leisure time for any such indulgences (Riess 1995:556). Eventually, with the gradual shortening of the workweek and a rise in income, ethnic teams with their ethnic spectatorship did become a significant social reality. During one period, basketball was especially important, although it scarcely qualifies as anyone's sacred heritage.

> During the 1920s and 1930s urban basketball maintained a very strong ethnic character. Ethnic fraternal groups organized athletic clubs for basketball and other sports to facilitate sporting competition and social events among the second generation who were unwelcome in prestigious WASP voluntary athletic organizations. In the 1930s there were Serbian, Lithuanian, and Polish national championships. Ethnic championship games in Chicago could draw in excess of 10,000 spectators. There was also inter-ethnic competition, which purportedly provided a broadening experience, though one might argue it encouraged as much ethnic hostility as friendship and understanding. (Riess 1992:202)

In contrast to basketball, a modern American invention, a few sports were successfully introduced from other lands. But golf,[8] skiing, and lacrosse (a Native American contribution) have quickly lost whatever original tinge of ethnic color they may have borne. Some other sports, notably boccie and jai alai, have not diffused beyond their ethnic bounds (Italian and Caribbean, respectively) and still help define the groups in question (as might the cricket imported from former British colonies). But, again, inherited athletic traditions are not indispensable for ethnic cohesiveness. Thus, in the case of "an extremely active American Indian Athletic Association" in Los Angeles, the major activities are softball, bowling, and basketball (Weibel-Orlando 1991:119–120). The fact that such sports are latter-day acquisitions does not negate their value as inner-directed expressions of ethnic togetherness and for the posting of barriers against other groups.

It is not too extravagant to claim that, in order to understand the contemporary ethnic scene in metropolitan America, one must delve into the sociology and geography of soccer (Escobar 1998). Here we have a competitive spectator sport that has generated intense passion virtually everywhere in the world except the United States, where it still remains almost entirely the domain of middle-class youngsters and recent immigrants. In the Washington metropolitan area, as in a good many others, "soccer plays a central role in structuring social and recreational life" (Cadaval 1989:277). Teams and leagues are composed of newcomers from Latin America, the Caribbean, Europe, and Africa, with each entity usually limited to players from a single ethnic group. Competition is generally intraethnic, but interethnic tournaments are not unknown, and the territorial range may be neighborhood, metropolis, or region. Most unfortunately, the only information available on this exceptionally important topic is journalistic, and that is sadly scattered and incomplete. What a glorious opportunity for the intrepid scholar!

No discussion of the social aspects of residual ethnic identity would be complete without considering the celebration of holidays (Waters 1990:121–124). These occasions exhibit the symbolically resonant intersection of religion, language, dress, foodways, pageantry, and other cultural legacies. A fair number of traditional holidays, but far from all (Guy Fawkes Day, Boxing Day, and the folkish May Day come to mind), have survived the shock of the American encounter. Within the Jewish calendar, for example, Rosh Hashanah, Yom Kippur, and Passover retain much of their original salience, while a distinctly Americanized Hanukkah has been growing in popularity. In rather similar fashion, the various ethnicized Eastern Orthodox Christmases, the Chinese New Year, the Vietnamese Tet, and certain powerfully meaningful Mexican dates have all been holding their own. It is likely that the same degree of visibility will be manifested by the major Islamic, Hindu, and Buddhist holidays as time goes on. Weddings also enter the picture with as rich a concentration of inherited customs as can be seen in any religious observance. Once again, ethnographic exploration in American venues could prove quite rewarding. One is not likely to confuse a Polish American wedding with the nuptials of a WASP Episcopalian couple.

Our knowledge is also hazy concerning a number of other aspects of the social behavior of immigrant and indigenous ethnic groups and whether or how they persist or alter within the modern American setting. Humor is one of the more interesting topics to be considered here (Sollors 1986:131–141). Although ethnic jokebooks and some lighthearted popular accounts may abound, little methodical scholarly work has been done on the particularities of in-group ethnic humor and the degree to which it aids and abets the lasting distinctiveness of the community. Similar observations apply to folklore, social etiquette, and all the many customs that may have been transmitted from other times and other places.

Built Landscape

In contrast to the spotty coverage of social behavior, geographers, folklorists, and other students of the American scene have devoted much attention to the ethnic imprint on the settlement landscape. Indeed the gathering of facts has been so extensive that we have two substantial surveys of the topic (M. P. Conzen 1990; Noble 1992). Two major generalizations can be ventured. First, during the early formative period of Euro-America, certain elements of the diversified European and African ways of constructing dwellings, sheds, barns, fences, wells, churches, public buildings, cemeteries, and other outdoor artifacts did manage to survive the trans-Atlantic passage and become embedded in particular sections of North America, though usually in simplified form (Harris 1977), even as nearly all the antecedent aboriginal landscape was obliterated.[9] Thus we can observe regionally distinctive settlement complexes in New England, Pennsylvania, the Deep South, southern Louisiana, and Quebec, if we venture northward, while certain corners of the Hispanic Southwest vividly remind us of their Old World ancestry. It also seems certain that the shotgun house of the American South was an African Caribbean import (Vlach 1976); and I suspect that, if and when someone performs a thorough investigation of the surviving African American churches and gardening and burial practices in the rural South, some definite Africanisms will be verified.

The second basic point is that once a standard, nationwide complex of house types, town patterns, commercial architecture, and other built objects had become prevalent — a process well under way by the 1850s but prefigured by the rectangular land survey system initiated in the 1780s — there was scant opportunity for any serious revisions by the millions of immigrants entering the country during the several decades leading up to World War I (Zelinsky 1990) or by more recent newcomers (Wood 1997). (But, as discussed below, some imported church building traditions do provide notable exceptions to the rule.)

Jerome Krase's conclusion, after studying Italian American neighborhoods in various cities, is applicable to other groups:

> Most of these [1880–1920] immigrant groups . . . established themselves in already built-up urban places, where they lacked the power to alter their environments radically, and adopted the environmental values of the dominant society as they became assimilated or Americanized. Consequently, only limited traces of traditional approaches to the design and use of buildings and space can be found in the new landscapes and places the immigrants created. (1993:48)

Judith Kenny duplicated Krase's findings in her study of Milwaukee's Polish South Side. "If we were to judge whether there are features of ethnic, immigrant culture surviving in the landscape of Milwaukee's major Polish neighborhood, the answer would be no. The Poles embraced new building patterns and outwardly conformed to American styles appropriate to their economic status" (1997:264).

What seems at first an obvious exception — the Chinese-appearing Chinatowns in a number of North American cities — does not stand up under critical scrutiny. In discussing San Francisco's Chinatown, Dell Upton notes that

> since Chinese immigrants were forbidden to own property, these buildings were designed by Caucasian architects and erected by Caucasian developers for Chinese and Chinese-American clients. . . . In other words, these "Chinese" buildings were designed by people who had never seen any buildings in China, and in some cases for clients who had never seen the originals themselves. (1996:4) [10]

The same sort of faux ethnic façade also developed in a British setting in the case of Liverpool's Chinatown (Dickenson 1998).

It was in Milwaukee toward the close of the nineteenth century that we find the sole metropolitan exception to the near-invisibility of immigrant influences, albeit a temporary one. This anomaly was the result of the extraordinary demographic, economic, and political clout of that city's German American community at the time.

> Only the Germans built a wide array of public and civic structures that reflected Old World patterns and motifs. . . . Only Milwaukee, with its unique ethnic power structure, employed its own interpretation of the dominant classical revival styles to create what architectural historians call the German Renaissance. . . . Just as a German ethnicity was being "invented" in Germany in the late nineteenth century, so was it being invented in Milwaukee during the city's German Renaissance building boom. Nowhere else in the United States is such a deliberate and successful adaptation of transplanted urban design to be found. (Hoelscher et al. 1997:386)

If we seek similar exceptions in rural America, that is, instances of latter-day immigrants ignoring national standards of landscape design, the only possibilities may be the Hutterite colonies of North Dakota and neighboring portions of Canada or the rather less confrontational efforts of Polish Americans in Portage County, Wisconsin, where they have been able to replicate part of their Old World ambience by erecting roadside crosses and shrines (Kolinski 1994).

But it cannot be denied that immigrants entering a predetermined settlement landscape are capable of adding their own special, if minor, accents to the scene. These appear in color schemes, house, lawn, and porch decorations, fencing, styles of gardening, and religious objects. Such modifications are noted, for example, in a field study of Polish and Italian neighborhoods in Brooklyn (Krase 1997). Even more readily visible is the Hispanicization of Mexican American housescapes in the Southwest, often involving structures acquired from Anglos (Arreola 1984a), or of the largely Puerto Rican sections of Manhattan's Loisaida (Fox 1996:233–236).

Undoubtedly there is much greater latitude for ethnic expression inside the home. Here the loyal ethnic family can indulge, to their heart's content, in some simulation of traditional décor. Safe from the critical gaze of others, they can try to replicate the homeland in furniture, carpets, shrines, plants, colors, objets d'art, dishware, and knickknacks of all sorts, as well as how rooms function and are scheduled for use. Once again, a cross-cultural, diachronic analysis should furnish valuable insights into the dynamics of assimilation as opposed to the inertia of cultural retention.

The only easily observable landscape element that may embody an obvious carryover from the homeland is the church building (Ostergren 1981). Not all immigrant groups tried to reproduce familiar designs. Some, like the Welsh Methodists of Wisconsin (Knowles 1997:293–294), simply acceded to standard American forms. Those who do opt for ethnic authenticity must inevitably do some compromising. Builders must meet local building codes; electricity, indoor plumbing, central heating, and parking lots — features probably unknown to their forebears — are adopted with few qualms; and almost always the exterior design contains some Americanisms.[11]

In any event, few casual sightseers would mistake the many Jewish synagogues with their allusions to eastern European or Mediterranean precedents for homes of Western Christian congregations. Similarly, the various Eastern Orthodox structures with their conspicuous onion domes can be spotted miles away. Some of the more recent communities — Moslems, Hindus, Buddhists, Sikhs, and Chinese — have created houses of worship that are so at visual odds with the conventional Euro-American landscape as to shock the more shockable of old-stock citizens (Prorok 1994).[12] However, although intent is always hard to read, it seems likely that these most costly and ambitious of physical statements of ethnic/religious identity are meant to address their congregations, to provide internal reassurance, rather than to be a form of lobbying, of staking claims within the civic polity.

Yet there may be more within these stone-brick-and-mortar affirmations than meets the eye immediately — specifically, ethnogenesis. In a study of the work of Victor Cordella, an architect responsible for many imposing Polish and eastern Slavic ecclesiastical projects in early twentieth-century America, we find these opinions: "No single church in Poland was the precedent for Cordella's structures in America and . . . this may have been a deliberate part of defining a new Polish-American identity that transcended a primary identity with a Polish locality or region" (Gyrisco 1997:43).

> In America, illiterate immigrants developed new European national consciousnesses, acquiring a new sense of identity in a larger nation. . . . The churches they built were material manifestations of an ethnic or national identity that extended beyond the locality or region that constituted their primary identity prior to immigration. Cordella designed most of this series of churches when there was no independent Ukrainian, Rusyn, Slovak, or Polish state. These churches were important symbols of community life and national identity that were not expressed on the political map of Europe. (Gyrisco 1997:51)

When we turn to still another landscape feature, the cemetery — one often affiliated with the church — it is to encounter another set of polysemous artifacts often infused with ethnic messages. Rather unexpectedly, the literature on the ethnic aspects of American cemeteries is a good deal ampler and deeper than the material on ethnic church buildings (Jackson and Vergara 1989:48–59; Meyer 1993a, 1993b, 1993c; Sclair 1995), but, once again, much remains to be investigated.

In times past, before the general availability of municipal and commercial burial places, spatial segregation of the American dead was the rule. Initially it was by church denomination and race, then later in terms of fraternal organizations and especially ethnic identity. Thus we find exclusively Roman Catholic, Jewish, Russian Orthodox, African American, and some Native American cemeteries in addition to those dedicated to Methodists, Baptists, Quakers, and all manner of other Protestant groups. Some immigrant communities generated the resources to operate their own large, elaborate cemeteries. Two outstanding examples are to be found in Chicago: the Bohemian National Cemetery (McGann 1990) and the Saint Casimir Lithuanian Cemetery (Hanks 1988; Sclair 1995).

When large, presumably ecumenical cemeteries became numerous, segregation within the grounds persisted for some time. More often than not, black or Chinese graves were relegated to the least attractive, least accessible corners. A study of cemeteries in Steelton, Pennsylvania, suggests strict segregation as late as the 1970s (Milspaw 1980). "Until 1948, racial segregation. . . . ruled the [Arlington] burial ground. Although Arlington resulted from a war which ended slavery, it conformed to the separation of grave sites for blacks and whites typical of military cemeteries until President Truman desegregated the armed forces by executive order" (Jackson and Vergara 1989:26–27).

Today the prevailing practice is to mingle at random the burial plots of persons of different faiths and ethnic background. In describing the current California situation, Irene Blevins (1993) notes that "ethnic cemeteries still exist, but few are started. Iranians, Moslems, Croats, Afrikaans, and Swedes lie side by side with bronze markers alike in the grass." But the urge toward exclusivity has not vanished totally.

Soviet immigrants bury their dead in plots adjacent to each other, not scattered throughout the cemetery. New York's Jewish cemeteries now have "Russian colonies" within them, whole sections where tombstones are engraved with Cyrillic lettering. . . . Even after death émigrés demonstrate their group identity, manifesting the symbolic boundary on the ground, in their sections of the graveyard. (Markowitz 1993:223)

Deliberately or otherwise, the grave sites of the foreign-born announce cultural affiliation in the design of gravestones, their language, text, and symbols, and grave decorations (Eckert 1998; McGuire 1988). And since cemeteries are only infrequently visited by the casually curious, we must assume such announcements are directed to compatriots. Inevitably, however, over time assimilationism takes its toll. The ancestral language gradually disappears, the older artistic motifs become less frequent, and gravestone styles converge with whatever is fashionable among the general population (Jansen 1991; Matturri 1993; McGann 1990). Thus, in a thoroughgoing analysis of cemeteries in Broome County, New York, Randall McGuire discovered that "increasingly in the last 10 years Jewish memorials are indistinguishable from the modest memorials of the Protestants and Irish, except for the Star of David and frequent use of Hebrew epitaphs" (1988:470).

Another interesting trend has set in recently — the use of the gravestone as a platform for declarations of neoethnicity or sympathy for the political and cultural struggles of the homeland. Thus, in discussing Lithuanian gravestone iconography, Milda Richardson finds that "the consistent use of this iconography becomes the vehicle of émigré protest as well as a repository of traditional Lithuanian symbols in America" (1995:5). Similarly, in another study, one dealing with a single cemetery in New Jersey, Thomas Graves (1993) documented the powerful elaboration of Ukrainian nationalism, with obvious reference to the long-suffering homeland, through the use of various symbols and religious motifs as well as the language itself. In the course of my own cemetery rambles, I have come across political / cultural manifestos of recent date inscribed upon, *inter alia*, Afghan, Albanian, Latvian, Lithuanian, Cossack, and Serbian gravestones. Like the earlier, less programmatic examples, such posthumous affirmations of identity speak to us of the residual power of ethnic feelings despite the steamroller impact of assimilation.

Dress and Bodily Adornment

Clothing, within the final category of residual attributes to be considered here, may well be the weakest, the least durable under American conditions. Immigrants and their children are seldom eager to flaunt their foreignness, or at least that was the case in times past. Being recognized as a newcomer could lead to taunts and all manner of unwelcome attention. Alien attire can be identified at some distance (as may also be true for body language and even facial expression), whereas one must stand close to the stranger in order to listen to a conversation in a foreign tongue or awkwardly accented English or sniff his or her breath for unfamiliar food aromas. And ascertaining that person's religious heritage usually calls for a certain amount of interrogation.

It is clear that there have been strong incentives for the newcomer to adopt the costume of the host population as quickly as possible. In the case of men, this might also mean discarding or trimming beards and mustaches so as to conform with current fashion. But the transition was not especially traumatic for European immigrants, and less so for men than for women. By the end of the nineteenth century at the latest, a generic style of male costume prevailed throughout the originating countries for ordinary daily use — rather plain jacket, trousers, boots, shirt, and hat or cap, together with topcoat as needed — but with visible social distinctions in style and quality. For the many African slaves, there was no element of choice. They wore whatever garments, new or hand-me-down, their owners saw fit to bestow upon them, and opportunities to express African tradition were minimal, except perhaps in ornaments and hair styling. But, as we shall see, there has been a recent surge of interest in the wearing and displaying of all things African among African Americans. The "Americanization" of Native American garb has apparently not been studied methodically, but the story is obviously complex. There are examples today of the maintenance of traditional dress among the more reclusive communities, and a good many individuals proclaim their ancestry, now that it is safe to do so, by mixing Euro-American with ancestral articles of clothing and by means of hair styling and jewelry. Perhaps the most distressing episode in America's sartorial chronicle was the treatment meted out to those nineteenth-century Chinese in the West who were unable or unwilling to acquire standard national garments and often continued to wear pigtails. These workers were mercilessly ridiculed, vilified, and often persecuted, in part because of their unacceptably foreign appearance.

Abandonment of inherited costume has not been total. Nuns and male clergy of a variety of faiths continue to wear Old World garb, and many ethnic groups feature traditional dress on festive and ceremonial occasions. In addition, of course, there are certain self-contained ethnic/religious communities for whom retention of the old ways is mandatory.

> In some special cases of minority group disidentification, as, for example, that of Hassidic Jews living in large American cities, the group's distinctive dress has remained essentially unchanged for hundreds of years. In these instances, as with such separatist, rural-based religious denominations as the Amish and Mennonites, not only does dress serve as testimony to the group's solidarity and oneness with their religious beliefs, but it quite purposefully erects a barrier to interaction with others in the society, thus keeping the group relatively isolated and safe from secular and other forms of moral contamination. (F. Davis 1992:180–181)

With the substantial influx of self-confident immigrants from non-European sources since 1965, along with a widening interest among the general population in all things exotic, the situation may be changing in interesting ways.[13] Perhaps the clearest departure from past assimilative practice may be found among newly arrived South Asians. An apparent majority of women from India, Pakistan, Bangladesh, and Sri Lanka are continuing to wear the sari and those from the Punjab, the *salvar kameez* while some of their spouses also wear their customary garments, the kurta pajama, in public. Similarly, many Islamic female immigrants and converts use the traditional headdress. Furthermore, no longer is it uncommon to see immigrant men and women in African dress on college campuses and the streets of our larger cities. Another intriguing development has been the number of pious Jewish males, otherwise indistinguishable in their business suits, who wear yarmulkes. This newfound pride in retaining, or reviving, the clothing of one's forebears has led to some perplexing legal and administrative dilemmas (Goodstein 1997). Whether nonconforming garments and hair styles should be tolerated in school, workplace, and the military is a question still being worked out in the courts and corporate and public offices.

This review of the available evidence clearly confirms the statement tendered at the outset of this section. There is no straightforward answer to the question of how much imported — and pre-Columbian indigenous — culture has survived assimilation into the dominant American system, thus remaining available for the expression of ethnic identity. And, although it is not a matter of crucial concern in this study, neither can we adequately specify or measure the contributions of individual cultures to the shaping of our contemporary national cultural complex. Many gaps in our knowledge remain to be filled. But when we have learned all that can be known, it is indisputable that the response to the question will be long and complex. As previously suggested, it will be contingent on the specific group being considered, the particular aspects of its culture, and the time frame within which the inquiry is cast.

EXTERNAL REPRESENTATION: THE BAD OLD DAYS

If simple generalizations about the viability of immigrant and other nonstandard cultures and their continued expression are beyond our grasp, there is no such problem in characterizing the ways in which the dominant Euro-Americans perceived and represented the strangers in their midst. Indeed the situation, at least as it developed in the past, was brutally simple and, in retrospect, in light of present day social values, brutally embarrassing. The western Europeans who created and ruled the republic brought with them from their natal lands a venerable set of antipathies toward alien communities. A latter-day racism directed toward persons lacking the proper complexion is a mind-set that seems to have been a concomitant of the modernization process (Hannaford 1996). But folklore and folk memories of ancient troubles may also contribute to various xenophobias. One need not actually meet the dreaded Other to loathe them. Thus Wu (1982:9–11) claims that the thirteenth-century Mongol invasion of Europe may help account for the persistent European antipathy toward East Asians, although most Europeans have never seen any. A similar situation prevails in some Appalachian localities where, despite the absence of Jews and African Americans, anti-Semitism and antiblack sentiment is traditional.

Simply put, in times past, anyone with the wrong (initially non-British) ancestry was inherently, irremediably inferior, and possibly subhuman. Consequently, there was little reason to study these creatures, learn their peculiar ways, or in any way interact with them as potential equals. The result was gross misrepresentation of alien cultures when they were accorded any attention at all and a widespread use of demeaning stereotypes. In fact, ignorance and willful unconcern were so prevalent that few old-stock citizens a century ago would have recognized Czechs as being a bit different from Slovaks, Slovenes, or Ruthenians, or would care to make the subtle distinction between Sicilians and Northern Italians.[14] "There is no avoiding the unpleasant reality that . . . one of the most salient facts of American history has been its roots as a 'white settler' society that through most of its history defined Blacks, Mexicans, Asians and Native Americans as internal and external Others: slaves, conquered 'mongrels,' 'coolies,' and 'savages,' respectively" (Goldberg 1992:210).

The first and still most rigorous attempt to systematize and rank-order components of the American racial/ethnic system was that of Warner and Srole (1945), more than a half-century ago in their classic account *The Social Systems of American Ethnic Groups*. In a tabular "scale of subordination and assimilation" (288), these scholars identified five "racial types," each subdivided into six "cultural types," in "descending" order: 1. light Caucasoids; 2. dark Caucasoids; 3. Mongoloid and Caucasoid mixtures with Caucasoid appearance dominant; 4. Mongoloid and Caucasoid mixtures that appear Mongoloid; 5. Negroes and all Negroid mixtures.

This form of "political correctness," one that prevailed for so many generations and seems rather less enlightened than the current brand, was hardly ever challenged, even by the best educated. Indeed many of those who bothered to think about the matter were convinced that the obvious physical, mental, and moral inequalities among the races (and between the sexes too, of course) were hereditary, divinely ordained, eternal verities not to be questioned by mortal beings. But the situation has never been wholly static. Recent social history has generally borne out Warner and Srole's expectations concerning future developments.

All of the six cultural types in Racial Types I and II we predict will change from ethnic groups and become wholly a part of the American class order. The members of each group, our Yankee City evidence shows, are permitted to be upwardly mobile in the general class order. But all of the six cultural types in each of the Racial Types IV and V are likely to develop into castes or semi-castes like that of the American Negro. (1945:295)

The social mobility of those darker Caucasoids, that is persons drawn from eastern and southern Europe and the Middle East, which progressed throughout the twentieth century, continues a trend beginning far back in the colonial period.[15] Thus the seventeenth- and eighteenth-century German settlers were obliged to run the gauntlet of hostility, derision, and discrimination before they were eventually certified as bona fide Americans by their neighbors. Even less friendly was the reception accorded the Irish coming to American shores from the 1830s onward. Their treatment in the British Isles was repeated, and they were racialized by earlier settlers as a debased lesser breed (T. W. Allen 1994). Many a year was to pass before the community of Irish Americans, now better fed, bathed and attired, and visibly scrambling up the socioeconomic ladder, were recognized as eligible Caucasians. Subsequently, Scandinavians, mid nineteenth-century German immigrants, and Jews from whatever land were to suffer many of the same indignities that were heaped upon the Irish.

But it was the vast swarm of newcomers from eastern and south-

ern Europe, materializing from the 1880s onward, that provoked
the greatest consternation and debates over racial identity. In any
event, among the American-born masses, the hostility toward these
strangers, thought to be semibarbarous, certainly contained a streak
of racism.

> During the nineteenth century, the category of "white" was sub-
> ject to challenges brought about by the influx of diverse groups
> who were not of the same Anglo Saxon stock as the founding im-
> migrants. In the nineteenth century, political and ideological
> struggles emerged over the classification of Southern Europeans,
> the Irish and Jews, among other "non-white" categories. Na-
> tivism was only effectively curbed by the institutionalization of a
> racial order that drew the color line *around*, rather than *within*,
> Europe. (Omi and Winant 1986 : 64 – 65) [16]

Historical happenstance hastened the process. "Once immigration
from Europe was effectively restricted [by World War I], the new immigrants were no longer defined as a threat to racial purity but as a
threat to political and economic order" (Pavalko 1980 : 56; also see
Hoelscher 1998 : 76 – 80). This perceived threat was key in initiating
the rather frantic Americanization programs that proliferated in the
1910s.

If the definition of "whiteness" has been relaxed and extended geographically over the years, no such reclassification has been experienced by "people of color." (A discussion of the broader implications
of race and racism is deferred until a later chapter.) From the very
earliest contacts, the invading Europeans have regarded Native Americans with mingled dread, contempt, and morbid fascination (Berkhofer 1978). If attitudes have softened and become sentimentalized
in recent years — hence the periodic resurfacing of the "noble savage"
theme — the aborigines are still regarded as a race apart, if potentially
redeemable.

Persons arriving from Mexico and other Latin American countries, whether aboriginal or mestizo in ancestry, have had poorer
luck, and continue to be perceived in strongly racialist terms. Al-

though many Asian Americans have fared well materially of late and have risen in status, the legacy of the "yellow peril," so pervasive in fiction, early films, and the popular imagination for so long, lingers on (M. Davis 1998:285–355; Marchetti 1993; Wu 1982), and even today overt or subtle discrimination persists in television and elsewhere in American life (Hamamoto 1994). But, of course, in terms of strength and durability, none of the other racialist visions of otherness match the great black-white schism, however cosmeticized it may have become in recent times. It is worth repeating that the ethnic/racial perceptions noted here and elsewhere are seldom based on close observation of the actual members of the groups in question.

In any event, such modes of perceiving the Other on the part of a dominant and often domineering Euro-American population have found external expression in a number of ways. Among the more obvious is the set of terms used to designate those who are ethnically or racially distinct from modal Americans. The sheer number of such epithets, which range from the jocular to the vicious, but mostly toward the latter, is truly amazing. It would be interesting to ascertain whether any other national lexicon can compete with the American in the amplitude and variety of this genre. A sample of the relatively more printable documented in the monumental *Dictionary of American Regional English* (Cassidy 1985, 1991, 1996) includes *bohunk, buck, Canuck, coonass, Frog, greaser, Guinea, Hebe, heinie, hunky, jigaboo, kike, Kraut, and Mick.*

Derogatory representations may also appear in material form. It is only recently that offensive toys have disappeared from store shelves (Nelson 1990). Nasty racial/ethnic stereotypes were staple items in the departed worlds of minstrel shows and vaudeville, in humorous postcards, early comic strips, radio, and commercial advertisements. The recent vogue for Polish jokes was only the latest in a series of snickering slights. But perhaps the most potent of all modes of representing the Other has been cinema.

In film, arguably the most popular and profitable form of culture in the last one hundred years, racist practices dominate the industrial, representational, and narrational history of the medium. Indeed, U.S. cinema has consistently constructed whiteness, the representational and narrative form of Eurocentrism, as the norm by which all "Others" fail by comparison. People of color are generally represented as either deviant threats to white rule, thereby requiring civilizing or brutal punishment, or fetishized objects of exotic beauty, icons for a racist scopophilia. (Bernardi 1996:405)

Verbal and visual denigration, so often a product of ignorance, can translate into sticks and stones quite literally. The deeply felt, albeit sometimes subconscious, antagonisms toward those of unfamiliar appearance and behavior have resulted in de jure or de facto exclusion in the past, and to some extent even today, from certain schools, crafts, professions, voting booths, shops, and sport and entertainment venues. The more comprehensive and revisionist of our history texts are crowded with tales of race riots, the violent harassment of Chinese and Japanese in the American West, the deportation of many Mexican Americans in the early twentieth century, the genocide and apartheid visited upon so many Native American communities, and other horrors. It is only a remarkably few years ago that state and local statutes prohibiting "miscegenation" or sustaining exclusionary zoning have been declared unconstitutional.

A NEW, MORE ENLIGHTENED ERA?

It is difficult to say just when a shift began to be evident in societal attitudes, when a genuine curiosity about, and incipient sympathy toward, the Other emerged from the malice and indifference of the past, or when the hitherto voiceless began clamoring for respectful notice from the citizenry at large.[17] It is even harder to explain why this development and others obviously akin to it happened how and when they did — and not just in the United States — a herculean task to be accosted in a subsequent chapter. If a guess must be hazarded about such a sea change in our collective psyche, perhaps the Great Depression of the 1930s, with its major political, social, and cultural convulsions, was a principal catalyst (Weiss 1979:585). This was also the decade that witnessed a surge of interest in folklore and regionalism. Then World War II, following immediately afterward, certainly energized whatever transformation may have been gestating. Another undeniable factor was the resumption of massive immigration in the 1960s, an influx unprecedented in character and source areas from anything known earlier. But whatever the reasons, who can deny that we now live in an era when "ethnics" strive to make themselves heard, seen, and appreciated in all kinds of ways, and that they may be succeeding.

But we should also be aware of another ambiguously relevant development, one antecedent to the positive ethnic self-expression discussed in the following pages, but something that is still very much with us. The phenomenon in question bears the rather awkward label of *anti-conquest*, a coinage proposed by Mary Louise Pratt (1992) in her study of Western travel writing about the non-Western world. On the face of it, the practice of adopting and cherishing selected aspects of the culture of conquered and subordinated "natives" might seem to be the generous, fraternal thing to do. But anti-conquest appears less benevolent under critical scrutiny. It involves "the strategies of representation whereby European bourgeois subjects seek to secure their innocence in the same moment as they assert European hegemony" (Pratt 1992:7).

This pattern of exculpation is a familiar one throughout virtually all of the United States, wherever we find presumably aboriginal placenames (often dreadfully mangled) attached to all sorts of landscape items, or in the marketing of pseudo-Indian goods (as often as not manufactured abroad). Another revealing example is the great popularity of relict, but more often recently fabricated Spanish-sounding placenames in such states as California, Arizona, and Florida.

The concept of anti-conquest is explored in some detail in R. D. K. Herman's (1999) article on the clash of cultures in Hawaii.

> The anti-conquest poses itself as a benign paternalism that puts the Other on a pedestal — a gesture of respect that is also an exclusion, an isolation, and a fixing of the Other into a historical space separate from the modern. In this case, anti-conquest is manifest as the promotion of things Hawaiian at the same time that

Hawaiians themselves are excluded from power. Anti-conquest is, therefore, a part of conquest in no way antithetical, but only masquerading as different by operating backwards. (1999:77)

The identity of anti-conquest as a variety of cryptoracism will become evident in the final chapter.

It is not too difficult to find instances in other places and other times of cultural traits being transferred among countries by immigrants, or of discriminatory or insulting behavior on the part of new settlers toward natives, or vice versa. However, the broadcasting of ethnic pride to the world at large by persons of immigrant background is something utterly novel and recent in social history, and nowhere more exuberantly developed than in the United States (Lopata 1976).

The Ethnic Festival

Of all the outwardly directed modes of exhibiting ethnic identity and pride, perhaps none is more vigorous, elaborate, and effective than the ethnic festival. It is also a relatively late development, a fresh version of a formula that communities long ago devised to impart some meaning to their collective existence. Indeed it is hard to imagine any semblance of community in a population that lacks periodic or occasional public performance of some ritual of abiding value. In premodern and early modern times, this function was almost always religious in character: the celebration of holy days, saints' days, and the like, frequently involving processions, music, dance, drama, special costume, feasting, and other out-of-the-ordinary, sometimes carnivalesque activities. Such traditional events are still with us, of course, though much diminished in number, potency, and their centrality to the health of the group. Some, like Saint Patrick's Day (Kelton 1985) or the church-related festivals that draw large crowds in Manhattan's Little Italy, have become essentially secularized and no longer limit their appeal to the faithful.

With the rise and triumph of nationalism in the modern nation-state, political commemorations usurped the role of the ecclesiastical and furnished a soul-stirring round of special days that fleshed out the importance of being a French, German, Mexican, Japanese, or Soviet citizen. And insofar as we can regard nationalism as ethnic identity writ large, these were indeed ethnic occasions. But much less so today. In the case of the United States, the emotional intensity of Independence Day, Washington's Birthday, or Memorial Day during generations past is beyond the comprehension of the blasé American of the early twenty-first century. The Fourth of July retains only vestigial resonance for the multitudes. The parades, decorations, picnics, orations, and other noises of yore are fading memories for most towns or a pale imitation of bygone days, perhaps little more than an excuse for an exhilarating fireworks display. Even more interesting has been the fate of Lincoln's Birthday, Flag Day, Columbus Day, Labor Day, and Armistice Day, occasions which post-office and bank patrons have come to regard more as annoyances than as cues for patriotic elation. In parallel fashion, Christmas, Easter, and other sanctified dates have shed most of their otherworldly significance.

Supplanting such nationwide and faithwide moments of worshipful affirmation has been a remarkable proliferation, indeed explosion, of more localized or specialized celebrations — a decidedly twentieth-century phenomenon. We now have in the United States uncounted thousands of daylong or weeklong periods of carefully engineered jubilation to extol the wonders of the locality's crops, biota, scenery, foods, crafts, sports, industrial products, architecture, music, folklore, heroes, beauteous maidens, historical events, and every other imaginable (and some unimaginable) claim for notoriety. Although mercenary motives are certainly not absent among the merchants and promoters, a more basic explanation for this largely spontaneous, widespread program for communal self-congratulation must be sought elsewhere. In a world in which traditional ligatures of personal, group, and place identity have been so badly frayed, such groping for anchorage in alternative harbors does make sense as a device to forge, reshape, and project identity (Danielson 1972 : 435–441), or at least to offer some consolation. The ethnic festival is a special subspecies of this latter-day mode of specialized excitement and an especially intriguing one.

There are two distinct periods in the evolution of the ethnic festival in America. The function of the first was ethnogenetic, to help fashion — along with other strategies, of course — a sense of peoplehood and shared identity among members of a specific immigrant or racial group. The most instructive example may be that of the largest such entity: the German American. As Kathleen Conzen (1985, 1989) has pointed out in her penetrating accounts of the invention of German Americanness, this was a population that "lacked a common religion, common regional or class origins, a common political ideology" (1989 : 48), and, one might add, a standardized German language. But, despite the serious divisions and antagonisms besetting this diversified assortment of human beings, "a common festive culture . . . drew them to one another and set them apart from other Americans" (K. Conzen 1989 : 46). Thus it came about that individuals of Germanic origin, and subsequently other groups, began to stage elaborate festivals, pageants, and parades, and were no longer content to be bit players within general holiday and communitywide celebrations.

These consensus-building exercises were not automatic, hardly the product of some collective epiphany. In a manner analogous to the creation of ethnic awareness and action in various nineteenth-century European settings that was manipulated by self-appointed members of an aggrieved intelligentsia, many of these festivals and related tactics were the doing of ethnic activists engaged in "a historically grounded act of cultural politics" (Schultz 1994 : 20). The outcome was the emergence of something new, as we have already noted, a community with no prior existence in homeland or America.

The process is set forth in great, revealing detail in a study of the 1925 Norse-American Centennial celebration in Minneapolis. It was, in effect, the fabrication of a cohesive Norwegian American image and sensibility, something previously dormant or absent (Schultz 1994). In this instance, the intent and accomplishment were overtly national in scope; in other cases the program may have been localized, but not without broader implications. But all such efforts were hyphenation projects and rife with ambiguity: the affirmation of the group's adoptive Americanness but, at the same time, a declaration of its specialness by virtue of a real or imagined sociocultural origin in a distant land. Thus this initial version of the ethnic festival, along with other gambits, was quite unlike the nation-building programs of European agitators whose aim was nothing less than separation and autonomy.

Akin in spirit and purpose to the festivals just discussed, and sometimes their convenient excuse, have been newly invented ethnic holidays. These are not the venerable, durable items arriving from overseas, such as Ramadan, Passover, Tet, the Chinese New Year, or a watered-down Saint David's Day intended to preserve some degree of Welshness, but instead rather recent, self-conscious devices designed to rouse or invigorate feelings of peoplehood under American conditions. A prime, relatively successful example is Kwanza, the harvest festival recently created by African Americans in obvious emulation of, and as a challenge to, the Thanksgiving and Christmas of the larger community. The elaboration of Chanukah, previously a relatively obscure episode in the Jewish calendar, is a parallel case. And it has only been since the 1960s that National Cherokee Day has been observed late every August. More localized an occasion, but perhaps as spirited as any in execution, is Juneteenth, the day on which black Texans rejoice over their emancipation in 1865. Some other such efforts have proved to be abortive or halfhearted, for example, the hope of turning Columbus Day into a major glorification of Italianness and the even less effective achievements of Leif Erickson Day and Kosciusko Day.

This first phase of the ethnic festival phenomenon has not been entirely inner directed. In some cases, non-insiders were permitted and eventually encouraged to watch, patronize, and even join in. That is what happened at the annual Swedish American festival in Lindsberg, Kansas, where the entire community, including the non-Swedish, became active participants (Danielson 1972). In southern Louisiana a recent spate of festivals — a practice initiated in 1936 but with examples now counted in the scores (Esman 1982:202–203) — has invigorated what had been a faltering sense of ethnic identity among the Cajuns. This occurred in good part because of its ratification by tourists arriving from far and wide. Indeed "for the Cajuns, the very fact of tourism has allowed a separate identity to survive"

(Esman 1984 : 465). Dutch American identity in southwestern Michigan could certainly have managed to endure without its popular, annual, tulip-laden festival, rooted as it is in other cultural elements, but the influx of hordes of visitors must serve nicely as a confidence builder (Sinke 1992). The practice of initiating single-group ethnic events is by no means extinct today. A fine example is the recent revival of Dyngus Day celebrations in Buffalo, New York, a development that seems to be a belated spasm of the Euro-American ethnic revival or, perhaps more realistically, recreational symbolic ethnicity (D. A. Silverman 1997).

In recent decades, the ethnic festival has undergone a basic transformation in keeping with the parallel evolution of Ethnicity itself. This metamorphosis may be signaled by a shift in the site or route of the event. The Puerto Rican experience is a case in point. Although in other cities the community's parades are held in Puerto Rican neighborhoods, in New York City, where something of a critical cultural breakthrough seems to have occurred,

> the parade is traditionally held along Fifth Avenue from 37th Street to 86th Street on a Sunday in early June. . . . It is an area where few Puerto Ricans live, yet is of symbolic importance for New Yorkers of all ethnic backgrounds. Long associated with the city's "establishment," it is the site of many parades, notably the St. Patrick's Day Parade, the Labor Day Parade, and that most curious ethnic ceremony of New York's social elite, the Easter Parade. (Kasinitz and Freidenberg-Herbstein 1987 : 334)

Appropriation of this elegant venue is not only an affirmation of ethnic self-esteem but an invitation to the larger world to gaze and admire.

Thus the essential attribute of the second phase of the phenomenon is a turning outward. Now that the immigrant-derived community has established its ethnic credentials to its own satisfaction, it is eager to proclaim itself to everyone, to invite interest and approval, and to share with outsiders its special cultural patrimony. But, in doing so, the celebrants seem to be transcending the uniqueness of their traditions, so that "increasingly, ethnic festivals have become celebrations of ethnicity itself rather than a particular ethnic heritage" (Alba 1990:104). Such transcendence takes the ethnic festival one logical step further into an ecumenical enshrinement of the general delights of Ethnicity. Consequently, the agenda has shifted from the legitimization of the single group toward an appreciation of the exotic many (Bodnar 1992:70–75).

In the case of Massachusetts in the 1980s, thirteen *multiethnic* festivals took place alongside fifty-four other events glorifying fifteen specific ethnic entities (Wilkie and Trager 1991:97).[18] More recently, and for the national scene as a whole, Robert Janiskee (1966) has documented no fewer than 3,360 ethnic festivals, and, as of 1995, at least 343 were multicultural.[19] Dozens of them attract one hundred thousand or more patrons, while a few draw more than one million visitors.

In certain major metropolises, the pluralism of ethnic extroversion occurs sequentially rather than simultaneously. On a central site dedicated to the purpose, one group may be assigned a given week, to be followed by others on a weekly basis during the festive season, all to the accompaniment of publicity calculated to entice the general population. The more common format for the multiethnic event is one in which several groups share space and facilities in nonhostile fashion. (But, it is essential to note, "plain vanilla" all-American culture is never featured.) The location of specific stalls and displays may or may not be random — that depends on organizers and participants — but usually a central stage or performance space is available to all at specified times.[20]

The attractions include ethnic music and dance, costumed vendors and performers, perhaps some dramatic presentations and speechifying, the opportunities to purchase ethnic handicrafts, articles of clothing, tape cassettes, flags, buttons, and all manner of other ethnically flavored merchandise, but, above all, food, whether for consumption on the spot, as is usually the case, or for later enjoyment at home. Indeed the exotic edibles may be the strongest drawing card, as it is at nonethnic festivals. In a study of a Midwestern urban ethnic festival featuring some twelve different food booths, Penny Van Esterik observes that the ethnic festival celebrates the cultural pluralism image of the new ethnicity, but the contradictions and ambiguities inherent in this position are expressed through the symbolic use of food. . . . Where ethnics were often negatively defined as people who eat smelly, spicy foods, these same smelly, spicy foods are now valued and utilized in redefining their ethnic identity. (1982:207, 217)

Certain festivals are planned with a quite specific objective in mind: the ethnogenesis or reinforcement of a *panethnic* entity. Thus every Labor Day weekend, New Yorkers of all ethnic persuasions are treated to the Caribbean Carnival held along or near Brooklyn's Eastern Parkway (Kasinitz 1992:133–159). The black and Hispanic groups who put on this colorful show are indeed creating a simulation, or emergent actuality, of togetherness that was decidedly weak or absent in the Antillean homelands. Thus much ethnic assertion today is in current terms, not just a salvage operation aimed at preserving traditional ways. Similarly, Washington's annual Hispano-American Festival, initially staged in the Adams-Morgan neighborhood but now in a downtown site, is "a powerfully integrating and participatory form [that] empowers the many voices of a diverse Spanish-speaking population to construct a social identity" (Cadaval 1989:286). That this event has been ethnogenetically effective seems plausible even though each year's program entails a great deal of bargaining and bickering among competing ethnic, political, and other special interests (Cadaval 1991).

But what is most thought-provoking, as the type of festival with the greatest ideological implications, is the event that seeks to draw in every group, whether resident in a particular neighborhood, as in Washington's Mount Pleasant (B. Williams 1988) or throughout an entire metropolis. An ideal exemplar of such a broader happening was Los Angeles' 1987 Cityroots Festival, a celebration intended to be a working model of an inchoate multicultural society on the metropolitan scale, and implicitly the national as well (Auerbach 1991). Thus

multicultural festivals like Cityroots are a small-scale, partial model of what cultural diversity looks like, sounds like, and tastes like. Festival time is special because of the abundance and juxtaposition of cultures represented, because of the easy access and proximity participants and audiences of various backgrounds have, because the differences highlighted are innocuously cultural rather than political or economic. . . . For audiences, then, multicultural festivals are an enjoyable and informative exercise in face-to-face encounters with diversity. They guide the public through a sort of harmlessly microcosmic tour of how cultural pluralism should work. The implicit message is that the prospect of diverse peoples cooperating and sharing, side by side, is not only possible but desirable. Creating such opportunities for exchange is as important as any specific knowledge transmitted about an ethnic community and its folklore. (Auerbach 1991:236)

It remains only to note, as Jo Anne Schneider has done in commenting on the presentation of Puerto Rican and Polish group identities through ethnic parades, that "the ethnic pluralism celebrated through these parades serves as a safety valve in a society which refuses to recognize class" (1990:50).

Ethnic Villages and Showplaces

By their very nature, ethnic festivals are temporary, though usually annually recurring, affairs, so that they seldom last longer than a week. But there is a less ephemeral alternative: maintaining a visibly, distinctively ethnic neighborhood, a permanent festival, so to speak, and one that clamors for attention by outsiders. Perhaps the best label is "ethnic epitome district" (Stansfield 1996). What is meant here is not the classic ethnic ghetto of first- and second-generation immigrants, a district dominated strongly or totally by a given group, although such a tract may eventually evolve into an epitome district or living museum, something quite different from its original incarnation. "Ethnic Epitome Districts, with their self-conscious and perhaps contrived packaging of ethnic culture to tourists and gentile shoppers in general, have developed an array of businesses aimed primarily at an external, transient clientele" (Stansfield 1996).

The clearest examples of these districts are the various Chinatowns to be found in our larger North American cities (K. J. Anderson 1987). In fact, in the case of the Washington metropolitan area, the only such district, indeed the only recognizably unitary ethnic neighborhood of any sort today, is its small Chinatown (M. Fisher 1995). Originally serving as the only places where Chinese immigrants were permitted to reside and conduct their own businesses (aside from laundries and restaurants), they now rely upon non-Chinese visitors and shoppers for much or most of their sustenance. Today most descendants of the earlier occupants and many of the newer arrivals live well beyond a Chinatown now populated largely by the retired elderly and the more impoverished of the newcomers. Without the domestic and foreign tourists who come to gawk at the extravagantly Sinicized building designs and décor, to indulge in exotic dishes, and purchase strange and wonderful objects from the Mysterious East, the viability of such districts would be questionable. Indeed virtually all the Chinatowns of the smaller western towns that failed to follow the touristic route by commodifying Sinicity have become things of the past.

Single-group neighborhoods, whether self-created or reined in by external forces, have certainly not vanished entirely from the American scene. Indeed, new ones, such as Miami's Little Havana or Chicago's Hispanicized Pilsen, have recently emerged. But the general ploy in fashioning ethnic epitome districts is to take over a faded neighborhood, most of whose original inhabitants may have departed some time ago, then refurbish it as it could or should have looked, elaborating its ethnic stigmata, and wait to see what sort of traffic some clever publicity can generate.[21] Following such a scenario, there have been several relatively successful ventures in the Germanic vein: Fredericksburg, Texas; Hermann, Missouri; New Ulm, Minnesota; the German Village of Columbus, Ohio; and downtown Milwaukee's recent German Renaissance (Hoelscher et al. 1997:395–402). Parallel examples include Detroit's Greek Town (where very few Greeks still reside); a carefully crafted Mexican epitome district in San Antonio; a rather tawdry Cherokee Village in western North Carolina; and its like elsewhere (Curtis 1997). Not to be left behind are the Danish American residents of Solvang, California, who have transformed their town, or at least its façade, into a "Scandinavian" tourist trap.

Perhaps the most instructive experiment in revitalizing an ethnic colony is the Swissification of New Glarus, Wisconsin, over the past sixty years (Hoelscher 1995a, 1995b, 1998; Hoelscher and Ostergren 1993). This small town, founded and settled by Swiss immigrants in the middle decades of the nineteenth century, initially relied heavily on the dairy industry for its livelihood. With the passage of time, the look and behavior of New Glarus and its citizens were becoming virtually indistinguishable from what could be seen in other Wisconsin localities. A few energetic local leaders, spurred in part by the vicissitudes of the dairy economy, realized the social and commercial dividends of refashioning the town into a fiercely authentic Swiss entity in terms of architecture, monuments, signs, museums, food, music, costume, organized tours, festivals, and ethnic societies. Evidently the plan has paid off handsomely. Not only is New Glarus being frequented by throngs of the non-Swiss but it has also attracted many Americans of Swiss ancestry and quite a few visitors from Switzerland itself, persons engaged in "heritage tourism." In a curious turn of events, "the village has taken on the role of international repository for the traditional Swiss culture that has all but vanished from the 'old world'" (Hoelscher 1995a : 488).

New Glarus is not unique in that respect. French tourists seeking the actualities of old France may find them in the New France of Quebec. Similarly, a rather romanticized version of early Finnish farms in Minnesota has been appropriated and manipulated by the more conservative wing of the Finnish American community for political and promotional purposes, so that "nowadays the landscape is a jewelry shop dispensing ethnicity in various hues, including items of recent manufacture in Finland and elsewhere which were unknown to the immigrant Finns, but of importance to contemporary culture brokers" (Kaups 1995 : 15).

If the examples cited represent defensible gestures at authenticity or at least claim some historical excuse, there are counterexamples with no redeeming cultural value whatsoever. As extreme a case as any is Leavenworth, Washington, which, much like its counterpart, Kimberly, British Columbia, was an ordinary small town that decided, quite arbitrarily, to transform itself into an ersatz Bavarian village. Despite the absence of any historical justification, the customers keep arriving in droves.

The phenomena described above embody the convergence of two developments in American culture, but something not limited to the United States. The more recent is the proliferation of historic villages and historically recycled neighborhoods with or without ethnic flavor, a practice apparently initiated with the Williamsburg, Virginia, project in the 1920s and imitated endlessly thereafter. Thus we may regard the ethnic epitome district as one of the subspecies of a grander population. Its older progenitor is to be sought in the history of major world's fairs. Beginning perhaps with the Paris Exposition of 1889, these elaborate showcases of the wonders and feats of the participating countries would not have been complete without a set of exotic "villages," simulacra of an actual landscape or a composite of such in the sponsoring nation complete with suitably bedecked natives doing their properly native things. Such exhibits were certainly much in evidence in the Chicago fairs of 1893, 1933, and 1934, among others, eventually to be supplanted, in Montreal's Expo 1967 and subsequent world's fairs by single structures whose outward design as well as internal displays were meant to convey the quintessence of the country's culture and economy. Extracting the core meaning of both those national villages of recent memory and the currently thriving ethnic epitome districts, we find them to be varieties of "human zoos." And perhaps it would be worthwhile to explore the parallelism in modern times between the evolution of zoological parks and that of synthetic ethnic landscapes.

Often associated with identifiably ethnic neighborhoods are specialized museums devoted to the group in question. In fact, it is only the most diffident of ethnic communities that have not maintained one or more museums and libraries, institutions that frequently include gift shops. Like so many other aspects of the quest for social identity, these relatively sedate expressions of ethnic pride are mostly recent in origin (Buttlar 1995; Wynar and Buttlar 1978).[22] Such establishments are dual in appeal, seeking to draw patrons from the general population as well as from the sponsoring community. In that respect they tend to differ from the multitudes of ethnic studies programs on American college campuses whose class lists are strongly dominated, if not totally monopolized, by students affiliated with the group in question.

All Manner of Signs

Less formal than museums, libraries, or college curricula, and less space-consuming than festivals, is still another device of recent vintage that has been projecting striking images of ethnic identity and pride both intraethnically and to the world at large: the outdoor mural.[23] Much remains to be learned about the historical geography of the phenomenon in the United States and elsewhere. What seems probable is that this form of public art, at least as manifested on exterior walls and fences, was either absent or of little consequence throughout the world before the 1920s. Its powerful development in Mexico began in that decade and has continued there ever since. The extensive New Deal subsidization of historical and inspirational murals on the interior surfaces of public buildings in the 1930s may have stimulated emulation in other venues in the United States and eventually, though on a modest scale, overseas.

These creations, which unlike advertising billboards are meant to endure, are not always ethnic in character. The content can be political-cum-ethnic or purely political or historical, or simply decorative. Murals can be used to tout the glories of the town, to commemorate local notables, or to convey some message about the neighborhood, while possibly transmitting some sort of ethnic signal. The more impressive examples can be heroic in dimension, clever in design and execution, the handiwork of skilled professionals, and deserving of critical respect, and they may be commissioned by the municipality, neighborhood, or other organizations. At the other end of the spectrum we have surreptitious graffiti, too often lacking serious content or artistic merit but perhaps, embodying ethnic material.

The mural movement has flourished in several, but not all, of the larger American cities, including New York, Chicago, Los Angeles, Philadelphia, and, most exuberantly of all, San Francisco (Drescher 1994). But surprisingly enough, the places in which you will most readily find Native American murals, some of which are quite memorable, are the small towns of Oklahoma, for example Pawhuska, not Oklahoma City or Tulsa. Of the various ethnic groups engaged in mural art, the most enthusiastic has been the Latino and especially the Mexican American, and not just in the Southwest (Arreola 1984b; Fox 1996 : 218; Olson n.d.). If the exploitation of murals to extol the worth and vitality of one's ethnic group is an accepted practice among Latinos, East Asians, Native Americans, and African Americans, it has never caught on among any of the European ethnic groups. This is perplexing in light of the peaking of the so-called European ethnic revival during the 1970s, just when the fervor for murals was becoming strong and widespread. Is the explanation to be sought in the relative power and socioeconomic status of the two categories of ethnic groups?

There are still other smaller, less obtrusive, less expensive ways in which to display one's ethnic identity beyond the immediate group, but they seem to have failed to capture the attention of scholars. The most pervasive are bumper stickers that grace the posteriors of so many private vehicles nowadays. In this instance, virtually all ethnic groups, from oldest to most recent, seem eager to indulge in a practice that, to the best of my recollection, was rare or unknown before the 1970s. Like many of the other items treated in this chapter, the specifically ethnic bumper sticker is just one facet of a broader recent development: the penchant for personal exhibitionism expressed via vehicles, clothing, ornament, and house and grounds. The object in question can be verbal and frequently jocular in tone and, if ethnic in intent, may contain nothing but the flag or colors of the homeland.

The human body and the various objects that cover and adorn it offer ample opportunity for the individual not just to project one's self-image, gender, age, social and economic status, occupation, personality, and aspirations but also his or her ethnic affiliation as well. As noted previously, such a display may be unselfconscious, the automatic retention of traditional attire and body management among immigrant or indigenous groups that have remained socially isolated (F. Davis 1992 : 180–181). But of greater relevance for analysis of recent developments is a quite different set of practices: the deliberate seeking out and affecting of styles of clothing, coiffure, beards and mustaches, facial and body makeup, color, ornament, and insignia presumed to be faithful copies of ancestral patterns. Or the message can be delivered by inscriptions on T-shirts, ties, caps, and buttons. Such a program of ethnic "outing," a matter of quotidian behavior, is something other than the temporary donning of costumes on festive and ceremonial occasions.

Clothing, jewelry, and hairdo may be the easiest ways to announce one's ethnic/racial preference, but advances in medical technology enable the cosmetic surgeon to do a great deal either to conceal or enhance one's visible identity, by remolding features so as to conform to the sought-after ideal.[24] A less costly option, but one not often seen in the United States, is the tattoo laden with ethnic overtones.

Of all the ethnic communities in the land the one that has most conspicuously exploited personal appearance as its manifesto is the African American, a concomitant, obviously, of the Black Pride movement.

> Through the 1970s and on into the 1990s, African-American men and women added and discarded an array of African-inspired clothes, jewelry, and hair-dos. Most items of dress adopted in the early years of rediscovering the West African past did not survive into the following decades. Looking back to that revolutionary period of the 1960s and 1970s, we can see that the kaftans did not last long as a daily fashion among the black American men involved in reclaiming their ties to West Africa, and within a decade African-American men and women had discarded the Afro and began braiding their hair or growing Rasta locks. (Griebel 1995: 224–225)

But whatever the specific, often transient, device that African Americans may adopt to announce their identity, what is revelatory is the decrease in efforts to simulate Caucasian Americans. Thus less often those costly, even painful, attempts to bleach skin and straighten hair, but rather the display of assertively African-related hairdos and other items (Campbell 1982; Rooks 1996; Shohat and Stam 1994: 325).

It seems predictable, then, that, although specific fads may come and go, African Americans will persist in exhibiting their African roots in one way or another, most clearly in clothing and body-related fashion, well into the future. But there is one interesting, venerable practice that has somehow survived intact past the trauma of the slave trade and American servitude and acculturation, going on recently to get its second wind, so to speak: the woman's headwrap. "It is a tradition which continues today in the last decade of the twentieth century, when black American women of all ages wear the headwrap for all manner of occasions. As such, the headwrap serves African-Americans as the fundamental symbol of self in relation to ethnic identity" (Griebel 1995:225).

Less widely noticed but perhaps as meaningful as this resurgence of Africanisms is a parallel development among many Native Americans. These individuals have chosen a return to traditional hair-styling and the wearing of selected garments and ornaments from the tribal past as conspicuous signals in their workaday encounters with the world.

> An even more telling, quite recent example of the power of dress to sustain or fabricate a sense of peoplehood under alien circumstances is that of the Hmong. The transformation of regional sub-styles of Lao Hmong dress into a cohesive Hmong American style can be interpreted as symbolic of Hmong American ethnicity. As the generation most acutely experiencing discrimination based on their ascribed ethnic identity, teenagers wear dress which expressed Hmong cohesiveness and pride. By wearing a mix of Hmong sub-styles teenagers visibly accept and celebrate their ascribed ethnic identity both as individuals and as corporate representatives of their families and communities. (Lynch 1995:265–266)

What makes this case worthy of special note is its ethnogenetic character. In their original abodes, the Hmong lacked any sense of sociocultural identity reaching beyond a given village and neighboring settlements. Thus the new synthetic Hmong American identity owes its existence to the mixing and sublimation of various previously isolated cultural complexes, of which dress happens to be the most visible.

Of course, the proclamation of ethnic pride by means of costume need not limit itself to the venerable and traditional. A case in point is the zoot suit craze among young Mexican Americans in southern California in the early 1940s (Fox 1996:80–81). These young men and their female companions created a distinctive image by donning deliberately provocative types of clothing and jewelry and inventing new hairdos, none of which had any visible reference to Mexico.

Any definitive study of the deployment of dress in the calculated promotion of ethnic awareness would encounter a major obstacle peculiar to our times. Unlike the situation in previous eras, when clothing and modes of bodily adornment were more or less geographically stable, fashions changed at a leisurely rate, and social station dictated wardrobe, today we have limitless choice and constant change — and much blurring of the sartorial division between the sexes. Styles and fads may be borrowed from anywhere in the world, as has been happening with popular music and cuisines, so that the cross-national sharing of new and traditional items has made everyday life into something of a veritable costume ball (F. Davis 1992; Eicher and Sumberg 1995). The ethnic zealot may be hard put to make a definitive fashion statement.

As noted earlier, first-generation non-British immigrants could do little to leave their impress on the settlement fabric and landscape of America, and even less is possible today. But if the construction of identifiably ethnic houses and other structures, aside from churches, is simply not feasible, there are opportunities for minor modifications that fall within the broad category of signs. Thus one might ask whether the colorful repainting of white or unpainted houses and barns by French Canadians in northern New England is a deliberate assertion of Québecois sentiment. The same sort of query could apply to the vivid color schemes Portuguese Americans have applied to older buildings in various cities. But ethnically militant persons of whatever ancestry can display flags or various ornaments on lawn or porch, items broadcasting an ethnic message. Or the relatively cosmetic changes implemented by immigrants acquiring preexisting housing may simply be the acting out of traditional norms, not necessarily a declaration of ethnic pride. Such seems to have been the case among the 1880–1920 generation of Italians in a Brooklyn neighborhood who, by means of added fencing, gardens, and changes in siding, imparted a distinctly Mediterranean flavor to their streetscape (Krase 1993).

Smaller and less often available for inspection than house and grounds, but presumably more durable, is another sort of sign in the built landscape that offers the ardent ethnic advocate a literally final chance to propagandize the cause: the gravestone. As suggested earlier, inscriptions above the final resting places of a significant minority of "hyphenated" Americans attest to undying devotion to their ethnic patrimony (Jackson and Vergara 1989:48–59). This is more than cultural inertia. The message may be verbal in the form of a political or cultural pronouncement or a sentimental poem, or it can be graphic — the flag or special emblem, logo, or musical motif sacred to the group, or a laser-printed reproduction of some hallowed site or object. The appropriation of this medium for ethnic expression is part of broader developments: the secularization of funerary practices and the free rein given personal expression in all conceivable media.

Language Again

The broader issues of language in the evolving ethnic scene in the United States are best dealt with elsewhere in this study. It is clear, however, that, as a device to mobilize ethnic passion, here is an item of far weaker salience than in many Old World situations, that the posture of ethnic enthusiasts is more defensive than defiant. Nonetheless, questions remain that invite serious research. How extensive and successful have been the efforts to sustain or resuscitate such ancestral tongues as Yiddish, Chinese (Petersen 1980:241), Ukrainian, Spanish (Fox 1996:7), or Welsh (Knowles 1997:297)? What effects, if any, do such programs have upon the external dealings of the community? Is it true, as argued by Crawford (1992) and Fox (1996), that a substantial number of recent immigrants wish to retain their birth tongue while becoming fluent in English? Are we witnessing more continuity of ethnic identity in personal names and less inclination to Americanize surnames among non-Anglophone immigrants than was usual in the past (Bennett 1976:165–174)?

One question we can answer has to do with the persistence and possible intensification of the linguistic barrier between two major camps of a divided society. It appears that comparative analysis of the given names recently bestowed on black and white infants leaves no doubt as to a continuing divergence between them along with the assertion of a distinctive black culture (Lieberson and Bell 1992; Lieberson and Mikelson 1995; McGregory 1985). Inasmuch as most of the black names in question are African or pseudo-African, one must assume an element of deliberate ethnic avowal in their adoption. It would be most interesting to learn about trends in patterns of personal names among Latinos, Native Americans, and other non–Euro-Americans in the United States and the extent to which they do, or do not, run parallel to changes occurring in the dominant population. Unfortunately, to the best of my knowledge, no such studies have been carried out to date.

Literary Outing

If one must reserve judgment regarding the efficacy of language maintenance as a weapon in the ethnic armory nowadays, there is little question about the potency of texts of various kinds in the English language, or English translations from foreign tongues, in advancing ethnic aspirations. Whether the deed is intentional or simply the byproduct of other developments, literary expression, in the form of novels, short stories, verse, essays, drama, criticism, reportage, and autobiography, along with related feats in cinema, television, music, dance, and the visual arts, has earned considerable attention, respect, and sympathy for *some* ethnic communities in recent decades. Limiting the discussion for the moment to the written word, note a remarkable recent switch in direction. Like many another phenomenon, literature, as both cause and effect, has been swept up in the broad stream of an ongoing cultural convulsion. No longer is discourse automatically confined to a hermetic immigrant community and in the ancestral language (with the obvious major exception of the African American situation, where English is the only choice). No longer is the magazine, newspaper, stage production, or work of fiction walled off from an uncomprehending, uninterested general public. Instead, the frequently monolingual second- or later-generation author thinks and writes in English, keeping in mind the opportunity, often the burning desire, to reach far beyond his or her coethnics.[25]

We have here an aspect of the American scene so vast and complex it would be utterly unreasonable to expect any scholar to cover it adequately, treating all the many relevant ethnic-literary communities and doing so in proper historical and critical depth. Evidently no one has ever thought of addressing such an awesome task. Also missing are accounts of ethnically flavored literature emanating from immigrant groups in other settler lands where the genre may be less well developed. What we do have is a rich body of works, including anthologies, critical surveys, and appreciations, dealing with specific ethnically defined literatures in the United States and, fortunately, a periodical dedicated to keeping track of a multifaceted phenomenon: *MELUS: The Journal of the Society for the Study of the Multi-Ethnic Literature of the United States* (1974 –).

There is considerable inequality among the various American ethnic entities in terms of the quantity and quality of their outwardly directed literature and the impact it has registered upon the general reading public. By any reckoning the three groups scoring the greatest success in recent decades have been the African American, Jewish American, and Southern. Indeed, if the writers in question were to form a literary cartel, they might conceivably dominate the contemporary world of serious American letters.

The oldest and perhaps most voluminous of the three ethnic oeuvres is the African American, with a history beginning in colonial times and steadily gathering force and momentum up to the present moment (B. W. Bell 1987; Gates 1997; Hill 1998). Beyond the sheer size and four-century duration of the community, it might be claimed that its published spokespersons have at their disposal an especially ample, promising mass of raw material, though all too much of it is rooted in oppressive, often tragic conditions. And indeed the more gifted authors have risen to the challenge with products rivaling those of any other ethnic or national school. The African American story has also gone beyond the printed page to reach stage and screen in recent years and an increasingly appreciative national, and occasionally international, audience. One must not overlook the connections with various black dance companies or the painters, sculptors, weavers, potters, and other practitioners of the fine, popular, and folk arts. The articulation of African American identity for both insiders and outsiders involves the interaction of all available media.

An even larger population that enjoyed literary notoriety and excellence during the twentieth century is the white Southern. Although it may not be customary to label Southerners as ethnics, they fully satisfy the objective criteria used to define an ethnic group, as previously argued (Killian 1970; Tindall 1976). Like the Québecois, Bretons, Kurds, Welsh, Sikhs, Catalans, Basques, and others, they may never have gained political autonomy, despite an exceedingly bloody effort, but, in the face of all the corrosive forces of modernity, they have managed to preserve and perpetuate a quite special cultural complex. The greatest of the Southern prose writers are towering figures who command worldwide admiration and are not only on a par with their Yankee peers but stand on equal footing with the finest of the British, French, Russian, and others.

In retrospect, the rise and triumph of the twentieth-century Jewish American writer might be viewed as a consummation preordained, given the intense bookishness of "the people of the book." The achievements of both major and minor authors in this fraternity are so widely recognized and covered in so many critical accounts (e.g., Guttmann 1971; Harap 1987a, 1987b; Shatzky and Taub 1997) that no extended comment is called for here. What is noteworthy is the degree to which Jewish American writings and other creative endeavors have converged with the mainstream — a far cry from the early ghettoization of the Yiddish scribe — a two-way process of naturalization and Judaicization of sensibilities, a reciprocal transaction between gentile and Jewish communities, instigated by immigrants and their progeny. As Daniel Walden has noted, "Millions of Americans have seen *Goodbye, Columbus*, the movie, and millions know *The Chosen*, the film. . . . The point is that with the passing of time, American Jewish writing has been able to penetrate middle America, for better or worse" (Shatzky and Taub 1997:xii).

Although the various immigrant groups, from the early British and African American onward, have monopolized the literary scene throughout the history of the nation, one must not overlook the indigenous communities. Their accomplishments and reputation in the creative realm have followed quite a different trajectory from that of bearers of Old World cultures. Unlike virtually all overseas newcomers, North America's pre-Columbian inhabitants were preliterate, yet rich in oral traditions and pictographic texts. Thus, for Native Americans, literature as we know it became possible only by learning the ways of the intruding Europeans. But before any appreciable body of printed matter could accumulate, connoisseurs, and soon much of the general public, had already discovered indigenous art and had begun collecting it and encouraging its production. This development is analogous to the nineteenth-century European discovery of the wonders of African arts and crafts and the much more recent Western excitement over the paintings and other productions of Australian aborigines. Indeed what has been happening in North America is just one example of a general lust among economically dominant populations for presumably authentic artifacts created by "natives" almost anywhere (Morley and Robbins 1995:114–115). And this appetite for the safely exotic Other is, obviously, intimately related to the explosive growth and spread of tourism at all its several levels (Löfgren 1999).

In the American case, three groups have been especially collectible, although others have not been neglected by any means: the Inuit of Alaska and Canada (Ray 1977), the Indians of the Pacific Northwest, and, above all, the native peoples of the Southwest. Somewhat ironically, the ceramics, carvings, jewelry, leatherwork, basketry, garments, weavings, and paintings so avidly sought after are, with some exceptions, not pristine objects from the precontact period but rather items stimulated and hybridized via dealings with Europeans and the acquisition of novel materials, techniques, and ideas. Another result of such cross-fertilization has been a belated entry into the world of letters. Unsurprisingly, the dominant motif in Native American fiction and nonfiction has been in the vein of protest and lamentation. It is more like the work of African Americans than the verbal output of European immigrant stock (Larson 1978; Krupat 1986).

Turning to non-English European immigrants, one might anticipate that the sheer size of a given group ought to correlate with the bulk and impact of its literary production. However, the actuality fails to bear out expectations. The largest of these populations, the German American, is virtually invisible in the literary bazaar. Two factors may account for the situation. After several generations, persons of German derivation have been so completely assimilated that any urge for ethnic self-expression may have faded away. And if any impulse to reach a non-German public had ever been felt, it was severely squelched by the antipathy toward the language and German culture in general occasioned by American participation in two world wars waged against Germanic militarism. But, paradoxically, similar arguments collapse in the case of Irish Americans — even though many members of this group may have been somewhat tepid in supporting the Allied cause as Americans fought alongside the despised British in the two conflicts. After more than a century and a half of successful assimilation and escalation on the socioeconomic scale, following initial humiliation not unlike the German experience, ethnic identity and pride remain more evident than among German Americans. Instead of dwindling away, the Irish American literary voice remains alive, loud, and well (Casey and Rhodes 1979; Fanning 1990).

Another substantial community, the Italian American, also succeeded in making itself heard amidst the Babel of twentieth-century American publications (Green 1974; Gardophe 1987). But, strangely enough, the Polish American, another sizable entity, roughly coeval with the Italian American, has failed to engender much memorable prose or verse in English. Lyra (1985) offers some plausible reasons for this curious silence.

The record is varied among those other communities that won a foothold on American soil in the nineteenth century or even earlier. Evidently the Welsh, Scots, and Dutch felt no pressing need to proclaim their encounter with the New World via the medium of literature as they merged smoothly into Anglo-American society. Among the less numerous entities, happenstance might bring forth a literary star or two whose broad readership exalted the image of their coethnics. Such was the good fortune of Norwegian Americans, whose early struggles as pioneers were immortalized by Knut Hamsun and Ole Rölvaag, while William Saroyan singlehandedly made much of the nation aware of the delights of being Armenian American (Shear 1986).

No such luck has befallen several other immigrant groups whose progeny are now into their third or later generations: the Czech, Serbian, Hungarian, Ukrainian, Greek, Finnish, Portuguese, or Lithuanian, among others. Other newcomers seem to have arrived too recently to create any sort of literary identity, among them Asian Indians, Koreans, Iranians, and Vietnamese. But in the case of that large though seldom noticed population, the Filipino American, some notable writing has recently begun to demand general attention (San Juan 1992:97–116).[26]

Among other immigrants deemed less acceptable by the more nativistic of Americans, two categories have been outstanding in terms of the heft and quality of literary effort: the Latino and the Asian. The diverse groups of persons labeled Hispanic or Latino have generated a goodly quantity of writing which has recently become accessible to a broader clientele, either in translation or in the original English (Gutiérrez and Padillo 1993). Each of the major regional/ national Latino literary traditions, including the Puerto Rican (Hernández 1997; Mohr 1982), Cuban American, Chicano, and Californian Mexican American has been robust enough to inspire anthologies and critical studies. In the Asian (largely Chinese) case, the English-language output has been growing vigorously while also attracting notice from non-Asians (Chin et al. 1974; E. H. Kim 1982; Ling 1990, 1992; S. C. Wong 1993). Even the smaller Middle Eastern influx has given rise to a body of Arab American verse significant enough to merit a book-length critical appreciation (Orfalea and Elmusa 1988).

Obviously, any author intent upon a realistic portrayal of his/her ethnic group that will find favor with a national or international audience must reckon with fearsome odds. But if there are few who win one of the major prizes in the literary lottery, the rewards, both cultural and financial, for those who do can be substantial. Such volumes as *Roots, Native Son, Studs Lonigan, Christ in Concrete, My Name*

Is Aram, The Education of H*Y*M*A*N K*A*P*L*A*N, Bury My Heart at Wounded Knee, and *The Joy Luck Club* come to mind. But the supreme example of what is possible, though drawn from a bygone era and composed under circumstances quite different from ours today and by an external observer, is Harriet Beecher Stowe's *Uncle Tom's Cabin*, a novel that did more to shape or accelerate the course of events than perhaps any other publication in American history. Limited though the author's knowledge of African American life may have been, her sympathetic treatment thereof was a crucial first step in upending hoary stereotypes.[27]

Film and Television

Remote though the prospect of a popular breakthrough may be, the knowledgeable writer need make only a minimal investment of funds. (A parallel statement could apply to musical composers.) All that is called for is a stack of paper, pen, pencil, or writing contraption, and enough time and private space as he or she works solo. With sufficient perseverance, the finished manuscript can eventually find a susceptible publisher or periodical editor, or, as a last resort, the author can try private publication or the electronic media. The downside is that in the vast majority of cases the fictional or nonfiction message may reach only a few hundred or a few thousand readers.

In contrast, the potential audience for a successful, or even mediocre, film or television program is some orders of magnitude greater: tens of millions viewers domestically and the possibility of hundred of millions internationally. But the obstacles to be overcome by the creative ethnic protagonist laboring in the realms of cinema and TV are simply enormous. This is not just because of the financial stakes but as much or more because of the many persons and interests involved in shaping the product. Beyond the writers, who conceive, nurture, cajole, bicker, and endlessly rewrite, there are bankers, producers, sponsors, directors, agents, actors, technical staff, public relations people, official or de facto censors, distributors, and local stations and theaters. Then, in any project dealing with a potentially sensitive topic there are special-interest groups with a stake in the outcome. The process, as played out in Hollywood studios dealing with black themes and actors from about 1939 to 1960, is set forth in excruciating detail in a study by Thomas Cripps (1993).

For those aspiring to entertain and instruct the general public, it is possible to circumvent all or most of the hassles and distortions inherent in the workings of major movie companies and television networks by turning to independent production. If the funding and personnel can be assembled, a feature or documentary with some semblance of ethnic verisimilitude may come to pass, then subsequently enjoy some kind of limited viewership via film or tape cassette in special cinematic venues, educational channels, the Internet, or, in a few lucky instances, general commercial distribution.

What is abundantly clear is that, from their very beginnings to the present, movies and television have been exceptionally powerful instruments in creating, perpetuating, or modifying ethnic/racial images. In doing so, they generally reflect and intensify majoritarian social attitudes. But there have been occasions in this dialectical dance involving the media and the general ethos when the imagemakers have ventured ahead of public sentiment and perhaps nudged it forward a bit. In any event, it is impossible to measure the extent to which film and TV have been either active or passive agents in the considerable shifts in ethnic/racial attitudes over the past several decades. But there is little doubt about the basic scenario and the direction of change therein. In contrast to the situation within the literary realm, a number of scholars have attempted critiques of the totality of at least the major "minorities" as they have been represented in film and/or television (Cortés 1984; L. D. Friedman 1991; James 1991; and, most notably, Shohat and Stam 1994). (For better or worse, radio is no longer a significant factor.) Their consensus is that there has been meaningful change for the better, but that the current situation still leaves much to be desired. Even if it is no longer acceptable to perpetuate the degrading stereotypes so prevalent in popular entertainment in the nineteenth and early twentieth centuries, rare is the show nowadays where we see fully rounded representations of ethnic/racial individuals or communities, or in which such persons have more than a token presence, or where they have genuine artistic control over the production.[28] Nonetheless, progress has been real, so that today a number of blacks, Latinos, and Jewish Americans in film and television, whether or not they create an ethnic persona, attract great numbers of fans from the population at large and command astronomical salaries.

The days of *Amos 'n Andy* and *Abie's Irish Rose* are gone beyond recall. The immediate reasons for the change are obvious enough.

> The steady increase in roles for minorities was hardly a surprise, given the growth of the minority consumer market in the United States, the civil rights movement, and the surge of "ethnic consciousness" during the 1970s. Such change was almost too obvious to report. . . . In 1973 the Michigan State University project on "Communication among the Urban Poor" . . . linked the improvements in minority representation and imagery in television to the growth of minority media and growing public sensitivity to ethnic and racial issues. (Woll and Miller 1987: 16–17)

But the turnabout may have overshot its goal inadvertently, especially in the case of African Americans. Their visibility, as role models in sport and as ordinary people in commercials and sitcoms enjoying all the blessings of an affluent society, may have lulled Caucasian viewers into believing that the fabled level playing field had really materialized. Thus the moral: No need for further policy initiatives (Farhi 2000). The actuality is, of course, rather different.

Perhaps no group better illustrates the maturing of attitudes toward unfamiliar peoples and cultures, as portrayed on movie screen and tube, than does the Native American. Not too long ago there was a wild seesawing of perceptions as the indigenes appeared as either fiendish redskins or noble savages. Recently, however, these venerable stereotypes have begun to fade away to be replaced by story lines and characters more closely approximating reality (Hilger 1995). As already suggested, the roles and images of African Americans in the mass entertainment media have also been experiencing something of a transformation, though, again, the process is far from complete (Bogle 1973; Cripps 1993; Leab 1975). Much the same must be said about the Latino situation, although too little of the community's creative ferment and sociopolitical agitation has yet to capture the attention of the general public in film or other media (Fregoso 1993; Noriega and López 1996).

The experience of Jewish Americans in popular entertainment venues is unique by virtue of their exceptionally strong involvement in the industry as both creators and managers throughout the twentieth century. At the outset, their situation was scarcely different from that of blacks, Native Americans, and other such entities. Like the others, Jews were invariably depicted in demeaning or patronizing terms, and only after decades of painful transition did they finally emerge as ordinary human beings (Erens 1984). Thus, alone among the various ethnic/racial constituencies, Jewish Americans currently have no grievances about the ways they are being exhibited to the world. This culmination did not come about because of an ethnic agenda being pushed by Jewish American insiders. Instead, the producers were simply responding to the facts of cultural assimilation and the reciprocal Americanization/Judaicization of the audience as they kept a vigilant eye cocked at box-office receipts and TV ratings.

Italian Americans can also claim some meaningful share of the Americanization process, although Michael Barone may be overstating the case when he argues that "the melting pot has worked: Italian Americans have become Americanized. But America has become, to some *considerable* extent Italian Americanized" (1994:494; emphasis added).

Much less reassuring has been the tale of how film and television have dealt with Asians and Middle Easterners (Bernstein and Studlar 1997; Hamamoto 1994). Overt or subtle misrepresentation persists, and the legacy of Charlie Chan and Fu Manchu lingers on, not to mention all those dark-skinned Arabs or sheiks with bedroom eyes. Orientalism still thrives in front of the camera. There may be a certain irony here, at least as far as the Chinese, Japanese, Koreans, and Vietnamese are concerned, for they have been recently type-cast as "model minorities." In cold fact, however, despite the remarkable academic and business achievements of some members of these communities, taken as a whole they have not yet reached parity with Caucasian Americans in material circumstances. Moreover, in the corporate world, virtually none of even the boldest and brightest have been able to pierce the glass ceiling. Attaining any semblance of cultural justice in film or television may have to await the day when these groups are able to wield sufficient clout in the marketplace.

Music

There is another cultural venue in which an unassimilated community can assert itself without most of the organizational and financial agonies besetting workers in film and television, namely, ethnic music. The most triumphant illustration of this claim is the impact African American jazz, folk songs, blues, and their derivatives have had on mainstream popular culture in the United States and elsewhere. Indeed the Euro-American receptivity to these musical idioms has been even broader and more fruitful in its consequences than is the case for African American literature, movies, or TV. Moreover, this cultural transfer has certainly not damaged the originating community's prestige or self-esteem.

Only two other exotic genres have had comparable effects on the musical life of the land in recent decades: the Latino-cum-Brazilian (Fox 1996:186–187) and Southern country music (Carney 1994). In fact, the latter craze diffused so widely and penetrated so deeply into the collective psyche that it is difficult to imagine late twentieth-century existence without the country sound. One can also make a case for an earlier absorption of the polka, Irish song, and some forms of German popular music into the general national heritage. Such acceptance assuredly served as a morale booster for the people in question. McCullough (1980) advances the claim that the promotion of traditional music and dance among Chicago's Irish Americans has enlivened their ethnic awareness.

There may be no foreign or regional musical style that has escaped the tourist ear and thus presumably has had no impact on the listeners, but relatively few beyond those already noted have won widespread or enduring popularity. Perhaps the best of the recent examples is Cajun, or zydeco, music (Kuhlken and Sexton 1994), which, not too coincidentally, achieved popularity at the same time as did Cajun cuisine. But in contrast to the relative authenticity of zy-deco, there is the cautionary tale of the incorporation of thoroughly degraded Hawaiian music into the American pop repertory.[29]

Thus far I have been setting forth the recent, largely self-conscious, purposeful efforts on the part of members of various ethnic groups to exhibit and validate their cultural worth in the eyes of the larger society. I believe it fair to say that the efflorescence of outwardly directed, Ethnicity-laden festivals, newly invented holidays, ethnic epitome districts and other forms of ethnic tourism, museums, murals and other modes of display, clothing and body management, personal names, literature, music, film, and television has succeeded in conveying the message though to differing degrees among the various ethnic entities. In the process, there has also doubtless been some spillover effect as the cause of Ethnicity benefits in a general way from the activities of the separate constituencies, even though such a relatedness of interests may never have entered their minds. To quote the tired old cliché, a rising tide has lifted all vessels.

The Globalization Factor

No less significant than the individual programs of ethnic self-promotion has been a related development: the general globalization of cultural elements. This vigorous, transnational sharing of all manner of ethnic attributes differs from the practices discussed in the preceding pages in that it arrives in the absence of any agenda for self-advancement. Most of what we see here is the handiwork of entrepreneurs seeking monetary gain in all those new ways made possible in our late stage of capitalism, as they exploit advanced technologies and marketing systems, and most basically, a worldwide restructuring of sensibilities and appetites. Among the results are indiscriminate glorification and commodification of Ethnicity — and a leveling of former barriers and prejudices.

Because of the disjunctive and unstable interplay of commerce, media, national policies, and consumer fantasies, ethnicity, once a genie contained in the bottle of some sort of locality (however large), has now become a global force, forever slipping in and through the cracks between states and borders. (Appadurai 1996:41)

An awareness of this novel state of affairs, that is the cultural dimensions of the grander process of globalization, is in the air. Nowadays journalists, popular writers of all stripes, and much of the general public seem to take for granted this unprecedented cultural panmixia, accepting it as a new fact of life. But, oddly enough, we have had precious little systematic investigation of this cultural transformation, whether perceived in its totality or from the perspective of any of its major components.

Thus, for example, we lack any overall account of transnational transfers or hybridizations of dance styles, in effect, the creation of a universal repertoire.[30] Similarly, in a manner reminiscent of the fabrication of genetically engineered organisms, something called "world music" has burst upon the aural scene lately. An awareness among musicians, and thus secondarily among their patrons, of a great variety of exotic folk and popular styles from all manner of countries has led to both an appreciation of their merits and the creation of new, hybrid, crossover forms, including the "indigenization" of imported items (Mitchell 1996; Robinson et al. 1991:227–232; T. D. Taylor 1997). However good or bad the results may be, one certain consequence is, at the very least, a tolerance or, more often, a heightened respect for all things ethnic — and a craving for all sorts of ethnic goods (Morley and Robbins 1995:114–115).

The array of globalized commodities and practices is large and varied. It includes, in addition to dance, music, film, and television, an endless profusion of gadgets and trinkets, food and drink, clothing, hair styles, toys, jewelry, and comic books. The sheer complexity of the phenomenon is such that it is not too surprising that only a single scholar has been bold enough to attack our new global culture holistically. In a seminal 1990 article and then in a 1996 book-length collection of essays, Arjun Appadurai confronted the transnationalization of culture and some of its implications. But his efforts must be regarded as a first approximation rather than the definitive exploration of a daunting assemblage of issues.

Cuisine

In the absence of any comprehensive treatment of a globalizing cultural system, there is, fortunately, one topic that has enjoyed a fair amount of academic and popular attention. As the set of practices rivaled only by language and religion in its centrality to the life of a community and in its potential for illuminating many questions about the community's history, ecology, and total culture, foodways can tell us a lot about the evolving role of Ethnicity in contemporary life. Truly "along with language the food complex becomes a basic badge of ethnicity" (Van den Berghe 1984:392).

Food has become the most accessible — and tempting — of entrées into alien cultures. Indeed for many Americans, cuisine may offer the only direct knowledge they have of Vietnamese, Jamaican, Greek, Afghan, Hindu, and other foreign ways of life. They are much more likely to patronize an ethnic restaurant than to learn the proprietor's language or to visit her church, to listen to the community's radio programs, witness a wedding or funeral, or ramble about the cemetery where her kith and kin are buried. Those scholars who have dealt with the role of ethnic food in American life have all noted its great and growing recent popularity and a multiplicity of relevant factors (Alba 1990:85–94; Brown and Musell 1984; Gabaccia 1998; Levenstein 1993:215–220; Pillsbury 1998; Van den Berghe 1984; Zelinsky 1985).

This post–World War II development may have begun among the elite and well traveled in America, as it has in other affluent countries, then diffused from the larger, more cosmopolitan metropolises to the smaller towns and shopping malls of the land. But it has not taken much time before the entire population has encountered and learned to relish a variety of previously unknown comestibles, however genuine or dubious their authenticity may be. This is a truly astonishing turn of events. Not too many decades ago, virtually all Americans regarded foreign cuisine with fear or disgust. Those who indulged in chop suey or spaghetti in rather unprepossessing establishments did so condescendingly and for reasons of price, not taste. As I can attest from personal experience, the grocery shops of the 1930s did not stock a single genuinely ethnic item on their shelves.

Today it would be difficult to find any supermarket anywhere in the country that does not feature an "ethnic foods" or "gourmet" section offering, at a minimum, Chinese, Italian, Mexican, and Jewish items, and frequently many others. For example, "Arab cuisine has become Americanized and popularized; Tabouli, Homous, and Baba Ghanouch are all popular 'American ethnic foods' as is 'Syrian bread,' which Americans refer to as 'pita'" (Younis 1995: 255–256). Perhaps the most telling or extreme case is the African American: "As . . . the idea that 'Black is beautiful' has gained acceptance, chitterlings and other soul foods are marketed not merely in Harlem grocery stores but in the gourmet section of supermarkets in predominantly white neighborhoods, often for a considerable price" (Van Esterik 1982: 221).[31]

Thus, in addition to the proliferation of ethnic restaurants catering to a general clientele, the increasing range and variety thereof, and the incorporation of ethnic dishes into the menus of ordinary eateries, these once strange, often dreaded imports from peoples and places other than the familiar northwestern European have become domesticated, appearing regularly on kitchen and dining room tables.[32] We have already seen the importance of exotic food at ethnic festivals visited by the general public. Further confirmation of a fundamental reversal of attitudes may be sought in the cookbooks Americans have been purchasing in such great quantities over the past century and a half. In a richly detailed analysis of no fewer than 1,309 such publications, Liora Gvion-Rosenberg (1991) has amply documented the shifting American attitudes toward Ethnicity as reflected in gastronomic discourse.

This respectability of ethnic cuisines in the United States and in other economically privileged countries as well, indeed a positive lusting after them, may be only the most obvious phase of that much broader phenomenon, a reconfigured relationship between Us and Them and the rise and triumph of Ethnicity as an absolute virtue. We cannot address that vast question at this point, nor can anyone else until we have had adequate monographic inquiry into the remarkable career of ethnic food since the middle of the twentieth century, along with a number of other germane topics. But it is obvious enough that this revolutionary redefinition of popular appetites is just one of several components of a manic tourism broadly defined that reaches everywhere and into everything in a world undergoing profound social and cultural transformation.

Whatever the larger meaning of the newly elevated status of ethnic cuisine in America, there are few commentators who would view this development other than benignly. One of those few is Sau-ling Cynthia Wong, who presents a blistering polemic on "food pornography" in the course of an explication of some recent Asian American fiction.

> Like exchanging sexual services for food, food pornography is also a kind of prostitution, but with an important difference: superficially, food pornography appears to be a promotion, rather than a vitiation or devaluation, of one's ethnic identity. . . . What in fact [food pornographers] do is to wrench cultural practices out of their context and display them for gain to the curious gaze of "outsiders." . . . They feed their white patrons "foreign matter" that has been domesticated, "detoxed," depoliticized, made safe for recreational consumption. . . . What appears to be hospitable acceptance of the outsider is really the ethnic's appeal for acceptance by the mainstream customer, who has the power to decide what is agreeably authentic and what is unthinkably outlandish. (1993:55–57)

Clearly there is some justification for such a protest, but perhaps less so now than a few decades ago. But the strength of Wong's argument is much diluted by the widespread adoption of ethnic foods in the American home as well as in a varied array of restaurants, and especially by the fact that such receptivity is no longer blemished by any observable hint of gastronomic racism or cultural slumming. If we reverse the terms of the debate and consider the export to the four corners of the planet of American carbonated beverages, breakfast cereals, hamburgers, chewing gum, bourbon, Spam, popcorn, potato chips, candy bars, and all manner of junk food, is that "gastronomic imperialism," or, more to the immediate point, another version of food pornography? What is being marketed abroad is scarcely representative of the "authentic," quite marvelous regional cuisines that still survive in some fortunate American localities.[33]

We cannot ignore the issue of authenticity when speaking of ethnic cuisine in the United States or anywhere else. Clearly the very act of transferring dietary items and methods of cooking, or any other cultural element, across space or ethnic boundaries creates serious difficulties for champions of ethnic purity. "To the extent that ethnic cuisine gets commercialized as a form of internal tourism, the problem of authenticity arises" (Van den Berghe 1984:394). "The secret of the acceptance of ethnic food resides in the harmonization and compromise between seemingly contradictory requirements: being authentic and being Americanized, maintaining tradition while consciously modifying it" (Lu and Fine 1995:547).

The necessary compromise, the amiable conspiracy, is apparent to both purveyor and consumer. This sort of accommodation, or pandering, to stereotypical perceptions of various ethnic cuisines is explored quite rewardingly in Magliocco's (1993) study of the Little Italy Festival of Clinton, Indiana. At this event the traditional regional, or "esoteric," dishes, for example polenta, *bagna cauda*, *riso al latte*, stewed rabbit, or *grissini* are bypassed while vendors push such items as pizza, Italian sausage sandwiches, Italian beef drowned in tomato sauce, and the more familiar pastas. But, however inauthentic such presentations may be, they are potent devices for building a sense of Italian American identity for both insiders and outsiders. In any event, however far the process of naturalization may have gone, Americans remain cognizant of the foreign origins or inspiration of the ethnic food and drink they ingest. This is true even for an extreme case, that of the sensationally popular pizza, which threatens to become as American as apple pie but never sheds its Italian aura.

The issue of authenticity is complicated by the identity of the persons who produce and sell the commodities in question. With increasing frequency, the proprietor and even the chef in an ethnic restaurant will have no firsthand acquaintance with the country whose foodways they are promoting, nor will either have been reared in its culinary traditions. Moreover, many are the establishments that advertise two or more different, sometimes wildly dissimilar, ethnic cuisines. In a parallel development, we are also seeing the fusion of previously isolated culinary complexes as innovators go about creating original, often intriguing hybrid dishes. At the manufacturing end of the business, the entrepreneur may have some ancestral connection with the product, but, as often as not, his or her only concern is mercenary. The seeker after ethnic thrills may be sorely disenchanted when visiting the plants whence pour forth soy sauce, frozen enchiladas, kielbasa, bagels, feta cheese, vodka, or chutney. It may be true, in the words of the classic subway poster, that "you don't have to be Jewish to love Levy's [Rye Bread]," but neither need one be Jewish to produce a reasonable facsimile thereof.

We must conclude, then, that when it comes to foodways, as in other realms of culture, the promoters of the virtues and delights of their specific ethnic community have succeeded all too well. In fact, they may have overshot the target while being overtaken by a grander sociocultural development. If just about all the varied ethnic cultures in the United States are now receiving their due as entities worth cherishing and celebrating, such acceptance comes at a potentially lethal cost: the risk of being swept into the embrace of an indiscriminate Ethnicity. When all things ethnic are deemed desirable but also interchangeable, what is the point of strict loyalty to a single tradition?

What has been happening in the realm of foodways is emblematic of the grander process of fabricating Ethnicity. We witness here a simplification of things, a taming of piquancies, the denaturing of the outlandish. The result is a reduction of the weird into a quasi-generic something, perhaps a blending of multiple alien cuisines or whatever, a fare acceptable by the timid multitudes. Such a smoothing over of real difference is clearly akin to the banalities of mass tourism. In another parallel development, there is the phenomenon of the "community church," the non- or interdenominational Protestant enterprise that has flourished of late in middle-class American neighborhoods. Gone are the fierce doctrinal squabbles within and between denominations that so enlivened the eighteenth- and nineteenth-century scene. In their place a comfortable social experience, a bland, one-size-fits-all, nonconfrontational theology, or lack thereof. There is little resemblance to the all-consuming passion, the spiritual agonies of the first-century martyrs and zealots.

ASSESSMENT

The moral should be plain by now. Whatever its parentage and pristine attributes, Ethnicity has erupted past the parochial, maneuvering across social and cultural boundaries to become something novel, delectable, and our common treasure. Although spokespersons for individual traditions may have striven to conserve and glorify the particularities of their own groups in all the ways discussed in this chapter, stronger trends have caught up with them.

We have seen how immigrant groups in the past, beset as they were by an unfamiliar social and physical environment and the pressures of assimilationism, were able to retain only residual fragments of ancestral cultures. Initially, then, there was scant opportunity to express their ethnic character to the host society in realistic terms. Instead it was the Anglo-American majority that monopolized the discourse, constructing a set of damaging stereotypes. Despite all the progress registered in recent years, some groups are still suffering the aftereffects, the malice and indignities resulting from such meretricious packaging. But the subsequent program of self-assertion has certainly had its triumphs and impacts. Eventually, however, all group-specific agendas have been swallowed up by a vaster development, that sublimation called Ethnicity, an apotheosis into a precious essence that transcends the particular community and sheds grace upon all.

The attentive reader may have discerned a second moral, or generalization, embedded throughout the foregoing mass of empirical matter, one as interesting and perhaps more significant than the first: that the external projections of ethnic traits follow two distinct and incompatible tracks. Thus we have, in the first instance, the retrospective, nostalgic celebration of ancestral stories, wishes, facts, and patterns prevailing among assimilated Euro-Americans. With the possible exceptions of the efforts of traditional Southerners, Cajuns, and Jewish Americans (and perhaps some Irish Americans), this is a form of what has come to be called symbolic ethnicity. The celebrants tout practices that are no longer integral to their usual, everyday routines but are rather trotted out only for special occasions or in backward-glancing literary and artistic endeavors. As often as not, they are nothing more serious than raw material for good-natured kidding.

Quite different are the outward expressions of people of color, most insistently African American but surely Latino, Native American, Middle Eastern, and Asian as well. Not only are their cultural assertions more intense and immediate, dealing with the here and now, than is the case for Euro-Americans, but they differ qualitatively as well. What they share with the Euro-American world are present-day realities, their actual lived experiences in a contemporary world where ultimate assimilation and cultural erasure are far from assured.

If the outward expression of ethnic identity among all manner of quasi-assimilated and immigrant groups — operations within cultural space, so to speak — if such activity has undergone remarkable change in recent decades, with ramifications reaching far into other sectors of the social scene, have there been parallel developments in the neighboring realm of social/geographic space? That is the question the following chapter may be able to answer.

3 HETEROLOCALISM

If we cannot adequately appraise the contemporary ethnic scene without taking into account its spatial aspects, it is also true that there is no *direct* connection between such matters and our central theme of Ethnicity. However, we do encounter the intriguing phenomenon of simultaneous origins. Of the three models of the sociospatial behavior of immigrant communities examined in this chapter, the latest, heterolocalism, is coeval with Ethnicity. Mere coincidence? Perhaps. Some subterranean relationship? Possibly. But what is certain is that heterolocalism is the only one of the three models that is compatible and can coexist with Ethnicity. The two phenomena share a common property: a propensity to leap over boundaries, whether territorial or cultural. The assimilation model makes no pretense of honoring difference; indeed it celebrates its obliteration. Pluralism, on the other hand, seeks to conserve and wall off ethnic particularities. Hence it is inherently incompatible with Ethnicity, a doctrine that professes, in its deceptive fashion, to cherish difference while actually nullifying it.

In discussing the three models — assimilationism, pluralism, and heterolocalism — I accept as axiomatic the principle that past and present placement and movements in physical space by non-British immigrant stock and nonwhite peoples in general have been intimately associated with, indeed are inseparable from, status and migration within social space.

ASSIMILATIONISM

Over the years, American social scientists and other scholars have devised two distinctly different models to describe and explain the sociospatial history of our "minorities" as it has materialized in actuality, or should have in an ideal world.

The first of the two, the assimilation model, initially articulated in the early twentieth century, has enjoyed great popularity ever since (Abramson 1980; Gans 1992; Gleason 1992; M. M. Gordon 1964; Hirschman 1983; Kantrowicz 1993; Kazal 1995; Magner 1974; Newfield and Gordon 1996; Nielsen 1985 : 133).[1] It constitutes an updated, nuanced version of the aspatial Anglo-conformity consensus of the 1800s. So obvious was the notion that all proper immigrants would eventually be absorbed into the Anglo-American sociocultural community that no one bothered to spell it out. The subsequent melting pot doctrine, popularized by Israel Zangwill (1911), and still devoid of a spatial component, posited a hypothetical two-directional process, with the immigrants contributing, as well as adapting, to the dominant cultural complex. However, in the subsequent general discourse dealing with the melting pot, the tendency has been to downplay and minimize the alien ingredients in the ultimate amalgam.

Following the work of Park and Burgess and the Chicago School of sociology in the 1920s,[2] we arrive at the standard, or ecological, model of assimilationism (Jordan-Bychkov et al. 1998 : 336; McKenzie 1925 : 76; Ward 1989 : 161–163). According to Alba and Logan, "the most fundamental tenets of the model are (1) that residential mobility follows from the acculturation and the social mobility of individuals, and (2) that residential mobility is an intermediate step on the way to more complete (i.e., structural) assimilation" (1991 : 432).

Thus, as significant numbers of immigrants from a given origin enter a large city in a nation like the United States, they will initially occupy less desirable tracts near its center. As they acquire higher educational and economic status and some measure of cultural assimilation, they or their descendants will shift upward and outward through social and physical space into the more attractive zones of the metropolis, eventually to be absorbed into the dominant community. In doing so, they replicate the path followed by earlier groups, and the expectation is that later, ethnically distinct streams of immigrants would follow, repeating the process (Massey 1985).

Implicit in the assimilation model is a close spatial fit between home and workplace, at least at first. During the 1800s and early 1900s, many immigrants lived and toiled in the same building or were able to walk between the two sites. After streetcar systems developed and private ownership of automobiles became common, the closeness of the connection may have loosened, but the overlap between employment and residence did not disappear (Stathakis 1996).

The durability of the assimilationist, or ecological, model, indeed the fact that it became part of the conventional wisdom of the educated layperson, attests to its adequacy in describing and explaining the changing metropolitan scene in the United States during much of the nineteenth century and the beginning of the twentieth. In fact, the correspondence between theory and reality was as neat as anyone could reasonably desire for such places as Chicago, Cleveland, or Philadelphia. But there may be reason to challenge the past or present applicability of the model to places of lesser magnitude, as suggested in studies of Omaha (Chudacoff 1973), Sacramento (Dingemans and Datel 1995), and Garden City, Kansas (Broadway 1986). Be that as it may, if we view matters in geographical and historical perspective, it seems the model *may* have been temporally and country specific, a creature of a unique period in American history.[3] As Waldinger has noted, "The ethnic neighborhood is not a timeless feature of American cities but rather the product of a particular moment in the technology of urban economics" (1987:2). Regrettably, the model's champions have never tested its merits in the metropolises of other settler countries, such as Buenos Aires, Montevideo, or Johannesburg, or, more recently, in Toronto, Sydney, or London.

The effectiveness of the assimilation model, at least until recently, is attributable in part to the fact that most immigrants fell into the broad racial classification of Caucasian and were members of the extended Western, or European, cultural community and of various branches of the Judeo-Christian faith (Lieberson and Waters 1988). It must be admitted that such commonalities may not have been visible immediately. Indeed, as noted earlier, many old-stock Americans tended to regard the newcomers from eastern and southern Europe as racially alien and inferior and more than a little suspect in religious terms. Nevertheless, dissimilarities in appearance, religion, and general cultural practice and the animosities between certain immigrant groups, while often obvious and sometimes unsettling, were not absolute. Time and the digestive processes of acculturation would presumably transform them into minor hindrances. As it happened, the great majority of the foreign-born flooding into America were of "lower" social, educational, and occupational status and equipped with little prior knowledge of American conditions or, excepting those from the British Isles and Canada, of the English language. For purposes of the model, it was both possible and convenient to treat the immigrants as a single undifferentiated class, so that distinction by country or community of origin and period of entry did not violate the structure of the model.

In recent years, and most notably since 1965, a massive influx of immigrants, refugees, and sojourners into the United States, along with a significant restructuring of the world economy and society, obliges us to reevaluate the spatial scenario as well as other aspects of the assimilationist perspective (Buell 1994; Hannerz 1992; M. J. White 1987:263). Most of the millions of recent newcomers hail from nations that contributed quite modestly, or not at all, to the earlier immigrant stream (Jasso and Rosenzweig 1990). In "racial" appearance, persons arriving from eastern, southeastern, and southern Asia, the Pacific Islands, Africa, the Caribbean, and Latin America are seldom mistaken for Europeans. Many adhere to such non-European creeds as Buddhism, Hinduism, Sikhism, Islam, santería, Vodun, the Bahai faith, or such formerly unfamiliar varieties of Christianity as those practiced in Ethiopia, Egypt, Palestine, Lebanon, and Iraq. They may also bear with them modes of social behavior and attitudes at variance with the Euro-American pattern. There is, for example, the matter of individual autonomy versus family togetherness. "One underlying assumption within the Chicago School model is . . . that residential choice is considered an individual or household decision as one's identity is as an individual. Many recent immigrant groups, however, hold collective or group identity as a high value, and consider individually based residential choices as a rejection of culture" (Miyares 1995:3).

Another departure from the situation of yesteryear is evident in the socioeconomic composition of the current wave of immigrants (Chiswick and Sullivan 1995; Rumbaut 1994). There are marked differences by country of origin, but, overall, a bimodal pattern prevails. Although the United States still receives a considerable complement of the disadvantaged — in the case of several national sources, a clear majority[4] — many of the New Americans are skilled, well-educated occupants of the higher-status occupational niches back home, and generally upwardly mobile. Although not all of these privileged individuals, bearing with them substantial human and sometimes financial capital, can immediately claim appropriate positions in their adopted country, a surprising number do just that and manage to flourish from the outset.

A further distinction between past and present is the amount of prior knowledge of the culture and language of the United States. Current immigrants often come from places where English is now the first or second language, and a goodly percentage arrive with a degree of comprehension and speaking ability. And whatever the social or educational rank of the newcomer, he or she will probably have some idea, however distorted, of what to expect at the destination because of the universal penetration of American-made or -influenced movies, television, and other popular media of entertainment and information.[5] In a sense, then, the foreign-born person seeking permanent or temporary domicile in the United States disembarks with assimilation already in progress.

There are two other flaws — or are they amendments to? — assimilationist doctrine that have escaped the notice of ethnic theorists, even though they should have been quite evident over the past two hundred years. First, the civilization into which the immigrant is destined to assimilate is not a static entity but rather a work in progress. Indeed, ever since its infancy, the American cultural system has been mutating and evolving at a pace that is readily observable, and never more rapidly than at present. Assimilating into a moving target is not a trivial challenge. More readily seen is the fact that, despite all those forces nudging national and global communities toward homogeneity, marked regional differences do persist in the United States. Thus the specific assimilationist path followed by the immigrant will depend upon just where and when he or she chances to settle. Disconformities in eventual outcomes can be quite striking. Compare the culturally, if not structurally, assimilated South Carolina Jews with their New York City coreligionists, Texas Germans with their co-ethnics in Milwaukee, or second-generation Mexican Americans in Reading, Pennsylvania, or Westchester County, New York, with those in San Antonio.

But what most concerns us immediately are the locational aspects of the recent stages of immigration or, more broadly, the phenomenon of mobility as it pertains to persons moving to the United States and, inferentially, to other corners of the world. We are in the midst of a profound remaking of the relationships between people and place that is both rapid and radical, a reordering of basic perceptions and behavior. If the technological underpinnings of this spatial quasi-revolution — near-universal access to automotive and airborne transportation as well as to the telephone and other modes of electronic communication — are clear enough, the social and cultural ramifications are still only sketchily explored. However, if we begin with the rudimentary chore of plotting foreign-born persons and their progeny in geographical space in the late twentieth century and the early twenty-first, and do so over time, using census data on residence, we will find that the assimilation model holds well for some groups but poorly for others.

And indeed it would be surprising to discover the new immigrants moving automatically through the familiar spatial ruts of assimilation, given not only their own unprecedented attributes but also the much altered morphology of the American metropolis and countryside.[6] With the passage of time, the spatial configuration of economic and residential districts has undergone a good deal of shifting and revision. Concurrently, there has also been considerable change in the intraurban transportation infrastructure and modes of travel. Moreover, for some groups "racial" blockage is frustrating any replay of the traditional assimilation scenario. In particular, the substantial African American and Latino populations that have so often filled the gaps left by the onward-moving European ethnics have succeeded only weakly in emulating the upward-and-outward trajectory of their predecessors (Denton and Massey 1991; Frey 1994; Massey and Denton 1988).

In any event, what we usually observe in those cities currently receiving substantial influxes of less privileged immigrants is hardly a recapitulation of the classic spatial scenario. Instead of clustering initially in the residential zone closest to the central business district, they tend to lodge in low-rent tracts some distance outward from the historic core. Examples include Chicago's Uptown neighborhood as the point of entry for natives of former French Indochina (Hein 1995:54–58), polyglot tracts in Queens and Brooklyn (Dinnerstein and Reimers 1988; C. Smith 1995), the development of multiethnic Latino and Asian communities in Greater Washington just beyond the District line in Montgomery and Prince Georges Counties, and those scattered nodes of recent immigrants mapped for the Los Angeles metro area by Allen and Turner (1997).[7]

THE PLURALIST VISION

The perception of assimilation as a smooth, unimpeded process was called into question as early as the 1910s, perhaps most eloquently in the writings of Randolph Bourne (1920; but also see Goldberg 1992:212). Another approach to coping with the diversity of immigrants had begun to take shape: the notion of pluralism (Kallen 1924; Ratner 1987). In lieu of fusion into a single sociocultural community within the melting pot, pluralists envision a mosaic of self-sustaining ethnic communities, each firmly engaged in the larger polity, economy, and society, that is, Americanized to a certain degree, but still retaining a traditional identity and complex of cultural practices in perpetuity (Abramson 1980; Fuchs 1990; Higham 1984:239; Matthews 1970; Hollinger 1992; Newfield and Gordon 1996; Zunz 1988). If there is a primary focus of interest in this model, it is in the relatively insular ethnic entity rather than the nation as a whole.

The term "mosaic" ("quilt" might be equally applicable) is more metaphorical than literal since, in the American case, the location of these communities is not well specified. To the extent that the mosaic has a geographic realization it presumably takes the form of a patchwork of ethnic enclaves persisting over time. At the metropolitan level, pluralism leads us to expect a population both highly diverse and highly segregated ethnically (Klaff 1980). At the group level, we infer spatial correlation among residential, economic, and social spheres to be strong, influenced in only a minor fashion, if at all, by upward mobility, English language acquisition, and other forces antecedent to dispersion in the assimilation model.[8] Unlike the carefully spelled out ecological principles associated with assimilation, there has been little effort by the pluralist school to offer an explicit locational statement. It seems to have been presented as a lofty ideal rather than as a reflection of existing realities or immediate possibilities.[9]

The early advocates of pluralism espoused a vision of comity among the divers communities, a convivial modus vivendi lacking any system of dominance and subordination. They seemed uninterested in, or unaware of, how pluralism was actually playing out in other parts of the world. In Lebanon, and in such plantation societies as Fiji, Malaysia, Mauritius, Guyana, and Trinidad, where pluralism has in effect been institutionalized, dealings among the various communities have been at best uneasy. The initial American version of pluralism was concerned only with recent European immigrants and old-stock Anglo-Americans. But, in fact, even though few scholars bothered to look at and comment on the situation, the United States has been a pluralistic society for some time, but inequitably so, given the social and political arrangements for African Americans, Native Americans, and Latinos.

Aside from an occasional semipopular treatment (e.g., Adamic 1940), pluralism failed to attract much public interest or serious academic attention in American circles before the 1960s. The reasons seem clear in retrospect. The idea of assimilation and conformity to national norms is deeply embedded in the reigning American ethos and is implicit in the notion of American exceptionalism, of the role of the United States in the "grand march of humanity" (Higham 1984:186–187). Thus pluralism runs decidedly against the American grain. In addition, with its recognition of group claims and rights, the role of the individual is downplayed, and nothing lies closer to the core of Americanism than individualism.

But the changing nature of the world has put matters in a new light. Simultaneously with developments in other Western nations

(Petersen 1980:238; Zwerin 1976), by midcentury various aggrieved American groups had begun to voice their complaints. In the vanguard was the Black Pride movement among African Americans, joined subsequently by a Red Power campaign among Native Americans and stirrings among Chicanos, Puerto Ricans, Cajuns, and some Asians. The limited applicability of the melting pot ideal to these groups caused academics to take heed (Glazer and Moynihan 1970; Gordon 1978:181–208; Newman 1973). So did the rise in the 1970s of the so-called European ethnics who sought acknowledgment of their persistent identity, most stridently in the writings of Novak (1972; also see Mann 1979; Schrag 1971; Weed 1973; J. A. Williams 1989). In the ensuing decades, academics have continued their hostile critiques of assimilationist doctrine, though without offering workable substitutes (e.g., Blaut 1987:142–171; Harrison and Bennett 1995; White et al. 1993).

Even though the Euro-American ethnic revival of the 1970s seems to have run its course, the cause of pluralism has taken on fresh life with the massive influx of post-1965 immigrants. Despite the inherent fuzziness of the pluralist perspective, it refuses to go away, and ongoing debates over "multiculturalism," "diversity," and kindred concepts, discussed in the final chapter, afford ample evidence of the essential vitality of the idea.

AN ALTERNATIVE MODEL

Given the serious shortcomings of the traditional assimilationist and pluralist models in describing and explaining the sociospatial behavior of recent immigrant groups in the United States, it seems appropriate to propose an alternative model more closely in accord with the new set of circumstances faced by such groups. In lieu of any preexisting word that captures the essence of this model, Barrett Lee and I have coined the term *heterolocal*. Rooted in the Greek *heteros* meaning "other" or "different," and the Latin *locus* meaning "place," this term is intended to convey the possibility that an ethnic community can exist without any significant clustering, that is, when the members of a particular group are scattered throughout a city, metropolitan area, or some larger spatial domain.

Heterolocalism is characterized by five of the attributes listed below that set it apart from the assimilationist and pluralist models. There is also a sixth (no. 5) that it shares with them.

1. There is immediate or prompt spatial dispersion of heterolocal immigrants within the host country.
2. Residence and workplace are usually widely separated, and, frequently, there is also a lack of spatial overlap between residence on the one hand and shopping districts and sites of social activity on the other.
3. Despite the absence of spatial propinquity, strong ethnic community ties are maintained via telecommunications, visits, and other methods at the metropolitan, regional, national, and even international scale.
4. Heterolocalism is a time-dependent phenomenon. Although we can detect some partial manifestations in earlier periods, its full development is conceivable only under the socioeconomic and technological conditions established in the late twentieth century.
5. As is the case with the other models, heterolocalism can exist in both metropolitan and nonmetropolitan settings.
6. In contrast to the other models, heterolocalism has implications for sociospatial behavior at the transnational, even global, scale.

I take up each of these propositions in turn.

Spatial Dispersion

Heterolocally inclined individuals and families currently enjoy a range of locational options in terms of residence, and also economic and social activity, much greater than anything known in the past. They become heterolocal by virtue of choosing spatial dispersion, or at most a modest degree of clustering, immediately or shortly after arrival, instead of huddling together in spatial enclaves. It would, of course, be naive to assert that their locational decision making is completely free. The tightness of the local housing market, the availability of appropriate economic niches, and the diversity of the local ethnic context all impose some degree of constraint. Also relevant is the character of the cultural baggage borne by the newcomers. Nevertheless, it is useful to think of heterolocalism as dispersion and variety, in contrast to localization and homogenization. Previous observers have noticed such relative freedom of spatial choice, but usually only in passing with reference to particular places or particular ethnic groups.[10]

The broadened range of residential possibilities exploited by heterolocals reflects more than the affluence of many of these foreign-born newcomers, though income does explain a good deal, as does the liberating effect of modern communications and transportation. The new territorial regime would not have been feasible without certain types of policy changes (e.g., the enactment of fair-housing legislation) and significant shifts in social attitudes and perceptions that have served to weaken locational barriers. Would it have been thinkable in the 1890s for a Brahmin scholar, a black Haitian merchant, a Japanese physician, or a Chinese banker to acquire a residence, and then survive, in one of Philadelphia's or San Francisco's upscale neighborhoods? The question answers itself.

In the United States, the residential dispersion connoted by heterolocalism varies considerably from one group to another. Even within a given group, it may be affected by the social history and geography of the specific metropolis in which group members settle (Foner 1987:5; Lee and Wood 1991:21). Thus extreme and instant dispersion characterizes recently arrived Asian Indians (Carlson 1978: 32; Dasgupta 1989:61–62; M. P. Fisher 1980; Helweg and Helweg 1990:163–169; Jyoti 1990; Sheth 1995:176; C. J. Smith 1995:6) and Iranians (Ansari 1992:61; Modarres 1992:103). Their homes are scattered throughout the suburban reaches of the metropolitan area (and widely throughout nonmetro America) with only moderate tendencies toward a loose sort of clustering. Equally striking is the spatial dispersion of the new influx of Filipinos, who have failed to create any recognizable neighborhoods, as was the case with the smaller, pre–World War II influx (Agbayani-Siewert and Revilla 1995; Allen 1977:205; Espiritu 1995:22; "Overseas Filipinos" 1974; Pido 1986: 71–72; C. J. Smith 1995:6). Similarly, the Thai tend to be scattered within the Los Angeles area (Desbarats 1979:316), and the Vietnamese have suburbanized quite quickly in the Washington, D.C., area and elsewhere (Wood 1997). Another intriguing example is that of recent Japanese immigrants and sojourners. They have sought out the most attractive suburbs while holding themselves spatially aloof from the already widely dispersed native-born Japanese Americans (Handelman 1991).

The case of the Koreans is more complicated, prompting questions for which I have no ready answers. Hurh and Kim's statement that "there is no sign yet that the Koreans will develop an ethnic neighborhood of their own as Italians and Poles did in the early stages of their immigration" (1984:63) seems valid enough for New York City (I. Kim 1981:184–185; Sakong 1990:23; Zhou 1992:195–196) and Washington (F. D. Lee 1980; E. R. Myers 1994:179), and probably Atlanta. Yet one can observe the coalescence of Korean residential and commercial neighborhoods in Chicago (Ahne 1995; Park 1994) and Los Angeles (Allen and Turner 1997; Min 1993; Sakong 1990: 23). However, such neighborhoods hardly qualify as classic, that is, early twentieth-century ethnic ghettos.

In another instance of the salience of the specific metropolitan setting, we have Cuban immigrants living in the Washington metro area who, unlike their coethnics in Miami, have failed to form any sort of distinct geographic enclave but are widely scattered in a number of neighborhoods (Boone 1989:17). The same pattern of dispersion holds for upper middle-class and professional Armenians (O'Grady 1981) and Sephardic Jews (Fredman 1981) who have gravitated to the nation's capital in recent decades. Rather surprisingly, the notion of heterolocalism also seems to apply to Haitian residents of the Chicago metropolitan area (Woldemikael 1989:160), but much more dubiously in Miami. Equally counterintuitive are the spatial choices of recent Chinese and Taiwanese immigrants of relatively advanced socioeconomic status. Many have bypassed preexisting Chinatowns to become instant suburbanites, most notably in the Los Angeles area (Li 1994, 1996; Tseng 1995), but elsewhere as well (Lin 1998; Zhou 1992:84).

Not all heterolocal groups are lodged within the more prosperous levels of the socioeconomic spectrum. An estimated forty thousand recent Bolivian immigrants of working-class status in Washington, D. C., and environs have not formed or joined any spatial enclave. They are instead spread widely throughout the Virginia suburbs, sustaining a lively sense of community through personal networking and a variety of formal and informal associations (Price 1996). The same pattern has materialized in the Tongan community within the San Mateo, California, metropolitan area (Small 1997:69–70).

We have still other instances of disadvantaged communities that are decidedly dispersed in spatial pattern but just as decidedly pluralistic in the tenacity with which most members cling to their unique social identity. For example, in Los Angeles, Seattle, and other metropolises to which Native Americans have migrated in substantial numbers since World War II — and where, incidentally, the process of ethnogenesis, that is, the formation of a supratribal or pan-Indian consciousness, has developed apace — residences are widely scattered and no distinct neighborhoods have formed (Nagel 1996:202–204; Weibel-Orlando 1991:23–31). The same sort of dispersion typifies the urban Gypsy population, a group that falls into a twilight zone between the pluralist and heterolocal models. Although they do not relish the attention of census takers or social scientists, it is clear enough that the Gypsies resist assimilation (Gropper 1975; C. Silverman 1991).

Despite its growing relevance, the heterolocal model obviously does not apply well to all ethnic groups, including a couple of the largest. In a manner reminiscent of times past, we can see the formation or enlargement of solidly Latino districts in a number of cities as well as the persistence of African American ghettos that have been expanding via natural increase, internal migration, and the acquisition and acculturation of West Indian and African immigrants. But even in these cases there are departures from earlier patterns of localization. Blacks, both native and foreign-born, have entered various suburbs in modest numbers. Similarly, as already noted, less affluent persons arriving from Southeast and Southwest Asia and the Caribbean frequently find homes in neighborhoods well beyond the innermost residential core.

Aside from such isolated cases as Miami's Little Havana and the Latino barrios of Los Angeles and Chicago, we are not witnessing any recent replications of ethnically homogeneous neighborhoods in the manner of the various old Chinatowns, Boston's intensely Italian North End or its equivalent in South Philadelphia, or the many classic examples — Polish, Jewish, German, Greek, and others — in the Chicago of yesteryear. Moreover, where new Chinatowns have sprouted, as in Los Angeles and New York City, they are not exclusively monoethnic, as in the past, since the Chinese may account for only a plurality of the inhabitants (Chen 1992:ix). Within the inner city, the prevailing pattern seems to be complex mixtures of several immigrant groups in a given neighborhood (Allen and Turner 1997; Fouron 1983:261; Winnick 1990) or even a single apartment complex (Conquergood 1992). The general point, as Denton and Massey (1991) amply document with census tract data, is that we have entered a new golden age of multiethnic neighborhoods. Indeed, future comparative research may reveal a greater degree of intermixing at the present than ever before known.

Spatial Disjuncture between Home and Work

Not readily apparent in the census data is another important attribute of heterolocalism: the spatial disjuncture between residence and workplace, and also, quite frequently, between residence and loci of social activity. Few more striking examples can be cited than that of the Korean American action-space in Greater Washington. My own field observations and those of others (F. D. Lee 1980:50–51; E. R. Myers 1994:179–180) indicate that, while Koreans operate hundreds of retail businesses within the District, virtually all these recent immigrants live, worship, and socialize in the suburban counties, but in the absence of any strong clusters.

Asian Indians further illustrate this point. Although they have not established noticeable residential concentrations in either suburban or central city locales (unlike the Koreans, who have done so in at least two instances), they have created no fewer than three thoroughly Indian shopping districts: one in Chicago and a pair in New York City, in addition to smaller clusters in the suburbs (Rangaswamy 1995:454). But none of these, including a diversified set of shops in Jackson Heights and a string of restaurants on Manhattan's Lower East Side, bear any relationship to the places the proprietors call home (Abu-Lughod et al. 1994:25; S. L. Myers 1993:B1, B19; R. B. Williams 1988:19). There is reason to expect similar findings for Iranians, Armenians, Japanese, Vietnamese, Filipinos, and other heterolocally inclined groups. If in all such cases one can discern little or no overlap between residence and workplace, it is likely that field investigation will confirm a similar disjuncture between home and places of worship (Livezey 2000), ethnic shopping areas, and sites of social activity. Indispensable to the social vitality of the widely dispersed ethnic group is the maintenance of a convenient meeting place whose specific address is of minor importance. Examples include the social center for the Iranian Jews of Los Angeles (Kelley 1993:104) and the recent dedication of Hindu temples in Edison, New Jersey, (Ojito 1996) and Lemont, Illinois.

Among the least advantaged segments of the urban population, such as working-class African Americans or Latinos, we find a general situation quite unlike that of Asian Indians and other heterolocal groups, but separation nonetheless between home and job. The former may be clustered within well-defined neighborhoods, but a large percentage of full- or part-time employees, especially domestic workers, gardeners, and casual laborers, earn wages by the day or hour almost anywhere within the metropolitan area, using whatever mode of transport is available to reach the job site. This phenomenon, dubbed "spatial mismatch," which has only recently begun to receive systematic attention (Hodge et al. 1996), is a distinct departure from the intrametropolitan circulation patterns of earlier generations of European immigrants.

Ethnic Community without Propinquity

"Liberated" social networks, that is, those that transcend narrow spatial boundaries, constitute a defining characteristic of what we might consider the "pure" or "strong" version of the heterolocal model, for they preclude the meaning attributed to dispersion — a severing of ethnic attachments — by assimilation theorists. Indeed the durability of such attachments in the face of dispersal, coupled with the pace at which a particular group scatters, is what enables us to distinguish between heterolocalism, on the one hand, and assimilation on the other. But, in broad outline, the ultimate ethnic settlement patterns predicted by the two models are rather similar.

Quite a few ethnic populations appear capable of sustaining lively, interactive communities without the aid of territorial clustering. The basic notion of "community without propinquity" was first proposed by Webber (1964) in a seminal essay more than thirty years ago that was not specifically concerned with ethnic matters. Since then, much empirical evidence has accumulated attesting to the vigor of the phenomenon, as seen in a variety of ethnically based social and economic networks. Among contemporary examples of aspatial ethnic communities in the United States are the suburbanized Japanese (Fugita and O'Brien 1991:10, 95), Cubans in Washington (Boone 1989:17), Koreans (Sakong 1990:107), recent Lithuanian and Jewish immigrants in Chicago (DeSantis and Benkin 1980), Estonians in suburban New Jersey (Walko 1989:72–73), Haitians (Basch et al. 1994:180; Woldemikael 1989:47–48, 160), and Danish Americans in Seattle (Chrisman 1981), in addition to the Asian Indians, Bolivians, Tongans, and others already discussed.

It is only fair to note that certain precursors of communities without propinquity existed many centuries ago in the form of networks of itinerant merchants, clergy, scholars, and other elite groups. However, such far-flung, interactive persons accounted for only a minor segment of whatever passed for an ethnic community in those days. On the other hand, we have the example of Jews living in the American South since the early 1800s, who illustrate the practicality and staying power of ethnic identity within a widely dispersed population subjected to all the pressures of social and cultural accommodation over an extended period. This minority has been present in southern cities both large and small throughout the region but almost never in numbers great enough to form residential clusters.

Thanks to intense long-distance dealings via individual visits, gatherings at major social and religious occasions, and summer camps, as well as contact through older and newer modes of communication, the southern Jewish community remains distinct and cohesive (Lipson-Walker 1991).

This type of heterolocalism is not uniquely American, of course, showing up as it does among Barbadian immigrants who are widely scattered throughout London (Western 1992:160). It must also be admitted that not all ethnic groups that are candidates for spatially liberated community actually avail themselves of such an arrangement. A conspicuous example is that of recent Israeli immigrants and/or sojourners in New York City who are content to go their isolated ways with no effort to realize any sort of ethnic cohesiveness (Shokeid 1988:100).

For the many heterolocal groups that do exhibit some degree of solidarity, the question arises about means. How is the deterritorialized community possible? Modern technology is a necessary if not sufficient factor in its genesis and operation. The specific agents include the telephone, the now universally available personal automobile, ethnic radio and television programs, and the newer modes of electronic communication (Agocs 1981:140; Boone 1989:17).

With ever greater frequency, this deterritorialized web of transactions is international rather than being confined to the United States (Kearney 1995a; Mountz and Wright 1996). Relatively cheap air travel enables immigrants to revisit homelands, family, and friends in a routine fashion that was unthinkable a generation or two ago. Fairly regular overland cross-border trips by car or bus between the United States, Mexico, and Canada are within the financial means of working-class immigrants and sojourners (Suro 1993). Among other strategies, the video camera has helped create and sustain a transnational community embracing persons from Ticuani and Chinantla, Puebla, residing in New York City (R. Smith 1993; Sontag 1998); special courier services, in addition to electronic media, perpetuate the ties between Haitians in Florida and New York City and their natal localities (Richman 1992:67–70); teleconferencing, aided and abetted by enterprises shipping parcels and currency to those at home, enable

Salvadorans in Washington and other American cities to retain their special identity (Farah 1996).

Personal mobility and instant electronic access to coethnics are only part of the story, however, because a salubrious ethnic community is not entirely divorced from specific sites. Much of the glue that holds it together exists in the shape of ethnic churches, business associations, athletic leagues, social and service clubs, bars, cultural centers, festivals, and other institutions, which may or may not be situated in neighborhoods where some modest measure of clustering can be detected. But a sense of community can be constructed and maintained even in the absence of formal organizations and activities if personal networks come into play. That is what has been observed in the case of Soviet Jews in New York City, who tend to hold themselves aloof from the older Jewish population with their quite different value system (Markowitz 1993 : 64, 235–236).

The advent and explosive growth of the Internet in the 1990s has added new potentialities for the heterolocal vigor of ethnic identity both within and well beyond the individual metropolitan area, embracing as it does the entire national, and even global, clientele. What has developed among the Iranian American elite is being duplicated by scores of other ethnic interests (Raghavan 1998).

> Since March 1990 a group of Iranian scientists, engineers, and students residing in the U.S. have created their own electronic [Internet] community, called Social, Culture Iranian. . . . The Iranian electronic community in the U.S. consists of those Iranian-Americans who are self-conscious of their ethnic identity but know each other only electronically. . . . This is a new kind of nonspatial community that is unlimited by geography. (Ansari 1992 : 139–140)

A preliminary report by Estaville (1996) indicates that as of March 1996 the number of ethnic-related Internet pages and websites, both commercial and nonprofit, within the United States had already climbed into the hundreds and that growth was continuing at an exponential rate. Such activity is also thriving at the global scale (Brunn, Jones, and Purcell 1994; Brunn and Purcell 1996).

Heterolocalism as a Time-Dependent Phenomenon

Although, as previously noted, we can identify earlier tendencies in the direction of heterolocalism, its full-blown development has become a reality only within recent decades. Its advent parallels the attainment of a certain threshold in the evolution of our global economy and the arrival of the newer technologies of travel and communication that have facilitated a much broader array of human action-spaces.

The very recency of the phenomenon renders futile any effort at prognostication. Thus it is impossible to guess whether heterolocalism will flourish for a considerable period or what future mode of sociospatial behavior might eventually supplant it. What does appear plausible is that we may be witnessing something like a steady-state system that, in the American case, could endure as long as a substantial volume of immigration continues and in the absence of major disturbances in the operation of the current globalized economy and society.

Adding to the likelihood of such a situation are the "racial," religious, and other cultural differences that distance the majority of the newer immigrants from the dominant Euro-American majority and inhibit structural assimilation. It is conceivable, then, that the "pure" expression of the heterolocal model may persist for some groups, and that a network of ties among coethnics will remain robust and lively despite the absence of enclaves or of any residual concentrations involving a preponderance of members of the same group.

The fact that it offers no temporal claims (despite being historically contingent) is another feature that distinguishes heterolocalism from the other two models. Pluralism, obviously enough, supposes a situation that remains static indefinitely, while the assimilation model implies the repetition over space and time of its ecological formula by successive groups — but implicitly, as with pluralism, in a changeless world.

Beyond the Metropolis

Given the liberating effects of technology, heterolocalism should hardly be thought of as an exclusively metropolitan affair. Neither, for that matter, should the assimilationist or pluralist scenarios. Although proponents of the latter two perspectives have little to say about the initial settlement of immigrants in nonmetropolitan America — in the farmlands, ranches, forests, mining areas, and smaller cities and towns — or their subsequent spatial shifts, the millions of persons in question have certainly played a major role in the ethnic history of the nation. It is clear, however, from the material offered in a multitude of studies, that the spatiotemporal careers of these newcomers parallel to some degree what took place in our larger cities, at least up through the early twentieth century.

Beginning in the colonial era, rural clustering was the rule for many Germans, Flemish, Highland Scots, and Cajuns, among others. Later chain and group migration created notable agrarian concentrations not only of Germans but also Czechs, Dutch, Ukrainians, Finns, Norwegians, Swedes, and others, including, belatedly, the successful Punjabi farmers of California's Sutter County (Leonard 1992). Cultural and social assimilation and some degree of spatial dispersion has ensued, but many of these early ethnic islands are still apparent in attenuated form.

At the same time, such pockets of rural ethnics have been losing ground to their city cousins for at least 150 years. Immigrants to the United States have sought out urban destinations to an extent unmatched by the native population, and, in recent decades, this cityward movement has intensified as a decreasing percentage of the foreign-born choose rural residence. Not surprisingly, then, students of contemporary ethnic and immigrant matters have focused heavily on the metropolitan scene. But changes emerging within the past quarter-century oblige us to include nonmetro America in any serious effort to upgrade old ethnic theories or construct new ones.

After many years during which the number of foreign-born in nonmetro counties suffered decline (as did the total population of such places in many instances), something of a turnaround materialized from 1970 onward (Johnson and Beale 1996). Absolute increments in the nonmetro foreign-born have been registered at the national level, even though this upswing has not rivaled the relative or absolute growth of such persons in metropolitan areas (table 2). And

TABLE 2. Foreign-Born Population by Metropolitan Status, 1950–1990 (in 1,000s)

Year	Metro	Nonmetro
1950	8,936	1,224
1970	8,809 (−1.4%)	721 (−41.1%)
1990	18,241 (+107.1%)	1,338 (+85.6%)

it has come about in many tracts, notably in the Southeast, where previously immigrants had been conspicuously rare. Indeed, statistical analyses of the level of ethnic/racial diversity at the county level have documented a significant increase throughout the nation during the 1980s (Lee et al. 1998; D. W. S. Wong 1998a, 1998b).

This current infusion of the foreign-born into much of rural and small-town America is not a replay of the epoch of pioneer settlement. There are few, if any, opportunities for yeoman farmers or for engagement in mining, forestry, or fishing. Yet a market does exist for menial, often dangerous employment in such enterprises as meat packing and the processing of poultry that have attracted the Mexican and Southeast Asian proletariat, while itinerant farmworkers from Mexico and the West Indies continue to circulate around the country.

If these movements vaguely resemble the classic succession of newcomers from central, southern, and eastern Europe posited in the assimilation model, a totally original phenomenon presents itself in the form of an influx of well-educated, upward-striving foreigners who are now widely distributed throughout nonmetro America in modest yet significant numbers.[11] Their far-flung ranks include physicians and nurses (Gordon et al. 1992; Kilburn 1991; Kindig and Movassaghi 1989; Muller 1993:124; Swearingen and Perrin 1977; O. White 1993), engineers and technicians, and business executives and managers, often operating foreign-owned enterprises, as well as a large group of motel keepers hailing from Gujarat (Gumprecht 1996). Equally intriguing are the many thousands of foreign-born faculty members, not to mention students, who have become such a noticeable presence on hundreds of college campuses in smaller towns as well as in major cities. Nothing like the current situation existed in pre–World War II years. I would anticipate that detailed analysis of the 2000 census data will reveal a nonmetro scene undergoing significant ethnic change. Then, in lieu of any existing or prospective studies, one can only speculate about the impact of increasing flows of foreign tourists, non-European as well as European, who frequent rural localities as well as the popular metropolitan attractions.

Although we still lack scholarly accounts of these medical, managerial, academic, and other personnel from distant sources,[12] it is reasonable to conjecture that, whether they are only sojourners or come with intentions of permanent residence, such individuals form part of the larger heterolocal panorama. Clearly any consideration of the heterolocal model must take them into account. Has their dispersion been as sudden as that of their metropolitan counterparts? Do they participate in, and identify with, an aspatial community of their co-ethnics despite their relative geographic remoteness? Affirmative answers seem likely in light of their human capital endowments and presumed inclination toward mobility. Only through further research, however, can we address in meaningful fashion such questions about these upscale members of the foreign-born nonmetro population.

TRANSNATIONALISM AS HETEROLOCALISM?

We must also reckon with another quite recent, apparently unanticipated manifestation of heterolocalism that has begun to engage scholarly attention. For lack of any generally accepted terminology, I resort to the terms *transnationalism* for the phenomenon and *transmigrants* for the participants therein, since those are the words adopted by the authors of an extended, path-breaking treatment (Basch et al. 1994) and in a concise, penetrating exposition of the concept (R. Smith 1993:2–6; also see Appadurai 1993:424–428 and Goldberg 1992). The concept also relates to claims concerning the "deterritorialization of the state." Thus it is not to be confused with the perennial involvement of ethnic organizations in the United States, for example, Cuban, Irish, Armenian, Serbian, in the political, economic, and environmental crises of the homeland (Halley 1985).[13]

How to define *transnationalism*? In the language of Basch and her colleagues, the word refers to

> the processes by which immigrants forge and sustain multi-stranded social relations that link together their societies of origin and settlement. We call these processes transnationalism to emphasize that many immigrants today build social fields that cross geographic, cultural, and political borders. Immigrants who develop and maintain multiple relationships — familial, economic, social, organizational, religious and political — that span borders we call "transmigrants." An essential element of transnationalism is the multiplicity of involvements that transmigrants sustain in both home and host societies. (1994:7)

The interesting political implications of transnationalism are spelled out by Jacobson (1996) and summarized by Robert Smith:

> Whereas under the sovereignty paradigm one's political membership is represented as citizenship conferred by the state, and political identity is centered on the states, contemporary migrants and states are forming and acting upon understandings of political community and identity which are transnational in scope. In these cases, membership is socially constructed around non-state identities and politics pursued within boundaries which do not conform to state borders. . . . I will argue that transnational migrant communities are imagined by their members and created through their social, cultural, and political practices; and they represent alternative, but simultaneous, political communities, inconsistent with our conventional notions of political community, identity, and membership. (1993:2–3)

And, of course, such transnational political communities are also ethnic groups of a novel and peculiar form.[14]

Like the types of heterolocalism already discussed, transnationalism entails a degree of freedom from spatial constraints — and from the "sovereignty paradigm" — coupled with the opportunity for attachment to one's own group, but at a higher level of geographic abstraction. In any case, the underlying axiom is the same: to a degree unknown in the past, ethnic individuals or groups can exercise some flexibility in choosing their location as well as identity, making both decisions contingent on personalized circumstances (Kivisto 1992).

We can flesh out the general definition of transnationalism with a specific, admittedly extreme example:

> The importance of the Pacific Rim connection to the economic activities of Los Angeles' Chinese immigrants can be seen in the emergence of hypermobile migrants who keep family in one society, business in the other, and are in constant motion between the two. With a "two-legged existence," one leg in the homeland and the other in the country of immigration, these newcomers — called "spacemen" by English media and known in Taiwan as "Tai Kun Fei Jen" (the equivalent term of "spacemen") — represent a unique class of Chinese immigrants shuttling comfortably between Taipei, Hong Kong, and such places as Los Angeles. (Waldinger and Tseng 1992:103–104)

Fong (1994) and Skeldon (1997:113–115) also discuss the phenomenon.[15]

It is almost superfluous to note that contemporary transnationalism and its attendant hypermobility have been rendered feasible, if not inevitable, by the invention and adoption of modern means of transport and communication and a radical cheapening in per-kilometer and per-unit costs for members of the working class as well as more affluent folks. Whereas in earlier times the transoceanic transmission of passengers, commodities, documents, and cash might take weeks or even months, today money and information can be transferred around the globe in the blink of an eye, while travel time for people and parcels between all but the most remote points is now measured in hours.

But something more fundamental than the merely technological has spawned the transnational phenomenon. Alejandro Portes (1987: 57; 1995) has counterposed the spatial-cum-economic initiatives of wage workers against the global grasp of capitalism. And, similarly, in their manifesto announcing a transnational perspective on migration, Glick Schiller et al. advance their line of reasoning by declaring that by maintaining many different social, national, and ethnic identities, transmigrants are able to express their resistance to the global political and economic situations that engulf them even as they accommodate themselves to living conditions marked by vulnerability and insecurity. These migrants express their resistance in small, everyday ways that usually do not directly challenge or even recognize the basic premises of the systems that surround them and dictate the terms of their existence. (1992:11)

Critics might challenge the uniqueness and theoretical and practical impact of transnationalism by pointing out that the present-day situation is no more than a logical continuation of historical trends. As previously noted, over the course of many centuries, a small but influential corps of merchants, clergy, mercenaries, skilled craftworkers, and scholars has circulated across wide distances. Indeed, many of those persons considered immigrants to the United States were actually sojourners who eventually returned to their original localities or even made several round trips in the course of a work life. And the world has long been acquainted with a number of international "tribes" that manage to sustain commercial, social, and cultural ties despite the diasporas that have strewn them far and wide. Among the more conspicuous examples are the Armenians, Jews, Lebanese, Chinese, and Gypsies of modern times and the Phoenicians and Hellenes of yore (Chaliand and Rageau 1995; Kotkin 1993). Moreover, the incidence, past and present, of return migration — upon retirement or for other reasons — and of annual cycles of international movement on the part of seasonal laborers and other transients has often reached magnitudes too great to be ignored.

But there are telling counterarguments to the charge that transnationalism is simply a new label for an old phenomenon. The most basic is that incremental quantitative change in technologies and social arrangements can result, sometimes quite abruptly, in serious qualitative change. Such was the case, I believe, with the advent of the electric telegraph and steam railroad in the mid nineteenth century. In parallel fashion, and thanks to the latest innovations in transportation, communication, and manipulation of information, we have recently experienced, indeed are still experiencing, rather sudden, mind-altering reconfigurations in our social, cultural, political, and economic dealings that may be even more consequential than the technological advances with which they are so intimately associated.[16] The transnational phenomenon is only one of the results.

Superficial similarities may blind us to the essential distinction between the traditional diaspora of a community that insists on clinging to its ancient identity and the novel attributes of the new transmigrants. Basch et al. suggest a crucial difference:

> The concept of diaspora is closely related to that of "nation," which envisions a people with a common past and a biological bond of solidarity who may or may not at any one time have its own state. In counterdistinction is the deterritorialized nation-state, in which the nation's people may live anywhere in the world and still not live outside the state. By this logic, there is no longer a diaspora because where its people go, their state goes too. (1994:269)

A striking example of such a free-floating nation, but one not involving standard immigrants or migratory laborers, is that of the virtually worldwide constellation of American military bases with their transient personnel and civilian dependents, a phenomenon that materialized with the onset of the Cold War. A parallel development is the widely scattered set of foreign retirement colonies inhabited by equally staunch members of the American sociocultural collectivity, in addition to the many businesspersons, technicians, missionaries, scholars, and students sojourning abroad at any given moment.

Perhaps the most compelling evidence for the unprecedented character of transnationalism appears in the attributes of the participants. It may be true enough that those "spacemen" shuttling between California, Hong Kong, Taiwan, Singapore, and wherever represent latter-day reincarnations of the vagabondish adventurers of long ago — but with a difference! Similarly, we can observe in the new Indian American residents of our land, with their enviable socioeconomic status, the inheritors of a venerable South Asian tradition, but now raised to a qualitatively novel degree of intensity, complexity, and social penetration. The frequency of international telephone calls and Internet postings, family visits, the traffic in prospective brides and grooms and entrepreneurs, the interchange of merchandise, gifts, and audio and video cassettes are all predicated on a comfortable income (Dugger 1998; M. P. Fisher 1980:91–106; Helweg and Helweg 1990:128; Lessinger 1992; R. B. Williams 1988:19). Similarly, the more well-to-do of Filipino immigrants have also been constructing "fluid and multiple identities that link them simultaneously to both countries" (Espiritu 1995:27–28).[17] The less affluent Tongans are behaving in much the same way (Small 1997:185–205). And it is likely that an investigation of Israelis throughout the United States (one of the groups to enjoy de jure as well as de facto dual citizenship) would detect symptoms of transnationalism as well.

But perhaps the most persuasive testimony for the reality of a new species of transnational ethnic community — or at least the example most intensively studied to date — comes from the people involved in the Caribbean–United States circuit (Basch et al. 1994; Sutton 1987, 1992; Sutton and Makiesky-Barrow 1987). And, as it happens, in this instance two processes are operating concurrently: the ethnogenesis of a pan-Caribbean identity occurring mainly in the United States; and transnationalization, a phenomenon involving the places and persons in question.[18]

What sets the current situation apart from the past, then, is the fact, so amply documented by Basch et al. (1994), that the actors fashioning the actual or nascent transnational entities are not elites but ordinary middle- and working-class individuals who originate in lands with no earlier pattern of diaspora. Most important, and consistent with heterolocalism at the national level, there are signs of sustained ambiguity, of dual allegiances that may continue indefinitely rather than of absorption into the host society as mandated by the dynamics of the assimilation model. According to Appadurai, "the landscapes of group identity — the ethnoscapes — around the world are no longer familiar anthropological objects, insofar as groups are no longer tightly territorialized, spatially bounded, historically unselfconscious, or culturally homogenous" (1991:191).

Alerted by the empirical work of Basch and her colleagues on underprivileged peoples from Grenada, Saint Vincent, Haiti, and the Philippines, we can expect similar transnational expressions of heterolocalism involving persons in the United States circulating to and from, and otherwise entangling themselves with, Brazil (Millman 1997:210–220), Mexico (Kearney 1995b), Jamaica, the Dominican Republic (Georges 1990; Grasmuck and Pessar 1991), and other Caribbean isles, as well as upscale Indians and Chinese. The vigorous to-and-fro movements of the Puerto Rican working class between island and mainland may also be classifiable as transnational, even though these travelers nominally inhabit a common political space. In related fashion, anyone seeking them out is bound to discover transnational communities of a nontraditional sort linking the United Kingdom with the British Caribbean, France with North Africa, and Germany with Turkey, while others are undoubtedly waiting to be discerned in other corners of the world.

IN SUMMARY

Recapitulating the central arguments of this chapter, the term "heterolocal" applies at the national scale to recent populations of shared ethnic identity that enter a given area from distant sources, then promptly adopt a dispersed pattern of residential location, all the while maintaining strong social cohesion by various means despite the lack of propinquity. Heterolocal arrangements are most readily observed in metropolitan settings, but such "communities without propinquity" can exist at the regional scale, within nonmetro territory, or, under the designation of "transnational," as something approaching "deterritorialized nations" that span the boundaries of two or more conventional nation-states. Although the most conspicuous of heterolocal communities involve relatively privileged persons, the concept is also valid for some less-privileged groups whose economic survival depends upon movement and transactions over long distances while retaining an older, or creating a new, sense of peoplehood.

Certain hints of heterolocalism are detectable in earlier times. However, its full maturation has become feasible only within the recent past, and there is no way to anticipate how it might play out in the future. Apart from the immediate effect of mutual acculturation generated by having large numbers of nontraditional migrants interacting with the native-born,[19] American society and culture are changing at an unprecedented rate in response to internal forces and the long-distance sharing of information, images, ideas, commodities, and problems with other parts of the world. Thus the sociocultural system into which our newer immigrants might be presumed to be assimilating, or resisting the process thereof, can be likened to an accelerating passenger train. And the pace of movement is far from negligible.

Against such a backdrop, we cannot discount the continuing utility of either the assimilationist or the pluralist model. Some immigrant groups entering the United States will undoubtedly assimilate into the larger society, whether or not they replicate the classic upward-and-outward movement of an earlier era. Similarly, other groups may stick to the pluralist path as they retain their cultural distinctiveness and territorial separateness. The African American community is perhaps the prime example, but various Latino groups (with the possible exception of the Cubans) clearly fall into this category, as do some Native Americans, the Cajuns, the more fundamentalist of the Mennonites, and other small isolated communities, old and new (e.g., Hutterites, Hasidic Jews) that cling zealously to their unique character.

In proposing a third model, I acknowledge that in the real world it fails to capture completely the reality of a number of communities, but note that the same qualification applies to the other two models. There are multiple instances of groups that fall through the cracks of "model space" by displaying the attributes of two or even three of the models. The extreme case may be that of the Jewish American community, whose predominantly metropolitan component has undergone much of the assimilation process — with its outward spatial progression, a fair degree of suburban dispersion, and much cultural adaptation — but in a pluralistic manner, without budging on the fundamental issue of a separate identity. At the same time, Jewish Americans in the South can best be classified as both heterolocal and pluralist. Similarly, many Chinese, especially in the Northeast, are enacting the spatial aspects of the assimilation model by anchoring initially in Chinatowns, then fanning outward to less constricted quarters while retaining their Chineseness, even as their Taiwanese and Hong Kong compatriots in California have been behaving heterolocally.

Applying any of the three rather abstract models to real people and real places is a difficult task, because the cultural baggage and history of a given immigrant group will determine in part which model it will follow in its adopted land. Equally determinative for those who are city-bound is the size, structure, economy, and general ambience of the urban destination. The date of entry is quite significant as well. A number of post-1965 immigrants differ markedly from their coethnics who arrived some generations earlier, not only in their personal characteristics but also by virtue of the fact that the homelands have experienced great change over the intervening years. As noted previously, much research remains to be done on the similarities and differences in the ways earlier and later contingents of Filipinos, Chinese, Poles, Czechs, Hungarians, Lithuanians, Armenians, and others have adapted themselves to new surroundings.

Also on the research agenda is the applicability of any of the three models to other settler countries that have received major influxes of immigrants, most notably Canada, Argentina, Brazil, South Africa, and Australia. What relevance does the American set of models have for such places? And when we turn to virtually all the nations of western Europe, formerly such vigorous exporters of emigrants, will it be necessary to contrive additional theoretical formulations, or does heterolocalism, with its transnational dimension, offer some hope?

Whatever the merits of the heterolocal model or the older perspectives, we can no longer confidently predict, as we did in years past, the ultimate structural assimilation of all recent immigrants into the mainstream of American society or that of other countries accepting sizable numbers of newcomers. In fact, the question of assimilation — how, where, at what speed, and under what circumstances it may occur — now seems obsolescent to the point of becoming a nonproblem, at least for a substantial portion of those populations that have been crossing and recrossing international boundaries. Their members are capable of retaining or inventing much of the ancestral culture while devising original amalgams of their heritage with what they find awaiting them in their new, perhaps provisional, abodes, and with no assurance of ultimate Americanization, Britishization, Gallicization, or whatever. This resourcefulness all but guarantees that the more general, hotly contested issue of multiculturalism will remain at the forefront of public discourse for the foreseeable future.

At a loftier level of abstraction, the ethnic phenomena with which we have been struggling represent a challenge to the Eurocentric master narrative of modernism: that in a rational, well-regulated world, all of the Other would eventually be recruited into the superior order of those who had already built the promised land. Happily, in my opinion, recent history has undermined the credibility of the Eurocentric view, but it has left us with a daunting task. In the new millennium, we must radically rethink the fundamental relationships among person, community, and place, as well as the meaning of ethnic identity, for all of us, not just for immigrants and traditional ethnic groups.

This presentation of heterolocalism as an important new consideration in the study of contemporary demographic, political, cultural, geographic, and ethnic matters still leaves us with some nagging questions. Perhaps the most obvious is the murkiness of the future. Whatever their shortcomings, the assimilation and pluralist models provide us with a comforting sense of predictability or finality. No such comfort is possible with heterolocalism. The vision it implies is one of continuing spatial flexibility and plasticity of identity. Is it necessary to wrestle with such immensities, the huge mysteries of identity, in order to grasp fully what it means to be ethnic? And, as we reconnoiter social space — this time with only fleeting reference to physical location — how will attacking the perplexities of personal and group identity aid us in dealing with ethnic matters nowadays? That is the business of our next chapter.

Deciphering the puzzlements of ethnic phenomena — and, specif-ically, the meaning and implications of Ethnicity — is a project be-yond our capabilities if we ignore the grander challenge of exploring the overarching *general* question of personal, group, and place iden-tity. Clearly, ethnic identity is nested within, is only one of the many dimensions of, that increasingly insistent problem of defining, label-ing, and plotting things within a world of unprecedented volatility. It also has an interesting relationship to that recent phenomenon we call Ethnicity.

THE ARRIVAL OF ETHNICITY

As Richard Handler has so correctly asserted, identity is just one of a surprisingly large set of concepts we have mistakenly come to take for granted as timeless components of our familiar Western world: "We should be as suspicious of 'identity' as we have learned to be of 'culture,' 'tradition' and 'ethnic group.' . . . The concept of 'identity' is peculiar to the modern Western world" (1994:2). The historical actuality is that, like Ethnicity, identity is relatively recent in origin as both word and idea. You will not find it in the Bible, nor did it form part of Shakespeare's capacious lexicon. The *OED*'s earliest citation of the term in anything resembling its current sense is dated 1638, and its definition is as good as any: "2a. The sameness of a person or thing at all times or in all circumstances; the condition or fact that a person or thing is itself and not something else; individuality; personality." Incidentally, *individuality* and *personality* are roughly contemporane-ous with *identity*, the earliest occurrences noted being 1658 and 1655, respectively.

My impression is that, during the first three centuries of its existence, *identity* remained a rather inconspicuous item in both our vernacular and scholarly vocabularies. Once again, the birth or maturation of a concept such as *identity* is not a casual occurrence; it usually signals a fresh development in social history. In any event, symptomatic of its previous obscurity is the absence of any entry on the general topic in the truly encyclopedic *Encyclopedia of the Social Sciences* (Seligman and Johnson 1930–35) several decades ago. But some three decades later the *International Encyclopedia of the Social Sciences* (Sills 1968–70) included two pertinent articles: "Identity, Psychosocial" and "Identification, Political."

In addition to other indicators, a spectacular upsurge in usage that began roughly fifty years ago offers quantitative evidence that a large, rapidly increasing portion of the world's population, and many of the places they inhabit, have begun agonizing over just who or what they are. Table 3 reveals the recency of this unprecedented pandemic *identity crisis*.[1] (*Identity angst* may be a more meaningful term, but *identity crisis* seems to have caught the public fancy.)

As was done with *Ethnicity*, we have in this tabulation the per-annum incidence of entries appearing under the heading *Identity* (but not *Identities*) in the *Social Sciences Citation Index* during the period 1956–1998. Quite significantly, the timing and pace of its upward trajectory closely parallels the experience of *Ethnicity* (table 1). It is quite likely that a count of titles of books and articles in the humanities would yield similar results, as would a content analysis of items appearing in newspapers and other popular periodicals.

TABLE 3. Entries under Heading of "Identity" in the *Social Sciences Citation Index*, 1956–1998

Year	*No.*	*Per Annum*	*Year*	*No.*	*Per Annum*
1956–65	688	69	1992	1,202	1,202
1966–70	1,131	226	1993	1,355	1,355
1971–75	1,360	272	1994	1,479	1,479
1976–80	2,739	548	1995	1,653	1,653
1981–85	3,270	654	1996	2,219	2,219
1986–90	3,813	763	1997	2,232	2,232
1991	780	780	1998	2,413	2,413

Although, as also happened with *Ethnicity*, Raymond Williams bypassed the opportunity to discuss *identity* in his admirable *Keywords* (1983), we are most fortunate in having Philip Gleason's searching inquiry into the semantic history of the term, one too subtle and detailed for brief recapitulation here (1992:123–149). It is not by chance that its recent meteoric career, described by Gleason, began in the United States, the country in the vanguard of twentieth-century social evolution. It was here that the brachiation of connotations rapidly luxuriated, then presumably diffused to more affluent countries. But, interestingly, it was the immigrant psychologist Erik Erikson who was the key figure in putting the word into general circulation. He coined the expression *identity crisis* and did more than anyone else to popularize *identity* (Gleason 1992:127).

THREE FORCES, THREE LANDSCAPES

But whatever the paternity of the term might be, the astonishing efflorescence of *identity* and related usages in the scholarly literature and in vernacular discourse, this seemingly abrupt development over the past half-century, calls for the most thoughtful sort of interrogation. In order to make some sense of the phenomenon, I offer some speculative, but plausible, hypotheses while insisting on situating our current dilemma within the broadest possible sweep of human history and prehistory, a metanarrative, if you please.

The Three Forces

Let me postulate the existence within human beings and their societies of three distinct drives, tendencies, impulses, or forces — I am unable to find any single noun that ideally expresses the idea in question. The oldest, indeed one we share with certain other species within the animal kingdom, I would like to call Force 1: the tendency to cling together, to huddle with our ilk. Its expression varies considerably over time and from community to community, but this is the universal adhesive, however attenuated it may be today, that binds together kinship, friendship, neighborhood groups, and intimate bands of coworkers, a concept roughly conveyed by the term *gemeinschaft*.

The second Force is unique to our species and indeed is one of the attributes that make human beings human, but something whose strength varies widely among individuals: the tendency to experiment, innovate, improvise, dissent, fantasize, to test the limits, to probe whatever possibilities are kindled by imagination and personal appetites. Social and environmental circumstances have seriously cribbed and confined Force 2 throughout nearly all of our species' existence. But it is its occasional successful expression that brings about all those advances, the personal, social, technological, and cultural speciations that have made the human chronicle so dynamic and unpredictable.

If the first two of our forces are presumably resident in our individual genomes, Force 3 is quite different in nature and origin, and I must apply to it that controversial term *superorganic*. It comes into being only after a society has grown past a certain threshold in terms of complexity of social organization and of technological prowess, and it operates over and beyond individual wills and only by means of complex corporate entities. A handful of nouns and adjectives will help characterize the concept, namely, hierarchy, dominance, stratification, conformity, bureaucracy, regimentation, authoritarian, militarization, centripetal.

In a final burst of foolrushery, I propose dividing our metanarrative into three qualitatively distinct epochs, three *longues durées*, to use Fernand Braudel's apt expression.[2] For each of these periods I also suggest the designations Landscapes 1, 2, and 3, following the seminal explorations of the American scene by the late J. B. Jackson (1984:147–157).[3] Although in Jacksonian parlance "landscape" refers only to the visible humanized tracts of the earth's surface, I use the term metaphorically so as to include the entire social fabric as well as physically tangible objects.

Landscape 1

This is the most protracted of the *longues durées* by some order of magnitude. During this lengthy prelude to the arrival of agriculture and its momentous consequences, it was simply impossible for Force 3 to manifest itself, while Force 2 was at low ebb, only rarely venturing to challenge the settled ways of the community. Over the several tens of thousands of years in question, Homo sapiens subsisted at the hunting-gathering-scavenging stage. Society was cellular, essentially egalitarian, and gender, age, lineage, physical condition, and perhaps special skills may have been the only important attributes distinguishing individuals.

In traditional societies, one's identity was fixed, solid, and stable. Identity was a function of predefined social roles and a traditional system of myths which provided orientation and religious sanctions to one's place in the world, while rigorously circumscribing the realm of thought and behavior. One was born and died a member of one's clan, a member of a fixed kinship system and a member of one's tribe or group with one's life trajectory fixed in advance. . . . Identity was unproblematical and not subject to reflection or discussion. Individuals did not undergo identity crises, or radically modify their identity. One was a hunter and a member of the tribe and that was that. (Kellner 1992:141)

Such persons were not individuals in our modern sense; their personhood emerged from a collective sense of identity, their will was directed according to a traditional and unquestioned moral order, their consciousness was not of a unique individual but of the inhabitant of a given destiny. (N. Rose 1996:301).

Our current concept of identity would have been utterly incomprehensible. Imagine, if you will, a time machine whisking us back to some typical community twenty-five thousand years ago, and a conversation with the brightest person in the band. Would it be possible for him or her to grasp the meaning of *identity* or of *alimony, vacation, boredom, alienation, underdevelopment, graft*, or *vitamins*? I seriously doubt it. And, of course, some of their most central, "primitive" concepts would be totally opaque to us.

Landscape 2

With the adoption of plant and animal domestication in several regions of the world and the growth of dense sedentary populations, larger, more complex societies gradually arose. There begins a slow but irreversible evolution of centralized, stratified, hierarchical societies. Landscape 2 had materialized.

This was also the time when "uneven development" first manifests itself, as certain regions proceed into Landscape 2 leaving other zones of humankind in a relatively timeless Landscape 1. It is the genesis of a zonation that has intensified and become more complex in the succeeding millennia. But if there has been lateral, or geographic, unevenness between communities at different stages of development, there is also a vertical sandwiching of landscapes within the community, so that even in hypermodern America or Japan we can detect older patches of Landscape 1 in the odd crevice and much ampler stretches of Landscape 2 resting under an ascendant Landscape 3.

As Landscape 2 crystallized, polities became bigger, more rigorously stratified in social and physical space, more complex in every dimension. A world had come into being where identity began to exist quietly, implicitly, so deep a strand in the social fabric that it needed no comment or naming. Hereditary class, caste, and occupation were universal, along with subservience of female to male. Establishing one's locus within the human realm was merely a matter of citing place of residence, gender, social station, kinship ties, and mode of livelihood.

With the ushering in of the modern age some five hundred years ago, we see a radical energizing and intensification of Landscape 2. Space is not available for even the sketchiest account of the many facets and filaments of the process, but the supreme achievement, the ultimate chapter in the biography of Landscape 3, was the fabrication of the nation-state, an episode begun in earnest some two hundred years ago. What sets this novel political institution apart from its predecessors is the appearance, for the first and probably last time in history, of a strong emotional identification with the state or, rather, nation-state, on the part of the citizenry. A sense of common peoplehood, of a shared history and destiny had come to pass, however artificial such a bond may be. Such a sentiment dissipates the need for forcible exploitation of a subjugated population that regarded their overlords with resignation or dread, if not outright loathing.

Despite the gradual rousing of Force 2 during the first centuries of the modern age, Force 3 and Landscape 2 moved ahead even more vigorously. With the maturation of capitalism and state socialism, an imperialist world order, the nation-state ideology, nationalism in Europe and elsewhere and the belated, imperfect export of the package to the rest of the world, Landscape 2 reached its climax during the early twentieth century. Its supremacy seemed beyond challenge. During this heyday any potential question as to identity was a non-question (and do keep in mind that the term *identity* was still inconspicuous in the lexicon.) One was automatically, primarily, and proudly a German, American, Japanese, Italian, Swede, or whatever.

Quite a few devices contributed to creating this unprecedented state of affairs (Zelinsky 1988a). The following list is a partial one: the production of celebratory histories, oratory, paintings, fiction, drama, opera, films, nationalistic songs and anthems; a standardized national system of education with appropriate textbooks; the apotheosis of national heroes; a series of national holidays with their parades and ceremonies; centralized systems of communication and propaganda; nationalistic placenames and personal names; the formation of citizen armies and adoption of uniforms by members thereof, as well as by the civil service; the provision of a social welfare system; the building or remaking of an emotionally overpowering capital city; the erection of historical and nationalistic monuments throughout the land; the dissemination of nationalistic graphic devices, perhaps including the flag; and, in some instances, a state church symbiotically meshed with other items in the foregoing arsenal.

So successful was the implementation of this program that, at the apogee of the nation-state, many of its adherents would willingly, even joyously, volunteer to sacrifice life, limb, and property in its encounters with hostile states. Less pleasing to the citizen than the developments listed above, but accepted as necessary evils for the smooth operation of the complex national apparatus, were the imposition of passports and various identity cards (social security, driver's license, medical insurance, voter registration, etc.) and eventually the creation of fingerprint files and dossiers on millions of individuals. Similarly, the modern nation-state absolutely requires periodic censuses and surveys of the population and various segments of the economy, not to mention the levying of taxes, and thus the accumulation and manipulation of enormous data banks covering individuals, households, business firms, and nonprofit organizations, just as is being done, clandestinely or otherwise, by many a profit-making corporation (Curry 1997). "Whatever rigidities the modern nation-state may have invented and imposed upon its citizens, choices of individual life-projects and the issue of personal identity began to surface, though seldom named as such or subjected to critical scrutiny" (Corbin 1990). "The person takes on a new form: that of the unique conscious, responsible, atomized, discrete, bounded, coherent, choosing, acting individual equipped with a personal consciousness and a personal conscience" (N. Rose 1996:301–302).

> In modernity, identity becomes more mobile, multiple, personal, self-reflective, and subject to change and revision. Yet identity in modernity is also social and Other-related. The forms of identity . . . are also relatively substantial and fixed; identity still comes from a circumscribed set of roles and norms: one is a mother, a son, a Texan, a Scot, a professor, a socialist, a Catholic, a lesbian — or rather a combination of these social roles and possibilities. Identities are thus still relatively circumscribed, fixed and limited, though the boundaries of possible identities, of new identities, are continually expanding. (Kellner 1992:141)

The Gestation of Landscape 3

Despite the apparent triumph of Landscape 2 in the early 1900s, rapid, profound change was just around the corner: the advent of our third *longue durée*, whose duration or ending is beyond our powers of prediction or imagining. The full unleashing of Force 2, and thus the shaping of Landscape 3, depended upon an interlocking series of technological and social developments. The most palpable of the proximate factors, it seems, were major innovations in communication and transportation.

The invention of writing several millennia ago initially and exclusively served the interests of rulers and merchants, and, as a skill monopolized by a small minority, including the clerisy, literacy continued to do so for many centuries. As a device for stabilizing and standardizing language, or at least retarding changes therein, writing also tended to strengthen the corporate structure of society.

However, eternally latent in the written word have been subversive opportunities for challenging or circumventing authority. This potentiality became obvious with the arrival of printing. Once again, a new technology was commandeered immediately to bolster the power of state, church, and market. But, just as promptly, the agents of dissent learned how potent a weapon the printing press could be in countering conformity and the Establishment. The truly pivotal development was the spread of universal literacy, a process essentially completed in affluent countries by the early twentieth century. What ensued was a reshaping of the minds and imaginations of the individual and of humanity in general. Now it became possible for Everyman to don mental seven-league boots, so to speak, to vault backward and forward through time, to visit real or imagined places far removed from one's humdrum surroundings, and perhaps to enter vicariously into other identities.

Progress toward Landscape 3 was also greatly facilitated later by the availability of electronic media, beginning with the telegraph, cable, and telephone, then the brave new world of television, tape cassettes, e-mail, the Internet, websites, and their inevitably even glitzier successors, not to mention photography and movies.

The building of networks of improved roads fitted readily into the centripetal programs of both ancient and modern states, as have the railroad systems of the past century and a half. But one of the peculiarities of such reinforcements of the regime is that they also facilitate outward and sideward, as well as inward, movement of people, commodities, and loyalty. And, with the passage of time, it became clear that faster, cheaper, more pervasive and efficient modes of travel — notably automotive and aeronautical — are doing as much to negate as to fortify hierarchical systems of collective existence.

As causative as the obvious technological developments in the transition from Landscape 2 to its successor have been alterations in social, demographic, economic, and psychological conditions. In terms of ultimate psychological impact, no single event was to have a greater role in paving the way for Landscape 3 than World War I. As of July 1914, Landscape 2, a would-be utopia, based on the nation-state system, a candidate for the pinnacle of human endeavor, seemed to have perfection almost within its grasp. But then, the horrific, senseless, massive slaughter of the following four years inculcated a much different lesson as the nation-state and its world began to look distinctly dystopian. Although the system remained intact and Landscape 2 continued to lurch onward for a few more decades, disenchantment and a certain numbness had set in, most noticeably in the arts and letters and among the intelligentsia in general. An even more cataclysmic World War II finally pushed Landscape 2 onto a visibly downward course. Among the many consequences of the two world wars were the initiation of the decolonization of the European, Japanese, and American overseas empires and, at least within Europe, the reshaping of new and old nation-states along ethnic lines. In general, the liberationist impulses sparked by the two conflicts subverted the rationale of Force 3. Be reminded that it was during the presumably placid 1950s, the decade when it is likely that Force 2 had finally caught up with Force 3, that identity began its extraordinary rise from relative obscurity.

Among the varied social and demographic developments that have been imperiling the well-being of Landscape 2, perhaps few are more directly threatening than the sheer vigor of population redistribution within and, more menacingly, among, our various sovereign states. Migration has, of course, always been a significant phenomenon as long as there have been complex societies, often involving migratory workers and occasionally mass transfers of entire populations. But, setting aside the less than voluntary movements of refugees, asylum seekers, and other such products of the accidents of history, which show no signs of abating, we have witnessed in recent times a remarkable increase in the voluntary mobility of individuals and families in terms of frequency and distances as well as volume.

One result has been a substantial influx of unfamiliar ethnic and racial groups (and adherents of unfamiliar faiths) into not just the settler countries with their tradition of liberal hospitality for familiar types of immigrants but also into a good many European nations previously characterized only as exporters of their surplus inhabitants. Even xenophobic Japan has begun to lower the barriers against non-Japanese sojourners, however reluctantly. And, as we have seen previously, compounding the situation has been the appearance of a nontrivial number of those heterolocal persons we call "transmigrants." In any case, this novel demographic mix in those states with the most advanced claims to a mature Landscape 2, has raised doubts about the wholeness and purity of the national community, also generating troubling questions concerning national identity. Many other profound changes have been going on, of course, but we must set them aside for the moment.

Symptomatic of a deep, metastasizing malaise among the inhabitants of Landscape 2 have been certain developments in the psychic realm. Most notably there are all those individual and collective attempts at escape (Freie 1998). The motivations underlying such ventures may not be recognized by the participants, but they are real enough nonetheless. The most compelling example may be that of science fiction. In its initial nineteenth-century incarnation, perhaps best displayed in the works of Jules Verne, it may have been an affirmation of the wonders of science and technology. But, in recent decades, as the genre has grown in popularity and sophistication, it has generally taken on a more somber tone. Consciously or otherwise, the authors and their readers and viewers — science fiction having exploded into film, television, and comix — as they devise alternative worlds, histories, and life forms, are expressing a decided disenchantment with the felicities of Landscape 2.

In parallel fashion, we have the discovery of time-travel as another mode of exit from a less than optimal here and now. Interestingly enough, the earliest fictional embodiment of the concept of which I am aware, *A Connecticut Yankee in King Arthur's Court* (in 1889, some seven years ahead of H. G. Wells's *Time Machine*), was the doing of Mark Twain, who matured into one of the most caustic of all commentators on his contemporary America. Other temporal excursions taking place outside the realm of imaginative literature involve many millions of volunteers. Indeed one of the more striking phenomena of recent years has been the boom in historic preservation, the pervasive cultivation of heritage, genealogy, historical museums, and other manifestations of antiquarianism and nostalgia. Also noteworthy is the ancient-music and period-instrument craze in classical music circles and the many backward-glancing gestures in postmodern architecture (Lowenthal 1985, 1996). One might also argue that one of the factors contributing to the recent surge of environmental activism is a traditionalist yearning to turn the calendar back to a mythical past when humankind and ecosystem presumably coexisted in salubrious balance (J. Friedman 1992:361). From a certain point of view it seems that, whether wittingly or not, those who indulge seriously in such activities are voting against the present (and future) while seeking emotional refuge and a more meaningful personal identity in other largely imaginary eras.

Landscape 3

By the 1960s, various cultural, social, and psychological tendencies that had been germinating and festering below the surface of public awareness burst into view rather abruptly. We have entered what, by general consensus — and for lack of a better term — we must call the postmodern era, as Landscape 3 challenges the hegemony of Landscape 2. Although we are still much too close to the event — this seemingly radical transformation of human affairs — to see or judge it with the cool rationality of some ideal twenty-second-century historian, some interim general observations seem feasible.

The new mode of perceiving, feeling, thinking, creating, and behaving is most readily apparent in architecture, literature, literary criticism, and much of popular culture; but postmodern sensibilities and anxieties have begun to reach into all departments of present-day existence, quite prominently in the United States but in other lands as well. Still, if there is any single dominant theme articulated or implicit in the relevant discourse, it is the dilemma of identity.[4]

At this point I can do no better than quote some characterizations of this dilemma more acute and eloquent than anything I am capable of.

> Postmodernity is the point at which modern untying (dis-embedding, dis-encumbering) of tied (embedded, situated) identities reaches its completion: *it is now all too easy to choose identity, but no longer possible to hold it.* At the moment of its ultimate triumph, the liberation succeeds in annihilating its object. . . . Freedom . . . has given the postmodern seekers of identity all the powers of a Sisyphus. (Bauman 1996:50–51; emphasis in original)

> From the postmodern perspective, as the pace, extension, and complexity of modern societies accelerate, identity becomes more and more unstable, more and more fragile. (Kellner 1992:143)

> Identity disturbance in general terms [is] part of a *meaning vacuum* which results from defective symbolic responses of one kind or another. We do not usually receive the kinds of responses from our fellow that will permit us to feel ourselves: deeply (in warm relationships or strenuous tests) as a unity or whole (continuously as the same kind of person), of inherent worth (creatively fulfilling inner potential), and living "for" something (a cause, value, or ideology in which one deeply believes). (Klapp 1969:19–20; emphasis in original)

> All fixed tradition and established habits seem to be questioned as never before by the breakdown of the stabilities of class and patterns of labour, the regularities of the domesticated nuclear family, the roles and divisions of men and women — those standardized forms of life promulgated by the modernization process of the nineteenth century. This novel multiplication of possible forms of life is reinforced by the images of lifestyle circulated by the mass media, and embedded within a relentless spiral of injunctions to consume in particular ways in order to become particular sorts of people. . . . Identity is no longer experienced as a natural, coherent and unchanging attribute of the individual, but as the uncertain and fractured result of personal decisions and plans. Biogra-

phy and identity become self-reflexive, to be constructed, worked upon, the outcome of choices — about clothes, marriages, relationships, diet — in which the individual himself or herself is the self-conscious centre of action. (N. Rose 1996:302)

And, speaking of clothes, we have in Fred Davis's historical account *Fashion, Culture, and Identity* (1992) a richly informative illustration of how one important aspect of material culture has evolved over time in form and meaning in tandem with the permutations of personal identity. During the earlier phases of Landscape 2, fashion, as we have come to know it in recent times, had not yet been born. With barely perceptible alterations from generation to generation, one's dress denoted station in life, occupation, gender, localized culture, and perhaps season. Then, in a development that was a harbinger of the gestating modern age, "fashion in the modern sense began in late medieval Europe, probably in Burgundy [appropriately enough in historic-geographic terms] in the late 13th, early 14th century" (Davis 1992:28–29). If members of the upper classes throughout Europe and, later, its overseas outposts zealously adhered to the slow swings and cycles in style, "the common people were for the most part excluded from fashion's orbit until the nineteenth century" (Davis 1992:33).

Then, in recent decades, as the "other-directed" individual of the high noon of modernism yielded to the "inner-directed" type, to adopt David Riesman's (1953) valuable insights, we have the unleashing of Force 2. The classic "long wave" fashion cycle, which formerly would in time dragoon all into the same stylistic camp, fell victim somehow, most certainly by the late 1960s, to the identity-defining reactivity elicited by late capitalist consumer culture" (Davis 1992:158).

The result has been our anarchic, carnivalesque situation today in which individuals from childhood onward enjoy virtually unlimited options for dress and personal adornment. Thus one can indulge in a wide repertory of identities, flitting from one costume to another following whim or circumstance. And the choice can vary by time of day, day of the week, or special occasion. The extreme form of such multiple role playing is the costume party, no longer the property of the privileged but available to any child or adult so inclined. Paradoxically, the person who strives to create a unique identity by means of personal appearance does so usually by assembling a mix of mass-produced commodities.

In any case, we have now reached the point where it is often literally impossible to distinguish paupers from millionaires by the clothes they wear or to use garb in guessing a stranger's ethnic background, class, or mode of employment. But the most convincing evidence for the blurring of the semantic value of garments and accessories may be the difficulty of ascertaining the gender of many young adults nowadays merely by looking at clothes, hair style, jewelry, or even tattoos.

As previously cited authors have strongly asserted, we find ourselves trapped in a curious world of contradictions, of unprecedented personal and group anxieties. The freedom to comparison-shop among lifestyles, to rotate among multiple identities, this culmination of millennia of human struggle and progress, such power and flexibility, all have failed to generate the bliss one might have anticipated or hoped for. Instead, an increasingly large segment of Landscape 3 populations, and incipiently others as well, has begun to wonder who or what they are — or should be.[5] It is almost needless to point out how psychotherapy in all its varied forms has become a growth industry in recent decades.

Thus choice has bred confusion, neuroses, and anomie rather than certitude. Obviously, not everyone is a full-time victim of this latter-day pandemic. Many millions are too preoccupied with the business of staying alive, of being fed, clothed, housed, and medicated to fret about anything beyond the daily grind. And, then, there is that blithe, talented fraction of humankind who revel in the late modern or postmodern opportunities for personal fulfillment by cultivating the creative arts, crafts, science, or advanced technologies in the company of their planetwide confrères — or who simply luxuriate in the euphoria of personal freedom. But even they are not totally immune to the general angst whenever they look up from their work or fun.

An additional source of nervousness, one seemingly quite opposite to the unbridled exercise of Force 2, is the ongoing globalization of all realms of human affairs, including material and nonmaterial culture as well as the economy (Barnet and Cavanagh 1994 : 13–22, 25–41). Subconsciously or otherwise, we have begun to worry whether we are all being ground down into universal sameness and anonymity. Hence the urge to be different, to search for one's own true self. This concern is observed readily enough in all those many cities, towns, and other localities that have become aware of the toxins of placelessness (Relph 1984) and strive to sustain or fabricate some semblance of distinctiveness.

Reflecting on all the materials presented above, one can scarcely help noticing a certain affinity between Landscape 3 and heterolocalism. Indeed it may be useful to think of heterolocalism as the territorial dimension of a multidimensional Landscape 3.

SHOPPING FOR IDENTITIES

Work and the Consumption of Places and Things

What to do? There are two general strategies — the individual and the collective — but they frequently operate in tandem. Beginning at the personal level, the most immediate question in concocting one's identity, for all but the beneficiaries of inherited wealth, is choice of occupation or means of livelihood. Gone are the days when one was simply born, or married, into a particular line of work. Perhaps as decisive a moment in social history as any was the one when adults began to ask youngsters, "What are you going to be when you grow up?" (Alas, we shall never be able to pinpoint date or place.) Whatever the juvenile responses, during their working years more and more individuals switch employers, types of job, or entire career paths, and do so with ever greater frequency. Such occupational churning has been eroding the ideal rigidities of Landscape 2 while also magnifying the dilemma of personal identity. We must conclude that, except for the minority with a single-minded, lifelong passion for a given vocation, profession, or craft, describing one's job does not pin down one's identity.

In the past, admittedly, successful business firms offered a seemingly solid, stable center of reality for their employees, their dependents, and frequently entire cities. Nowadays, in our advanced (and final?) stage of capitalism such intimate bonds have been badly frayed or severed. Driven by the bottom line, more and more companies have abandoned their initial sites and long-term workforce. In the process, many towns have lost much of what unique identity they claimed previously. (Think of Akron and rubber, Pittsburgh or Bethlehem and steel, Manchester and textiles, Cremona and violins, Belfast and shipbuilding, Lynn and shoes.) And the same must be said of the corporation in terms of geographic specificity. What places, if any, spring to mind when you hear the names IBM, Exxon, Pepsi-Cola, Xerox, Shell, Nike, Burger King, Time Warner, or AT&T? And the firms themselves are susceptible to identity angst, so that many go to great lengths to fabricate some sort of instantly recognizable image via logo and carefully crafted print and TV ads.

For the individual, an increasingly popular option involves territorial mobility. The person engaged in an identity quest may realize a certain measure of satisfaction by migrating to a place whose physical and social qualities are consonant with his or her inner proclivities (Zelinsky 1974). Created thereby are "voluntary regions," such as southern Florida, or specialized cities or smaller tracts blessed with unquestionable individuality. Such places may have some degree of permanence or may be only temporary gatherings.[6] By sharing in this geographic specialness he or she has helped to form, the migrant has found a compatible nest where, wittingly or not, all those appetites and qualities that may have been only latent previously can be nurtured. But there is no guarantee that the place in question can retain its uniqueness indefinitely. In any event, of all the stratagems to be reviewed here, this may be the only one that, partially or temporarily, assuages the craving for authentic identity. On the other hand, not everyone has the means or knowledge to gravitate to such exceptional sites. Even those who do cannot totally evade the perplexities, the identity challenges, of the wider world beyond their enclave.

Much more widespread is a ploy generated by our consumerist, postindustrial economy with its relentless pressures to seek personal fulfillment by buying, and presumably enjoying, more and more commodities and experiences. Thus many of us classify ourselves and others by the cars we drive, the style and price of the houses we inhabit, the beverages we drink, the entertainments we indulge in, the designer clothes we wear, or the vacation spots we frequent. But all such items, houses partially excepted, are essentially ephemeral, fads subject to swift obsolescence. The shifting sands of our purchases or the mix of credit cards in our wallets do not make for solid foundations of personal identity.

There is, however, one costly acquisition that can mark us for life: a college education. American parents and children usually expend a good deal of time and thought in deciding upon an appropriate institution as they factor in not just cost and travel distance but other less quantifiable variables. And, during the four years or more of residence, the young person certainly absorbs a specific collective identity, something a tireless alumni organization will never permit the grad to forget. Class reunions revive and fortify bygone togetherness, and, for an even larger share of the population, reunions of high school classes serve the same purpose (Vinitzky-Seroussi 1998). Similarly, for millions of veterans, the bonding bred by military service and perpetuated by subsequent clubs and periodic gatherings often proves to be the defining social experience of a lifetime. But for even the most devout alumnus, alumna, or veteran, this receding episode does not supply the wherewithal for the totality of postschool or postmilitary identity formation.

Still another way to create personal identity that has boomed in recent years is membership in one or more of the countless voluntary associations that cater to every imaginable form of human interest and curiosity. Such quasi-communities can now congregate in cyberspace as well as through the traditional conventions, newsletters, and other publications.[7] The proliferation of such flocks of far-flung individuals with shared appetites and impulses is an intriguing paradox. Here we have as full an expression of Force 2 as one could desire, as the atomized person casts about to realize a unique destiny within Landscape 3 while at the same time he or she seeks to appease a primordial hunger that harks back to Landscape 1. But such pseudo-identities fall short of filling the need even, or especially, when a person affiliates with several of the organizations in question. Total immersion of self into any such entity is difficult to realize.

The Nation-State Option

If solo efforts to forge meaningful personal identities in an increasingly bewildering world are proving fruitless, the questing individual might logically turn to grander entities to learn who he/she really is, or should be. As we have seen, two of the more obvious options — the large business corporation and the special-interest voluntary association — are less than ideal solutions to the dilemma. But we are still left with that ultimate mass institution of the recent past, the nation-state. Until recently, for almost the entire citizenry, this was the absolute, rock-solid core of group and individual identity. But that was then.

Today, as Landscape 3 encompasses more and more of our social, cultural, and economic terrain, the legitimacy of the nation-state, its monopolistic title to loyalty and shared identity, has been mortally compromised (Castells 1997:242–308).[8] Perhaps no one has diagnosed the plight of the nation-state, and the ongoing transition to a new kind of world we cannot yet describe, more insightfully and disturbingly than Jean-Marie Guéhenno (1995).[9] Although we twenty-first-century creatures find it mind-boggling to try imagining a world bereft of the nation-state, Guéhenno rightfully characterizes it and its two-century career as no more than a brief, passing episode within the vaster stream of human history, while documenting all of its incurable ailments at the end of the last millennium.

We have already seen how the debacle of World War I began the demystification of the nation-state, how doubts were sown concerning its goodness and inevitability. But more directly challenging is the threat posed by a chronic economic and social crisis that had become impossible to ignore as of 1973 and still has no end in sight. As the long-term rise in real personal income among the populations of developed nations came to a halt and many incomes even began to recede, as the myth of perpetual progress becomes tarnished, as the state becomes less and less able to honor the social contract with its citizens, its claims upon the hearts and minds of the populace begin to sound hollow, even frivolous.

And there has been a remarkable sea change in the popular disposition toward the state and its governmental apparatus. I am old enough to remember the period when national leaders were accorded considerable deference by the masses. Indeed in many countries they were regarded with awe, as objects of veneration or, at the very least, with sullen respect. Today, in contrast, I have difficulty citing a single example (perhaps the Czech Republic's Havel or South Africa's Mandela?) where admiration or adulation describes the prevailing attitude of the ruled toward their rulers. Instead, almost universally, we find the rank and file envisioning those at the top of the political heap as incompetents or scoundrels, as self-serving, meretricious, or worse, as objects of suspicion, derision, or contempt.

The crumbling of its moral legitimacy dims the prospect for the long-term survival of the nation-state. In fact, one can argue that this was one of the key factors in the disintegration of the Soviet Union, the bifurcation of Czechoslovakia, and the calamitous dismembering of Yugoslavia. In still other instances, such as India, Mexico, Russia, Indonesia, and the recent Zaire, one can detect ominous signs of an impending crisis of legitimacy. A good many observers have pointed out other grave challenges to the integrity of the nation-state. Most often cited are the multinational corporations with their global reach and mighty accumulations of wealth and power. Then there are the many nongovernment offices (NGOs), including grass-roots environmental and social-issues organizations, whose missions and activities may run counter to the interests of sovereign states, as do various international treaties and conventions that circumscribe their operations. It is also difficult to overlook the many intranational campaigns for greater political and cultural autonomy, if not outright secession, on the part of certain regional entities, such as those in Great Britain, France, Italy, Russia, Spain, Canada, Iraq, Sudan, and Sri Lanka.

Nevertheless, reports of the imminent demise of the nation-state are greatly exaggerated. However shaky its emotional hold may have become, the state still monopolizes police and military power, along with judicial systems, and remains the decisive agent in many phases of economic and social life. Furthermore, recent technological advances in surveillance and control have meant an even greater potential for manipulating the citizenry. Not even the mightiest of multinational firms or the most ambitious of international agencies has the capability or desire to manage all of humankind's affairs. Thus we dare not ignore the huge facticity of the nation-state, that looming presence that is still so much with us.[10]

Other Alternatives?

A venerable alternative is available in the form of the church, despite the fact that the state has so often coopted it. One of the more striking developments of recent times has been a virtually worldwide resurgence of fundamentalism (another form of time travel?) among substantial numbers of worshipers. We are also witnessing the spawning of many denominations and cultures, groups ranging along the entire spectrum from the most traditional all the way to the most esoteric and outlandish. Some would characterize such rekindled religiosity as a side effect of globalization and a response to the shortcomings of the modernization project (Robertson and Chirico 1985). But, however interesting such stirrings may be, the fact remains that the truly devout, who may very well attain the personal-cum-group identity they crave, account for only a small minority of humankind. Secularism continues to claim more and more people. But even relatively observant, church-going (but not-yet-born-again) parishioners are unlikely to think of themselves primarily in religious terms.[11]

Another increasingly popular expedient revolves around region or locality. The recent efflorescence of regional sentiment in the United States and some European countries, generally in the absence of any political agenda, has yet to be studied definitively, but one can speculate about a yearning for rootedness in place, for a shared geographic identity, as one causative element. In any case, many cities have indulged in some ingenious gestures to proclaim their (and thus their inhabitants') particularity. Some fortunate localities can capitalize on the renown of their illustrious dead. Such examples as Bayreuth, Weimar, Stratford, Salzburg, Arles, Lourdes, Hannibal (Missouri), Springfield (Illinois), Oxford (Mississippi), Charlottesville (Virginia), Jim Thorpe (Pennsylvania), Salinas (remember Steinbeck?), and Memphis (of Elvis fame) come readily to mind.

Or the strategy may rely on a recurrent spectacular event, for example New Orleans' Mardi Gras, Calgary's Stampede, Charleston's

Spoleto Festival, or Pasadena's Tournament of Roses. Where manageable, the creation, refurbishing, or embalming of a historic district is also helpful in the image-building process. But almost every town or city can conjure up some excuse for uniqueness by virtue of its being the birthplace of some minor celebrity, the gateway to, or center of, some region, or the "capital" of some esoteric activity. And such credentials will be flaunted in the shape of distinctive logos, slogans, monuments, welcoming signs, billboards, and other types of publicity (Zelinsky 1988b).

Within North America, an almost universal formula for fabricating group identity has to do with spectator sports, arguably the last vestige of old-fashioned community. Beginning gradually in the late nineteenth century but reaching an almost hysterical climax lately is a powerful emotional commitment to the local professional football, baseball, hockey, or basketball team or, in the case of the presumably amateur college football or basketball program, the enmeshment of an entire state or region. And, of course, during the periodic Olympic and World Cup excitements, the nation's identity seems to hang upon the fortunes of its athletes. What is truly strange about this rather spurious kind of place identity, one that excludes that sizable minority uninterested in sports, is the willful, open-eyed self-deception it entails. Even the most fanatic of fans is well aware of the fact that the players are mobile professionals or subsidized amateurs, usually born and reared elsewhere, with their eye on the main chance, wherever it may be, and that indeed (except for the collegiate) the franchise itself is portable and can be whisked away at any time at the whim of the owner. Such blind devotion to a business enterprise with no binding commitment to the locality bespeaks a certain desperation.

The Ethnic Choice

The quandary remains. The individual adrift in Landscape 3 can nowhere espy the stable, identity-affirming mooring so avidly sought. All the larger aggregations, the quasi-ideal communities we have considered so far — nation-state, business firm, college class, other voluntary associations, born-again congregation, sport-fandom, boosterish town — seem to meet the identity needs of far fewer than the totality of any contemporary society, and perhaps do so only temporarily or problematically. Is there any other possibility, any potential magic formula still waiting to be appraised? Perhaps.

> The sweet warmth of the community, with its one-dimensional simplicity, is . . . a very natural temptation. To those who see the idea of the nation become more and more abstract, to those who do not participate in the integration of the enterprise, to those that the enterprise isolates, rather than unites, the [ethnic] community is likely to appear as the natural framework within which everyone may rediscover his identity. Without any links to a territory, "nomadic," and nevertheless imprisoned in a function, without an overarching perspective to give a meaning to a given task, modern man, a social nodule infinitely reproduced and nevertheless always single, solitary, is condemned to find in a search for origins a difference that he needs in order to share with others, as different as he is, a feeling of common heritage. (Guéhenno 1995 : 45)

And so, after this lengthy (seemingly endless?) detour, we have finally circled back to the ethnic group and the central business of this study. Is the latter-day ethnic community the unbreakable safety net in which, when all else fails (to muddle metaphors), we find our bearings?

There are certainly those who would like to have us think so. However, we have already seen that the self-conscious ethnic group is a modern social construct that may or may not have some claim to primordiality. We have also learned about the ambiguities as well as artificialities of this recent invention and how tentative, fickle, and multiply contingent membership therein can be.

Looked at coolly and objectively, then, any campaign to mobilize latent, or contrived, ethnic sentiment into some semblance of genuine community, whether among Caucasians or non-Caucasians, is a quixotic enterprise.[12] "The search for community turns into a major obstacle to its formation" (Bauman 1992 : 139). What is created, pursuing the ethnic strategy, is what Michel Maffesoli and Zygmunt Bauman label as "neo-tribalism" (Bauman 1992 : 136 –137).[13] "Such communities will never be anything like Tönnies's cosy and unreflective (cosy *because* unreflective) homes of unanimity. Tönnies-style communities fall apart the moment they know of themselves as communities" (Bauman 1992:136–137; emphasis in original). Thus these neotribes are products of willful effort, not the Tönnies-style communities of remote, Landscape 1 antiquity where gemeinschaft prevailed. But, however fragile and evanescent they may prove to be, such recent social constructs can still have major political and other consequences.

Their instigators, too often with ignoble motives in mind, have been able to capitalize on the tensions engendered by modernism and, more acutely of late, by globalization. Much of their appeal derives from recovered or invented traditions and also the fiction that their popular movement, as a corrective to the coercive top-down homogenization mandated by the nation-state, is a spontaneous, people-based phenomenon. Rather ironically, the nation-state has been an active collaborator in initiating neotribes.

For a variety of administrative, political, and other reasons, as we have seen, the national bureaucracy, for all but the most homogeneous states, has seen fit to categorize the population into convenient pigeonholes. Such standard measures as age, sex, class, occupation, and residence do not suffice. Almost always the preferred option has been an ethnic/racial taxonomy. (Religion can be equally important in some countries.) In many instances, as we have also learned, the designations and definitions are arbitrary with only a tenuous relationship, if any, to anthropological actualities. But the impact of administrative fiat can be substantial. The case of South Africa during its apartheid era may be extreme, but in the United States, as elsewhere, the census classification system has certainly been a factor in channeling the collective behavior of various constituencies. If you are officially informed that you belong to a given group, you may begin to believe it.

The situation is especially tricky for people of color. Indeed we face a mighty paradox in considering the quandaries of those "minority" persons who, on the face of it, ought not to entertain the slightest hesitation in acknowledging their ethnic/racial, hence total, identity. If they are perceived to belong to such and such a group by official decree or the opinion of the general public, and if there has been such a lively campaign to assert their worth and cultural vitality, why should anyone challenge the obvious? But challenge many of them have, whether singly or collectively.

Even the simple issue of nomenclature reveals a certain degree of apprehension. Should we call ourselves Latino, Hispanic, Spanish American, Chicano, or what? Or note the awkward, sometimes fractious progression from colored to Negro to black to African American, and what tomorrow? Labeling by outsiders often fails to match self-classification. How many Cuban Americans would consent to being lumped together with Hondurans or Dominicans? What to do with Brazilians? Which category for a Puerto Rican or a Somali with decidedly Negroid features? Will recent immigrants from the Bahamas or the Cape Verde Islands agree to African American status? Furthermore, as suggested earlier, the spread of panethnicity complicates the issue. Samoans may think of themselves as Samoans but hardly as bearing the sobriquet Asian and Pacific Islanders, and Cherokee may prefer identification as Cherokee rather than as Native American. In any case there may be simple uncertainty as to one's niche within a vertically structured, nested hierarchy and also as to lateral affiliation with one or more cultural communities. Such fuzziness means that, while a flat "racial" tag may suffice for the Euro-American observer, it is of questionable worth for many a questing person of color.

In addition, the increase in absolute and relative numbers of persons of mixed ancestry means wilder complications in an already muddled situation. To add to all the other qualifications, one must deal with the insidious fact that the advent of the notion of Ethnicity has eroded whatever virtue or credibility may have once inhered in the verification of a specific ethnic identity. And even when external impressions of identity correlate with self-evaluation, does such affiliation always satisfy one's craving for certitude, for a stable locus in a volatile world? Is it really feasible to retrieve that subconscious sense of belongingness, the taken-for-grantedness of the intimate proto-ethnic community of the premodern past, something not treasured until it had been shattered?

Setting "racial" considerations aside for the moment, in general how well has the ethnic strategy worked in packaging individual and group identity? The short answer is: imperfectly in the most successful of cases, not at all in the others. A fundamental difficulty is that, by their very nature, neotribes are transient, subject to corrosion, and beset by centrifugal tendencies.

Furthermore, not all eligible participants are eager to buy into the scheme, and the increasing incidence of intermarriage may limit the pool of candidates. Then there is the basic contradiction between a backward-glancing mind-set and the compelling realities of our current future-oriented age. The complex movements and action-spaces of neotribal people, the transnationalization of information and all manner of cultural items, and the globalization of the economy all militate against the snugness of a self-contained, perhaps territorially defined ethnic cell. And, finally, the most elemental question of all: If one must ask oneself, as our postmodern ethnic wanna-bes are obliged to do periodically, "Who am I?" — how trustworthy is the response?

Despite such reservations, we must acknowledge the intensity, even fierceness, of devotion to the ethnic cause among *some* members of certain societies in Europe, Asia, and Africa, for example Catalans, Corsicans, Bretons, Albanians in Serbia, Ibo, Afrikaaners, Palestinians, Kurds, Welsh, Tamils, and Transylvanian Magyars. For such adherents there is no doubting the primacy of the ethnic label. Nothing fully comparable exists in the United States at the subnational level, and we must ask why. One answer concerns territory. If all the examples cited above involve claimants to ancestral turf, the only American possibilities, with the marginal exception of the Cajuns, concern non-European peoples. Even though some immigrant groups from Europe did maintain a heavy multigenerational presence in some tracts, it was never to the total exclusion of other communities. Americans should be profoundly thankful, given the relative tranquillity we enjoy as a result.

The territorial story of the Native Americans is quite different, of course, but hardly comparable to the case of, say, the Basques, Québecois, or Frisians. Many of North America's earliest communities were nomadic or frequenters of tracts with vague, contested bound-

aries. Since their disastrous encounter with the invaders from overseas, shifts hither and yon, voluntary or otherwise, followed by intermarriage and urbanization, have weakened or broken attachments
to ancestral locales. If, however belatedly, Native Americans are advancing territorial claims in courts and legislatures with some success, for only a minority of these nations is identification with place
the critical component of ethnic identity. A parallel assertion applies
to the burgeoning Latino population. Excepting some Chicanos in
the Southwest for whom a mythical homeland shines brightly in the
imagination, location is incidental or irrelevant in constructing a
sense of Hispanic American peoplehood. And its relevance may be
even less for African Americans, despite historical concentrations in
the South. For Asian Americans the territorial issue is a nonissue.
Thus, important though it may be for many communities, place
bonding is not an absolute prerequisite for the existence of an ethnic
group. The diasporic Gypsies, Jews, and Lebanese are obvious counter examples of robust peoplehood, if not full-fledged ethnic identity, in all its modern dimensions.

If immigrant Europeans fail to furnish any convincing exceptions,
given their inability to maintain strong ethnic cohesiveness after spatial dispersal, we must still consider the abortive Euro-American
"ethnic revival" of the 1970s. Why did it fizzle by the 1980s, even
though other ethnic movements in the United States and abroad continue to display some vitality? Two or three reasons come to mind.

First, there was the initial encounter of the European immigrant
with an overpowering American cultural system. Thus the Old World
cultural heritage was quickly, mortally compromised as soon as assimilation got under way. By the latter half of the twentieth century,
the process was so far along that symbolic ethnicity became the dominant condition for those nth-generation persons of foreign stock
who gave the matter any thought at all. The *coup de grâce* may well
have been the rise of Ethnicity, as set forth in an earlier chapter. The
sublimation of specific ethnic complexes into a transcendent entity
whereby various cultures become essentially interchangeable has
meant discrediting the campaign of any individual Euro-American
group for gaining autonomy or special recognition.

Must we conclude that the ethnic ploy is missing from the inventory of identity alternatives available to the modal American? Not at all. As argued earlier, membership in the national cultural community means participation in a macroethnic group. But as it happens, unlike in such contentious cases as, say, Bosnia, few Caucasian American individuals have reason to think about this crucial affiliation in the course of everyday activities. It is only during episodes of international strife or in their travels abroad that most Americans are jolted into some appreciation of their primal ethnic identity.

A more reasonable conclusion is that, for those Euro-Americans who still comprise a majority of the population, being an American is only one of the many ways they can use to define themselves. Thinking of oneself as an American is normally a fitful practice without the immediacy or definitional completeness that comparable thought may have for a Japanese, Israeli, Maltese, or Cuban. Under usual circumstances, it is far from a definitive, soul-nourishing response to that nagging postmodern query: Who am I really?

If this chapter or something like it were being composed in 1965, this would be a fitting place to write finis. And the final comment might have been that ethnic identity had dwindled into insignificance, while other options for identity formation had come to the fore. Or there would have been no excuse then for this chapter or even for essaying this entire study. But by the 1980s and 1990s, ethnic issues had come roaring back in the United States and most other advantaged countries because of two developments. First, and especially in the American case, the earliest of subordinated groups — people of color — had become vociferous in demanding their place in the sun; and, secondly, a massive, predominantly non-Caucasian influx of immigrants and sojourners, so foreign in appearance and frequently also disconcerting in terms of religion, language, and other cultural attributes, had made their presence felt.[14] In neither category does numerical growth show any sign of slackening. Furthermore, the rate and extent of assimilation remains problematic (Edmonston and Passel 1994). Indeed there is no assurance that ultimate amalgamation is possible.

We see, then, that what had become a moribund issue, namely, a concern with ethnic groups, has taken on a new, extended lease on life, more than incidentally a development concurrent with the invention of Ethnicity. This turn of events is not confined to the United States. Parallel situations have arisen in other non-European lands, notably Canada and Australia, and in Europe itself with such instances as the Pakistanis in Britain, Surinamese in the Netherlands, Turks in Germany, Albanians in Italy and Greece, and Algerians in France. The subordinated groups in question may or may not welcome recognition of their ethnic distinctiveness, but they have little choice in the matter. If they do not cultivate and cherish their identity themselves, it is thrust upon them by official designation or by the attitudes of the host population. Under the conditions of American life, hardly a day (or hour?) goes by when an African American or a Latina or a Chinese American is not reminded of her ethnic/racial status, especially in dealings with members of the majority. The reverse situation is uncommon. Whatever the company, the Euro-American, whether "hyphenated" or old stock, is seldom obliged to contemplate the ethnic label that is so visible to the Other.

What must we conclude from all this? First, in posing the question "How relevant are ethnic considerations in finding solutions or palliatives for our pandemic identity angst?" the answer, again, is tentative and disappointing: Quite important in some instances, trivial or irrelevant in others. We also learn that the advent of Ethnicity has seriously compromised the prospect that the ethnic option can serve as *the* ideal answer to the identity quandary. If we come to believe that all ethnic groups are essentially the same beneath their varied veneers, what do we gain by adhering to one and abjuring the others?

But there is a still greater message embedded in all the preceding pages: that ethnic identity and Ethnicity are deeply interwoven not just with the currently unanswerable questions "Who am I?" and "What are we?" but with most of the more pressing social, cultural, and political problems of our day. In the final chapter, I begin to explore, to try making explicit, however provisionally, the nature and implications of these involvements.

But, before doing so, I must admit again that the frustrating conclusion to this inquiry into the contemporary world's identity crisis is that there are no satisfactory solutions available for either individuals or social groups, nor are any likely in the near future. Such confusion or rootlessness is a core component of the postmodern condition. It will pass away, or be replaced by some other pathology, only when humankind enters another utterly unpredictable phase of its social evolution.

In this concluding chapter I take stock, as best I can, of the current ethnic scene in the United States, and I peer, most hesitantly, into a decidedly undecided future. If asked for a single term that best captures the present-day situation, the uncontested choice would have to be *multiculturalism*. Reversing the practice followed heretofore, I find it prudent to postpone the effort to define the term precisely — or rather three distinct versions of it — until a later point. The reader's patience will be rewarded.

The United States is not the only country in which this concept has set off a heated discourse (Bauböck et al. 1996). Similar debates are enlivening public life in, *inter alia*, Canada, the Netherlands (Penninx 1996), Sweden (Hannerz 1996; Runblom 1994), Australia (Smolicz 1997), and New Zealand (Spoonley 1988 : 104 –105), but nowhere else has it generated so much noise and discord.[1] Although the uproar may be recent, the underlying situation is not. From the earliest years of European colonization, America has been multicultural or pluralist in social structure. It has served the interests and conscience of the dominant population to remain blind to that reality. Truly

> America has always been multicultural, but it has been a peculiar kind of multiculturalism: not equally powerful cultures enriching one another on a reciprocal basis, but a dominant culture set against subservient cultures fighting to secure places for themselves. Today's immigration creates the possibility that the United States may become a country without a dominant race and without a dominant culture. (Isbister 1996 : 191–192)

Recent Immigration

It seems sensible, then, to examine the facts and implications of recent immigration briefly before coming to grips with contemporary multiculturalism in all its controversial dimensions.

After centuries of huge, relatively unrestricted immigration into the United States, overwhelmingly from European sources, the severe limits imposed by Congress in the early 1920s, a major depression, World War II, and altered conditions in the traditional countries of origin resulted in a mere trickle of newcomers over the forty-year period preceding the 1960s. And, during that interval, the structural assimilation of foreign stock made substantial headway within America, producing a relatively unified Euro-American community (Massey 1995). The passage of the Hart-Celler Act in 1965, which effectively eliminated the pre-existing restrictive national quotas, not only reopened the country to a greatly augmented influx of the foreign-born, but, contrary to the hopes and intentions of its sponsors, it drew these immigrants predominantly from nontraditional sources.

The fact that there were concurrent developments in other lands obliges us to note another qualitative departure from earlier international movements. No longer can we frame such migrations within a simplistic push/pull model involving just a pair of countries. It has become impossible to ignore the complexities of an increasingly weblike globalized world society. In the words of Portes and Böröcz:

> A perspective on immigration as a process internal to the global system offers a more superior point of departure than the traditional view of the movement as something taking place between separate nation-states, and to be evaluated exclusively in terms of its domestic impact. The frontier for theory and research in this field has moved beyond an exclusive concern with immigrant adaptation to focus on relationships between immigration and other international processes. Movements of capital, technology, institutional forms and cultural innovations — like displacements of workers and refugees — criss-cross the world and interact with each other. (1989:626; also see Kritz 1987)[2]

Temporary relocations and ambiguous identifications with two or more sovereign entities, noted previously in the discussion of transmigration as an aspect of heterolocalism, are common in the present-day scene. Consequently, and for better or worse, the traffic in migrants to and from (and within) the United States is only one element in a complicated, worldwide tangle of both nondemographic and demographic relationships. The United States may be the largest, most conspicuous player in this game, but it is only one among many.

But whatever qualifications we may accept, the fact remains that the United States has been receiving (as well as emitting) impressive flows of migrants and sojourners, both legal and undocumented, whose racial/ethnic/religious identities are transforming the national society (Harrison and Bennett 1995).[3] Indeed it is clear that, when we project current trends into the near future, immigration will account for virtually the entirety of population growth and that non-European stock will begin to outnumber the Euro-American at some point during the first half of the twenty-first century (Edmonston and Passel 1992, 1994). But even now, thanks to the geographic pervasiveness of the Other, partly heterolocal in character, it has become impossible to evade multicultural issues.

Can history repeat itself? Would it be feasible for the American government to alter the provenience of immigrants in addition to reducing the volume of intake, as was done so effectively in the past? Or, put simply, is there any way to reverse the direction of racial/ethnic change in the composition of the American population? In the absence of unforeseen events of major magnitude, the answer must be: Most unlikely.[4]

> Whatever the motive for the apparent rise in sentiment against non-white immigrants, those concerned with the changing ethnic composition will have to acknowledge that the demographic changes set in motion by the 1965 and 1990 immigration laws and the penetrability of the common border with Mexico are *irreversible*. (Muller 1993:322; emphasis in original)

And, aside from other considerations, the porosity of both of the country's land borders and certain fissures in the approaches by sea and air render the United States open to continuing incursions by determined would-be Americans. Official measures to subdue the incoming waves would have Uncle Sam doing an impersonation of King Canute.

It is quite conceivable that Congress will decide to cap the total annual volume of immigration somewhere below the present figure and to revise the relevant statutes in relatively minor ways. Indeed such policies were being considered seriously at the time of this writing. But any attempt to whiten the influx substantially by setting discriminatory national quotas or by administrative procedures is politically (if not ethically) unthinkable. It would also be hard to restrain our altruistic impulses (and perhaps political calculations) if another major political, military, or environmental disaster were to direct streams of refugees in our direction, as has happened repeatedly during the past fifty-odd years.

But, most immediately, and unlike the situation in times past, the proimmigration constituencies (substantially, but not entirely, ethnically based) are too well entrenched, too effective in lobbying and in influencing the votes of the electorate to be ignored by the powers that be. A much more basic consideration is the fact previously alluded to, namely, that the connectivities between the economy and society of the United States and the remainder of the global system are now so powerful, so deeply enmeshed in the workings of our collective existence, that any serious interruption to the relatively free flow of individuals (just as for capital, information, or commodities) could be fatal. Try to imagine the consequences, geopolitical as well as economic, if the United States were to reenact the exclusionary laws that for several decades kept virtually all Chinese and Japanese from entering the country legally. Indeed, if by some magical act all international movements on the part of illegal travelers could be halted at the Mexican border — something many nativists have been clamoring for — and at other points of entry, there is every likelihood of the collapse of some significant sectors of the economy.

Reactions to the Post-1965 Immigration

The changes already wrought by the latest episode of immigration and the prospect of even greater transformations in the near future have provoked the widest possible range of reactions by observers of the current scene. At one end of the spectrum, we find those who greet the reshaping of American society with unqualified glee as they credit the newcomers with the enrichment of our social, cultural, and intellectual lives and a strengthening of the economy (Millman 1997: 91–97; 366–373; Ungar 1995) or, more specifically, with revitalizing cities and neighborhoods that had been all but written off as disaster areas (Muller 1993; Winnick 1990).[5] Their polar opposites are the commentators who view the developments in question as an unmitigated calamity, as leading to the "disuniting of America" and to the economic, moral, and social impoverishment of the nation. They would, if they could, completely staunch, or severely limit, the intake of "aliens" (Bouvier 1992; Brimelow 1995; Schlesinger 1992).[6] And, of course, there are still others (e.g., Dormon 1981; Hollinger 1992; Massey 1995) who inhabit the more temperate middle ground and balance the pluses and minuses against each other.

Those who are alarmed by the ethnic/racial dynamics of early twenty-first-century America have mainly directed their baleful gaze at two issues: the economic and the linguistic. A considerable literature has appeared in recent years, one too large and technical for even cursory review here, that deals with the economic impact of recent immigration. It is based on detailed analyses of data concerning such aspects as the effect on wages paid the native-born, and earnings received and taxes paid by, and the costs of social benefits accruing to, the newcomers. The consensus appears to be that, in the aggregate, recent immigrants contribute more to the national economy than they extract from it. But one must add the proviso that, if their impact is positive at the national or even regional scale, there are some localities that do incur an undue financial burden created by unemployed or low-income foreign-born residents. One must also take into account the fact, already mentioned, that an embargo on immigrants would cause great distress for many businesses and institutions relying upon a steady supply of trained professionals and technicians. Then, toward the humbler end of the economy, how could we do without the labor of immigrants in such callings as agriculture, restaurant work, meat processing, landscaping, and janitorial and domestic service?

Perhaps as widespread and as emotional as any collective fretting about the economic implications of recent immigration has been an-

guish over the supposed plight of the English language in its confrontation with alien tongues. Several groups have materialized of
late that have been agitating vigorously at the national, state, and local levels to make English our one and only official language and to
discourage or prohibit the use of others in schools, courts, ballots, and
governmental services (Crawford 1992; Schmidt 1993). They have
won some campaigns and lost others.

At this point I must abandon any pretense of appearing dispassionate. It seems clear enough that the proponents of English First
or similar movements, or at least the well-educated members thereof,
are not acting in good faith as they shed crocodile tears in pursuit of a
hidden agenda. Language becomes a useful flanking strategy when it
is no longer good etiquette to mount a frontal assault on the Other.
The laughable truth is that, of all the world's many languages, English is the least endangered. Indeed at both the global scale and
within the United States it is engulfing or outstripping all rivals.
Where it is not already the first language, English has become the
preferred second language, inasmuch as the vast majority of the
world's upwardly striving inhabitants find that fluency therein has
become indispensable to one's economic, cultural, scholarly, and social well-being.

One of the concerns of the English-Firsters is that many communities may become and remain bilingual — a rather peculiar bit of hy-
pocrisy. Although it may be praiseworthy for the "better" elements
in the native-born population to acquire a second language through
schooling or travel, retaining one's ancestral tongue is somehow sus-
piciously un-American. Furthermore, the guardians of the linguistic
ramparts do not seem overly upset by the fact that most of those
Americans who are permanent or temporary residents abroad make
little or no effort to become fluent in the local language, something
their essential logic would mandate.

The substantial growth of the Latino population and the vigor of
the Spanish language (along with bilingualism) within American territory has become a particular source of apprehension (Massey 1995:
647–648). Will the speakers of Spanish arriving from Latin America
and the Caribbean and their offspring acquire the language of their

adopted land, or will clusters of such people eventually squeeze out English? Perhaps nowhere are such concerns more insistent than in southern Florida. Fortunately, we have a reassuring answer. Reporting the results of a rigorous study of linguistic practices in Miami, Portes and Schauffler state that

> English is alive and well in Miami. This is the American city most heavily affected on a relative basis by recent immigration and, hence, the one where the demise of English dominance, so feared by nativist organizations, should be most evident. Our results indicate that such fears are unfounded. Second-generation youth not only report widespread competence in English, but also demonstrate an unambiguous preference for it in everyday communication. Children raised in the core of the Spanish-speaking Miami community (those attending bilingual schools) are actually the most enthusiastic in their preference for the language of the land. These results indicate that, contrary to nativist fears, what is at risk is the preservation of some competence in the languages spoken by immigrant parents. (1996:442)

Casual observation, however, can be deceptive. Even though time is clearly on the side of American English, the rapidity and extent of second- and third-generation linguistic assimilation is masked by the sheer volume of ongoing non-Anglophone immigration.[7]

Another tactic recently adopted by the antiimmigration forces is to point with alarm at the environmental havoc that would be generated by immigration-fueled population growth in the United States. This strategy has had only limited success, in part because of its flawed logic. It remains to be shown that the foreign-born pose a greater burden on the environment per capita than do our native citizens. Furthermore, ecological problems can be global in extent, so that it is hard to imagine how keeping potential immigrants tethered to their homelands would improve the health of the planet's ecosystem.

It is even more difficult to avoid the conclusion that the fuss over economic, linguistic, and environmental issues on the part of the nativistically inclined is incidental to a much more elemental sort of anguish. As Douglas Massey has so shrewdly observed,

Given the apparent animus toward immigrants and the imperviousness of public perceptions to the influence of objective research findings, one suspects that deeper forces are at work in the American psyche. This consternation may have less to do with ascertainable facts about immigration than with unarticulated fears that immigrants will somehow create a very different society and culture in the United States. . . . The demographic reality suggests the real nature of the anti-immigrant reaction among non-Hispanic whites: a fear of cultural change and a deep-seated worry that European Americans will be displaced from their dominant position in American life. (1995:632)[8]

Adjusting to their imminent role as something of a minority — although still accounting for a solid plurality of total numbers — will undoubtedly be emotionally traumatic for the outnumbered Euro-American community, quite apart from the stressful institutional and social rearrangements mandated by the numerical shift. In any event, the influx of New Americans is just one outcome of a massive set of processes penetrating all corners of the world, a phenomenon propelled by forces beyond the control, or even comprehension, of governments, corporations, think tanks, and other institutions.

DEFINING MULTICULTURALISM

Whatever the fears or hopes of the partisans in this momentous debate over the swiftly changing composition of the American population, the concept of multiculturalism has become central to the discourse. Until recently, it was possible to ignore the fact that the United States has always been a stratified, caste-ridden society, practicing a rather primitive form of multiculturalism. Now, given our altered circumstances, with the quantitative growth, increasing complexity, and activism of the minority populations and the globalization of social and cultural processes, multiculturalism has come out of the closet, so speak.[9] But what precisely do we mean when we speak about "multiculturalism"?

In searching for an answer, we stumble across a tangle of ambiguities, indeed utter confusion. Unfortunately, writers who discuss the phenomenon usually neglect to offer definitions, precise or otherwise, or may have in mind a wide range of meanings. The assumption is that the reader will intuit the meaning of the term. Our better dictionaries are only modestly helpful. The *OED* simply characterizes *multicultural* as "of or pertaining to a society consisting of varied cultural groups," with the earliest citation dated 1941.[10] It offers no definition for *multiculturalism*, but its earliest example is rather recent: 1965. The *Random House Dictionary* entries are a bit more enlightening. After defining *multicultural* in much the same manner as the *OED* and suggesting 1940–45 as the period of origin, these lexicographers define *multiculturalism* as "1. The state or condition of being multicultural" and, more usefully, as "2. The preservation of different cultures or cultural identities within a uniform society, as a state or nation [1960–65]."

Upon reflection, it may seem odd that no term existed before the mid twentieth century for a phenomenon that had prevailed for so many generations in various parts of the world. But, once again, it appears that new words are contrived only when there is some compelling social need for their deployment. Belated though their genesis may have been, these neologisms have enjoyed a meteoric rise in popularity.[11] Turning once again to the *Social Sciences Citation Index*, we find a mere eleven entries for *multiculturalism* for the entire 1956–65 period, but a staggering 642 for the single year 1996. (One can document a similar trajectory for the term *diversity*.)

Much of the difficulty in achieving a definitive definition of *multiculturalism* results from an overlap in meaning with respect to other widely used but rather less inflammatory terms. It may not be synonymous with *pluralism*, another wriggly concept we have already noted as eluding absolute definition, but it certainly shares some of its semantic territory.[12] There is also an intimate relationship with relatively innocuous *diversity*. Almost everyone nowadays is willing to acknowledge, if perhaps grudgingly, that diversity is a good thing and even to celebrate it publicly, much like *brotherhood*, *tolerance*, and *democracy*. Unlike multiculturalism, it does not brandish a red flag in the faces of the watchdogs of America's sacred traditions. But, it is worth noting, such acceptability is rather late in arriving. Before

FDR's first term, presidential pronouncements and other authorita-
tive utterances invariably promoted the notion of national homogeneity (Fuchs 1990:363).[13] In any event, the concept of diversity is
so broad and absorbent that exploring it does little to illuminate the
mysteries of multiculturalism.

Even less helpful is *cosmopolitanism*, another related ism. As Hollinger has pointed out, "Cosmopolitanism is more oriented to the
individual, whom it is likely to understand as a member of a number
of different communities simultaneously, while pluralism [and mul-
ticulturalism] is more oriented to the group, and is likely to identify
each individual with reference to a single, primary community"
(1992:83).

Multiculturalism is even further removed from another important
concept: *creolization*. This is the process whereby a new, relatively homogeneous culture is created via the hybridization of two or more
antecedent cultures, usually the consequence of the migration and
confluence of populations that previously had been located some distance apart. Although the classic examples of creolized societies are
found in the Caribbean, the phenomenon is actually quite widespread over recent centuries and millennia. Indeed one can argue that
the United States, like the English "mother country" before it, has
undergone significant creolization. Multiculturalism *may* be a condition preceding the formation of a creole society, but so long as the
various ethnic groups retain their individuality, creolization has nothing to tell us about what it means to be multicultural.[14]

In this frustrating quest for the core meaning of a term that has
become so conspicuous in academic and general public debate, the
only safe generalization is that we are dealing with a protean concept.
Thus the upshot of our inquiry finds us without a single firm definition, even one as long and nuanced as that for *ethnic group*. Multiculturalism means different things — good, bad, and neutral — to all the
varied participants in the colloquy, and implies a substantial set of in-
tractable questions. How much separation or autonomy on the part
of the various ethnic/racial/religious groups does it suggest? What
relationship, if any, with spatial distribution? Who sets the terms for
the multicultural matrix? What degree of interaction among the var-

ious parties? How stable a phenomenon is it? How much, or how little, assimilation into the dominant culture? Does it imply equal status or a hierarchical arrangement among the communities?

No clear answers are forthcoming. But if we must learn to live with the ambiguities, I believe some progress is thinkable if we recognize one fact about multiculturalism that seems to have been pretty much overlooked: that it is no single, timeless, absolute state of affairs. Instead, multiculturalism is a time-dependent phenomenon, one calling for multiple definitions, a social development that has experienced two distinct phases to date and aspires, in the utopian vision of its advocates, to still another manifestation quite preferable to its predecessors. The historically persistent version of multiculturalism is the situation in which two or more distinctly dissimilar ethnic groups inhabit a common political space but one of the groups dominates all others, economically, politically, and in all other power relationships. On closer consideration, this condition breaks down into two subphases, which, in lieu of better descriptive labels, I would designate as multiculturalisms 1 and 2.

The former refers to the protracted period in the American (and other) pasts when the highly unequal status of the various ethnic communities was given the silent treatment. As part of the divine order of things, Multiculturalism 1 was simply not a topic for polite scholarly or social discourse. With the upsurge of dissent, of group self-awareness and assertiveness over the past several decades, in the wake of much structural change in society and the economy, Multiculturalism 2 has emerged and continues to dominate the national dialogue. This is the situation in which there is constant, often obstreperous jousting for advantage, prestige, social and cultural power among the contending groups, the playing out of "identity politics." Amidst the cacophony we hear no consensus, no clear responses to the questions posed above, only the clash of agendas.

In contrast, what I designate as Multiculturalism 3 is a simpler, if elusive, proposition, belonging as it does, to a different realm of ideas, with the appeal of a near-ideal world that may never come to pass. As discussed in fuller detail at a later point, we have here the vision of a society where divers ethnic groups coexist on a truly level playing field, freely interacting culturally and socially while still husbanding their special identities. It is a vision with the power to inspire, though the program for implementation remains obscure. Also unclear is whether the realization of Multiculturalism 3 must engage the entire society advancing en masse or whether it could be attained piecemeal, group by group. The reason for entertaining the notion of any such consummation with any degree of seriousness is that, as detailed below, at least one community seems to have achieved multicultural grace already, while others may be on the verge.

But, however cloudy and contested the definition of multiculturalism, past, present, or potential, few would deny the arrival of at least one version (2) thereof and its conspicuous presence in two major American metropolitan areas, Miami and Los Angeles, and in the state of Hawaii. Furthermore, one can make a case for the increasingly multicultural complexion of three other cities (and possibly even more) that have been polyglot ever since their founding — New York, Chicago, and San Francisco — and two that have not: Washington and Atlanta.

Viewing the broader regions of the country, it is hard to challenge the plausibility of Carlos Fuentes' (1992:341–355) forecast of a "Hispanic U.S.A." that might embrace much more American territory than just the southwestern quadrant. In fact, Joel Garreau (1981) has argued persuasively for the existence of an emphatically multicultural (or bicultural) "Mex-America" that embraces a broad swath of northern Mexico as well as the United States borderlands.

DECODING ETHNICITY: THE HISTORICAL PERSPECTIVE

We come, finally, to the cluster of questions for which all the preceding pages have served as prologue: Why did Ethnicity appear on the scene just when it did? How does it relate to other contemporaneous developments? What is its real function, its real significance? Invoked here is that most primitive of all axioms in geographic scholarship, one that could apply equally well to all the social and earth sciences: *Everything is connected to everything else*. And I must add another equally primitive, basic historical axiom: The present can never fully replicate the past no matter how influential that past may be and no matter how deceptively some aspects of the current scene may mimic bygone phenomena.

To begin the search for answers, there is patently some sort of connection between our heightening concern over multiculturalism and the simultaneous advent of Ethnicity. It is equally self-evident that the two phenomena are enmeshed within a much vaster complex of changes in a period of unprecedented social and psychological convulsion. We have already examined the identity crisis, another notable component in the ongoing restructuring of humankind's mode of thinking and behaving. But there are many more mutations we participant-observers can hardly fail to notice. Some are benign and to be welcomed most heartily, others are troubling, even pathological, still others must await future appraisal. In any case, few of these developments could have been anticipated several decades ago.

I can do no more here than simply list some of the more conspicuous elements contributing to the immense late twentieth- and early twenty-first-century transformation of human affairs as Landscape 3 began to take shape. Most have no direct relevance to Ethnicity, at least at present, but I am convinced that eventually, in the fullness of hindsight, social historians will be able to chart their meaningful interrelationships, just as I believe in the reality of their linkages with heterolocalism.

Few developments have been as noteworthy as the women's movement, a phenomenon that has spread worldwide, and evidently associated with it are the sexual revolution and the restructuring of the family. The triumph of consumerism and the hegemony of the multinational firm are hard to ignore, and so too, paradoxically, their polar opposite, environmentalism. Mass tourism, on a scale unimaginable a few generations ago, can also be linked with consumerism, while a "pandemic of compassion" displays kinship with several of the developments noted here. In coining this term, I have in mind sympathy for and activism on behalf of the homeless and gays and lesbians, as well as endangered species, not to mention the animal rights movement. Then there is the chronic crisis in the creative arts, something that became noticeable as early as 1900. It has intensified in recent years as novelists, poets, composers, painters, architects, choreographers, and even filmmakers, those practitioners of the liveliest of modern arts, flail about, struggling to find firm footing and direction, some shared set of values and purpose.

I find it convenient to divide the latter two-thirds of the American twentieth century into two qualitatively distinct eras. The first, extending from the 1930s into the early 1970s, was essentially an epoch of optimism, of confidence in a brighter future, and one of progressive social activism and change (when liberalism was not a dirty word) and some genuine aesthetic accomplishment — this despite the worst economic depression and military conflict the world has ever endured. And the period after 1945 was also a time of remarkable economic expansion and rising personal affluence.

Then, around 1973, we encounter a basic change of mood and objective circumstance, one that has persisted to the present moment in the new century. As basic a visible cause as any has been what appears to be a long-lasting stalling of the economy as we bump into the basic contradictions of the capitalist system, as real income levels stagnate or decline and we observe a steady widening of inequities in the distribution of wealth. This not to deny genuine growth in some sectors of the economy and in certain localities during the "bubble economy" of the 1990s. But, taking the broad view, stasis or strain is the theme, and parents are no longer hopeful, as in the past, of greater material and moral well-being for their children. Equally troubling is a growing social and personal malaise that is expressed in many ways, including political cynicism and voter apathy. Insofar as there is any pervasive political mood, it is distinctly rightward of the temper of the preceding period, and a critical mass of the intelligentsia has migrated into the neoliberal camp, one virtually synonymous with the neoconservative.

It would seem that, after some three hundred years or more, our collective faith in the idea of progress and the Enlightenment project has withered, that the future is no longer the shining, inviting place we once envisioned. Although new discoveries in the physical, biological, and earth sciences show no sign of slackening, and all manner of technological innovations continue to bedazzle us, the axiomatic belief in a better tomorrow has begun to collapse and the prattle of the hucksters leaves us unconvinced. I suspect we have just slouched past one of the great turning points in the human chronicle.

One inescapable symptom of altered sensibilities is the switching of temporal gaze from future to past. As noted in a previous chapter, nostalgia has become a growth industry, and historical preservation and heritage worship are only two small parts of it. Retrospection threatens to dominate creative activity of every variety, and "retro" is the appropriate adjective for much that passes for trendy today in clothing styles, domestic architecture, entertainment, food, music, personal names, and moviemaking.

Another trend with much more obvious bearing on the Ethnicity question (and not unrelated to the do-goodism already mentioned) is a veritable boom in social tolerance. Beginning in the 1930s and continuing without interruption past the watershed period of the early 1970s, there has been a remarkable change in the ways Americans behave toward, and apparently feel about, persons whose racial, ethnic, or religious identity differs from their own. And as attitudes have mellowed, we see a growing curiosity about the culture of groups once shunned or despised and an eagerness to sample their wares. (This development is parallel, of course, to the changing relationships between males and females.) Anyone who, like myself, has lived through this transition can attest to its reality — and incompleteness — but the documentation, both statistical and anecdotal, is abundant. Thus public opinion polls conducted since the 1930s reveal a dramatic increase in tolerance with respect to religion and race (Ladd 1998; Reimers 1992:82–83; Spickard 1989:198–199; Taylor et al. 1978).[15] And other evidence indicates a decline in anti-Semitism (Bershtel and Graubard 1982:65–67; Higham 1984:95–174).

There has also been a notable transformation in both the scholarly and pedagogical historiography of racial and ethnic topics in terms of both attitude and focus. Although Rudolph Vecoli (1970) was complaining bitterly as recently as a generation ago about the persistent neglect of such material by his disciplinary colleagues, the situation had already begun to change in striking fashion. Nowhere is this development more visible than in the schoolbooks used in American elementary and secondary classrooms (FitzGerald 1979:74–105). As Glazer and Ueda commented in their analysis of such publications, "We see a new civic morality whose major ingredients are understanding, sympathy and respect for the humanity of all ethnic minorities" (1983:160).[16]

This attitudinal quasi-revolution is also plain to see in the realms of commerce and entertainment. Ethnic images in toys and games have evolved over the years from demeaning stereotypes to neutral or positive representations (Nelson 1990), and the same trend is even more obvious in advertisements (Stern 1984). Indeed nowadays it is almost obligatory to include at least one token black or Latino in television commercials and in newspaper ads while zealously avoiding any words or illustrations that could be construed as ethnically or racially derogatory. And, as noted earlier, there has been a decided, if less than complete, improvement in the depiction of "minorities" in American film and television (Wilson and Gutierrez 1995; Woll and Miller 1987). The new civility, one so different from the nastiness of two generations ago, is such that no one in the fields of government, sport, or entertainment dares utter publicly any of the forbidden epithets or any remark that could be regarded as a racial or ethnic slur.

How and why did this change of heart — or at least of outward demeanor — come about? This is a profound question, one that calls for some truly difficult scholarship and cogitation, and, to the best of my knowledge, no one has yet essayed the task. Ruling out any sudden mutation in human nature or some sort of spiritual contagion, we can point to such proximate factors as legislative and judicial decisions. But, as often as not, such actions reflect the climate of public opinion, responding to, rather than initiating, social change.

In this connection, there is the obvious question of why the Hart-Celler Act became law in 1965.[17] Although it was consistent with the *Zeitgeist* of the 1960s, its sponsors certainly did not intend the sort of dramatic change in immigration patterns that did ensue. If one may indulge in counterfactual history, however, the increase in tolerance during the past few decades was not confined to the United States. Similar developments with respect to immigration and social behavior took place in other developed countries. It is likely — nay, virtually certain — that, if not in 1965, then shortly thereafter, the economic, moral, and social pressures of the times would have led to a significant rewriting of immigration law in the United States.

But, returning to the larger issue, if I may hazard a crude hypothesis, I suspect that the transformation of social mores and the breaking down of overt barriers to the advancement of "minority" individuals in recent years may be analogous to the emancipation movement of the nineteenth century. It had become obvious then that prolongation of the chattel slavery system was incompatible with the efficient operation of the ascendant capitalist economy of the period. Is it not imaginable that, in its current incarnation, the capitalist economy realizes benefits from the *partial* relaxation of restrictions on the social, economic, and spatial opportunities of ethnic and racial groups that so recently had been suffering severe discrimination? But one is also entitled to wonder whether such an unsubtle economistic explanation will fully suffice.

But heartening as the new civility and all our professions of good will may be, one dare not forget that the amelioration of interracial and interethnic dealings in the United States still has far to go before all prejudices and conflicts vanish. Thus, in summarizing their analysis of recent survey data, Herring and Amissah tell us what a host of other observers have noted, namely that

> despite the supposed declines in racial intolerance and prejudice and years of legislation and regulation, there are still sizable segments of the U.S. population who do not want their children to go to school with black children, who do not want to live in the same neighborhoods with black people, who do not want to be led by black leaders, and who definitely do not want their relatives to be married to a black person. (1997:142)

And one must assume that many Euro-Americans harbor similar sentiments toward Moslems, Hindus, Latinos, Laotians, and other foreign groups — and vice versa.

Further progress toward genuine acceptance of the Other is likely to be slow and qualified, and there has been, of course, some disturbing backsliding in the political arena. Nevertheless it seems safe to believe that any future reversion to the barbarities of old-fashioned racism is unthinkable for good and sufficient political, economic, and social-psychological reasons.

CRYPTORACISM AND ETHNICITY

We cannot avoid facing an enormous, harrowing set of contradictions. On the one hand, the truly hateful, naked forms of racism have been banished to the lunatic or near-lunatic fringes of the American and other "advanced" societies. Official rhetoric and policies condemn discrimination, the authorities even occasionally punish racist behavior, and we have many formal programs designed to foster better relations among racial and ethnic groups. There has been conspicuous success in desegregating the armed forces.[18]

Nowadays ordinary citizens by the millions profess tolerance and fraternal sentiments toward members of other cultures, and some go to great lengths to demonstrate their sincerity. The rise of a substantial middle class among African Americans and other people of color should gladden the hearts of persons of good will. So too the recent, unprecedented accomplishments of those talented or lucky few members of "minorities" in politics, sport, entertainment, academic endeavor, and the creative arts who are situated at or near the pinnacle of their particular worlds. Then, on the face of it, one might feel obliged to rejoice also in the advent, concurrently, of Ethnicity, that doctrine of the parity of all ethnic essences and the celebration of the entirety of all those exciting Othernesses.

But when we look at American life in its totality, the rejoicing seems premature: "Racism is ultimately indivisible from the rest of American life, a fact few of us wish to face." (Kovel 1970:177). Indeed, there is a great deal to be alarmed about in the ethnic/racial scene. The literature on the various pathologies is so huge it could literally fill a good-sized library, much too extensive for even selective citation here. (But for a worthwhile overview and entrée, see Hacker 1992 and Waldinger 1996.) Especially distressing is the growth in absolute numbers and intensifying spatial segregation of the so-called underclass as we witness the development of "hyperghettos" (Massey and Denton 1993; Wacquant 1994).[19] Their inhabitants are over-whelmingly African American and Latino, but the syndrome of so-cioeconomic maladies to which they are subjected is not unknown among some Asian communities and the relatively spatially unfet-tered Native Americans.[20] Moreover, purely economic and social dis-crimination and general material deprivation can be just as crushing to body and spirit as being physically isolated from one's "betters."

Another troubling development has to do with recent immigra-tion. A significant fraction of the newcomers, especially those who arrive with substantial social and other forms of capital, do manage to enter the middle and upper economic ranks of American society rather promptly and often display heterolocal behavior. But out-numbering them are those who follow a different track. As Portes and Rumbaut have pointed out, after observing 1.5 and second-generation kids in Miami and San Diego, "Today . . . immigrants do not enter a society with a monolithic culture but rather a consciously pluralistic society in which a variety of racial and ethnic subcultures coexist" (1996:13). Thus, continuing in the words of Alejandro Portes,

> the important consideration is *to what sector* of the receiving soci-ety a particular immigrant group assimilates. Instead of a rela-tively uniform "mainstream" whose values and norms dictate a homogeneous path of integration, it is possible to distinguish to-day several paths. One of them replicates the time-honored pat-tern of growing acculturation and parallel integration into the ma-jority white middle class; a second leads straight in the opposite direction to permanent poverty and assimilation into the under-class; a third links economic mobility with preservation of the im-migrant community's solidarity. (1995:251; emphasis in original)

All too many of the immigrants and their offspring travel the second path rather than the first or third, thereby perpetuating and intensifying the bifurcation (or is it trifurcation?) of American soci-ety.[21] Indeed this twenty-first-century United States may come to resemble the two nations of nineteenth-century Britain as described by Benjamin Disraeli, rather than a nineteenth-century America in which the actuality or promise of homogenization seemed quite plausible. Enthusiasm over the blessings of Ethnicity is of only limited value in dissipating our qualms.

But should we not take heart over the apparent demise of overt racism and the dawning of our era of warm and cuddly intergroup rapport? After all, we have those spectacular examples of super-achievers, persons who happen to have been born black, Latino, or Asian, who have won glory and accumulated great fortunes and renown in sport, government, the armed forces, show business, and financial endeavors. However, after further reflection, one is inclined toward a certain cynicism concerning the role of these role models. The existence of such individuals, just like the availability of lottery tickets, is an anodyne, offering hope to the hopeless and thus reducing the threat of a social upheaval. They are also commercially useful in breaking into an ethnic/racial market whose size and purchasing power has been growing, just as has the electoral clout of "minority" groups.[22]

If America's business is business, then the level of success of people of color (and women of whatever hue) in the corporate world might well provide a meaningful index of their attainment of the American Dream. The facts are discouraging. The men and women in question, who comprise well over 60 percent of the total population, account for only 3 percent of senior management positions in the Fortune 1000 industrial corporations (United States Department of Labor 1991). I am willing to wager that fewer than 1 percent of the CEOs of those firms are nonwhite. Perhaps equally depressing is the fact that, despite all the widely touted efforts to "level the playing field," African American men with professional degrees earn only 79 percent of the amount received by white males who hold the same degrees and are in the same job categories. Taking the charitable view and assuming no deliberate disparity of treatment, then clearly some subtle, perhaps subconscious, forces are at work to prolong discriminatory practices.

The "glass ceiling" is a reality in the social realm as well as in the world of work. Many members of the widely admired "model minority," that is Asian Americans, and especially the Chinese and Japanese, the latter virtually honorary Caucasians, have prospered economically, but no matter how impressive their incomes, education, worldly goods, and general deportment, they find themselves excluded from the loftiest strata of American society.

> Hong Kong immigrants seeking to break into the highest social circles encounter limits to their attempts at flexible cultural accumulation. Their class distinction, as displayed in consumer objects, university degrees, and a jet-setting life, is not sufficient to attract the embrace of the local white upper classes [in the San Francisco Bay area]. . . . The buzz word is "glass ceiling," a term more often applied to women and middle-class minority professionals whose rise in corporations are [*sic*] obstructed by an invisible barrier of discrimination. (Ong 1992 : 135–136)

As for Japanese Americans, Hamamoto (1994 : 64) attacks the widespread notion of their success in overcoming all barriers, noting that they still must deal with the glass ceiling everywhere, except perhaps in Hawaii (also see Cheng and Yang 1996).

Thus the daily lived experience of nonwhites in the United States leaves little doubt as to the stubborn vitality of what might be called *cryptoracism*. The situation is all too easy to demonstrate. The standard examples are the plight of an African American male, well dressed or not, trying to hail a cab in a white neighborhood, or what happens to the black youth sporting dreadlocks as he strolls through a posh white residential area.

Only a few authors have explicitly recognized the phenomenon and dealt with it in any depth, and each has devised his own nomenclature. To the best of my knowledge, the first scholar to confront what he labeled "metaracism" was the psychologist Joel Kovel (1970) in an extraordinary volume dealing with the psychohistory of white racism, a work whose originality has gone virtually unheeded by the academic community. An excessive burden of Freudian dogma might explain that neglect, or Kovel may simply have been too far ahead of his time. But in recognizing the existence and perniciousness of metaracism, he identified its essence unerringly. "Metaracism — *the illusion of non-racism co-existing with the continuation of racism's work —* exists wherever in this subtle balance of human and anti-human forces, destructivity predominates no matter what the gains in 'racial equality'" (1970 : 218).[23]

In an important recent essay, sociologist Lawrence Bobo and his associates (1997) have delivered a devastating analysis of what they refer to as *laissez-faire racism*, which they characterize as a "kinder, gentler anti-black ideology." Although concerned solely with the white-black situation, their observations could be applied readily to all disadvantaged ethnic/racial groups, not just the African American. The historical logic of their thesis runs as follows:

> We argue that Jim Crow racist ideology reflected the economic and political needs, as well as the prevailing cultural ideas, of a specific historical period and set of actors. The setting was the post–Civil War South. The critical actors were the old Southern planter elite. The cultural trend was the rise and scientific legitimacy accorded notions of biological racism. As the economic and political power of these historic conditions and actors waned, as cultural trends turned against biological racism, and as the power resources of the black community rose, Jim Crow social structures and, ultimately, Jim Crow ideology were defeated. Rising from the collapse of Jim Crow racism, we argue, is laissez-faire racism. The latter set of ideas legitimates persistent black oppression in the United States, but now in a manner appropriate to a modern, nationwide, postindustrial free labor economy and polity. (1997 : 21)

The results?

> Rather than relying on state-enforced inequality as during the Jim Crow era . . . modern racial inequality relies on the market and informal racial bias to re-create, and in some instances sharply worsen, structured racial inequality. Hence, laissez-faire racism. . . . Laissez-faire racism involves persistent negative stereotyping of African Americans, a tendency to blame blacks themselves for the black-white gap in socioeconomic standing, and resistance to

meaningful political efforts to ameliorate U. S. racist social conditions and institutions. (1997:17, 16)

Noel Jacob Kent (1993) has advanced the same idea under the designation of *symbolic racism*. Its logic is "to attribute racial inequalities to the shortcomings of individual blacks, while affirming the elasticity and openness of the American opportunity structure to all who strive" (1993:63).[24] Then, in their remarkable exegesis of *The Cosby Show*, Sut Jhally and Justin Lewis (1992) have coined the expression *enlightened racism* and use it in a manner not entirely tongue-in-cheek. In analyzing the impact of this immensely popular sitcom on an American public besotted with television, the authors discovered to their surprise that their "evidence suggests . . . that the presence of these apparently benign images of black people on television constitutes, for African Americans, a serious step backward" (1992:71). For white viewers at least, the example of the prosperous, ever-so-likable, beautifully adjusted Huxtable family confirmed their delusion that racism had become a thing of the past, that anyone can now make it on his/her own on our level postindustrial playing field. We have here a seductively welcome notion that negates any lingering impulse for social or political action.[25]

Closely allied with our present-day cryptoracism is the new interracial etiquette, a comforting ideology of self-delusion. Calling it *friendship orthodoxy*, Benjamin DeMott (1995a) has examined its development and characteristics in a blistering book-length attack.[26] Paralleling Bobo et al., he sets his presentation within a historical framework. The current period of feel-good white-black camaraderie (and, implicitly, interactions with other peoples of color), a period also featuring a turn to conservatism, is the fourth in a series that begins with the epoch of slavery, then proceeds to the "nadir" of interracial dealings (1870–1920), which yields in turn to the years of progress centered in the 1960s. His central thesis is that

> the theme of interracial identity-under-the-skin amounts to no more . . . than a mere pacifier useful in periods of crisis. It has become a critical element of the same mind-set in which antipathy to "dependence" finds a place. Through its ubiquity in an ex-

traordinary range of media, it seems, indeed, to be fashioning a new secular orthodoxy: the friendship orthodoxy of our time. (1995a:4)

In effect, domination with a human face. Cryptoracism may be the last refuge of privilege.

So what does all this have to with Ethnicity? As it happens, everything. The relationship between cryptoracism and Ethnicity is intimate; each pattern of thought nourishes the other. If race is always the current subtext of ethnic identity, Ethnicity does its part by fostering the illusion of the level playing field. But evidently only a single author, Epifanio San Juan, Jr., (1992) has expounded this crucial actuality in any depth, in another volume that seems to have been pretty much ignored by mainstream scholars. In a collection of five angry but highly perceptive essays, he has mounted an attack on the "ethnicity school" and the "ethnologues," claiming that their output has furthered the recidivist social and economic policies of the Reagan-Bush-Clinton era. In essence, San Juan's argument is that

> by conflating the two concretely disparate experiences of white European immigrants and the colonized — slavery (Africans), colonization (Chicanos), racially based exclusion (Chinese, Filipinos), genocidal pacification (Native Peoples), forced relocation (Japanese Americans) — the ethnicity school perpetrated a pseudo-universalism that in effect gutted the progressive gains of the civil rights movement in the conservative Reagan era. (1992:69)

In effect, the doctrine of "merge and conquer" has supplanted "divide and conquer."

With great vigor, San Juan confronts and rebuts the current tendency to regard race as just another category of ethnic identity.

> Race, not ethnicity, is the explanatory and hermeneutic concept needed to describe the heterogeneous terrain of conflicting cultures in the United States. Race, not ethnicity, articulates with class and gender to generate the effects of power in all its multiple protean forms. Ethnicity theory elides power relations, conjuring an illusory state of parity among bargaining agents. It serves

chiefly to underwrite a functionalist mode of sanctioning a given social order. It tends to legitimize a pluralist but hierarchical status quo. (1992:5)

Or, putting the matter as succinctly as possible, "to relabel race ethnicity doesn't make it so" (San Juan 1992:33).[27]

A number of other authors have discerned the political agenda concealed behind the beguiling façade of Ethnicity but without charting the connections with cryptoracism. The following samples certainly reinforce the interpretation I have been presenting.[28] "Ethnicity . . . must be understood not as nostalgia for a perceived authentic past, nor as a symbolic invention divorced from historical realities. It must be understood instead as a historically grounded act of cultural politics" (Schultz 1994:20). "Ethnicity has become a commodity packaged in a form which supports the dominant ideology of the United States" (Schneider 1990:52). "All ethnicities are not equal; all are not symbolic, costless, and voluntary. When White Americans equate their own symbolic ethnicities with the socially enforced identities of non-White Americans, they obscure the fact that the experiences of Whites and non-Whites have been qualitatively different in the United States and that the current identities of individuals partly reflect that unequal history" (Waters 1996:450).

Perhaps most telling are the findings of Lutz and Collins (1993), because their subject is the photographic imagery appearing in *National Geographic*, probably the country's most widely read or ogled periodical (next perhaps to *TV Guide*).

To anyone writing in the early 1990s, when new forms of racism and intolerance are reasserting themselves, criticizing even a conservative brand of humanism seems self-defeating. Images are always read in their historical context, and in eras of racial and cultural tension, images of shared underlying values may be understood as direct contradictions of racist ideology. Yet in the end such images may not contribute to social change in the ways that we would hope a political photography would do. They contribute to an erasure of the forms of difference which impel social struggle, at the same time that they conserve notions of ethnic and other identities as stable enclosures that preclude real forms of empathy and communication. . . . By arguing that people are basically the same under the veneer of culture, *National Geographic* photography both denies fundamental differences and reifies the cultural boundary that it depicts. (1993:277–278)

Cryptoracism in Action

It may be useful to reflect on the tangible ways in which Americans actually encounter Ethnicity or cryptoracism and how such interactions play out ideologically. One of the more obvious examples is ethnic tourism in all the many forms already noted, including both international and domestic sightseeing and, of course, indulgence in ethnic restaurants and cuisines. The recent proliferation of shops retailing a potpourri of exotic goods from just about every developing country, places catering to a middle-class clientele, is another symptomatic development. Dean MacCannell has penetrated to the heart of the matter.

> Perhaps what really happens in ethnic tourist contexts is only the rhetoric of ethnic relations changed to create the impression of progress while older forms of repression and exploitation are perpetuated below the surface. . . . In other words, it appears that tourism has helped in getting beyond the phase of ethnic relations where minorities are kept in place with light salaries, heavy prison terms, and redneck cruelty. But one may have come full circle. Insofar as the larger society extends its acceptance conditional upon the minority restricting itself to an "authentic" image of itself, one is only doing with admiration what he earlier did with dogs and guns. As the rhetoric of hostility toward minorities is replaced with a rhetoric of appreciation, the circle of their potential exploiters is dramatically expanded. Now blacks can exploit blacks, Indians, etc., all with a clear conscience under the rubric of the development and preservation of culture. (1984:388–389)

A particularly revealing development is the multiethnic festival. Consider the following fictitious but altogether plausible scenario. It is a warm Sunday afternoon in a major American city, and two families are visiting a festival, staged in a central site and featuring displays and performances by most of the city's ethnic communities (although, oddly enough, there is almost no representation of the large, completely assimilated Euro-American population).[29] The first family, decidedly WASP in character, has driven in from one of the "better" suburbs, the second, obviously "minority" in appearance, has arrived from their inner-city neighborhood.

Both families have had a grand time eating and drinking strange and interesting foods, listening to all sorts of music, unfamiliar or otherwise, admiring the dancers and their costumes, and strolling among the booths while being tempted by all the unusual goods on display. Interestingly, some of the individual stalls are offering wares from several different countries, some of them ethnically alien to the group doing the displaying. The two families have accidentally jostled each other at one of the booths and may actually have exchanged smiles and a polite remark or two. Both families are impressed by the good spirits and friendliness of the crowd. Feelings of commonality, of being brothers and sisters under the skin, help make a happy scene even happier.

When fatigue finally sets in, Family A, arms and bags loaded with goodies and nearly inebriated with the milk of human kindness, picks up their air-conditioned van at a nearby garage and makes it home quickly and comfortably. Family B has the option of a long walk home or a ride on a hot, crowded bus. The next morning Family A's dad heads off to the executive suite in an Edge City office complex. Mom begins a long day of arranging for the approaching European vacation and keeping the children on time for dental appointments and tennis lessons at the country club, during her shift as a computer specialist for a suburban business. At a hurried supper they will discuss which colleges their eldest child would like to apply to.

Meanwhile, Family B is following a rather different trajectory. The father arrives late by bus at the restaurant where he washes dishes at the minimum hourly rate only to learn that he will be laid off at the end of the week. The mother shares a cab with neighbors to get to her cleaning job at a suburban motel, all the while wondering whether, how, and when she can get an appointment at a free medical clinic downtown. The older son is a dropout and just hangs out all day in a scruffy neighborhood park. His younger sister, who flunked math and English in the spring, goes to makeup summer classes in a public school building that the authorities are ready to condemn because of imminent structural failure. The other daughter, who is babysitting the younger son, spends much of the morning chasing down the building superintendent to see what can be done about the plumbing. But not to despair. The memory of that idyllic Sunday afternoon will glow just as warmly in the memories of Family B as it does for those ethnic enthusiasts they bumped into yesterday.

The moral? If ethnic identity is an inadequate solution for our identity crisis, Ethnicity does help substantially in handling another annoying problem: masking the deep fissures and injustices in our society. Once again, one cannot help wondering about how Ethnicity was born and why it happened just when it did. In any event, we must avoid the delusion that by quaffing the elixir of Ethnicity we can somehow purge ourselves of the contrarieties of racism.

If we now have domination with a human face, it is not the result of a willful conspiracy in the sense of a clandestine committee plotting dastardly deeds behind locked doors in some secret retreat. Instead, what happened could have followed a pattern analogous to Darwinian evolution. Random behavioral and attitudinal mutations are forever occurring among individuals and groups. Most are ephemeral because they lack social utility. A few, like the idea of Ethnicity, survive and thrive because they enhance the life chances of the larger social organism, in this instance the preexisting system of domination and exploitation of the many by the few. Thus Ethnicity serves to calm and stabilize a potentially unruly situation.

THE MULTICULTURAL MUDDLE AND BEYOND: THE NEW AMERICAN DILEMMA

If the preceding pages have shed some light on the nature of Ethnicity and some related concepts, my final chore is to suggest how these findings may help us to come to grips with multiculturalism.

This is not a casual or simple challenge. Setting aside the prospect of a truly major ecological or military disaster or economic collapse — not wholly improbable events — it is difficult to imagine a graver national issue, one more decisive in shaping the American future, than multiculturalism. But, before confronting it, let us step back a moment to review the lessons emanating from what has gone before. Some of the notions in question are familiar, essentially a repackaging and repositioning of the thoughts of others, but one or two may be original with this author and open to debate. The order of presentation is largely arbitrary.

Findings and Hypotheses in Summary

First and most basic: The fact, really the axiom, of constant change, the mutability of all things human. Thus no matter how unsettling the realization might be, we must learn to live with the actuality that virtually anything we wish to regard as fixed and primordial is a product of specific historical period. The ethnic group, or the idea of its existence, is no exception. It is an innovation appearing rather late in the modern age and in different places at different times.

I have arrived at a definition of that modern social construct, the ethnic group, that is broader and more comprehensive than what has been envisioned in conventional usage.

In addition, I have argued that ethnogenesis, a peculiarly latter-day phenomenon, operates at various levels of magnitude, the most capacious being the panethnic group and the more or less perfected nation-state. Furthermore, some social entities that are indubitably ethnic do not acknowledge themselves as such, mainly because being ethnic smacks of Otherness and sociocultural inferiority. The Euro-American population is an outstanding example.

Ethnicity, which I define as the generic condition of being ethnic, is an even more recent invention than the ethnic group, having arrived on the scene no earlier than the mid twentieth century. This concept tends to erase whatever significant cultural and historical differences may exist among ethnic groups, replacing them with an imaginary, socially acceptable quintessence, some presumed universal quality common to all. Upon critical examination, the concept of Ethnicity is exposed as both tautological and deceptive. The reality is that all ethnic groups are by definition unique unto themselves and lack any transcendent quiddity shared with all others.

Despite certain laudable, but limited, advances in ethnic/racial relations in the cultural, economic, and political realms, and the public banishment of ugly old-fashioned racism, the fundamental inequities besetting less privileged groups and the presumably subconscious mind-sets that help produce them have enjoyed a fresh lease on life recently, thanks to a new mode of social relations. This newer behavioral pattern — egalitarian and polite on the surface but seriously discriminatory in effect — we can call cryptoracism.

During the late twentieth century, the synergistic effects of new modes of travel and communication, as well as the economic arrangements created by advanced capitalism and changing social conditions, have produced for many members of immigrant ethnic groups a novel locational regime called heterolocalism. In this new system, individuals and families that are spatially dispersed over metropolitan areas or broader distances in terms of residence and other activities can maintain social cohesion by means of telecommunications and travel rather than relying on propinquity. The simultaneous birthing of heterolocalism and Ethnicity appears to be more than mere coincidence. In any event, this new situation is obviously pregnant with implications for multiculturalism.

Although the great majority of recent immigrants reside in a small number of metropolitan areas, this influx of the foreign-born involves much of America's rural as well as urban territory, and often in heterolocal fashion. Moreover, the action-spaces (physical and otherwise) of the newcomers are often transnational in character. We cannot deal with the geographical and other attributes of these New Americans, and many

of the native-born as well, without also reckoning with the
lands beyond America's borders.

The quest for ethnic identity on the part of groups and individuals — again a recent development — is just one phase of a pandemic identity crisis that has infected a growing portion of
the world's population. Although the ethnic option is only
one of many strategies adopted to respond to the questions
"Who am I?" and "What are we?" and, like all others, is ultimately futile, no other type of identity quest has had such important social and political consequences.

Taking a broad view, what I aspire to have accomplished thus far
is to situate ethnic phenomena in the contemporary United
States within three varieties of space-time: the cultural, spatial, and social. All three sets of dimensions bear interestingly
upon the vexed question of multiculturalism.

We can discern significant differences in behavioral tendencies
within all three of these modes of space-time between the
dominant Euro-American population and the various non-
European minorities, whether native or foreign-born. After
a long period during which the cultural attributes of non-
British immigrants and aboriginal communities suffered denigration and severe attrition or extinction (but not without
contributing to the making of the national and regional cultural complexes), in recent decades the groups in question
have begun asserting their special characteristics and stories
energetically, even exuberantly. Thus they are, or have recently become, more aware of their real or imagined cultural
heritage than is the case with Euro-Americans. Similarly, they
are more inclined as individuals or groups to engage in identity quests that result in ethnic affiliations. In contrast to such
ethnic assertiveness, virtually the entire majoritarian European
contingent, now effectively assimilated into a single Euro-
American community, has been losing whatever subnational
ethnic self-consciousness it may once have had, resorting now,
at most, to the fitful practice of symbolic ethnicity.

The United States, and British North America before it, has been multicultural from the very beginning, but this condition has not been fully acknowledged or even named as such until quite recently.

Finally, it is clear that more than chance was at work in the simultaneous birthing of Ethnicity and Multiculturalism 2, and that these phenomena are somehow dialectically related as responses to a shifting social landscape. But it is even more obvious, upon reflection, that the two entities are not synonymous. As a perverse form of assimilationism, Ethnicity tends to wash out all meaningful cultural and historical distinctions among subordinated groups — and between them and the dominant Euro-Americans. In contrast, whatever else it may happen to be, multiculturalism seeks to preserve, energize, and foster the particularities of the communities at risk, and "explicitly recognizes the interrelationships between various racial/ethnic/national and cultural groups along the multiple dimensions that define social life" (Manning 1995a: 150). It would appear, then, that the two phenomena do exist within a dialectical embrace, one serving as the antidote to the other.

Defining Multiculturalism 3

Before proceeding onward, we must return to the troublesome chore of defining multiculturalism, especially in its current and prospective forms, that "overloaded term, a symbolic container that is not capable of containing the range of investments that it attempts to carry" (Cruz 1996: 33), or at least ascertaining what it is not.

The preceding discussion might mislead one into believing that multiculturalism could be another name for pluralism. Nothing could be further from the truth, even though the two concepts do share some attributes. "In the disjuncture of economic expansion and cultural compression, multiculturalism becomes a new and profoundly contentious social mixture that is not captured — indeed it is obscured — in the framework of pluralism" (Cruz 1996: 32). And even more sharply to the point,

The debate about multiculturalism . . . at its most fundamental, represents a shift from the notion of a pluralist society — a society composed of a mosaic of separate cultures — to a view of America as a complex but common social system, one that has propagated and, most strikingly, produced significant cultural differences within itself. (Buell 1994:157–158)

Thus the multicultural vision parts company from the pluralistic, which is essentially static and inward-looking. But the question of specifying the special nature of Multiculturalism 3 remains. The crux of the problem of defining, predicting, interpreting, and assessing such a fluid and dynamic form of multiculturalism, something quite distinct from Multiculturalisms 1 and 2, lies in describing the topology and physiology of interconnections among multiple sociocultural entities. These, as we have learned, are forever in the process of becoming, dwindling, mutating, blending, or undergoing mitosis. We must try to visualize a web of transactions tied into the grander national polity, and perhaps even into global arrangements.[30]

Perhaps the most meaningful way to define the essence of a potential Multiculturalism 3 is to picture a sustainable, diversified national community in which each of its varied participating ethnic/racial groups fully and freely collaborates in building and operating a symbiotic national culture while still maintaining its peculiar identity *in both the national forum and inside its own social boundaries*. Such a situation, it must be repeated, is quite distinct from either a cellular pluralist society or one in which assimilation prevails. Of course, such a "perfect society," in the words of David Shipler, is a project nowhere near consummation in the United States, or anywhere else for that matter.

All the American subcultures, whether black or Chicano or Chinese, are also American, a point too often forgotten in the whirlwind of debate over multiculturalism and "political correctness." They are parts of the whole, and the whole would be diminished without them. They do not escape the influence of the American common ground, just as the common ground is not insulated from them. In this symbiosis, aided by boundaries that are permeable and blurred, citizens may move to and fro across lines, engaging in the great American compromise [i.e., Multiculturalism 2]. That means checking at the gateway to the common ground their particular subcultural attributes of language, dress, manner, and perhaps values. These can be picked up on the way out — every evening or every holiday or just when the older generation is gathering. In a perfect society [i.e., Multiculturalism 3] each American would be permitted to keep this cultural baggage with him as he enters the common ground; he would be allowed to advance and excel without relinquishing his cultural attributes. But it is not a perfect world: America's common ground remains rather unwelcoming to other, non-Anglo cultural styles. (1997: 72–73)

But if the United States is by no means wholeheartedly committed to genuine Multiculturalism 3 as just defined, nor has it passed the point of no return in the passage toward it, that is clearly the desideratum toward which the grander logic of this era is propelling the country. But the resistance to any such transformation is formidable.

An unsettling of the presumed homogeneity of American society signals a call for more cultural repression to nip an emerging "tribalism" in the bud, and equates the renewal of civic virtue and a return to traditionalism with an antimodernist intolerance articulated in the shadows of a receding American dream. (Cruz 1996:33)

And no doubt the scholarly manifestos of such guardians of a bygone monocultural Eden as Brimelow (1995), Heller (1996), Ravitch (1990), Schlesinger (1992), and Schwarz (1995) give voice to the misgivings of many rank-and-file Euro-Americans.[31]

We face, then, a new American Dilemma. It is obviously akin to the older predicament, that of slavery and its aftermath so effectively articulated by Gunnar Myrdal (1944) and his associates. Once again, we experience the clash between the foundational principles of the republic, on the one hand, and, on the other, all those baser universal impulses driving most individuals and institutions. But there are some substantial differences between the two dilemmas, quite apart from the unlikelihood of a military convulsion in the twenty-first century. This time a multiplicity of new parties are embroiled in the controversy, along with the eternal black versus white partisans. Furthermore, we now have lively public awareness of, and concern over, the multicultural dilemma, in contrast to the avoidance or amnesia concerning the plight of African Americans in the eight decades or so following Emancipation.

Another novel dimension of our latter-day dilemma is its international or transnational character. The difficulties so ably depicted by Myrdal and his crew were really particular to the American scene, although one can find pale analogies in Brazil and the Caribbean. Today a number of other countries are confronting their own problems in coping with unprecedented multicultural situations. And a few, the Netherlands and Sweden most notably, have apparently achieved an enviable level of comity among their divers communities. But what we behold is not simply a set of isolated instances but rather a process that is global in its reach. "The challenge of diasporic pluralism is now global and . . . American solutions cannot be seen in isolation. . . . Neither popular nor academic thought has come to terms with the difference between being a land of immigrants and being one node in a postnational network of diasporas" (Appadurai 1996 : 171).

An Exceptional United States?

But, having recognized commonalities between the American and kindred cases abroad, I must contend that there is something genuinely unique about the current American dilemma. At this point we accost that long-running, stalemated controversy over American exceptionalism (D. Bell 1975b; Veysey 1979). However platitudinous it may sound, the truism that every nation — indeed every place, every individual — is exceptional in some way is valid enough. But the United States of America is exceptional in a truly exceptional way, one that is both its glory and its burden, and has had some remarkable consequences. It has "a strongly universalist mythology" (Hollinger 1993 : 334), the nation's conviction of its providential role in fulfilling a divine destiny, not just for itself but for humankind in general (Zelinsky 1988a : 235–237, 285–286).[32] This messianic complex is the outcome of a process conceived in the turmoil of Europe's Reformation and germinating in early British North America, thanks to a set of unusual historical-geographic conditions, then bursting into full evangelistic, self-congratulatory vigor with the rise of the young republic.

One consequence of becoming "God's country" is that the United States was to develop as "an open and free society resting on universal self-evident principles rather than any exclusive origins, a society dedicated to the separation of church and state and the elimination of all barriers to mobility and opportunity, a society of individuals rather than groups" (Higham 1984:186–187), and thus welcoming all (European) immigrants of whatever class, religious creed or political persuasion.[33]

Such an ideology has enabled the country to evolve gradually, but not without much strife and soul-searching, from a white Protestant nation into a richly diversified society that pays at least lip service to the doctrine of inclusiveness, tolerance, and the license to pursue all possible routes to personal fulfillment. The American Dream, then, is not simply a matter of material betterment for one's self and progeny or of the Four Freedoms (of speech and worship and from fear and want) so nobly enunciated by FDR in 1941. It also embraces the even more visionary, indeed utopian, project of building a "city set on a hill," an ideal society that serves, *inter alia*, as an enlightened haven for the oppressed and downtrodden of the world.

Needless to note, there has been many a slip between ideal and deed, between aspiration and realization, and many an ugly episode in the collective behavior of Americans when they have grossly violated basic precepts. But afterward an aching conscience may come back to haunt us. Thus there have been a number of belated apologetic gestures. As notable as any was the congressional decision, a half-century after the event, to grant reparations to the Japanese Americans who lost homes and property in 1942, or the dedication in 1998 of a memorial in Washington to the black combatants in the Civil War a century and a third after their service. But, whatever the qualifications, there can be little doubt that this universalistic faith, the sense of chosenness in the national ideology, plays a critical role in the fierce debate over multiculturalism. What sort of policy are we to pursue if we must also remain faithful to our sacred heritage?[34] If the question is not frequently uttered openly, it still resonates at some deep level of the national conscience.

In any event, does an authentic Multiculturalism 3 fit within an expanded American Dream? Such is the appealing goal, envisioned by Shipler and others, of a delicate equilibrium in which all participating communities interact freely and equitably in the national playing field, without disavowing their particularities by leaving them outside in the parking lot, while simultaneously cherishing and practicing their sociocultural attributes within the privacy of the individual community. This idealized situation goes by a variety of names: *postnational* (Appadurai 1996); *postethnic* (Hollinger 1995); *adhesive adaptation* (Hurh and Kim 1984); *polycentric multiculturalism* (Shohat and Stam 1994); and perhaps others as well. Whatever the label, the essential goal is virtually the same. The crucial issue, of course, is whether there is even a remote possibility of reaching that goal.

Surprisingly enough, Americans have already taken a meaningful step toward the ideal multicultural destination, even if it is a development limited to the marketplace of pleasure and entertainment. In an illuminating study of the role of ethnic foods in American culture, Donna Gabaccia has argued that

> Americans have not been as tolerant of and curious about their neighbors as they have about their neighbors' foods (1998: 228). . . . Americans have been far more willing to celebrate multi-ethnic eating than the pleasures of cross-cultural sex and marriage (231). . . . But creole American eating is not an isolated example of multi-ethnic identity in American culture. It has important counterparts wherever Americans seek pleasure, most notably in the history of American music [and dance] (229). . . . The marketplace, and its consumer culture, may be a slim thread on which to build cross-cultural understanding. But given the depths of American fears about cultural diversity, it is better to have that thread than not. (231)[35]

Meaningful multiculturalism — once again, a free and equal display of ethnic-specific properties in the public arena combined with their firm retention within the communal space — has come a long way in the United States as far as foodways, music, and dance are concerned, indeed, probably a good deal further among Americans than in those other countries where similar trends can be seen. (Another argument for American exceptionalism?) We are entitled to some mild rejoicing over such multicultural progress.

Blacks and Jews: Two Divergent Paths

But the issues become ever so much stickier when we venture into those places where fundamental life-patterns are shaped, into residential, social, educational, economic, and political realms. There the institutional and psychic barriers against structural change can be formidable, to say the least. In judging the possibility of mastering the odds, of surmounting the barriers, the question might be posed at two levels: that of the general society, and a case-by-case consideration of individual ethnic/racial groups.

Since the former strategy can be no more than speculative at best, let me begin with the latter, keeping in mind the truism that no single ethnic group, or even a pair thereof, provides an adequate swatch of America's complex ethnic quilt. Any of the communities one might choose has lived through a unique history before and after arrival, carrying along its own distinctive material and nonmaterial cultural baggage, including a set of particular values, beliefs, memories, talents, and practices.

I offer for inspection two major, sharply contrasting populations: the African American and the Jewish American. In both cases the focus is on the modal majority and, for the latter group, the second and later generations, that is, persons who have undergone considerable cultural assimilation. Excluded are those individuals toward the far ends of the spectrum: the ultra-orthodox, unhyphenated Jews and the Afrocentric extremists in one direction and, toward the other, persons so thoroughly immersed in the national society and culture that ties to ethnic brethren are tenuous or broken.

Despite many obvious differences, the two communities do share a number of attributes. Among them is longevity on the American scene. Both have been on hand almost from the very beginning of the European presence in North America, though blacks have always greatly outnumbered Jews. For several generations, both were objects of suspicion, fear, ridicule, hatred, and various forms of persecution, and until recently all self-respecting Christian white folks shunned both blacks and Jews. As central as anything to the vitality of these societies have been church and synagogue. To a critical degree, especially in the past, the life of both communities revolved around their congregations and their two quite dissimilar, but emotion-laden, modes of worship and communion. And after death both populations have inhabited their own segregated cemeteries or sections of larger burial grounds. Both groups have sent children to their own parochial and public schools, whether identified as such de jure or de facto. And, although nominally open to all comers, we still have many black colleges and a few Jewish universities. Within both societies we find a great profusion of fraternal and other social and cultural organizations, many newspapers and magazines, and group-specific museums, libraries, and scholarly research.

In recent decades, both entities have been highly active politically at the national as well as local level.[36] Another political parallelism is in the realm of foreign relations — intense with respect to Eastern Europe, the former USSR, and, especially, Israel in the Jewish instance, rather less so but still importantly in the case of the African homelands. Finally, something not immediately visible to the casual observer but a matter of the utmost significance is the possession of a set of social mores specific to each community, patterns that guide personal and group behavior.

Interesting and meaningful as all these commonalities and still others may be, the real point of this exercise is to plot the great split, the two divergent, collectively chosen or mandated paths traveled by African Americans and Jewish Americans during the last century. One crucial factor that has helped push the former along its separate route is scarcely a matter of choice: bodily features. The fact that all but a small minority appear to be African in ancestry has facilitated African American separation from the bulk of a basically racist society. (Belatedly, of course, whether by choice or necessity, such "racial" physical distinctiveness has been actively cultivated, becoming a source of pride.) On the other hand, and despite the folk belief that all Jews look alike and are characterized by "Semitic" features, nowadays we can identify relatively few simply by virtue of appearance. Having clambered up the educational, occupational, and economic ladders, the vast majority of this community are dressed and groomed like everyone else and share much of the same body language and speech patterns of the population at large. Many could pass for northwestern European; others could be easily mistaken for Poles, Russians, Italians, Portuguese, Greeks, Armenians, or Iranians.

At least equally potent in intensifying pluralistic tendencies among African Americans is another factor over which they have minimal control: spatial segregation. As noted earlier, despite the abolition of legal restrictions and the trickle of families escaping the ghetto for more desirable tracts, any number of studies using a variety of spatial measures have failed to report any meaningful decrease in the level of racial segregation within American metropolises. In contrast, Jewish Americans, once almost equally bereft of spatial options, have begun to range far and wide residentially; indeed a fair number qualify for the heterolocal category.

In any event, African Americans, still rejected (Would you really wish to live next to one of them?) and rejecting full partnership in the national "common ground," remain obstinately pluralist. They have fashioned a parallel world, a rich, complex comfort zone (in certain respects more culturally creative and exciting than the white world) that is indubitably American but on its own *African* American terms. Persuasive evidence of the institutional completeness of this parallel world appears, for example, in the existence and vitality of national television networks catering to the 12 percent of the national population who inhabit it, in addition to all those local radio stations that are exclusively African American in format. There is no such autonomous support structure for Jewish Americans.[37]

Whereas the Yiddish theater of yore, so lively and sometimes wonderful, is now a fading memory as is the language despite lastminute efforts at resuscitation, and whereas tracking down a decent authentic Jewish restaurant or deli nowadays takes a certain ingenuity, African American theater, in spite of its many tribulations, manages to thrive, and so too does traditional soul food. Moreover, Black

English remains alive and well, to the consternation of its many critics, just as there is no mistaking the force of identity-confirming body language, dress, coiffure, dance, and etiquette among our inhabitants of an alternative cultural universe. Then, within the once almost exclusively Caucasian game of basketball, note how African Americans, with their special moves, have *almost* succeeded in transforming this wildly popular pastime into their own special reserve. When it comes to literature and music, the African American contribution is separate from, and at least comparable in quality to, its competitors. It is decidedly more of the here and now than most Jewish efforts, so generally nostalgic in tone. If it were possible to devise a valid quantitative index of the gap between African American culture and that of the American mainstream, I dare say we would learn it has stabilized or perhaps widened in recent decades (DiMaggio and Ostrower 1990).

But, however praiseworthy its intrinsic merits, African American culture cannot overcome a most negative sort of liability: the class (or caste) stigma of its practitioners. Black culture, or "blackness," is fatally tarnished in the minds of all too many nonblacks as smacking of membership in the lowest of social classes, in the dreaded "underclass." Notwithstanding occasional episodes of cultural slumming by those Caucasians who sample soul food or experiment with African hairdos or dashikis, self-respecting 100-percent Americans generally avoid contact with such lifestyles.[38] In order to be acceptable to the larger national community, à la Colin Powell, Ralph Bunche, or the Huxtables, the ambitious African American must shed nearly all reminders of stereotypical traits or of ancestry, except complexion.

In contrast to the socially and culturally sequestered African American, the typical contemporary Jewish American, who frequently claims gentiles as close colleagues, friends, and even in-laws, can move back and forth between the larger public realm and his/her ethnic circle with minimal psychic stress or discomfort and without disguising the fact of Jewishness. And that ethnic identity, albeit much modified from its European origins and still evolving, remains intact and precious to its participants. (On this point, see Bershtel and Graubard 1982; Goldscheider and Zuckerman 1984:225–226; Higham 1984:95–174; Showstack 1990; and Waldinger and Lichter 1996.)

One can argue, then, that we have no choicer current American example — though certainly not yet a totally ideal one — of the feasibility of membership in a fully matured multicultural society than the Jewish American. Indeed it would seem to be unique to date. The drastic difference in the status of the pluralistic African Americans as compared to the multiculturalized Jewish Americans is best illustrated by the great strain involved in the role-switching the former must enact when temporarily engaged in the everyday world of school or work.[39]

Are there other promising candidates for Multiculturalism 3? Possibly. Judging from the historical record, eligibility for entrance into this realm of multicultural grace, whose sole tenant to date is the Jewish American community, depends on meeting all of the following four criteria: (1) a distinctive cultural complex, either preexisting as such or given the ingredients for its ethnogenetic construction; (2) a significant degree of upward socioeconomic development; (3) a population numbering a certain, but still to be determined, size; and, alas, (4) a population among which a great majority of members could pass for Caucasians.

I can think of only four ethnic/racial groups in today's America that *might* pass muster: Cubans, Iranians, Asian Indians, and Lebanese. (But the last may be questionable in terms of quantity.) At least five East Asian groups — the Koreans, Japanese, Chinese, Vietnamese, and Filipinos — satisfy all but the final criterion But it may be some time before these speculations can be confirmed or refuted. After all, it took more than a century for the Jewish community to arrive at its current status.

The two examples I have chosen to illustrate the attainability of Multiculturalism 3 were not random selections. The Jewish American case would seem, again, to be the only possible success story to date. The inescapable African American counterexample, one too large to ignore, tells us how difficult, perhaps impossible, the odds are for genuine multiculturalism for ethnic, or rather ethnic/racial, groups with less promising preconditions. In order for the black population to enter into a viable multicultural compact with other Americans they must first approach national norms en masse in terms of occupation, education, income, and other indicators of middle-class success. Sad to say, the prospects for such an ascent are exceedingly dim during any foreseeable future. Furthermore, even if such a transformation were to come to pass, and assuming that other Americans would be amenable, one would be indulging in extreme optimism to forecast the voluntary multiculturalization of the African American masses (once again, excluding the atypical fringe members of the community). Given the absence of class barriers and the dwindling of racial prejudice, the African American community, perhaps like some other non-European groups, may be so deeply comfortable within its own cultural nest that Multiculturalism 3 would have questionable appeal — a sobering thought as we assess the likely patterns of future ethnic dealings in the United States.

PARTING THOUGHTS

It is time for a final review of strategies. In the light of all we have learned so far, what options are available to a nation-state such as the United States in coping with a multiplicity of ethnic/racial groups. I can discern only four.

The first is hideous. But the historical reality is that it was not only contemplated formerly but actually implemented: the extermination of undesirable aliens. This was the implicit official policy — and an overt one on the part of many individuals — with respect to Native Americans until the late nineteenth century. At this late date, however, it seems safe to claim that, for all but the lunatic fringe, genocide is unthinkable.

Not so readily dismissed is the second option, namely, the deliberate, forced segregation or expulsion of those we regard as superfluous, disagreeable, or threatening, or who happen to be proprietors of interesting property. That policy has a venerable history. Among the more notorious examples have been the expulsion of Jews from thirteenth-century Britain and from Spain in 1492, the Huguenot flight from France, the *millet* system of segregation within the Ottoman Empire, and, in the twentieth century, among too many other examples, we have the forced reshuffling of Greeks and Turks from one state to the other, the removal of East Indians from Uganda, South African apartheid, the Nazi atrocities throughout their short-lived European empire, and the recent ethnic "cleansing" in the former Yugoslavia.

But the American record is far from unblemished. It is difficult to overlook the forced westward relocation of so many Native American nations in the nineteenth century and their subsequent incarceration in reservations, the Back to Africa movement that actually resulted in the transfer of several thousand persons to their ancestral continent, the extralegal repatriation of Mexicans from Texas in the early twentieth century, or the inexcusable uprooting of Japanese Americans from California, Oregon, and Washington during World War II. Once again, there is little likelihood that, at this late date, such a strategy could be officially pursued ever again, even though the more rabidly xenophobic among us would not object to the deportation of millions of certain newcomers. On the other hand, some small ethnic/religious communities do voluntarily fence themselves off socially and/or physically from the surrounding world and thus render moot any policy debate.

The two remaining strategies both take multiculturalism into account as they wrestle with the complexities of a globalizing world. The first of the pair is raw, unrefined, muddling-along Multiculturalism 2. It is the situation in which we find ourselves mired currently, one that entails the maintenance of a rickety status quo now that we have become aware of the existence of the phenomenon but are at loggerheads as to what to do about it. On the one hand, there is the celebration of Ethnicity, the "feel-good" policy that papers over the fissures and inequities of an unjust social system; on the other, the closely allied practice of cryptoracism. In essence, we have denial, making genuine multiculturalism into a nonissue. Much more boisterously, we have also a series of angry debates, the constant squabbling among competing ethnic/racial interests and the Establishment, and clashing ideologies concerning agendas and the allocation of power and prestige among the contestants, but with only incidental attention to the transnational dimensions of the discourse. Not the least of the issues is how history should be written or rewritten. At the moment, no end is in sight, no cease-fire acceptable to all the belligerents, only more of the same well into the future and quite possibly with even greater incivility.

The fourth strategy, our final option, envisions the attainment of genuine Multiculturalism 3 as previously defined. If, for the sake of argument, we assume that such an objective is desirable (and many would demur, of course), there would seem to be two ways to realize it. The first is the piecemeal approach, the advance of one formerly disadvantaged group after another from lowly status to parity and a healthy symbiosis with the dominant majority. As already indicated, the good fortune of the Jewish American community provides the most nearly ideal example of the process to date. One can only conjecture about the prospect that other groups could emulate their delicate balancing act, rising to the same level of acceptance while sustaining addresses in two overlapping sociocultural worlds. But even under the best of circumstances, the outcome would be an incompletely multiculturalized country. Groups dwelling near the bottom of the heap — Haitians, Laotians, Gypsies, Mexicans, Salvadorans, Navajo, Menominee, and Somalis, among others — obviously would have much tougher going on the path toward a genuine multicultural collectivity.

The other approach is radical and visionary, indeed thoroughly revolutionary in character. It envisions a nation and, by implication, an entire world in which domination has been banished and all ethnic/racial groups coexist, interacting freely as they maintain their identities and enjoy mutual trust and respect. It is a program most fully enunciated by Hollinger (1995) and Shohat and Stam (1994). The "radical polycentric multiculturalism" espoused by the latter authors globalizes the phenomenon. It "is not about 'touchy-feely' sensitivity toward other groups; it is about dispersing power, about empowering the disempowered, about transferring subordinating institutions and discourses. Polycentric multiculturalism demands changes not just in images but in power relations" (1994:48).

A glorious goal, no doubt, and many Americans might agree we should begin working toward it, although probably many more would have their reservations. Unfortunately, its proponents fail to offer the step-by-step scenario whereby we can arrive at such a wondrous destination. And compounding the challenge of realizing Multiculturalism 3 is the fluid, contingent nature of ethnic identity. With their uncertain boundaries and memberships of variable loyalty, how are the competing entities to fabricate a formula for mutual accommodation? In any event, the only certainty about any such process is that it presupposes a truly profound political and economic reordering of the world, something not likely to be accomplished without much trauma or a series of unpredictable calamities.[40]

A further cautionary note is in order. Utopias, or the routes heading that way, can be dangerous places, even if they exist only in the social imagination. History presents us with all too many horrendous examples of the dystopic results of utopian programs undertaken with the utmost earnestness. Indeed if the chronicle of the past two centuries teaches us nothing else, we should have learned how fallible, even pernicious, is the doctrine of human perfectibility. As Maffesoli has observed in a characteristically gnomic utterance,

> Imperfection is a sign of life; perfection a synonym for death. It is only in its hodge-podge, its effervescence, its disordered and stochastic aspects, its touching naivete, that the vitalism of the people is of interest to us. It is because it is in this *nothingness* which gives shape to everything that, relatively speaking, we can see an alternative to decline; but at the same time it tolls a bell for modernity."
> (1996 : 389; emphasis in original)

Do not misunderstand me. I do not end with a counsel of despair. There is much that can and should be done to improve our lot, or even to preserve past gains, and to inch our way forward, zigzagging toward a predominantly, genuinely multicultural, if still imperfect, society. I trust that the findings presented in this study can nurture the process. The rate of forward movement may be glacial, and even holding our own will not be easy, but try we must.

How frustrating it is to conclude this work without some sort of grand flourish or the least hint of certitude. All I can do is to remind the reader of the alternatives, the two possible, or thinkable, multicultural futures in store for us.

The choice is ours. Or is it?

NOTES

1. A truly anomalous, perhaps amusing, situation occurs when, as so often happens in discussions of American minorities, we include females in that category. The fact is, of course, that they now comprise an absolute majority of the total population.

2. Strictly speaking, Japan is not a nation totally free of caste. A relatively small, endogamous group called the Eta are treated as social outcasts by their neighbors for reasons that are quite obscure. To the non-Japanese observer they are indistinguishable from the rest of the population.

3. Even though we now have a pretty clear notion as to the origins and development of racism among the learned, we are still in the dark concerning the history of "vulgar racism" among the masses. Was it concurrent with beliefs and attitudes in scholarly circles? In any event, what was the relationship between the two levels of the phenomenon? Answers will be hard to come by because of the meagerness of documentation.

4. For especially valuable insights into the history, nature, and significance of racism, see Kovel (1970) and Spoonley (1988).

5. In William Petersen's (1997) penetrating and scorching critique of the ways in which officialdom collects and classifies data on race and ethnicity, we have as definitive an account as one could desire.

6. In recent decades, censual designations of race in the United States are no longer left to the discretion of the enumerator. The persons filling out the questionnaire now may check off an appropriate response from among a menu of choices (T. W. Smith 1980).

7. "If a lesson can be drawn from this discussion, it may well be that the current system of racial classifications should be abandoned. . . . A preferred mode of measurement might be simply to ask people for their ancestry" (S. M. Lee 1993 : 91).

8. But over the course of several decades (1850–1936), census officials did conduct the Census of Religious Bodies, an operation based on soliciting information from the central offices of church organizations rather than by interrogating the general citizenry (Zelinsky 1961 : 141–142).

The resulting tabulations were incomplete and seriously flawed in many ways.

9. The Canadians have faced similar perplexities in their efforts to frame meaningful questions related to ethnic identity in their 1986 and 1991 enumerations (Boyd 1992).

10. But self-identification is far from being an effective panacea. As Lieberson and Waters (1993) have discovered, responses among Euro-Americans are increasingly unstable and inconsistent. Also see Cresce et al. (1992).

11. The cartographic and analytical potentialities generated by the ancestry data are splendidly realized in the two atlases created by Allen and Turner (1988, 1997).

12. For further discussion of our latter-day flexibility in ethnic self-identification, see Albers and James (1986), Cresce et al. (1992), Fuchs (1990:326–339), Hollinger (1993:33), Kivisto (1992), Nagel (1994), Okamura (1981), and Staub (1989:9).

13. The phenomenon is deeper, wider, and older than most of us realize. "The proportions may vary, but the fact of racial heterogeneity obtains almost everywhere, including in the U.S. But while Latin Americans have known their continent to be *mestizo*, many Euro-Americans have resisted the recognition that North American culture is also *mestizo*, mixed, hybrid. While the syncretic nature of other societies is 'visible,' the syncretic nature of North American society often remains hidden" (Shohat and Stam 1994:241).

14. It was only in 1962 that the United States Supreme Court finally struck down the various state laws proscribing interracial marriage.

15. The boundary may be something other than a line drawn on the ground. "An ethnic category, network, or group . . . offers, from the social point of view, communality in language, a series of customs and symbols, a style, rituals, an appearance, and so forth, which can penetrate life in many ways. These trappings of ethnicity are particularly attractive when one is continually confronted by others who live differently, as happens in New York, Brussels, and Amsterdam" (Roosens 1989:17).

16. "By its own nature, [ethnicity] offers a broad field for the use and manipulation of symbols. To begin with, the ingredients used in ethnic discourse seem quite natural: descent, biological origin, belonging together, land, culture, and history all seem eminently real and constitute what many people consider to be palpable realities. At the same time, they are extremely vague in their definition. Nobody can deny that a given group of people has ancestors, that they have a past, a culture, a

biological origin, or that they have been living somewhere, on some piece of land. These facts constitute the eminently solid, genuine, irreducible side of ethnicity, ethnic identity, and ethnic feelings. But who exactly these ancestors were, where they lived, what type of culture they transmitted, and the degree to which this culture is an original creation, and what their relationships were with other, similar ethnic groups in the past — all these are frequently open questions for the open mind. Political discourse and ethnic politics, of course, need not imply an open mind. And even if they do, the lack of definition of the things involved, their imprecision, their predominant arationality, makes them remarkably flexible and useful as building materials for an ethnic ideology. In the ethnic arsenal you can partially forget what you know if others do not notice or do not mind. You can add things if exact knowledge is not available. You can choose a suitable variant if different theories exist. You can combine and transplant. You can inject vigor and authenticity . . . . Almost anything and everything are [*sic*] possible, as long as no falsehoods are told that are too obviously refuted by common knowledge and as long as the adversary is not too strong" (Roosens 1989:160–161).

17. "I think there is considerable doubt about the historical continuity of ethnic divisions. While there are many examples of groups with long histories, there are many populations whose numbers appear to have declined through amalgamation and/or absorption by other populations" (Hirschman 1991:45).

18. "It was not until after the French and American Revolutions and the social upheavals which followed that the idea of race was fully conceptualized and became deeply embedded in our understandings and explanations of the world. In other words, the dispositions and presuppositions of race and ethnicity were introduced — some would say 'invented' or 'fabricated' — in modern times and were the outcomes of a vast excrescence of recent thought on descent, generation, and inheritance" (Hannaford 1996:6). "The answer to the bland, amoral universalism of consumer society is commitment to a specific people — one's own people — and to place, not only its sights, but also its exclusive odors, myriad sounds and tactile qualities. The answer, in short, is ethnicity and nationalism" (Tuan 1996:948). Also see Berlin (1972:28).

19. In his "Aztlán Rediscovered," Chávez (1984:129–155) has shown how the repositioning of the American Southwest as the mythical ancestral homeland has been a significant component of the Chicano Revival.

20. "The melting pot was not . . . a failure. Rather, it succeeded in trans-

forming weak, fragmented, and unclassifiable bundles of immigrants into self-conscious, active, and easily identifiable groups" (Sarna 1978: 375).

21. "The first level in the evolution of nationalism is ethnic naïveté. The overwhelming bulk of East European, German, and Italian immigrants were at this stage. They both possessed and practiced certain cultural characteristics of their group . . . but they had little or no feeling of membership in an ethnic nation. Whether in Europe or America, they may have sensed that they were different from other nationalities, but when asked for their own group identification, they probably would have responded by naming their regional or local origins — their village or more likely their province. Very few would have replied 'Polish,' 'Lithuanian,' 'German,' or 'Italian,'" (Greene 1975:3).

22. "The Italian immigrants faced a strange situation: although they all came from the same country, they did not share a common culture or even a language with which to communicate. The various regions of Italy had developed widely different cultures and dialects due to a number of political, social and economic factors. The immigrants, being largely from the peasant class, knew only their local dialects and had no knowledge of literary Italian, which is based on the Tuscan dialect, and in any case had only recently been designated as the official Italian language. Thus they could not communicate effectively with other Italians who spoke a different dialect" (Magliocco 1993:110).

23. "Community and group consciousness among 'Southerners' [Italians] in the United States did not cross the Atlantic, but developed in the new homeland" (Nelli 1970:5).

24. Benkin and DeSantis (1982) focus on the differences and relationships between pre–World War I and post–World War II Eastern European Jews and Lithuanians in Chicago.

25. In contrast to the North American situation, some residuum of tribal identity was retained among the African populations of Brazil, Cuba, and Haiti.

26. "This study of Haitian immigrants shows us that black America is also a 'melting pot' for black immigrants just as white America serves as a 'melting pot' for European immigrants. Thus, there are two 'melting pots' in American society, one for Americans of European descent and one for Americans of African descent" (Woldemikael 1989:171) — and additional melting pots for Latinos, non-Hispanic Caribbeans, and possibly East Asians?

27. There is an interesting analogue in the sudden appearance and coalescence of the modern Israeli nation, but as recent as this process has been, it was, at least in part, a refashioning of an ancient antecedent.

28. Perhaps the most concise and insightful statement concerning the unique character of the American ethnos is that offered by Philip Gleason (1982). Within a splendid essay that merits study in its entirety, we find the following key passage: "The generation of the founding fathers understood very well that building a new nation required the development of a national sense of peoplehood. They were quite self-consciously concerned over the establishment of what they called the national character. Because four out of five whites were of British derivation, because virtually all were Protestant, and because blacks and Indians were not considered part of the national community, Americans of that era may be considered highly homogeneous in culture. Dedication to freedom and self-government was an integral element in their British heritage and in their recent American experience, so there was naturally a close correspondence between the sense of peoplehood of the cultural majority (the founders, or core group, or WASPs) and the national sense of peoplehood they projected for the nascent republic. Yet American nationality was not simply 'WASP ethnicity' writ large. On the contrary, it was regarded as something novel and distinctive; it was oriented toward the future rather than the past; and, most important, it rested on a commitment to universalist political and social principles rather than particularist cultural features such as language, religion, or country of origin. Thus the ethnic consciousness-of-kind of the American core group was closely related to, but not identical with, the American nationality that was to be formed" (138).

29. Defining the range and edges of the population sheltered under the broad tent of the American ethnos has never been an easy proposition. In the words of Edward Said, "Before we can agree on what the American identity is made of, we have to concede that as an immigrant settler society superimposed on the ruins of a considerable native presence, American identity is too varied to be a unitary and homogeneous thing; indeed the battle within it is between advocates of a unitary identity and those who see the whole as a complex but not reductively unified one. This opposition implies two different perspectives, two historiographies, one linear and subsuming, the other contrapuntal and often nomadic (1993 : xxv).

30. This is by no means a uniquely American problem. "One of the things which happens in England is the long discussion, which is just beginning, to try to convince the English that they are, after all, just another ethnic group. I mean a very interesting ethnic group, just hovering off the edge of Europe, with their own language, their own peculiar customs, their rituals, their myths" (Hall 1997 : 21).

31. We might also speculate about the potential emergence of a sixth pan-

ethnic entity: the Middle Eastern. The census has not accorded it special attention, and its prospective components are quite varied in terms of language, religion, ideology, and ethnic attributes, but on occasion there have been efforts to rally the groups in question in support of a "pan-Arab" cause (Haddad and Smith 1994: Younis 1995:249–265). Any pan-African project would encounter even greater difficulties (Selassie 1996:272–273).

32. This habitual practice of lumping together the disparate populations of the "Mysterious Orient" is clearly another manifestation of the orientalism that has so fully pervaded European and American thought for centuries (Lewis and Wigen 1997; Said 1978).

33. The archipelagic array of Germans strewn across central and eastern Europe before 1939 is a classic example of such a supranational entity.

34. The remainder of this discussion by Sollors (1986:23–26) merits close attention, as does his introductory essay in *The Invention of Ethnicity* (1989), but the most nearly definitive account of the semantic history of *ethnicity* is that by Philip Gleason (1992).

35. A more poetic definition also solicits our attention: "Ethnicity is only a public metaphor, like sexuality or age, for a knowledge that bewilders us" (Rodriguez 1989:9).

36. One finds food for thought in the divergent careers of the cognate terms *ethnicity* and *Nationalism*. Strictly speaking, as noted earlier, *ethnie* and *nation*, though Greek and Latin in origin, respectively, are, or should be, identical in meaning. But while Ethnicity has gone on to glory as a Good Thing, *nationality* claims absolutely none of its cachet, and our feelings about *nationalism* are complicated and often contradictory. Patriots and jingoists may shout the praises of a specific nationalism but the generic concept has few champions.

37. "Interestingly, one group about which all too little has properly been written is White Anglo-Saxon Protestants, especially the English. To argue that most of American history in general has already been written about these people is to miss the point, much the same way that the male bias of past scholarship hardly diminishes the need today to study maleness as a cultural network" (Ibson 1981:299).

38. "The radical attempt to escape from freedom [via fundamentalism or romantic ethnicity] is itself a specifically modern phenomenon. The interplay between different kinds of such 'syndromes' is itself part and parcel of the drama of modernity" (Lechner 1984:253). Also see Sollors (1989).

39. But the impulse has energized even some relatively obscure groups such as the Sephardic Jews (Lavender 1975).

40. "I argue that in order to understand ethnicity in late twentieth-cen-

tury America, we must consider thinking about it less from a macro-structural and more from a symbolic perspective. Ethnicity persists because it means something important to many contemporary Americans. Its meaning resides primarily in the private and familial realms of life, although it may insinuate itself in the public realm and structural processes in interesting ways. Ethnicity is a symbol of group and family identity and history. Its power and persistence reside in its place in a conscious and unconscious discourse among ethnic group members about the distinctive history of a group, about what constitutes membership in the ethnic group, and about the role of families in sustaining that membership" (Kellogg 1990:28–29).

CHAPTER 2. EXPRESSIONS

1. Consider, *inter alia*, the following non-British contributions to the standard contemporary American cultural scene: lacrosse, skiing, canoes, vodka, the polka, bagels, pizza, rodeos, moccasins, log cabins, the rumba, Christmas trees, and Santa Claus.

2. In addition to linguistic losses automatically hastened by cultural assimilation, there was the further impetus of the English language instruction that was so central in the Americanization curricula of the early twentieth century and the outright ban on aboriginal tongues in the federal schools enrolling Native American children.

3. "Today Americans of Spanish-speaking ancestry who do not speak the language often try to learn it, and most want their children to learn it, too. The growth of Spanish-language television makes this easier, since they learn by watching soap operas and other entertainment. It also tends to standardize the emerging North American dialect of Spanish and increases its usefulness" (Fox 1996:7).

4. Kaups (1978–79) deals definitively with the Finnish impact on the toponymy of northern Minnesota.

5. But generally, in the short term, and for some groups in some localities over a longer period, foodways have served as a significant key to ethnic identity, however doubtful their role in political and organizational strategies. For extended discussion of the ethnic dimensions in American cuisine, see Gabaccia (1998), Pillsbury (1998), and Shortridge and Shortridge (1998).

6. As a child in Chicago, I attended and enjoyed the lively programs arranged by my father's large *verein* (derived from Mogilev, Belorus) and my mother's smaller group (Bratslav and Nemerov, Ukraine). See Kliger (1992).

7. An institution apparently uniquely confined to the Jewish American populations of our larger cities was the family or cousin club (Mitchell

1978). I was once affiliated with one such (on my mother's side), but, like virtually all other such groups, ours simply petered out when many of the third-generation kinfolk and all of the fourth generation lost interest.

8. Golf does not qualify as an immigrant import. Although, as is well known, the sport originated in Scotland, the source of many early American settlers, it did not arrive with such relatively indigent people. Instead, affluent WASPs introduced it into the northeastern United States in the late nineteenth century.

9. The obvious exceptions are the hogans of the Navajo and the traditional dwellings still built and maintained by the Hopi, Zuni, and certain other groups in the Southwest. Partially or fully acculturated Native Americans seem to prefer Anglo-American styles of building. Perhaps the only aboriginal structures or designs (aside from the play tepee) to be adopted by the invaders were the brush arbors and camp meeting layouts used for religious occasions that seem to have been acquired by Christian Caucasians from their vanished originators in the Southeast.

10. Much of the remainder of Upton's commentary merits attention. "This is particularly likely since the Chinese architectural elements in San Francisco's Chinatown allude to the northern Chinese classical architectural tradition, although nearly all overseas Chinese originated in a small area of southern China. . . . These images suited non-Chinese landowners and Chinese tenants, for both wanted Chinatown to be a revenue-generating tourist attraction. They are distilled, highly stylized, commodified images of a mythical 'heritage' that respond to the outsider's imposition of difference and to the insider's adoption of ethnicity as a distinguishing identity. . . . Chinatowns and ethnic churches place us in the realm that the historians Eric Hobsbawm and Terence Ranger have labeled 'invented tradition.' They are not 'vernacular' buildings; for political reasons they reject vernacular images in favor of high-cultural forms, such as baroque churches. Neither are they 'traditional,' for they have little connection with the Old-Country lifeways of their builders. Consequently, they are not 'authentic' signs of 'true' identities in any conventional sense. Yet these fragments of an idealized high culture serve very effectively in a multiethnic society as metonyms of identity" (1996 : 4–5).

11. African American church structures deserve special comment. There may not have been any overt transmission of architectural practice from the homelands, but I suspect that careful study of rural southern black churches will reveal certain Africanisms in their design. In the larger cities, one apparently unique feature of the African American ec-

clesiastical landscape is the abundance of storefront churches, i.e., former retail shops, movie theaters, etc., converted into places of worship. The only changes visible to the passerby are in signage and decoration of doors and windows.

12. It is the more flamboyant of Hindu temples that have aroused the greatest consternation, but many Christian Americans also find Islamic mosques offensive. One notable exception, a unique, breathtakingly lovely structure that seems immune to adverse comment, is the Bahai Temple in Wilmette, Illinois.

13. Among these interesting ways is a general tropicalization of informal American dress, especially during the warmer months (along with certain tropical leanings in latter-day house design). There may be a Latin American and Caribbean connection here, combined with the allure of the Hawaiian theme.

14. In just the same way, most Anglo-Americans today are unaware that any distinctions exist between Jamaicans and Barbadians, Salvadorans and Nicaraguans, or Puerto Ricans and Dominicans.

15. Warner and Srole avoided any forecasts concerning racial type 3, i.e., Mongoloid and Caucasoid mixtures with Caucasoid appearance dominant, which we may assume to include, *inter alia*, most Middle Easterners, some East Indians and Polynesians, perhaps Filipinos, and the offspring of pairings involving Caucasians. And such silence may have been sensible. Even now it is not possible to predict the future status of such persons within the American value system.

16. From the early career of the noted photojournalist Weegee (Arthur Fellig), we have a most revealing comment concerning the symbolic and social importance of literal whiteness. "The people loved their children and, no matter how poor they might be, they managed to dig up the money for my pictures. . . . I would finish the photographs on the contrastiest paper I could get in order to give the kids nice, white, chalky faces. My customers, who were Italian, Polish, or Jewish, like their pictures dead-white" (M. Barth 1997:15).

17. An interesting aspect of this change has been the realization by Euro-Americans that there is much to be admired, and commercialized, in the cultures of North America's first nations. Obvious examples include the aboriginal communities of the Pacific Northwest, Hawaii, and, most especially, those of the Southwest. Such attention is not universally welcome. For the Hopi, intrusions by outsiders have occasioned considerable annoyance (Howes 1996).

18. Certain events are transnational in character. "Some, mostly in cities on the Mexican border, are hands-across-the-border celebrations. Others celebrate sister city relationships, the international character of uni-

versity student bodies, or the cultures of foreigners who own manufacturing plants in a particular locale. The majority [of multicultural festivals] celebrate international cultures in potpourri fashion, and many highlight a different country or world region each year. A good example of the multicultural genre is the renowned Memphis in May International Festival, which spotlighted Brazil in 1997" (Janiskee 1997:4).

19. Ethnic festivals are not unknown in other lands, e.g., Canada and Australia, but are far less numerous outside the United States.

20. It is not unusual to have disputes between organizers and political activists as to whether any demonstrations or leafleting should be permitted and, if so, just when, how, and where.

21. For the recent development of such enterprises in other countries, see Oakes (1997a, 1997b).

22. There are at least two museums that are catholic in their approach: Philadelphia's Balch Museum, whose exhibits and library cover the full range of the nation's ethnic groups, and San Antonio's museum, a legacy of that city's world's fair, that honors all the various native and immigrant communities of Texas.

23. The literature on this intriguing phenomenon is still spotty, but worthy of attention are Arreola (1984b); Cockcroft et al. (1977); Dowler (1996); Drescher (1994); Environmental Communications (1977); Fleming and Von Tscharner (1987); and Pocock (1980).

24. "Doctors are making efforts to preserve ethnic features while enhancing beauty. Since the aesthetics of surgery has historically been tailored for Caucasian faces, surgeons now face a 'two-pronged challenge.' First, they need to define beautiful features for African-Americans, Hispanics, and Asian-Americans, and, second, they must determine how to modify standard operations to achieve these goals. The ideal nose or shape of face is subject to ethnic variation, and the concept of beauty varies among people of different ethnic groups. . . . Hence, patients must choose physicians experienced in operating on their specific ethnic group. Improved surgical techniques and a better understanding of the anatomical differences among people of different races have greatly aided surgeons' attempts to preserve ethnicity" (Rubinstein 1995:163–164). But such mortifications of the flesh and hair are not always aimed at enhancing one's visible links with the ancestral stock. Shohat and Stam speak of the Eurocentric gaze that is "spread not only by First World media but even at times by Third World media, [which] explains why *morena* women in Puerto Rico, like Arab-Jewish (Sephardic) women in Israel, dye their hair blonde, why Brazilian TV commercials are more suggestive of Scandinavia than of a Black ma-

jority country, why 'Miss Universe' contests can elect blonde 'queens' even in North African countries, and why Asian women perform cosmetic surgery in order to appear more Western. . . . A patriarchal system contrived to generate neurotic self-dissatisfaction in *all* women (whence anorexia, bulimia, and other pathologies of appearance) becomes especially oppressive for women of color by excluding them from the realms of legitimate images of desire. At the same time, recently, there have been reverse currents linked to the central role of African-Americans in mass-mediated culture: Whites who thicken their lips and sport dreadlocks, fades or cornrows" (1994:322).

25. This recent development reminds one of an earlier phenomenon, the "cultural cringe" that afflicted so many American authors, artists, and musicians, especially in the early nineteenth century, and the efforts to overcome it. Considered colonial and inferior by the cultural elite of Great Britain and Western Europe, a number of these creative individuals went to great pains to revise foreign opinion. But it was not until well into the twentieth century that the battle was finally won.

26. It is worth noting that, thanks to the numbers and cultural liveliness of the newcomers, the ethnic press is staging a strong comeback (Sreenivasan 1996). Whether it will suffer the same fate as the publications that once flourished among the immigrant stock from Europe depends on future social and political development, as well as immigrant flows that cannot be predicted.

27. Mrs. Stowe's gripping masterpiece is evidently one of those works more often referred to than read. Thus if the eponymous hero were better known, we would realize that the epithet "Uncle Tom" is wildly off target. The author depicts the fictional character as a strong, noble, altogether admirable human being, not the cringing Stepinfetchit stereotype of popular misconception.

28. But there has been an interesting recent turn of events in the world of television soap opera. "After decades of racial exclusion or tokenism, racial-ethnics were finally portrayed as leading characters on most of the daytime television dramas during the 1980s. The serials are viewed by 50 to 70 million viewers a week and broadcast 260 episodes a year. Therefore, soap operas have the potential to raise ethnic consciousness" (James 1991: Abstract).

29. Taking a much broader view, American consumers of contemporary popular music and their counterparts everywhere else are being exposed to what is called, rather problematically, "world music" (Mitchell 1996:49–64). This genre expropriates presumably traditional musical idioms from anywhere and everywhere, often hybridizing them with Anglo-American and other styles. And, again, whatever accep-

tance such cultural products enjoy redounds to the credit of the ethnic groups in question.

30. Instead, there are tantalizing snippets, such as in descriptions of how the polka and other types of Slavic and German music and ethnic and folk dance have found favor among ordinary Americans from the 1920s onward (V. Greene 1990:19–20, 148–158).

31. "The rise of black nationalism in the late 1960s had brought a new appreciation for the southern black culinary tradition, now called 'soul food.' On New Year's Eve well-off urban blacks ostentatiously eschewed steak and roast beef for the ham hocks, peas, and collard greens of their rural forbears. One entrepreneur set up shop importing prepared soul food directly from North Carolina to affluent blacks in New York City" (Levenstein 1993:218).

32. For the geography and something of the history of ethnic restaurant cuisines in North America, see Zelinsky (1985).

33. For Mark Twain's mouth-watering manifesto on the glories of American vittles, regional or otherwise, see Clemens (1880:574–575).

CHAPTER 3. HETEROLOCALISM

1. This may be as good a point as any to mention the famous thesis proposed by Marcus Lee Hansen (1938) some six decades ago, in essence that what the third generation tries to remember of its ethnic heritage the second generation had tried to forget. Perhaps the only direct empirical test, a survey of Italian Americans in two Rhode Island suburban communities (Roche 1982), failed to find any support for this notion. However, the so-called ethnic revival of the 1970s, which I discuss elsewhere in this study, did provide some confirmation, but of a quite partial, temporary sort.

2. For a brief commentary on the ideological agenda of the Chicago School of sociology, the principal exponent of the assimilation model, see Basch et al. (1994:41).

3. Furthermore, "relatively little work has been done on non-Caucasian groups or on immigrants whose method and location of entry was other than the European tradition of booking voluntary passage to the colonies, Boston harbor, Ellis Island and the port of New York" (Arce 1981:178).

4. But contrary to the general public impression of a frequently stigmatized group, "these Haitian boat people are not the starving, landless, poverty-stricken wrecks described in the popular literature. . . . Certainly by Haitian standards they are far from poor" (Lawless 1986:46).

5. For insights into the ways in which cinema, television, and VCR tech-

nology have reshaped the global cultural order and enhanced the role of imagination in social life, see Appadurai (1991), especially p. 198.

6. For richly informative and provocative discussions of the postmodern American metropolis, see Dear and Flusty (1998) and Knox (1993).

7. But, despite the ongoing transformation of the American metropolis, Allen and Turner still argue valiantly for the enduring value of the assimilation model. "Thus, ethnic concentrations are no longer exclusively located in older centralized areas, and the areal differentiation of relative assimilation is often weaker than that implied by the model of spatial assimilation. Nevertheless, changes in the characteristics of immigrants and a radically expanded metropolitan geography over the last half-century have not invalidated the general spatial pattern of relative assimilation that once characterized European immigrants and their children" (1996:154).

8. Are pluralism and multiculturalism synonymous? That is a question taken up in the final chapter, but it may be relevant to note that the latter concept, unlike pluralism, does not consider spatial location either explicitly or implicitly.

9. However, a recent study of immigrant groups in London does test the two standard model within a geographic framework by applying data on residential location and rates of intermarriage (Peach 1997). The results indicate that assimilationism, being played out by the Caribbeans, and pluralism, the path followed by Bangladeshis and to a lesser extent by a diversified East Indian population, can coexist in the same metropolis during the same period.

10. Relevant material is to be found in Alba and Logan (1993:1418); Alba et al. (1995); Allen and Turner (1996); Bartel (1989:375); Bhardwaj and Rao (1990:207–208); Bozorgmehr (1992:166–170); Carlson (1975, 1978); Laguerre (1984:30); Lam (1986: Abstract); Lobo et al. (1996: 16); Min (1988:27, 69–70); Mahler (1996:14–15); Manning (1994a: 12); Newbold (1999); Rangaswamy (1995:444, 454); Tsai and Sigelman (1982); Waksberg and Tobin (1984:111); and Waldinger et al. (1990:114, 121).

11. It is surprising how little systematic attention has been paid to this striking new development, but for a stimulating introductory sketch on the topic, see Fuchs (1990:289–304).

12. "Immigrant professionals are . . . more likely to be geographically dispersed because they tend to rely more on their qualifications and job offers than on preexisting kinship networks and ethnic communities (as do working-class immigrants and entrepreneurs)" (Rumbaut 1995:8).

13. Benedict Anderson has forcefully stated the perils of this brand of ab-

sentee political meddling, something, again, quite distinct from genuine transnationalism. "Today's long-distance nationalism strikes one as a probably menacing portent for the future. First of all, it is the product of capitalism's remorseless, accelerating transformation of all human societies. Second, it creates a serious politics that is at the same time radically unaccountable. The participant rarely pays taxes in the country in which he does his politics; he is not answerable to its judicial system; he probably does not cast even an absentee ballot in its elections because he is a citizen in a different place; he need not fear prison, torture, or death, nor need his immediate family. But, well and safely positioned in the First World, he can send money and guns, circulate propaganda, and build intercontinental computer information circuits, all of which can have incalculable consequences in the zone of their ultimate destinations. Third, his politics, unlike those of activists for global human rights or environmental causes, are neither intermittent nor serendipitous. They are deeply rooted in a consciousness that his exile is self-chosen and that the nationalism he claims on E-mail is also the ground on which an embattled ethnic identity is to be fashioned in the ethnicized nation-state that he remains determined to inhabit. That same metropole which marginalizes and stigmatizes him simultaneously enables him to play, in a flash, on the other side of the planet, national hero" (1994:327).

14. Many of the more interesting of these novel transnational ethnic communities are anchored, at one end, in New York City. For richly informative journalistic accounts of the systems developed there and in the originating towns by Dominicans, Mexicans, and East Indians, see Sontag (1998) and Sontag and Dugger (1998).

15. "Historically, the pattern of Chinese immigration was for the men to come alone and work and earn money, while the wife and family stayed behind. But in the late 1970s it was not uncommon to see wives and children living in Monterey Park [California] while the husbands commuted across the Pacific. Sometimes both parents stayed in Asia and the children were sent over as students; they were set up with a home and sometimes a car, if they were old enough. Once the children were established as permanent residents, they could help the parents immigrate" (Fong 1994:48–49).

16. A related development still awaiting adequate documentation and analysis is the recent surge of international tourism involving coethnics. Such trips are different from the periodic circulation or return migration of immigrants of the past. They entail not only descendants of European (and some African?) immigrants frequenting ancestral sites but also such visits as those of German tourists to New Ulm, Min-

nesota, or the Swiss heading for New Glarus, Wisconsin (Hoelscher and Ostergren 1993; Hoelscher 1995:449–450, 484–486).

17. "Immigrants with professional backgrounds tend to settle in suburban neighborhoods, beyond the reach of their compatriots, and form their own communities and organizations. Having minimal ties to the pre-1965 Filipinos, these professionals join voluntary associations that cater primarily to their particular class interests and needs" (Espiritu 1995; also see pp. 27–28).

18. "It is the emergence of this transnational socio-cultural system which suggests that the model of immigrant/ethnic incorporation into a 'culturally pluralistic' American society is not the destiny of migrant Caribbeans. For unlike most European immigrant/ethnic groups whose heritage became confined to their private, personal lives as they became incorporated into the economy and polity of U.S. society, the cultures and identities of Caribbean migrants are public, politicized issues. Moreover, Caribbean cultures are being replenished by the transnational system created by the continuing inflow of Caribbean peoples and by circular migration. This provides grounds for affirming a separate cultural identity. It is perhaps ironic that in the U.S. this affirmation of a separate Caribbean identity, especially among Puerto Ricans, is equated with a puzzling resistance to the process of becoming 'Americanized' whereas in the Caribbean region there is concern with a loss of their distinctive Caribbean identities as the region has become increasingly 'Americanized' both economically and culturally" (C. R. Sutton 1987:20).

19. Striking examples of such mutual acculturation can be seen in the "Mex-America" of the Southwest (Haverluk 1998) and in Miami with its substantial recent intake of Haitians, Nicaraguans, and especially Cubans. Portes and Stepick observe that "the overlap of parallel social systems in the same physical space has given rise to acculturation in reverse — a process by which foreign customs, institutions, and language are diffused with the native population. As a consequence, biculturalism has emerged as an alternative adaptive project to full assimilation into American culture. Opponents of biculturalism, immigrants and natives alike, must either withdraw into their own diminished circles or exit the community" (1993:8).

CHAPTER 4. THINKING ABOUT IDENTITY

1. The earliest lexicographic notice of *identity crisis* I have come across is dated 1954 in the 1993 edition of *Merriam-Webster's Collegiate Dictionary*. Both of its definitions are apposite in this discussion: "1: personal psychological conflict esp in adolescence that involves confusion about

one's social role and often a sense of loss of continuity to one's personality. 2: a state of confusion in an institution or organization regarding its nature or direction."

2. These three epochs are quite plausible, indeed generally recognized, even though the reader may be entitled to some skepticism regarding the trinity of forces I am suggesting.

3. In a rather polemical essay, Timothy Luke (1996) also sets forth a succession of three "natures" that rather closely parallel Jackson's scheme.

4. There has been a truly explosive growth in recent years in the scholarly literature devoted to questions of contemporary personal and group identity. I cannot pretend to have read and digested more than a modest fraction of all these publications. But much of the time spent in perusal was time wasted. All too many of these books and essays are confused and confusing, written in nearly incomprehensible jargon. It would be too unkind to cite examples, but the worst of them sound like spoofs. On the positive side, I have encountered several items that are lucid, illuminating, and quite useful. In addition to the writings by Kellner and N. Rose already cited, I have found especially valuable what appears to be the earliest, but still highly stimulating, book-length discussion of postmodern identity: Orrin Klapp's *Collective Search for Identity* (1969). Although obviously a creature of its feverish times, this is a remarkably perceptive inquiry into the nature, causes, and possible antidotes to the identity dilemmas besetting advanced societies in the 1960s. Virtually no mention of ethnic issues, but Klapp does treat fads, fashion, cults, crusades, hero and celebrity worship, and the pursuit of fun in all its varied forms. Also recommended for its provocative, sprightly examination of the fluidity and uncertainties of personal identity as experienced by Americans and others is Kenneth Gergen's *The Saturated Self* (1991), and for acute insights into not only identity questions but larger contemporary sociological issues as well, the works of Zygmunt Bauman (1992, 1996) offer rich helpings of food for thought. For deep historical-cum-philosophical disquisitions on identity, see Dunn (1998); despite its clotted prose, Hoffman-Axthelm (1992); or Charles Taylor's massive and erudite *Sources of the Self* (1989). Although focused on just one aspect of culture, Fred Davis's *Fashion, Culture, and Identity* (1992) presents a highly stimulating historical perspective on how our current bizarre situation vis-à-vis clothing styles and, inferentially, other components of postmodern culture came to be.

5. "But freedom and globalization has also brought in its wake a need for cultural and ethnic self-identification, as people become uncomfortable with the borderless global community and feel a loss of control" (Burayidi 1997:1). "The old essentialisms, such as the Marxist idea that

social identity could be reduced to class identity, are now redundant. Rather gender, age, disability, race, religion, ethnicity, nationality, civil status, even musical styles and dress codes, are also very potent axes of organization and identification. These different forms of identity appear to be upheld simultaneously, successively or separately and with different degrees of force, conviction and enthusiasm" (R. Cohen 1997:129).

6. Although the full development of voluntary regions is a late twentieth-century phenomenon, there is ample precedent in the profusion of utopian colonies and communes, both religious and secular, that have flourished in America from colonial days to the present (Holloway 1951; Porter and Lukermann 1976). Such social experiments are not unknown in other lands, but nowhere else have they been so numerous and variegated as in the United States.

7. Paul Adams (1998:100–101) has shown how the computer has enabled a person to engage in masquerades, "to alternate quickly among several identities," in cyberspace.

8. "There are crucial differences between the periods loosely known as 'modernity' and 'the age of globalization.' One of the most important features of modernity was that the leaders of powerful, hegemonizing nation-states sought to make exclusive citizenship a sine qua non. The world is simply not like that any more; the scope of multiple affiliations and associations that have been opened up outside and beyond the nation-state has allowed a diasporic allegiance to become both more open and more acceptable. There is no longer any stability in the point of origin, no finality in the points of destination and no necessary coincidence between social and national identities. What nineteenth-century nationalists wanted was a 'space' for each 'race,' a territorializing of each social identity. What they got instead is a chain of cosmopolitan cities and an increasing proliferation of subnational and transnational identities that cannot easily be contained in the nation-state system" (R. Cohen 1997:174–175). Applying such notions specifically to the United States, we have the observation that "three powerful currents are undermining the integrity of national boundaries. The first is a long history of military, economic, and political intervention by the United States beyond its frontiers. The second is the growing transnational character of capitalism, its need to organize markets at a regional level. The third current undermining the nation state is that of migration. . . . Having spent the last century and a half violating, militarily, economically, politically, and culturally, the national boundaries of the region, the center now finds itself incapable of defending the violation of its own national borders. The costs of doing so are administratively, politically, and, most important, economically too high. Trade and the international division

of labor follow the flag. But they also set in motion what tears it down" (Patterson 1987:260).

9. For further commentary on the forces eroding the integrity of the nation-state, see Appadurai (1996:4; Hollinger (1995); Jacobson 1996: 107–138; and Young (1993).

10. Certain states and would-be nation-states have suffered chronic identity crises from the moment of inception, or even earlier. Two prominent examples are Canada, a country forever trying to characterize itself, and Israel with its never-ending dispute over what sort of state it is, theocratic or secular, Zionist, socialist, capitalist, or whatever. The United States has never overcome this kind of collective nervousness. "It is probable that only in the United States would a national body, appointed by the head of the state, embark on a study of the national purpose, as President Eisenhower's Commission on National Goals did in 1959" (Nye 1966:167).

11. As a thought experiment — but something any intrepid investigator could actually perform — consider the responses one might elicit by confronting a random sample of pedestrians on the street of an American city and asking them to volunteer a single term that best identifies them. I am willing to bet that religious or denominational affiliation would rank low among the responses.

12. "I am . . . skeptical that holding on to national or to ethnic or to any other form of particularistic culture can be anything more than a crutch. Crutches are not foolish. We often need them to restore our wholeness, but crutches are by definition transitional and transitory phenomena" (Wallerstein 1991:104).

13. We would also do well to question the authenticity not just of "neo-tribes" but of conventional tribes as well, social constructs we usually tend to regard as primordial and stable. There are many instances of Native American tribes (the Seminoles are a particularly strong example) that came into being in post-contact times as a result of governmental policy and actions. The African situation is scarcely different. To take two groups that have been much in the news recently, historians have ascertained that Ruanda's Hutu and Tutsi are the products of political machinations during the colonial period (Chrétien 1993:314–334; Mugiraneza 1988).

14. We dare not disregard the "racial" factor. As indicated earlier, it was certainly an element in the Anglo-American perceptions of eastern and southern European immigrants prior to World War I, although eventually these people were also recognized as Caucasians. Such an accommodation will be more problematic when so many of the post-1965 newcomers are so different from the western European ideal in terms of complexion and other visible bodily features.

CHAPTER 5. EXPLICATING THE AGE OF AUTHENTICITY

1. "A century after Whitman, it is useful to think of America as a polyethnic nation among polyethnic nations instead of *the* nation of nations. After all, polyethnic countries are the rule and not the exception in the world today, so that if diversity is the touchstone for divinely chosen peoplehood, then there must be many nations among the elect" (Sollors 1986:260).

2. "Contemporary immigration is a direct consequence of the dominant influence attained by the culture of the advanced West in every corner of the globe" (Portes and Rumbaut 1990:13).

3. For a richly informative account of the recent increase in number of denominations in the United States and the general diversification of the religious scene, see Kosmin and Lachman (1993), a volume based largely on the 1990 National Survey of Religious Identification.

4. "Rather than having the opportunity of a 60-year 'breathing space' within which to absorb and accommodate large cohorts of immigrants, the United States will more likely become a country of perpetual immigration. Unlike the European ethnics of the past, today's Latin Americans and Asians can expect to have their numbers continuously augmented by a steady supply of fresh arrivals from abroad. Rather than being a one-time historical phenomenon, immigration has become a permanent structural feature of the post-industrial society of the United States" (Massey 1995:643).

5. One is tempted to compare the influx of exotic immigrants with the many, sometimes intentional, intercontinental invasions of alien plants, animals, and microorganisms that have transformed so much of the world's biota in recent centuries. The difference is that the impact of the latter is often detrimental, whereas the introduction of alien cultures into the United States and other economically privileged countries has had, on balance, salutary cultural and economic effects. This is apparent most immediately in the realm of cuisine.

6. Among the more agitated expressions of concern over recent ethnic change in the United States, we have this: "Should current immigration levels be maintained or increased, the future of the United States, as a twenty-first-century national community, is dim" (Bouvier 1992:204); and "Without the dominance that once dictated, however ethnocentrically, what it meant to be an American, we are left with only tolerance and pluralism to hold us together. Unfortunately, the evidence from Los Angeles to New York, from Miami to Milwaukee, shows that such principles are not so powerful as we had believed or hoped" (Schwarz 1995:67).

7. The recent uproar in academe over the contents of the canon, i.e., the standard literary works that should form the core of a liberal educa-

tion (see, e.g., Fox-Genovese [1990], Ravitch [1990], and Schlesinger [1992]), obviously parallels and is related to the controversy over immigration.

8. "Public acknowledgment of language diversity as fully *American* . . . symbolizes acceptance of 'cultural' diversity and therefore of a broader range of the full identities of non-European Americans. In any case, this 'reconstruction' of American national identity means that European-origin Americans are themselves being constructed anew as 'ethnics' (for example, as 'Anglos' or 'Euro-Americans') rather than as 'just Americans.' A truly multi-cultural and multi-racial understanding of American national identity, in short, would mean that European-origin Americans would be 'reduced,' from being the standard, the prototype, against which all the *Others* are to judge their own 'Americanness' to being one ethnic group among many in a 'decentered' multi-cultural polity" (Schmidt 1993 : 88; emphasis in original). "How does an ethnic group that has historically been dominant in its society adjust to a more modest and balanced role? . . . As the population of the United States shifts to embrace ever-larger numbers of previously marginalized groups, there is an emerging need to take a close look at the changing role of white Americans. . . . As our percentage of the population declines, our commitment to the future must change. Even though we are undeniably connected by history and ethnicity with a long legacy of oppression, this identification with the oppressor is not our only means of defining ourselves" (Howard 1993 : 36). Also see Crawford (1992).

9. The best bibliographic guide to the literature on American multiculturalism I have come across, though a bit dated now, is Buenker and Ratner (1992).

10. The term *polyculture* has only biological significance. The *OED* offers no entries for *polyethnic* or *multiethnic*.

11. "The word 'multicultural' has had a fitful beginning in the World War II era, appearing in non-trendsetting situations such as a *New York Herald-Tribune Books* attack on prejudice on 27 July, 1941, or, in 1959, a description of Montreal as multicultural (*Oxford English Dictionary*). . . . The word had a far more developed existence in British Commonwealth countries such as Canada and Australia. . . . The United States' understanding of multiculturalism will remain incomplete until it develops a picture of other international varieties" (Newfield and Gordon 1996 : 94). The career of the term *globalization* closely resembles that of *multiculturalism*. "Use of the noun 'globalization' has developed quite recently. Certainly in academic circles it was not recognized as a significant concept, in spite of diffuse and intermittent usage prior to that,

until the early, or even middle, 1980s. During the second half of the 1980s its use increased enormously, so much so that it is virtually impossible to trace the patterns of its contemporary diffusion across a large number of areas of contemporary life in different parts of the world. By now, even though the term is often used very loosely and indeed, in contradictory ways, it has *itself* become part of 'global consciousness,' an aspect of the remarkable proliferation of terms centered upon 'global'" (Robertson 1992:9).

12. In reviewing pluralism and similar concepts, one should keep in mind the fact that the definitions thereof are part of a larger debate and that "the debate about multiculturalism, . . . at its most fundamental, represents a shift from the notion of a pluralist society composed of a mosaic of separate cultures — to a view of America as a complex but common social system, one that has propagated and, more strikingly, produced significant cultural differences within itself. Correspondingly, the conceptualizations of ethnicity reviewed represent a movement from nationalist mystification to postnational self-reflexivity" (Buell 1994: 157–158).

13. "The movement for cultural democracy helped define the ambience of the New Deal years. The increased power of ethnics and the drive to unify the country against fascism called forth a new set of cultural imperatives. Diversity became legitimate, even desirable. Prejudice and intolerance became pathologies to be studied and cured. Minorities acquired cultural rights in addition to legal ones. The generation of the 1930s failed to fulfill its promise of ethnic democracy, but the ideal speaks to us still" (Weiss 1979:585).

14. The multiple definitions and perceptions of multiculturalism reflect more than semantic confusion. The meanings depend upon who is using the term and to what ends. "The concept of 'multiculturalism,' then, is polysemically open to various interpretations and subject to diverse political force-fields: it has become an empty signifier onto which diverse groups project their hopes and fears. In its more coopted version, it easily degenerates into a state or corporate-managed United-Colors-of-Benetton pluralism whereby established power promotes ethnic 'flavors of the month' for commercial or ideological purposes. In institutional terms, Ada Gay Griffin posits a spectrum of models of multiculturalism, varying in their degree of participation by POC (people of color): the IBM model (White executive staff plus a few token Blacks); the Spook model (a POC plots to empower other POCs); the Benetton model (POCs are visually conspicuous but decision-makers are White); the Abolitionist model (progressive Whites consult with POCs but retain power); the Nkrumah model (POCs trans-

form a White institution into an organ responsive to their own concerns); and the Mugabe model (in a multiracial coalition, POCs enjoy
decision-making power). In other national contexts, multiculturalism
radically alters its valence. In Canada, it designates official largely cosmetic government programs — the object of satire in Srinivas Krishna's
Massala, 1991 — designed to placate the *québecois*, Native Canadians,
Blacks, and Asians. In Latin America, intellectuals worry about a new
'multicultural' neocolonialism" (Shohat and Stam 1994:47). "Some
of these conflicts over the basic meaning of the mere word 'multiculturalism' follow from the remarkable range of uses to which it's been
put. It has indeed referred to 'the life of various ethnic groups, racial
diversity, gender differences, international issues, non-Western culture,
cross-cultural methodologies, sexual preference, and the physically
challenged. But the term also manifests mainstream American irreso-
lution about these four conflicts. Does a democratic United States have
one or many centers? Will the bottom or the top control intergroup
conflict — will control be relatively popular or relatively elite?" (Gordon and Newfield 1996:7).

15. "The stereotypes of an earlier day were far more hateful and far more
cruel than those today. Today, one seldom encounters [as I did in the
1940s] people who regard the Japanese as cruel, sly, and treacherous or
who fear that Jews will kidnap their young children for ritual blood
sacrifices. Fewer people today accept negative ethnic-group stereotypes than at the time of the civil rights movement. Changes have also
occurred in the motivation of people to discriminate against others
in everyday settings: in public accommodations (i.e., restaurants), in
schools and in the workplace, in voting practices, and in political office.
To be sure, neighborhood segregation persists in almost all cities and,
in many, has gotten worse. Intergroup friendships that cross ethnic
and racial lines are still not as frequent as within-group friendships. Although the prevailing social norms still prescribe considerable social
distance between many ethnically different people in intimate settings,
much less distance is prescribed in public and casual settings" (Pincus
and Ehrlich 1994:4–5). "For all the history of separation and name-
calling, stereotyping and oversimplification, Americans now see race
relations in hues far more subtle than black and white. . . . What's perhaps most striking in these [opinion poll] data is the increase over the
past couple of decades in the proportions of both [racial] groups reporting interactions with members of the other group as friends and
neighbors" (Ladd 1998:50).

16. Not all observers were pleased by this turn of events, e.g., Niemonen
(1993), who criticizes the unexamined liberal axioms of the authors.

17. We still await a comprehensive monograph on the history, circumstances, and consequences of Hart-Celler, but, for useful interim accounts, see Millman (1997:60–69) and Winnick (1990:xii–xvii).

18. "The paradigmatic example of metaracism is modern Army life. Here is a system, immensely powerful and capable of exercising its will upon individual personalities, which has elevated the lot of black men within its ranks to the highest general level that they have enjoyed in American history. The top echelons are [or were] pure white, to be sure, but in any number of lesser positions, Negroes have done well, are accorded an equality much closer to actuality than that obtainable outside, and indeed are quite frequently in positions of command over white troops. No wonder then that the Moynihan Report proclaimed the military as perhaps the best way to black manhood. Yet what kind of manhood is so fostered by military life? Isn't it simply the mechanized — indeed robotized — reduction of humanity to selfless tools of the will of culture, the grind of both black and white into gray? Nowhere in our culture is there less freedom, less autonomy, less originality, joy and affirmation; nowhere is there more cold calculation, more mindless regimentation, more dullness, more banality — and more racial equality. And nowhere else is the integrated anal-sadistic wish of the Western matrix raised to such a pitch of perfection, nowhere else is the exteriorized destructivity of our culture so perfectly expressed" (Kovel 1970:216–217).

19. "These findings very clearly reinforce the conclusions of all earlier studies that race remains a more dominant basis for segregation than does class, that class variation can only explain a small part of racial segregation. . . . Middle-class and rich Asians have succeeded in suburbanizing and integrating to a meaningful degree. But, even in liberal Seattle, without a large, poor underclass black ghetto, upper-class black households are not significantly suburbanized or integrated, and they remain as segregated as poor blacks" (Morrill 1995:39–40).

20. Too often overlooked is the fact that in absolute numbers poor whites comprise the largest portion of any socioeconomically defined underclass. Furthermore, they do tend to be segregated spatially in most cities.

21. "Children of nonwhite immigrants may not even have the opportunity to gain access to the white mainstream, no matter how acculturated they become. Joining those native circles to which they do have access may prove a ticket to permanent subordination and disadvantage" (Portes 1995a:274). For further discussion of the phenomenon, see Buriel and De Ment (1995), Hurh and Kim (1984:162–163), Keefe and Padilla (1987:191, 193), Lieberson (1980), and Waters (1994).

22. "'Demonstration Negroes' are summoned up to improve a corporation's image or when advertisers need them to sell more synthetic junk to keep the wheels of production turning" (Kovel 1970:217). But the visibility of such role models imposes a heavy penalty upon their community. "Television, despite the liberal intentions of many of its writers, has pushed our culture backward. White people are not prepared to deal with the problem of racial inequality because they no longer see that there *is* a problem. *The Cosby Show*, our study showed, is an integral part of this process of public disenlightenment. Commercial television becomes Dr. Feelgood, indulging its white viewers so that their response to racial inequality becomes a guiltless, self-righteous inactivity. Television performs an ideological conjuring trick that plays neatly into the hands of free market proponents in the Republican party, with their irresistible recipe of 'don't worry, be happy'" (Jhally and Lewis 1992:136).

23. Kovel's extended discussion of metaracism (1970:215–225) merits close consideration.

24. Kent also offer this succinct definition: "The core of symbolic racism: *the chasm between the change in racial norms and the absence of commitment to equalizing conditions*" (1993:70; emphasis in original).

25. "Although television portrays a world of equal opportunity, most white people know that in the world at large, black people achieve less material success, on the whole, than white people. They know that black people are disproportionately likely to live in poor neighborhoods and drop out of school. How can this knowledge be reconciled with the smiling faces of the Huxtables? If we are blind to the roots of racial inequality embedded in our society's class structure, then there *is* only one way to reconcile this paradoxical state of affairs. If white people are disproportionately successful, then they must be disproportionately smarter or more willing to work hard. The face of Cliff Huxtable begins to fade into the more sinister and threatening face of Willie Horton. Although few respondents were prepared to be this explicit (although a number came close), their failure to acknowledge class or racial barriers means that this is the only other explanation that makes any sense" (Jhally and Lewis 1992:136).

26. The sidebars in DeMott's magazine article tell the tale: "Day after day the nation's corporate ministries of culture churn out images of racial harmony"; "These messages and images allow the comfortable white majority to tell itself a fatuous untruth"; "Acts of private piety substitute for public policy while the possibility of political action disappears into a sentimental haze"; "We diminish historical catastrophes affect-

ing millions over centuries and inflate the significance of brief racial tendernesses."

27. The foregoing observations are hardly exclusively American in relevance. For the comparable situation in New Zealand, see Spoonley (1988:104–105).

28. Is it mere coincidence that the next five authors to be cited all happen to be female?

29. In writing about "white culture," Dean MacCannell (1992:122) asks, "How is consensus achieved on this matter, a consensus which extends to include both the groups in power and the ethnic peoples out of power? This consensus structures our institutions so that, for example, in tourism we have ethnic cuisine but no white cuisines; in the university we have ethnic studies programs, but no white studies programs. This structural imbalance is fundamental, operating on grammar and rhetoric as well as in social and economic relations."

30. For reasonably objective surveys and discussions of American multiculturalism, see Gordon and Newfield (1996), Hollinger (1992), Isbister (1996:186–194), Kisubi (1997), and Manning (1995a).

31. Although he never says so outright, Benjamin Schwarz (1995) strongly implies that only "ethnic cleansing" can provide the country with long-term stability.

32. In his *White Jacket* Herman Melville offers us a peroration on the American mission that, for sheer perfervid passion, would be difficult to match. "Escaped from the house of bondage, Israel of old did not follow after the ways of the Egyptians. To her was given new things under the sun. And we Americans are the peculiar, chosen people — the Israel of our time: we bear the ark of the liberties of the world. Seventy years ago we escaped from thrall; and, besides our first birth-right — embracing one continent of earth — God has given us, for a future inheritance, the broad domains of the political pagans, without bloody hands being lifted. God has predestined, mankind expects, great things from our race; and great things we feel in our souls. The rest of the nations must soon be in our rear. We are the pioneers of the world; the advance-guard, sent on through the wilderness of untried things, to break a new path in the New World that is ours. In our youth is our strength; in our inexperience, our wisdom. At a period when other nations have but lisped, our deep voice is heard afar. Long enough have we been sceptics with regard to ourselves, and doubted whether, indeed, the political Messiah had come. But he has come in *us*, if we would but give utterance to his promptings. And let us always remember that with ourselves, almost for the first time in the history of

earth, national selfishness is unbounded philanthropy; for we cannot do a good to America, but we give alms to the world" (1850:180–181). However, below the surface of his later writings, the implicit message concerning America's role in human history is a good deal less exuberant.

33. "The search by Americans for a precise definition of their national purpose, and their absolute conviction that they have such a purpose, provide one of the most powerful threads in the development of American ideology. All nations, of course, have long agreed that they are chosen peoples; the idea of special destiny is as old as nationalism itself. However, no nation in modern history has been quite so consistently dominated as the United States by the belief that it has a particular mission in the world, and a unique contribution to make to it" (Nye 1966:164).

34. For a subtle, carefully argued programmatic statement advancing the thesis that there is a middle ground, one both desirable and feasible, between the extreme positions of the partisans in the ongoing debate over multiculturalism, see Hollinger (1992).

35. Also see Yang et al. (1997) for an exceedingly thorough, breezy, and entertaining account of Asian influences on virtually every aspect of American culture, popular and otherwise.

36. Neither has stinted when it comes to lobbying activity, but there is no overt Jewish equivalent to the congressional Black Caucus.

37. The Yiddish-language radio programs that were regularly scheduled in major metropolitan listening areas a generation or two ago seem to have vanished, as has also *The Goldbergs*, a radio serial that won the loyalty of a large general public for a good many years. Among our contemporary stand-up comedians on television and stage, the number who are aggressively Jewish is far smaller than that of their black counterparts.

38. In a certain sense, a quite derogatory form of cultural slumming began in the mid nineteenth century when minstrel shows, presented before white audiences, used white performers in blackface. Racist degradation was raised to an exquisitely painful level in the 1920s when highly talented black artists appeared in performances at Harlem's Cotton Club, from which black patrons were excluded.

39. For an extended, lacerating account of the psychological and behavioral difficulties encountered by African Americans as they circulate between their own cultural domain and that of Euro-Americans, see Shipler (1997).

40. The multicultural problem as it plays out in the United States is a local manifestation of a general dilemma to be encountered in many

other lands: How are unlike ethnic/racial groups to arrive at some am-
icable formula for coexistence? Within a broad spatial arena, it relates
also to those clashes between sovereign states that are based on perceived cultural antagonisms. Failure to find solutions, at either the domestic or international level, has led in the past to considerable bloodshed, injustice, and all manner of misery. And, as for the future, this
sociocultural challenge bears the potential to breed further lethal
strife. It is one, if the least immediate, of three macrocrises threatening the well-being, if not survival, of civilization, the others being
maintenance of a wobbly globalized economy that may be in the
throes of a terminal pathology; and the devising of a sustainable
modus vivendi between a hyperactive human species and a belea-
guered planetary ecosystem. (At some profound level, these three
huge problems may well be linked together.) Even though no plausible scenarios have been set forth that could address the latter two
crises, we may take some comfort in having the destination for the
first, a perfected Multiculturalism 3 to contemplate, however remote
the prospect of serious implementation in the absence of a clearly
marked road map. But confronting and overcoming any or all of the
three macrocrises will do little or nothing to alleviate still another crisis. Even though it may not result in loss of life, livelihood, or habitat,
the world's increasingly virulent identity crisis is deeply debilitating
psychologically, and its long-term effects unpredictable but baleful.
Even in that highly unlikely consummation of a multiculturally bliss-
ful, economically and ecologically viable world, we shall probably still
remain haunted and torn by the questions "Who am I?" and "What
are we?" But perhaps I have wandered too far afield.

REFERENCES

An asterisk indicates an item of special interest or importance.

Abramson, Harold. 1980. "Assimilation and pluralism theories." In Stephan Thernstrom, ed. *Harvard Encyclopedia of American Ethnic Groups*, 150–160. Cambridge: Harvard University Press.

Abu-Lughod, Janet L., et al. 1994. *From Urban Village to East Village: The Battle for New York's Lower East Side*. Cambridge, Mass.: Blackwell.

Adamic, Louis. 1940. *From Many Lands*. New York: Harper & Brothers.

Adams, Paul. 1998. "Network topologies and virtual place." *Annals of the Association of American Geographers* 88 : 88–106.

Agbayani-Siewert, Pauline, and Linda Revilla. 1995. "Filipino Americans." In Pyong Gap Min, ed. *Asian Americans: Contemporary Trends and Issues*, 134–168. Thousand Oaks, Calif.: Sage.

Agocs, Carol. 1981. "Ethnic settlement in a metropolitan area: A typology of communities." *Ethnicity* 8 : 127–148.

Ahne, Joseph. 1995. "Koreans of Chicago: The new entrepreneurial immigrants." In Melvin G. Holli and Peter d'A. Jones, eds. *Ethnic Chicago: A Multicultural Portrait*, 463–500. 4th ed. Grand Rapids, Mich.: William B. Eerdmans.

*Alba, Richard D. 1985a. *Italian Americans: Into the Twilight of Ethnicity*. Englewood Cliffs, N.J.: Prentice-Hall.

———. 1985b. "The twilight of ethnicity among Americans of European ancestry: The case of Italians." In Alba, ed. *Ethnicity and Race in the U.S.A.: Toward the Twenty-First Century*, 134–158. London: Routledge & Kegan Paul.

*———. 1990. *Ethnic Identity: The Transformation of White America*. New Haven: Yale University Press.

———. 1993. "Minority proximity to whites in suburbs: An individual-level analysis of segregation." *American Journal of Sociology* 98 : 1338–1427.

Alba, Richard D., and John R. Logan. 1991. "Variations on two themes: Racial and ethnic patterns in the attainment of suburban residence." *Demography* 28 : 431–453.

Alba, Richard D., Nancy A. Denton, Shu-yin Leung, and John R. Logan. 1995. "Neighborhood change under conditions of mass immigration:

The New York City region, 1970–1990." *International Migration Review* 29 : 625– 656.

Albers, Patricia C., and William R. James. 1986. "On the dialectics of ethnicity: To be or not to be Santee (Sioux)." *Journal of Ethnic Studies* 14 : 1–28.

Allen, James P. 1977. "Recent immigration from the Philippines and Filipino communities in the United States." *Geographical Review* 67 : 195–208.

*Allen, James P. and Eugene J. Turner. 1988. *We the People: An Atlas of America's Ethnic Diversity*. New York: Macmillan.

———. 1996. "Spatial patterns of immigrant assimilation." *Professional Geographer* 48 : 140–155.

*———. 1997. *The Ethnic Quilt: Population Diversity in Southern California*. Northridge: California State University, Center for Geographical Studies.

Allen, Theodore W. 1994. *The Invention of the White Race*. Vol. 2 of *Racial Oppression and Social Control*. London: Verso.

Almirol, Edwin B. 1985. *Ethnic Identity and Social Negotiation: A Study of a Filipino Community in California*. New York: AMS Press.

Alter, Robert. 1972. "A fever of ethnicity." *Commentary* 53 : 68–73.

Anderson, Benedict. 1983. *Imagined Communities: Reflections on the Origin and Spread of Nationalism*. London: Verso.

———. 1994. "Exodus." *Critical Inquiry* 20 : 314–327.

Anderson, Kay J. 1987. "The idea of Chinatown: The power of place and institutional practice in the making of a racial category." *Annals of the Association of American Geographers* 77 : 580–598.

Anderson, Margo, and Stephen E. Fienberg. 1995. "Black, white, and shades of gray (and brown and yellow)." *Chance* 7 : 15–18.

Ansari, Mahoud. 1992. *The Making of the Iranian Community in America*. New York: Pardis Press.

*Appadurai, Arjun. 1990. "Disjuncture and difference in the global cultural economy." In Mike Featherstone, ed. *Global Culture: Nationalism, Globalization and Modernity*, 295–310. London: Sage.

———. 1991. "Global ethnoscapes: Notes and queries for a transnational anthropology." In Richard G. Fox, ed. *Recapturing Anthropology: Working in the Present*, 191–210. Santa Fe: School of American Research Press.

*———. 1993. "Patriotism and its futures." *Public Culture* 5 : 411–430.

*———. 1996. *Modernity at Large: Cultural Dimensions of Globalization*. Minneapolis: University of Minnesota Press.

Apraku, Kofi K. 1991. *African Émigrés in the United States: A Missing Link in Africa's Social and Economic Development*. New York: Praeger.

Arce, Carlos. 1981. "A reconsideration of Chicano culture and identity." *Daedalus* 110:177–191.

Armstrong, John A. 1982. *Nations before Nationalism*. Chapel Hill: University of North Carolina Press.

Arreola, Daniel D. 1984a. "Mexican American housescapes." *Geographical Review* 74:299–31.

———. 1984b. "Mexican American exterior murals." *Geographical Review* 74:409–424.

Auerbach, Susan. 1991. "The brokering of ethnic folklore: Issues of selection and presentation at a multicultural festival." In Stephen Stern and John Allan Cicala, eds. *Creative Ethnicity: Symbols and Strategies of Contemporary Ethnic Life*, 223–238. Logan: Utah State University Press.

Aversa, Alfred. 1978. "Italian neo-ethnicity: The search for self-identity." *Journal of Ethnic Studies* 6:49–56.

Axtell, James. 1985. *The Invasion Within: The Contest of Cultures in Colonial North America*. New York: Oxford University Press.

Bakalian, Anny. 1993. *Armenian-Americans: From Being to Feeling American*. New Brunswick, N.J.: Transaction Publishers.

Barnet, Richard J., and John Cavanagh. 1994. *Global Dreams: Imperial Corporations and the New World Order*. New York: Simon & Schuster.

Barone, Michael. 1994. "A turning point in the Italian-American experience." In Lydio F. Tomasi, Piero Gastoldo, and Thomas Row, eds. *The Columbus People: Perspectives in Italian Migration to the Americas and Australia*, 491–495. Staten Island: Center for Immigration Studies.

Bartel, Ann P. 1989. "Where do the new U.S. immigrants live?" *Journal of Labor Economics* 7:371–391.

Barth, Fredrik. 1969. Introduction to Barth, ed. *Ethnic Groups and Boundaries: The Social Organization of Cultural Difference*, 9–38. Boston: Little, Brown.

Barth, Miles. 1997. *Weegee's World*. Boston: Little, Brown.

*Basch, Linda, Nina Glick Schiller, and Cristina Szanton Blanc. 1994. *Nations Unbound: Transnational Projects, Postcolonial Predicaments, and Deterritorialized Nation-States*. Langhorne, Pa.: Gordon and Breach.

Bauböck, Rainer, Agnes Heller, and Aristide R. Zolberg, eds. 1996. *The Challenge of Diversity: Integration and Pluralism in Societies of Immigration*. Aldershot, U.K.: Avebury, 1996.

*Bauman, Zygmunt. 1992. *Intimations of Postmodernity*. London: Routledge.

———. 1996. "Morality in the age of contingency." In Paul Heelas,

Scott Lash, and Paul Morris, eds. *Detraditionalization: Critical Reflections on Authority and Identity*, 49–58. Oxford: Blackwell.

Beale, Calvin L. 1994. "Asian and Pacific Islanders in rural and small town America." Unpublished paper. Washington, D.C.

Bell, Bernard W. 1987. *The Afro-American Novel and Its Tradition*. Amherst: University of Massachusetts Press.

*Bell, Daniel. 1975a. "Ethnicity and social change." In Nathan Glazer and Daniel P. Moynihan, eds. *Ethnicity: Theory and Experience*, 141–174. Cambridge: Harvard University Press.

———. 1975b. "The end of American exceptionalism." *Public Interest* 41:193–224.

Benkin, Richard L., and Grace DeSantis. "Creating ethnicity: East European Jews and Lithuanians in Chicago." *Sociological Focus* 15: 231–248.

Bennett, Linda A. 1976. Patterns of ethnic identity among Serbs, Croats, and Slovenes in Washington, D.C. Ph.D. dissertation, American University.

———. 1981. "Washington and its Serbian émigrés: A disinctive blend." *Anthropological Quarterly* 54:82–88.

Berkhofer, Robert F., Jr. 1978. *The White Man's Indian: Images of the American Indian from Columbus to the Present*. New York: Knopf.

Berlin, Isaiah. 1972. "The bent twig: A note on nationalism." *Foreign Affairs* 51:11–30.

Bernardi, Daniel, ed. 1996. *The Birth of Whiteness: Race and the Emergence of U.S. Cinema*. New Brunswick: Rutgers University Press.

Bernstein, Matthew, and Gaylyn Studlar. 1997. *Visions of the East: Orientalism in Film*. New Brunswick: Rutgers University Press.

Bershtel, Sara, and Allen Graubard. 1982. *Saving Remnants: Feeling Jewish in America*. New York: Free Press.

Bhardwaj, Surinder M., and N. Madhusudana Rao. 1990. "Asian Indians in the United States: A geographic appraisal." In Colin Clarke, Ceri Peach, and Steven Vertovec, eds. *South Asians Overseas: Migration and Ethnicity*, 197–217. Cambridge: Cambridge University Press.

Binder, Frederick M., and David M. Reimers. 1995. *All the Nations under Heaven: An Ethnic and Racial History of New York City*. New York: Columbia University Press.

Blanck, Dag. 1989. "Constructing an ethnic identity: The case of the Swedish-Americans." In Peter Kivisto, ed. *The Ethnic Enigma: The Salience of Ethnicity for European-Origin Groups*, 134–152. Philadelphia: Balch Institute Press.

Blaut, James M. 1987. "The myth of assimilation." In *The National Question: Decolonising the Theory of Nationalism*, 142–171. London: Zed.

Blevins, Irene. 1993. Personal communication, September 20.

* Bobo, Lawrence, James R. Kluegel, and Ryan A. Smith. 1997. "Laissez-faire racism: The crystallization of a 'kinder, gentler' anti-black ideology." In Steven A. Tuch and Jack K. Martin, eds. *Racial Attitudes in the 1990s: Continuity and Change*, 15–42. Greenwood, Conn.: Praeger.

* Bodnar, John. 1985. *The Transplanted: A History of Immigrants in Urban America*. Bloomington: Indiana University Press.

———. 1992. *Remaking America: Public Memory, Commemoration, and Patriotism in the Twentieth Century*. Princeton: Princeton University Press.

Bogle, Donald. 1973. *Toms, Coons, Mulattoes, Mammies and Bucks: An Interpretive History of Blacks in American Films*. New York: Viking.

Bonacich, Edna. 1980. "Class approaches to ethnicity and race." *Insurgent Sociologist* 10 : 9–22.

Bonnett, Aubrey W. 1990. "West Indians in the United States of America: Some theoretical and practical considerations." In Bonnett and G. Llewellyn Watson, eds. *Emerging Perspectives on the Black Diaspora*, 149–163. Lanham, Md.: University Press of America.

Boone, Margaret S. 1989. *Capital Cubans: Refugee Adaptation in Washington, D.C.* New York: AMS Press.

Bourne, Randolph. 1920. *History of a Literary Radical, and Other Essays*. New York: B. W. Huebsch.

Bouvier, Leon F. 1992. *Peaceful Invasions: Immigration and Changing America*. Lanham, Md.: University Press of America.

Boyd, Monica. 1992. "Measuring ethnicity in the future: Taking winding paths down slippery slopes and into murky swamps." Paper presented at the Joint Canada–United States Conference on the Measurement of Ethnicity, Ottawa, April 1992.

Bozorgmehr, Mehdi. 1992. Internal ethnicity: Armenian, Bahai, Jewish, and Muslim Iranians in Los Angeles. Ph.D. dissertation, University of California, Los Angeles.

Bradshaw, Carla K. 1992. "Beauty and the beast: On racial ambiguity." In Maria P. P. Root, ed. *Racially Mixed People in America*, 77–88. Newbury Park, Calif.: Sage.

Brimelow, Peter. 1995. *Alien Nation: Common Sense about America's Immigration Disaster*. New York: Random House.

Broadway, Michael J. 1986. "Indochinese refugee settlement patterns in Garden City, Kansas." *Transactions of the Kansas Academy of Science* 90 : 127–137.

Brown, Linda Keller, and Kay Musell, eds. 1984. *Ethnic and Regional*

Foodways in the United States: The Performance of Group Identity.
Knoxville: University of Tennessee Press.

Brunn, Stanley D., Jeffrey A. Jones, and Darren Purcell. 1994. "Ethnic
communities in the evolving 'electronic' state: Cyberplaces in
cyberspace." In Werner A. Gallusser, ed. *Political Boundaries and
Coexistence: Proceedings of the IGU Symposium*, 415–424. Basle,
Switzerland, 24–27 May 1994. Berne: Peter Lang.

Brunn, Stanley D., and Darren Purcell. 1996. "Ethnic 'electronic
communities': New immigrant linkages in a wired world." In Matjaz
Klemencic, ed. *Fraternalism in Immigrant Countries*, 337–343.
Maribor, Slovenia: Univerza v Maribor.

* Buell, Frederick. 1994. *National Culture and the New Global System*.
Baltimore: Johns Hopkins University Press.

Buenker, John D., and Lorman A. Ratner. 1992. "Bibliographical essay."
In *Multiculturalism in the United States: A Comparative Guide to
Acculturation and Ethnicity*, 231–258. Westport, Conn.: Greenwood
Press.

Burayidi, Michael A. 1997. "Multicultural nations in a monocultural
world: An introduction." In Burayidi, ed. *Multiculturalism in a Cross-
National Perspective*, 1–14. Lanham, Md.: University Press of America.

Buriel, Raymond, and Terri De Ment. 1995. "Immigration and
sociocultural change in Mexican-, Chinese-, and Vietnamese-
American families." Paper presented at the National Symposium
on International Migration and Family Change, Pennsylvania State
University, November 1995.

Buttlar, Lois. 1995. "Ethnic cultural institutions in the United States: A
statistical analysis." *Ethnic Forum* 15:61–77.

Cadaval, Olivia. 1989. The Hispano-American festival and the Latino
community: Creating an identity in the nation's capital. Ph.D.
dissertation, George Washington University.

———. 1991. "Making a place home: The Latino festival." In Stephen
Stern and John Allan Cicala, eds. *Creative Ethnicity: Symbols and
Strategies of Contemporary Ethnic Life*, 204–222. Logan: Utah State
University Press.

Calhoun, Craig. 1993. "Nationalism and ethnicity." *Annual Review of
Sociology* 19:211–238.

Campbell, Bebe Moore. 1982. "What happened to the Afro? Changing
hairstyles reflect new roles and new definitions." *Ebony* 37:79–85.

Carlson, Alvar W. 1975 "Filipino and Indian immigrants in Detroit and
suburbs." *Philippine Geographical Journal* 19:199–209.

———. 1978. "The mapping of recent immigrant settling in Cleveland

and Cuyahoga County based upon petitions for naturalization."
Ecumene [East Texas State University] 10:27–34.

Carman, J. Neale. 1962. *Foreign Language Units of Kansas. 1: Historical Atlas and Statistics*. Lawrence: University of Kansas Press.

Carney, George O. 1994. "From down home to uptown: The diffusion of country music radio stations in the United States." In Carney, ed. *The Sounds of People and Places: A Geography of American Folk and Popular Music*, 161–175. 3rd ed. Lanham, Md.: Rowman & Littlefield.

Cary, Francine Curro, ed. 1996. *Urban Odyssey: A Multicultural History of Washington, D.C.* Washington: Smithsonian Institution Press.

Casey, Daniel J., and Robert E. Rhodes, eds. 1979. *Irish-American Fiction: Essays in Criticism*. New York: AMS Press.

Cassidy, Frederic G., ed. 1985, 1991, 1996. *Dictionary of American Regional English*. 3 vols. Cambridge: Harvard University Press.

Castells, Manuel. 1997. *The Power of Identity*. Oxford: Blackwell.

Chaliand, Gerard, and Jean-Pierre Rageau. 1995. *The Penguin Atlas of Diasporas*. New York: Viking.

Chávez, John R. 1984. *The Lost Land: The Chicano Image of the Southwest*. Albuquerque: University of New Mexico Press.

Chen, Hsiang-shui. 1992. *Chinatown No More: Taiwan Immigrants in Contemporary New York*. Ithaca: Cornell University Press.

Cheng, Lucie, and Philip Q. Yang. 1996. "Asians, the 'model minority,' deconstructed." In Roger Waldinger and Mehdi Bozorgmehr, eds. *Ethnic Los Angeles*, 305–344. New York: Russell Sage Foundation.

Chin, Frank, Jeffrey Paul Chan, Lawson Fusao Inada, and Shawn Hsu, eds. 1974. *Aiiieeeee! An Anthology of Asian-American Writers*. Washington: Howard University Press.

Chiswick, Barry R., and Teresa A. Sullivan. 1995. "The new immigrants." In Reynolds Farley, ed. *State of the Union, America in the 1990s*. Vol. 2. *Social Trends*, 211–270. New York: Russell Sage Foundation.

Chrétien, Jean-Pierre. 1993. *Burundi: L'Histoire retrouvée*. Paris: Karthala.

Chrisman, Noel J. 1981. "Ethnic persistence in an urban setting." *Ethnicity* 8:256–292.

Chudacoff, Howard P. 1973. "A new look at ethnic neighborhoods: Residential dispersion and the concept of visibility in a medium-sized city." *Journal of American History* 60:79–93.

Clark, Dennis. 1986. *Hibernia America: The Irish and Regional Cultures*. Westport, Conn.: Greenwood Press.

Clemens, Samuel L. 1880. *A Tramp Abroad*. Hartford: American Publishing Co.

Clifford, James. 1997. *Routes: Travel and Translation in the Late Twentieth Century*. Cambridge: Harvard University Press.

Clifton, James A. 1990. "Introduction: Memoir, exegesis." In Clifton, ed. *The Invented Indian: Cultural Fictions and Government Policies*, 1–28. New Brunswick, N.J.: Transaction.

Cockcroft, Eva, John Weber, and Jim Cockcroft. 1977. *Toward a People's Art: The Contemporary Mural Movement*. New York: Dutton.

Cohen, Abner. 1981. "Variables in ethnicity." In Charles F. Keyes, ed. *Ethnic Change*. 306–331. Seattle: University of Washington Press.

Cohen, Robin. 1997. *Global Diasporas: An Introduction*. Seattle: University of Washington Press.

Cohen, Ronald. 1978. "Ethnicity: Problem and focus in anthropology." *Annual Review of Anthropology* 7:379–403.

Conquergood, Dwight. 1992. "Life in Big Red: Struggles and accommodations in a Chicago polyethnic tenement." In Louise Lamphere, ed. *Structuring Diversity: Ethnographic Perspectives on the New Immigration*, 95–171. Chicago: University of Chicago Press.

Conzen, Kathleen Neils. 1985. "German-Americans and the invention of ethnicity." In Frank Trommler and Joseph McVeigh, eds. *America and the Germans: An Assessment of a Three-Hundred-Year History*, 131–147. Philadelphia: University of Pennsylvania Press.

———. 1989. "Ethnicity as festive culture: Nineteenth-century German America on parade." In Werner Sollors, ed. *The Invention of Ethnicity*, 44–76. New York: Oxford University Press.

———. 1991. "Mainstreams and side channels: The localization of immigrant cultures." *Journal of American Ethnic History* 11:5–20.

* Conzen, Kathleen Neils, David A. Gerber, Ewa Morawska, George E. Pozzetta, and Rudolph J. Vecoli. 1990. "The invention of ethnicity: A perspective from the USA." *Altreitalie* (April):37–62.

Conzen, Michael P. 1990. "Ethnicity on the land." In Conzen, ed. *The Making of the American Landscape*, 221–248. Boston: Unwin Hyman.

———. 1993. "Culture regions, homelands, and ethnic archipelagos in the United States: Methodological considerations." *Journal of Cultural Geography* 13:13–25.

———.1995. "The German-speaking ethnic archipelago in America." In Klaus Frantz and Robert Sauder, eds. *Ethnic Persistence and Change in Europe and America: Traces in Landscape and Society*, 67–92. Innsbruck: Veröffentlichungen der Universität Innsbruck.

Corbin, Alain. 1990. "The secret of the individual." In Michelle Perrot, ed. *A History of Private Life*. *4. From the French Revolution to the Great War*, 457–547. Cambridge and London: Harvard University Press.

Cortés, Carlos E. 1984. "The history of ethnic images in film: The search for a methodology." *MELUS* 11:63–77.

* Crawford, James. 1992. *Hold Your Tongue: Bilingualism and the Politics of "English Only."* Reading. Mass.: Addison-Wesley.

Cresce, Arthur R., Susan J. Lapham, and Stanley J. Rolark. 1992. "Preliminary evaluation of data from the race and ethnic origin questions in the 1990 Census." Paper presented at the annual meeting of the American Statistical Association, Boston, August 1992.

Creuzinger, Clementine G. K. 1987. The preservation of Ukrainian culture in Chicago with special reference to the role of the church. Master's paper, University of Chicago, Department of Geography.

Cripps, Thomas. 1993. *Making Movies Black: The Hollywood Message Movie from World War II to the Civil Rights Era*. New York: Oxford University Press.

Cruz, Jon. 1996. "From farce to tragedy: Reflections on the reification of race at century's end." In Avery F. Gordon and Christopher Newfield, eds. *Mapping Multiculturalism*, 19–39. Minneapolis: University of Minnesota Press.

Curry, Michael R. 1997. "The digital individual and the private realm." *Annals of the Association of American Geographers* 87: 681–699.

Curtis, James R. 1997. Personal communication, December 9.

Daniel, G. Reginald. 1992. "Passers and pluralists: Subverting the racial divide." In Marcia P. P. Root, ed. *Racially Mixed People in America*, 91–107. Newbury Park, Calif.: Sage.

Daniels, Roger. 1990. *Coming to America: A History of Immigration and Ethnicity in American Life*. New York: HarperCollins.

Danielson, Larry William. 1972. The ethnic festival and cultural revivalism in a small midwestern town. Ph.D. diss., Indiana University.

Dasgupta, Sathi S. 1989. *On the Trail of an Uncertain Dream: Indian Immigrant Experience in America*. New York: AMS Press.

* Davis, Fred. 1992. *Fashion, Culture, and Identity*. Chicago: University of Chicago Press.

Davis, Mike. 1998. *Ecology of Fear: Los Angeles and the Imagination of Disaster*. New York: Henry Holt.

Dear, Michael, and Steven Flusty. 1998. "Postmodern urbanism." *Annals of the Association of American Geographers* 88: 50–72.

* DeMott, Benjamin. 1995a. *The Trouble with Friendship: Why Americans Can't Think Straight about Race*. New York: Atlantic Monthly Press.
———. 1995b. "Put on a happy face: Masking the differences between blacks and whites." *Harper's Magazine*, September, 31–38.

* Denton, Nancy A., and Douglas S. Massey. 1991. "Patterns of neighborhood transition in a multiethnic world: U.S. metropolitan areas, 1970–1980." *Demography* 28,1: 41–63.

* DeSantis, Grace, and Richard Benkin. 1980. "Ethnicity without community." *Ethnicity* 7 : 137–143.

Desbarats, Jacqueline. 1979. "Thai migration to Los Angeles." *Geographical Review* 69 : 302–318.

De Vos, George. 1975. "Ethnic pluralism. Conflict and accommodation." In De Vos and Lola Romanucci-Ross, eds. *Ethnic Identity: Cultural Continuities and Change*, 5–41. Palo Alto: Mayfield.

Dickenson, John P. 1998. Personal communication, June 18.

DiMaggio, Paul, and Francie Ostrower. 1990. "Participation in the arts by black and white Americans." *Social Forces* 68 : 753–778.

Dingemans, Dennis, and Robin Datel. 1995. "Urban multiethnicity." *Geographical Review* 85 : 458–477.

Dinnerstein, Leonard, and David M. Reimers. 1988. *Ethnic Americans: A History of Immigration*. 3rd ed. New York: Harper & Row.

Dormon, James H. 1981. "Ethnicity in contemporary America." *American Studies* 15 : 325–339.

Dowler, Lorraine. 1996. Gendered prisons, gender, identity and place in Belfast, Northern Ireland. Ph.D. diss., Syracuse University.

———. 1997. Personal communication, September 24.

Drescher, Timothy W. 1994. *San Francisco Murals: Community Creates Its Muse, 1919–1994*. Saint Paul: Pogo Press.

Dugger, Celia W. 1998. "In India, an arranged marriage of 2 worlds." *New York Times*, 20 July, A1, A14–15.

Dunn, Robert G. 1998. *Identity Crises: A Social Critique of Postmodernity*. Minneapolis: University of Minnesota Press.

Eckert, Eva. 1998. "Language and ethnicity maintenance: Evidence of Czech tombstone inscriptions." *Markers 15: Annual Journal of the Association of Gravestone Studies*: 204–233.

Edmonston, Barry, and Jeffrey S. Passel. 1992. *The Future Immigrant Population of the United States*. Washington: Urban Institute.

———, eds. 1994. *Immigration and Ethnicity: The Integration of America's Newest Arrivals*. Washington: Urban Institute Press.

Edmonston, Barry, and Charles Schultze, eds. 1994. *Modernizing the U.S. Census*. Washington: National Academy Press.

Eicher, Joanne B., and Barbara Sumberg. 1995. "World fashion, ethnic, and national dress." In Eicher, ed. *Dress and Ethnicity: Change across Space and Time*, 295–306. Oxford: Berg.

Eisen, George, and David K. Wiggins, eds. 1994. *Ethnicity and Sport in North American History and Culture*. Westport, Conn.: Greenwood Press.

Eller, Jack David, and Reed M. Coughlan. 1993. "The poverty of primordialism: The demystification of ethnic attachments." *Ethnic and Racial Studies* 16:183–202.

Environmental Communications. 1977. *Big Art: Megamurals and Supergraphics*. Philadelphia: Running Press.

Erens, Patricia. 1984. *The Jew in American Cinema*. Bloomington: Indiana University Press.

Escobar, Gabriel. 1998. "The other pro soccer: In area's Latino leagues, part of the game is profit, and the best players are paid." *Washington Post*, 29 November, A1, A18–19.

Esman, Marjorie R. 1982. "Festivals, change, and unity: The celebration of ethnic unity among Louisiana Cajuns." *Anthropological Quarterly* 55:451–467.

———. 1984. "Tourism as ethnic preservation: The Cajuns of Louisiana." *Annals of Tourism Research* 11:451–467.

Espiritu, Yen Le. 1992. *Asian American Panethnicity: Bridging Institutions and Identities*. Philadelphia: Temple University Press.

———. 1995. *Filipino American Lives*. Philadelphia: Temple University Press.

Espiritu, Yen Le, and Ivan Light. 1991. "The changing ethnic shape of contemporary urban America." In M. Gottdiener and C. G. Pickvance, eds. *Urban Life in Transition*, 35–54. [*Urban Affairs Annual Review* 39.]

Estaville, Lawrence E. 1996. "American ethnic geography on the Internet." Paper presented at the Ninety-second Annual Meeting of the Association of American Geographers, Charlotte, April 1996.

Evans, E. Estyn. 1965. "The Scotch-Irish in the New World: An Atlantic heritage." *Journal of the Royal Society of Antiquaries of Ireland* 95:39–49.

Evinger, Suzanne. 1995. "How shall we measure our nation's diversity?" *Chance* 7:7–14.

Fanning, Charles. 1990. *The Irish Voice in America: Irish-American Fiction from the 1760s to the 1980s*. Lexington: University of Kentucky Press.

Farah, Douglas. 1996 "For Salvadoran émigrés, video is the tie that binds." *Washington Post*, 16 February, A1, A28.

Farhi, Paul. 2000. "TV's skin-deep take on race." *Washington Post*, 13 February, G1, G7.

Farley, Reynolds. 1990. "Race, ancestry and Spanish origin: Findings from the 1980s and questions for the 1990s." *1990 Proceedings of the Social Statistics Section of the American Statistical Association*, 11–16.

———. 1991. "The new census question about ancestry: What did it tell us?" *Demography* 28:411–429.

Fenton, John Y. 1988. *Transplanting Religious Traditions: Asian Indians in America*. New York: Praeger.

Fischer, David Hackett. 1989. *Albion's Seed: Four British Folkways in America*. New York and Oxford: Oxford University Press.

Fisher, Marc. 1995. "If the price is right, we sell." *Washington Post Magazine*, 29 January: 9–13, 18–22.

Fisher, Maxine P. 1980. *The Indians of New York City: A Study of Immigrants from India*. Colombia, Mo.: South Asia Books.

Fishkin, Shelley Fisher. 1995. "Interrogating 'whiteness,' complicating 'blackness': Remapping American culture." *American Quarterly* 47: 428–466.

Fishman, Joshua. 1966. *Language Loyalty in the United States*. The Hague: Mouton.

———. 1980. "Language maintenance." In Stephan Thernstrom, ed. *Harvard Encyclopedia of American Ethnic Groups*, 629–638. Cambridge: Harvard University Press.

* Fishman, Joshua, Michael Gergner, Esther G. Lowry, and William G. Milan. 1985. *The Rise and Fall of the Ethnic Revival: Perspectives on Language and Ethnicity*. Berlin: Mouton.

FitzGerald, Frances. 1979. *America Revised: History Schoolbooks in the Twentieth Century*. Boston: Little, Brown.

Fleming, Ronald Lee, and Renata Von Tscharner. 1987. *Place Makers: Creating Public Art That Tells You Where You Are*. New York: Harcourt Brace Jovanovich.

Foner, Nancy. 1987. "Introduction: New immigrants and changing patterns in New York City." In Foner, ed. *New Immigrants in New York*, 3–33. New York: Columbia University Press.

Fong, Timothy P. 1994. *The First Suburban Chinatown: The Remaking of Monterey Park, California*. Philadelphia: Temple University Press.

Fouron, Georges E. 1983. "The black immigrant dilemma in the U. S.: The Haitian experience." *Journal of Caribbean Studies* 3: 242–265.

Fox, Geoffrey. 1996. *Hispanic Nation: Culture, Politics, and the Constructing of Identity*. Secaucus, N.J.: Birch Lane Press.

Fox-Genovese, Elizabeth. 1990. "Between individualism and fragmentation: American culture and the new literary studies of race and gender." *American Quarterly* 42: 7–34.

Fraser, Nancy, and Linda Gordon. 1992. "A genealogy of dependency: Tracing a keyword of the welfare state." In Paul James, ed. *Critical Politics: From the Personal to the Global*, 77–109. Melbourne: Arena Publications.

Fredman, Ruth Gruber. 1981. "Cosmopolitans at home: The Sephardic Jews of Washington, D.C." *Anthropological Quarterly* 54: 61–67.

Fregoso, Rosa Linda. 1993. *The Bronze Screen: Chicana and Chicano Film Culture*. Minneapolis: University of Minnesota Press.

Freie, James F. 1998. *Counterfeit Community: The Exploitation of Our Longings for Connectedness*. Lanham, Md.: Rowman & Littlefield.

Frey, William H. 1994. "Minority suburbanization and continued 'white flight' in U.S. metropolitan areas: Assessing findings from the 1990 census." *Research in Community Sociology* 4 : 15–42.

Friedman, Jonathan. 1990. "Being in the world: Globalization and localization." In Mike Featherstone, ed., *Global Culture: Nationalism, Globalization and Modernity*, 311–328. London: Sage.

———. 1992. "Narcissism, roots and postmodernity: The constitution of selfhood in the global crisis." In Scott Lash and Jonathan Friedman, eds. *Modernity and Identity*, 331–366. Oxford: Blackwell.

Friedman, Lester D., ed. 1991. *Unspeakable Images: Ethnicity and the American Cinema*. Urbana: University of Illinois Press.

* Fuchs, Lawrence H. 1990. *The American Kaleidoscope: Race, Ethnicity, and the Civic Culture*. Hanover, N.H.: Wesleyan University Press.

Fuentes, Carlos. 1992. *The Buried Mirror: Reflections on Spain and the New World*. Boston: Houghton Mifflin.

Fugita, Stephen S., and David J. O'Brien. 1991. *Japanese American Ethnicity: The Persistence of Community*. Seattle: University of Washington Press.

* Gabaccia, Donna R. 1998. *We Are What We Eat: Ethnic Food and the Making of Americans*. Cambridge: Harvard University Press.

* Gans, Herbert J. 1979. "Symbolic ethnicity: The future of ethnic groups and cultures in America." *Ethnic and Racial Studies* 2 : 1–20.

———. 1992. "Comment: Ethnic invention and acculturation: A bumpy-line approach." *Journal of American Ethnic History* 12 : 42–52.

Gardophe, Fred L. 1987. "Italian-American fiction: A third generation renaissance." *MELUS* 14 : 69–85.

Garreau, Joel. 1981. *The Nine Nations of North America*. Boston: Houghton Mifflin.

Gates, Henry Louis, Jr., ed. 1997. *The Norton Anthology of African American Literature*. New York: W. W. Norton.

Gedmintas, Alexandras. 1989. *An Interesting Bit of Identity: The Dynamics of Ethnic Identity in a Lithuanian-American Community*. New York: AMS Press.

Georges, Eugenia. 1987. "A comment on Dominican ethnic associations." In Constance R. Sutton and Elsa M. Chaney, eds. *Caribbean Life in New York City: Sociocultural Dimensions*, 297–302. Staten Island: Center for Migration Studies of New York.

———. 1990. *The Making of a Transnational Community: Migration, Development, and Cultural Change in the Dominican Republic*. New York: Columbia University Press.

Gergen, Kenneth J. 1991. *The Saturated Self: Dilemmas of Identity in Contemporary Life*. New York: Basic Books.

*Glazer, Nathan. 1983. *Ethnic Dilemmas, 1964–1982*. Cambridge: Harvard University Press.

*———. 1988. Introduction to Glazer and Moynihan, eds. *Ethnicity: Theory and Experience*, 1–26. Cambridge: Harvard University Press.

Glazer, Nathan, and D. P. Moynihan. 1970. *Beyond the Melting Pot*. 2d. ed. Cambridge: MIT Press.

Glazer, Nathan, and Reed Ueda. 1983. *Ethnic Groups in History Textbooks*. Washington: Ethics and Public Policy Center.

*Gleason, Philip. 1982. "American identity and Americanization." In William Petersen, Michael Novak, and Gleason. *Concepts of Ethnicity*, 57–143. Cambridge: Harvard University Press.

*———. 1992. *Speaking of Diversity: Language and Ethnicity in Twentieth-Century America*. Baltimore: Johns Hopkins University Press.

Glick Schiller, Nina, Linda Basch, and Cristina Blanc-Szanton. 1992. "Transnationalism: A new analytic framework for understanding migration." In Glick Schiller et al., eds. *Towards a Transnational Perspective on Migration*, 1–24. [*Annals of the New York Academy of Sciences* 645, July 6].

Godfrey, Brian J. 1988. *Neighborhoods in Transition: The Making of San Francisco's Ethnic and Nonconformist Communities*. Berkeley: University of California Press.

Golab, Caroline. 1977. *Immigrant Destinations*. Philadelphia: Temple University Press.

Gold, Gerald L. 1979. "The French frontier of settlement in Louisiana: Some observations on culture change in Mamou Prairie." *Cahiers de Géographie du Québec* 23:263–280.

*Goldberg, Barry. 1992. "Historical reflections on transnationalism, race, and the American immigrant saga." In Nina Glick Schiller, Linda Basch, and Cristina Blanc–Szanton, eds. *Towards a Transnational Perspective on Migration*, 201–215. [*Annals of the New York Academy of Sciences* 645, July 6].

Goldscheider, Calvin. 1992. "What does ethnic/racial differentiation mean? Implications for measurement and analyses." Paper presented at Joint Canada–United States Conference on the Measurement of Ethnicity, Ottawa, April 1992.

Goldscheider, Calvin, and Alan S. Zuckerman. 1984. *The Transformation of the Jews*. Chicago: University of Chicago Press.

Goodstein, Laurie. 1997. "Women in Islamic headdress find faith and prejudice, too." *New York Times*, 3 November, A1, A21.

Gordon, Avery F., and Christopher Newfield. 1996. Introduction to

Gordon and Newfield, eds. *Mapping Multiculturalism*, 1–126. Minneapolis: University of Minnesota Press.

*Gordon, Milton M. 1964. *Assimilation in American Life*. New York: Oxford University Press.

———. 1978. "Assimilation in America: Theory and reality." In *Human Nature, Class, and Ethnicity*, 181–208. New York: Oxford University Press.

Gordon, Rena J., Joel S. Meister, and Robert G. Hughes. 1992. "Accounting for shortages of rural physicians: Push and pull factors." In Wilbert M. Gelser and Thomas C. Ricketts, eds. *Health in Rural North America: The Geography of Health Care Service and Delivery*, 153–178. New Brunswick: Rutgers University Press.

Grasmuck, Sherri, and Patricia R. Pessar. 1991. *Between Two Islands: Dominican International Migration*. Berkeley: University of California Press.

Graves, Thomas E. 1993. "Keeping Ukraine alive through death: Ukrainian-American gravestones as cultural markers." In Richard E. Meyer, ed. *Ethnicity and the American Cemetery*, 36–76. Bowling Green, Ohio: Bowling Green State University Popular Press.

Green, Rose Basile. 1974. *The Italian-American Novel: A Document of the Interaction of Two Cultures*. Rutherford, N.J.: Farleigh Dickinson University Press.

Greene, Victor. 1975. *For God and Country: The Rise of Polish and Lithuanian Ethnic Consciousness in America, 1860–1910*. Madison: State Historical Society of Wisconsin.

———. 1990. "Old-time folk dancing and music among the second generation, 1920–50." In Peter Kivisto and Dag Blanck, eds. *American Immigrants and Their Generations*, 142–163. Urbana: University of Illinois Press.

Griebel, Helen Bradley. 1995. "The West African origin of the African-American headwrap." In Joanne B. Eicher, ed. *Dress and Ethnicity: Change across Space and Time*, 207–226. Oxford: Berg.

Gropper, Rena C. 1975. *Gypsies in the City: Culture Patterns and Survival*. Princeton, N.J.: Darwin Press.

Guéhenno, Jean-Marie. 1995. *The End of the Nation-State*. Minneapolis: University of Minnesota Press.

Gumprecht, Blake. 1996. "Geographically isolated Asian Indians in the rural United States: A research proposal." Unpublished paper, University of Oklahoma.

Gutiérrez, Ramon, and Genero Padillo. 1993. *Recovering the U.S. Hispanic Literary Heritage*. Houston: Arte Publico Press.

Guttmann, Allen. 1971. *The Jewish Writer in America*. New York: Oxford University Press.

Gvion-Rosenberg, Liora. 1991. Telling the story of ethnicity: American cookbooks, 1850–1990. Ph.D. diss., State University of New York–Stony Brook.

Gyrisco, Geoffrey M. 1997. "Victor Cordella and the architecture of Polish and East-Slavic identity in America." *Polish American Studies* 54 : 33–52.

Hacker, Andrew. 1992. *Two Nations: Black and White, Separate, Hostile, Unequal*. New York: Charles Scribner's Sons.

Haddad, Yvonne Yazbeck, and Jane Idleman Smith, eds. 1994. *Muslim Communities in North America*. Albany: State University of New York Press.

Hall, Stuart. 1997."The local and the global: Globalization and ethnicity." In Anthony D. King, ed. *Culture, Globalization and the World-System: Contemporary Conditions for the Representation of Identity*, 19–39. Minneapolis: University of Minnesota Press.

Halley, Laurence. 1985. *Ancient Affections: Ethnic Groups and Foreign Policy*. New York: Praeger.

Hallowell, A. Irving. 1959. "The backlash of the frontier: The impact of the Indian on American culture." In *Smithsonian Report for 1958*, 447–472. Washington: Smithsonian Institution.

Halter, Marilyn. 1993. *Between Race and Ethnicity: Cape Verdean American Immigrants, 1860–1965*. Urbana: University of Illinois Press.

Hamamoto, Darrell Y. 1994. *Monitored Peril: Asian Americans and the Politics of TV Representation*. Minneapolis: University of Minnesota Press.

Handelman, David. 1991. "The Japanning of Scarsdale." *New York* 24 (29 April) : 40–45.

Handler, Richard. 1994. "Is 'identity' a useful cross-cultural concept?" In John R. Gillis, ed. *Commemorations: The Politics of National Identity*, 27–40. Princeton: Princeton University Press.

Handlin, Oscar. 1951. *The Uprooted*. New York: Grosset & Dunlap.

Hanks, Jacqueline. 1988. "St. Casimir Cemetery." *Stone in America* 101 (November) : 28–37.

* Hannaford, Ivan. 1996. *Race: The History of an Idea in the West*. Washington and Baltimore: Woodrow Wilson Center Press and Johns Hopkins University Press.

Hannerz, Ulf. 1992. *Cultural Complexity: Studies in the Social Organization of Meaning*. New York: Columbia University Press.

———. 1996. "Stockholm: Doubly creolizing." In *Transnational Connections: Culture, People, Places*, 150–159. London: Routledge.

Hansen, Marcus Lee. 1938. *The Problem of the Third-Generation Immigrant*. Rock Island, Ill.: Augustana Historical Society.

Harap, Louis. 1987a. *Creative Awakening: The Jewish Presence in Twentieth-Century American Literature*. New York: Greenwood.

———. 1987b. *In the Mainstream: The Jewish Presence in Twentieth-Century American Literature, 1950s–1980s*. New York: Greenwood.

Harris, R. Cole. 1977. "The simplification of Europe overseas." *Annals of the Association of American Geographers* 67 : 469–483.

Harrison, Roderick J., and Claudette E. Bennett. 1995. "Racial and ethnic diversity." In Reynolds Farley, ed. *State of the Union: America in the 1990s*. Vol.2. *Social Trends*, 141–210. New York: Russell Sage Foundation.

Harrison, Roderick J., and Daniel H. Weinberg. 1992. "Racial and ethnic residential segregation in 1990." Paper presented at the Population Association of America meeting, Denver, May 1992.

Haverluk, Terence W. 1998. "Hispanic community types and assimilation in Mex-America." *Professional Geographer* 50 : 465–480.

Hein, Jeremy. 1995. *From Vietnam, Laos, and Cambodia: A Refugee Experience in the United States*. New York: Twayne Publishers.

Heller, Agnes. 1996. "The many faces of multiculturalism." In Rainer Bauböck, Heller, and Aristide R. Zolberg, eds. *The Challenge of Diversity: Integration and Pluralism in Societies of Immigration*, 25–41. Aldershot, U.K.: Avebury.

Helweg, Arthur W., and Usha M. Helweg. 1990. *An Immigrant Success Story: East Indians in America*. Philadelphia: University of Pennsylvania Press.

Herman, R. D. K. 1999. "The Aloha state: Place names and the anti-conquest of Hawaii." *Annals of the Association of American Geographers* 89 : 76–102.

Hernández, Carmen Dolores. 1997. *Puerto Rican Voices in English*. Westport, Conn.: Praeger.

Herring, Cedric, and Charles Amissah. 1997. "Advance and retreat: Racially based attitudes and public policy." In Steven A. Tuch and Jack K. Martin, eds. *Racial Attitudes in the 1990s: Continuity and Change*, 121–143. Westport, Conn.: Praeger.

Herskovits, Melville. 1941. *The Myth of the Negro Past*. New York: Harper & Row.

Hertzberg, Hazel W. 1971. *The Search for an American Indian Identity: Modern Pan-Indian Movements*. Syracuse: Syracuse University Press.

Higham, John. 1984. *Send These to Me: Immigrants in Urban America*. Rev. ed. Baltimore: Johns Hopkins University Press.

———. 1990. "From process to structure: Formulations of American immigration history." In Peter Kivisto and Dag Blanck, eds. *American Immigrants and Their Generations*, 11–41. Urbana: University of Illinois Press.

Hilger, Michael. 1995. *From Savage to Nobleman: Images of Native Americans in Film*. Lanham, Md.: Scarecrow Press.

Hill, Patricia Liggins, ed. 1998. *Call and Response: The Riverside Anthology of the African American Literary Tradition*. Boston: Houghton Mifflin.

Hirschman, Charles. 1983. "America's melting pot reconsidered." *Annual Review of Sociology* 9 : 397–423.

———. 1991. "Ethnic blending in historical perspective." Paper presented at the annual meeting of the American Sociological Association, Cincinnati, August 1991.

Hobsbawm, Eric. 1983. "Introduction: Inventing tradition." In Hobsbawm and Terence Ranger, eds. *The Invention of Tradition*, 1–14. Cambridge: Cambridge University Press.

Hodge, David C., et al. 1996. "Focus: Exploring spatial mismatch." *Professional Geographer* 48 : 417–467.

Hoelscher, Steven D. 1995a. The invention of ethnic place: Creating and commemorating heritage in an Old World Wisconsin community, 1850–1995. Ph.D. diss., University of Wisconsin.

———. 1995b. "Conspicuous construction: Ethnic architecture in America's Little Switzerland." *Wisconsin Preservation* 19 : 9–12.

———. 1998. *Heritage on Stage: The Invention of Ethnic Place in America's Little Switzerland*. Madison: University of Wisconsin Press.

Hoelscher, Steven, and Robert C. Ostergren. 1993. "Old European homelands in the American Middle West." *Journal of Cultural Geography* 13 : 87–106.

Hoelscher, Steven, Jeffrey Zimmerman, and Timothy Bawden. 1997. "Milwaukee's German Renaissance twice-told: Inventing and recycling landscape in America's German Athens." In Robert C. Ostergren and Thomas R. Vale, eds. *Wisconsin Land and Life*, 376–409. Madison: University of Wisconsin Press.

Hoffman-Axthelm, Dieter. 1992. "Identity and reality: The end of the philosophical immigration officer." In Scott Lash and Jonathan Friedman, eds. *Modernity and Identity*, 196–217. Oxford: Blackwell.

Holli, Melvin G., and Peter d'A. Jones, eds. 1995. *Ethnic Chicago*. 4th ed. Grand Rapids, Mich.: William B. Eerdmans.

* Hollinger, David A. 1992. "Postethnic America." *Contention* 2 : 71–96.

———. 1993. "How wide the circle of the 'We'? American intellectuals and the problem of the ethnos since World War II." *American Historical Review* 98 : 317–337.

* ———. 1995. *Postethnic America: Beyond Multiculturalism*. New York: Basic Books.

Holloway, Mark. 1951. *Heavens on Earth: Utopian Communities in America, 1680–1880*. London: Turnstile Press.

Horowitz, Irving Louis. 1975. "Race, class, and the new ethnicity." *World View* 18 (January): 46–53.

Hout, Michael, and Joshua Goldstein. 1994. "How 4.5 million Irish immigrants became 40 million Irish Americans: Demographic and subjective aspects of the ethnic composition of white Americans." *American Sociological Review* 59: 64–82.

Howard, Gary R. 1993. "Whites in multicultural education." *Phi Delta Kappan* 75: 36–41.

Howes, David. 1996. "Cultural appropriation and resistance in the American Southwest: Decommodifying 'Indianness.'" In Howes, ed. *Cross-Cultural Consumption: Global Markets, Local Realities*, 138–160. London: Routledge.

Hurh, Won Moo, and Kwang Chung Kim. 1984. *Korean Immigrants in America: A Structural Analysis of Ethnic Confinement and Adhesive Adaptation*. Cranbury, N.J.: Associated University Presses.

Ibson, John. 1981. "Virgin land or Virgin Mary? Studying the ethnicity of white Americans." *American Quarterly* 33: 284–308.

Isaacs, Harold R. 1975. *Idols of the Tribe: Group Identity and Political Change*. New York: Harper & Row.

Isajiw, Wsevolod W. 1974. "Definitions of ethnicity." *Ethnicity* 1: 111–124.

———. 1992. "Definition and dimensions of ethnicity: A theoretical framework." Paper presented at the Joint Canada–United States Conference on the Measurement of Ethnicity, Ottawa, April 1992.

*Isbister, John. 1996. *The Immigration Debate: Remaking America*. West Hartford, Conn.: Kumarian Press.

Jackson, John Brinckerhoff. 1984. *Discovering the Vernacular Landscape*. New Haven: Yale University Press.

Jackson, Kenneth T., and Camilo José Vergara. 1989. *Silent Cities: The Evolution of the American Cemetery*. New York: Princeton Architectural Press.

Jacobson, David. 1996. *Rights across Borders: Immigration and the Decline of Citizenship*. Baltimore: Johns Hopkins University Press.

James, Cathy Lynette. 1991. Soap opera mythology and racial-ethnic social change: An analysis of African-American, Asian/Pacific and Mexican/Hispanic American storylines during the 1980s. Ph.D. dissertation, University of California.

Janiskee, Robert L. 1996. "Celebrating ethnic diversity: Multicultural festivals in the United States." Paper presented at the Ninety-second Annual Meeting of the Association of American Geographers, Charlotte, April 1996.

———. 1997. "America's ethnic festivals: A geographic inventory and analysis." Paper presented at the Sixth Annual Festival and Events Research Symposium, Montreal, October 1997.

Jansen, Lee. 1991. "The new ethnic symbolism." *Stone in America* 104: 32–39.

Jarvenpa, Robert. 1985. "The political economy and political ethnicity of American Indian adaptations and identities." In Richard D. Alba, ed. *Ethnicity and Race in the U.S.A: Toward the Twenty-First Century,* 29–48. London: Routledge & Kegan Paul.

Jasso, Guillermina, and Mark R. Rosenzweig. 1990. *The New Chosen People: Immigrants in the United States.* New York: Russell Sage Foundation.

Jenkins, Richard. 1994. "Rethinking ethnicity: Identity, categorization and power." *Ethnic and Racial Studies* 17:197–223.

Jhally, Sut, and Justin Lewis.1992. *Enlightened Racism: The Cosby Show, Audiences, and the Myth of the American Dream.* Boulder: Westview.

Johnson, Kenneth M., and Calvin L. Beale. 1996. *The Reemergence of Population Growth in Nonmetropolitan Areas of the U.S.: The Rural Rebound.* Demographic Change and Fiscal Stress Project, Working Paper no. 10. Chicago: Loyola University.

Johnson, Ronald C. 1992. "Offspring of cross-race and cross-ethnic marriages in Hawaii." In Maria P. P. Root, ed. *Racially Mixed People in America*, 239–249. Newbury Park, Calif.: Sage.

Jordan-Bychkov, Terry G., and Donna Domosh. 1998. "Ethnic geography." In *The Human Mosaic: A Thematic Introduction to Cultural Geography*, 335–373. 8th ed. New York: Addison Wesley Longman.

Judd, Eleanore Parelman. 1990."Intermarriage and the maintenance of religio-ethnic identity. A case study: The Denver Jewish community." *Journal of Comparative Family Studies* 21:251–265.

Jyoti, [Ms.].1990. Asian Indians in Chicago: An examination of residential pattern, business activities, and cultural institutions. Master's paper, University of Chicago, Committee on Geographical Studies.

Kadaba, Lini S. 1998. "Ethnic TV takes immigrants home." *Philadelphia Inquirer*, 27 October, B1, B6.

Kallen, Horace M. 1924. *Culture and Democracy in the United States.* New York: Boni & Liveright.

Kantrowicz, Edward R. 1993. "Ethnicity." In Mary Kupiec Cayton, Elliott J. Gorn, and Peter W. Williams, eds. *Encyclopedia of American Social History*, 453–466. New York: Charles Scribner's Sons.

Kasinitz, Philip. 1992. *Caribbean New York: Black Immigrants and the Politics of Race.* Ithaca: Cornell University Press.

Kasinitz, Philip, and Judith Freidenberg-Herbstein. 1987. "The Puerto Rican parade and West Indian carnival: Public celebrations in New York City." In Constance R. Sutton and Elsa M. Chaney, eds. *Caribbean Life in New York City: Sociocultural Dimensions*, 327–349. Staten Island: Center for Migration Studies of New York.

Kaups, Matti. 1978, 1979. "Finnish place names as a form of ethnic expression in the Middle West, 1880–1977." *Finnish Americana* 1 (1978): 51–59; 2 (1979): 28–49.

———. 1995. "Cultural landscape: Log structures as symbols of ethnic identity." *Material Culture* 27, 2: 1–19.

*Kazal, Russell A. 1995. "Revisiting assimilation: The rise, fall, and reappraisal of a concept in American ethnic history." *American Historical Review* 100: 437–471.

Kearney, Michael. 1995a. "The local and the global: The anthropology of globalization and transnationalism." *Annual Review of Anthropology* 24: 547–565.

———. 1995b. "The effects of transnational culture, economy, and migration on Mixtec identity in Oaxacalifornia." In Michael Peter Smith and Joe R. Feagin, eds. *The Bubbling Cauldron: Race, Ethnicity, and the Urban Crisis*, 226–243. Minneapolis: University of Minnesota Press.

Keefe, Susan, and Amado M. Padilla. 1987. *Chicano Identity*. Albuquerque: University of New Mexico Press.

Kelley, Ron, ed. 1993. *Irangeles: Iranians in Los Angeles*, Berkeley: University of California Press,

Kellner, Douglas. 1992. "Popular culture and the construction of postmodern identity." In Scott Lash and Jonathan Friedman, eds. *Modernity and Identity*, 141–177. Oxford: Blackwell.

Kellogg, Susan. 1990. "Exploring diversity in middle-class families: The symbolism of American ethnic identity." *Social Science History* 14: 27–41.

Kelton, Jane Gladd. 1985. "New York City's St. Patrick's Day parade: Invention of contention and consensus." *Drama Review* 29, 3: 93–105.

Kendis, Kaoru Oguri. 1989. *A Matter of Comfort: Ethnic Maintenance and Ethnic Style among Third-Generation Japanese Americans*. New York: AMS Press.

Kenny, Judith T. 1997. "Polish routes to Americanization: House form and landscape on Milwaukee's Polish South Side." In Robert C. Ostergren and Thomas R. Vale, eds. *Wisconsin Land and Life*, 263–381. Madison: University of Wisconsin Press.

Kent, Noel Jacob. 1993. "To polarize a nation: Racism, labor markets, and the state in the U.S. political economy, 1965–1986." In Crawford

Young, ed. *The Rising Tide of Cultural Pluralism: The Nation-State at Bay?*, 55–76. Madison: University of Wisconsin Press.

Kikumura, Akemi, and Harry H. L. Kitano. 1973. "Interracial marriage: A picture of the Japanese-Americans." *Journal of Social Issues* 29 : 67–81.

Kilburn, Peter T. 1991. "Foreign doctors flocking to rescue long-shunned areas of dire poverty." *New York Times*, 2 November, 8.

Killian, Lewis M. 1970. *White Southerners*. New York: Random House.

Kim, Elaine H. 1982. *Asian American Literature: An Introduction to the Writings and Their Social Context*. Philadelphia: Temple University Press.

Kim, Illsoo. 1981. *New Urban Immigrants: The Korean Community in New York*. Princeton: Princeton University Press.

Kindig, David A., and Hormoz Movassaghi. 1989. "The adequacy of physician supply in small rural counties." *Health Affairs* 8, 2 : 63–70.

Kisubi, Alfred T. 1997. "Ideological perspectives on multicultural relations." In Michael A. Burayidi, ed. *Multiculturalism in a Cross-Cultural Perspective*, 15–35. Lanham, Md.: University Press of America.

Kivisto, Peter. 1990. "The transplanted then and now: The reorientation of immigration studies from the Chicago School to the new social history." *Ethnic and Racial Studies* 13 : 445–481.

*———. 1992. "Beyond assimilation and pluralism: Toward situationally sensitive theoretical models of ethnicity." Paper presented at the annual meeting of the American Sociological Association, Pittsburgh, August 1992.

Klaff, V. Z. 1980. "Pluralism as an alternative model for the human ecologist." *Ethnicity* 7 : 445–481.

* Klapp, Orrin E. 1969. *Collective Search for Identity*. New York: Holt, Rinehart & Winston.

Kliger, Hannah, ed. 1992. *Jewish Hometown Associations and Family Circles in New York: The WPA Yiddish Writers' Group Study*. Bloomington: Indiana University Press.

Knowles, Anne Kelly. 1997. "Religious identity as ethnic identity: The Welsh in Waukesha County." In Robert C. Ostergren and Thomas R. Vale, eds. *Wisconsin Land and Life*, 282–299. Madison: University of Wisconsin Press.

Knox, Paul L. 1993. "The postmodern urban matrix." In Knox, ed. *The Restless Urban Landscape*, 207–236. Englewood Cliffs, N.J.: Prentice-Hall.

Koehn, Peter H. 1991. *Refugees from Revolution: U.S. Policy and Third-World Migration*. Boulder: Westview Press.

Kolinski, Dennis. 1994. "Shrines and crosses in rural central Wisconsin." *Polish American* Studies 51, 2 : 33–47.

Kornblum, William. 1974. *Blue Collar Community*. Chicago: University of Chicago Press.

Kosmin, Barry A., and Seymour P. Lachman. 1993. *One Nation under God: Religion in Contemporary America*. New York: Harmony Books.

Kotkin, Joel. 1993. *Tribes: How Race, Religion, and Identity Determine Success in the New Global Economy*. New York: Random House.

* Kovel, Joel. 1970. *White Racism: A Psychohistory*. New York: Pantheon.

Krase, Jerome. 1993. "Traces of home." *Places* 8 : 46–54.

———. 1997. "Polish and Italian vernacular landscapes in Brooklyn." *Polish American Studies* 54 : 9–31.

Kritz, Mary M. 1987. "The global picture of contemporary immigration patterns." In James T. Fawcett and Benjamin V. Carino, eds. *Pacific Bridges: The New Immigration from Asia and the Pacific Islands*, 29–51. Staten Island: Center for Migration Studies.

Krupat, Arnold. 1989. *The Voice in the Margin: Native American Literature and the Canon*. Berkeley: University of California Press.

Kuhlken, Robert, and Rocky Sexton. 1994. "The geography of zydeco music." In George O. Carney, ed. *The Sounds of People and Places: A Geography of American Folk and Popular Music*, 63–76. 3rd ed. Lanham, Md.: Rowman & Littlefield.

Ladd, Everett C. 1998. "The American ethnic experience as it stands in the Nineties." *Public Perspective* 9, 2 : 50–65.

Laguerre, Michel S. 1984. *American Odyssey: Haitians in New York City*. Ithaca: Cornell University Press.

Lal, Barbara Ballis. 1983. "Perspectives on ethnicity: Old wine in new bottles." *Ethnic and Racial Studies* 6 : 154–173.

Lam, Frankie King-sun. 1986. Residential segregation of Chinese and Japanese-Americans in the United States suburban areas: 1960, 1970, and 1980. Ph.D. dissertation, Purdue University.

Larson, Charles R. 1978. *American Indian Fiction*. Albuquerque: University of New Mexico Press.

Lavender, Abraham D. 1975. "The Sephardic revival in the United States: A case of ethnic revival in a minority-within-a-minority." *Journal of Ethnic Studies* 3 : 21–32.

Lawless, Robert. 1986. "Haitian migrants and Haitian-Americans: From invisibility into the spotlight." *Journal of Ethnic Studies* 14, 2 : 29–70.

Leab, Daniel J. 1975. *From Sambo to Superspade: The Black Experience in Motion Pictures*. Boston: Houghton Mifflin.

Lechner, Frank J. 1984. "Ethnicity and revitalization in the modern world system." *Sociological Focus* 17 : 243–256.

Lee, Barrett A., Stephen A. Matthews, and Wilbur Zelinsky. 1998. "The spatial contours of racial and ethnic diversity in the United States."

Paper presented at the Eastern Sociological Society Annual Meeting, Philadelphia, March 1998.

Lee, Barrett A., and Peter B. Wood. 1991. "Is neighborhood racial succession place-specific?" *Demography* 28, 1:21–40.

Lee, Dong Ok. 1992. "Commodification of ethnicity: The sociospatial reproduction of immigration entrepreneurs." *Urban Affairs Quarterly* 28:258–275.

———. 1995. "Koreatown and Korean small firms in Los Angeles: Locating in the ethnic neighborhoods." *Professional Geographer* 47: 184–195.

Lee, Frederick David. 1980. The Korean community of metropolitan Washington, D.C. Master's thesis, George Washington University.

*Lee, Sharon M. 1993. "Racial classifications in the US Census: 1890–1990." *Ethnic and Racial Studies* 16:75–94.

Leonard, Karen Isaksen. 1992. *Making Ethnic Choices: California's Punjabi Mexican Americans*. Philadelphia: Temple University Press.

Lessinger, Johanna. 1992. "Investing or going home? A transnational strategy among Indian immigrants in the United States." In Nina Glick Schiller, Linda Basch, and Cristina Blanc-Szanton, eds. *Towards a Transnational Perspective on Migration*, 53–80. [*Annals of the New York Academy of Sciences* 645, July 6].

Levenstein, Harvey. 1993. *Paradox of Plenty: A Social History of Eating in Modern America*. New York: Oxford University Press.

Lewis, Martin W., and Karen E. Wigen. 1997. *The Myth of Continents: A Critique of Metageography*. Berkeley: University of California Press.

Li, Wei. 1994. "Geographical study of ethnicity: Comparison between downtown and suburban Chinese in metropolitan Los Angeles." Paper presented at the annual meeting of the Association of American Geographers, San Francisco, April 1994.

———. 1996. "Los Angeles' Chinese ethnoburb: Overview of ethnic economy." Paper presented at the annual meeting of the Association of American Geographers, Charlotte, April 1996.

Lieberson, Stanley. 1980. *A Piece of the Pie: Blacks and White Immigrants since 1880*. Berkeley: University of California Press, 1980.

———. 1985. "Unhyphenated whites in the United States." *Ethnic and Racial* Studies 8:159–180.

Lieberson, Stanley, and Eleanor O. Bell. 1992. "Children's first names: An empirical study of social taste." *American Journal of Sociology* 98:511–554.

Lieberson, Stanley, and Kelly S. Mikelson. 1995. "Distinctive African American names: An experimental, historical, and linguistic analysis of innovation." *American Sociological Review* 60:928–946.

*Lieberson, Stanley, and Mary C. Waters. 1986. "Ethnic groups in flux: The changing ethnic responses of American whites." *Annals of the American Academy of Political and Social Science* 487:79–91.

———. 1988. *From Many Strands: Ethnic and Racial Groups in Contemporary America*. New York: Russell Sage Foundation.

———. 1993. "The ethnic responses of whites: What causes their instability, simplification, and inconsistency?" *Social Forces* 72: 421–450.

Light, Ivan. 1981. "Ethnic succession." In Charles F. Keyes, ed. *Ethnic Change*, 53–86. Seattle: University of Washington Press.

Light, Ivan, and Parminder Bhachu, ed. 1993. *Immigration and Entrepreneurship: Culture, Capital, and Ethnic Networks*. New Brunswick, N.J.: Transaction.

Lin, Jan. 1998. *Reconstructing Chinatown: Ethnic Enclave, Global Change*. Minneapolis: University of Minnesota Press.

Ling, Amy. 1990. *Between Worlds: Women Writers of Chinese Ancestry*. New York: Pergamon.

———. 1992. *Reading the Literature of Asian America*. Philadelphia: Temple University Press.

Lipson-Walker, Carole. 1991. "Weddings among Jews in the post–World War II American South." In Stephen Stern and John Allan Cicala, eds. *Creative Ethnicity: Symbols and Strategies of Contemporary Ethnic Life*, 171–183. Logan: Utah State University Press.

Livezey, Lowell W., ed. 2000. *Public Religion and Urban Transformation: Faith in the City*. New York: New York University Press.

Lobo, Arun Peter, Joseph J. Salvo, and Vicky Virgin. 1996. *The Newest New Yorkers 1990–1994: An Analysis of Immigration to NYC in the Early 1990s*. New York: New York City Department of City Planning.

Löfgren, Orvar. 1999. *On Holiday: A History of Vacationing*. Berkeley: University of California Press.

Lopata, Helena Znaniecki. 1976. *Polish Americans: Status Competition in an Ethnic Community*. Englewood Cliffs, N.J.: Prentice-Hall.

*Lopez, David, and Yen Espiritu. 1990. "Panethnicity in the United States: A theoretical framework." *Ethnic and Racial Studies* 13: 198–224.

Lowe, Lisa. 1991. "Heterogeneity, hybridity, multiplicity: Marking Asian American differences." Diaspora: A Journal of Transnational Studies 1:24–44.

Lowenthal, David. 1985. *The Past Is a Foreign Country*. New York: Cambridge University Press.

———. 1996. *Possessed by the Past: The Heritage Crusade and the Spoils of History*. New York: Free Press.

Lowry, Ira S. 1992. "The science and politics of ethnic enumeration." In Winston A Van Horne and Thomas V. Tonnesen, eds. *Ethnicity and Public Policy*, 42–61. Milwaukee: University of Wisconsin.

Lu, Shun, and Gary Alan Fine. 1995. "The presentation of ethnic authenticity: Chinese food as a social accomplishment." *Sociological Quarterly* 36 : 535–553.

Lucas, Pam. 1995. Emerging patterns: Asian cultural and religious imprints on the landscape within commercial cemeteries in Fairfax County, Virginia. Unpublished paper, George Mason University.

Luke, Timothy W. 1996. "Identity, meaning and globalization: Detraditionalization in postmodern space-time compression." In Paul Heelas, Scott Lash, and Paul Morris, eds. *Detraditionalization: Critical Reflections on Authority and Identity*, 109–133. Oxford and Cambridge, Mass.: Blackwell.

Lutz, Catherine A., and Jane L. Collins. 1993. *Reading National Geographic*. Chicago: University of Chicago Press.

Lynch, Annette. 1995. "Hmong American New Year's dress: The display of ethnicity." In Joanne B. Eicher, ed., *Dress and Ethnicity: Change across Space and Time*, 255–267. Oxford: Berg.

Lyra, Franciszek. 1985. "Following the cycle: The ethnic pattern of Polish-American literature." *MELUS* 12, 4 : 63–71.

MacCannell, Dean. 1984. "Reconstructed ethnicity: Tourism and cultural identity in Third World countries." *1984 Annals of Tourism Research* 11 : 375–391.

———. 1992. *Empty Meeting Grounds: The Tourist Papers*. London & New York: Routledge.

Machado, Deirdre Meintel. 1981. "Cape Verdean Americans." In Joan H. Rollins, ed. *Hidden Minorities: The Persistence of Ethnicity in American Life*, 227–250. Lanham, Md.: University Press of America.

Maffesoli, Michel. 1996. *The Time of the Tribes: The Decline of Individualism in Mass Society*. London: Sage.

Magliocco, Sabina. 1993. "Playing with food: The negotiation of identity in the ethnic display event by Italian Americans in Clinton, Indiana." In Luisa Del Guidice, ed. *Studies in Italian American Folklore*, 107–126. Logan: Utah State University Press.

Magner, Thomas F. 1974. "The rise and fall of the ethnics." *Journal of General Education* 25 : 253–264.

Magocsi, Paul Robert. 1987. "Are the Armenians really Russian? Or how the U.S. Census Bureau classified America's ethnic groups." *Government Publications Review* 14 : 133–168.

Mahler, Sarah J. 1996. *American Dreaming: Immigrant Life on the Margins*. Princeton: Princeton University Press, 1996.

*Mann, Arthur. 1979. *The One and the Many: Reflections on the American Identity*. Chicago: University of Chicago Press.

Manning, Robert D. 1994a. Multicultural Washington, D.C.: The changing social and economic landscape of a post-industrial metropolis. American University, Department of Sociology.

———. 1994b. From city to suburbs: The "new" immigration, native minorities, and the post-industrial metropolis. American University, Department of Sociology.

*———. 1995a. "Multiculturalism in the United States: Clashing concepts, changing demographics, and competing cultures." *International Journal of Group Tensions* 25, 2 : 117–168.

———. 1995b. "Washington, D.C.: The social transformation of the international capital city." In Silvia Pedraza and Ruben G. Rumbaut, ed. *Origins and Destinies: Race, Immigration and Ethnicity in America*, 373–389. New York: Wadsworth.

Marchetti, Gina. 1993. *Romance and the "Yellow Peril": Race, Sex, and Discursive Strategies in Hollywood Fiction*. Berkeley: University of California Press.

Margolis, Maxine L. 1994. *Little Brazil: An Ethnography of Brazilian Immigrants in New York City*. Princeton: Princeton University Press.

Markowitz, Fran. 1993. *A Community in Spite of Itself: Soviet Jewish Émigrés in New York*. Washington: Smithsonian Institution Press.

Mass, Amy Iwasaki. 1992. "Interracial Japanese Americans: The best of both worlds or the end of the Japanese American community?" In Maria P. P. Root, ed. *Racially Mixed People in America*, 265–279. Newbury Park, CA: Sage.

Massey, Douglas. 1985. "Ethnic residential segregation: A theoretical synthesis and empirical review." *Sociology and Social Research* 69 : 315–350.

*———. 1995. "The new immigration and ethnicity in the United States." *Population and Development Review* 21 : 631–652.

Massey, Douglas, and Nancy A. Denton. 1988. "Suburbanization and segregation in U.S. metropolitan areas." *American Journal of Sociology* 94 : 592–626.

———. 1993. *American Apartheid: Segregation and the Making of the Underclass*. Cambridge: Harvard University Press.

Matthews, Fred H. 1970. "The revolt against Americanism: Cultural pluralism and cultural relativisim as an ideology of liberation." *Canadian Review of American Studies* 1, 1 : 4–31.

Matturri, John. 1993. "Windows in the garden: Italian-American memorialization and the American cemetery." In Richard E. Meyer, ed. *Ethnicity and the American Cemetery*, 14–35. Bowling Green: Bowling Green State University Popular Press.

McCullough, Lawrence. 1980. "The role of language, music, and dance in the revival of Irish culture in Chicago, Illinois." *Ethnicity* 7: 436–444.

McGann, Tom. 1990. "Chicago's Bohemian National Cemetery." *American Cemetery* 63,6: 22–25, 52–54; 63,7: 25–29.

McGregory, Jerrilynn M. 1985. Aareck to Zsaneka: African American names in an urban community, 1945–1980. Master's thesis, Cornell University.

McGuire, Randall H. 1988. "Dialogues with the dead: Ideology and the cemetery." In Mark P. Leone and Parker B. Potter, Jr., eds. *The Recovery of Meaning: Historical Archaeology in the Eastern United States*, 435–480. Washington: Smithsonian Institution Press.

* McKay, James. 1982. "An exploratory synthesis of primordial and mobilizationist approaches to ethnic phenomena." *Ethnic and Racial Studies* 5: 395–420.

McKenney, Nanpeo R., and Arthur R. Cresce. 1992. "Measurement of ethnicity in the United States: Experiences of the U.S. Census Bureau." Paper presented at the Joint Canada–United States Conference on the Measurement of Ethnicity, Ottawa, April 1992.

McKenzie, Roderick D. 1925. "The ecological approach to the study of the human community." In Robert E. Park, Ernest W. Burgess, and McKenzie, eds. *The City*, 63–79. Chicago: University of Chicago Press.

McWhiney, Grady. 1987. *Cracker Culture: Celtic Ways in the Old South*. Tuscaloosa: University of Alabama Press.

Meinig, D. W. 1986. *The Shaping of America: A Geographic Perspective on Five Hundred Years of History*. Vol. 1. *Atlantic America, 1492–1800*. New Haven, Yale University Press.

Melville, Herman. 1850. *White Jacket, or the World in a Man-of-War*. New York: Harper & Brothers.

Meyer, Richard E., ed. 1993a. *Ethnicity and the American Cemetery*. Bowling Green: Bowling Green State University Popular Press.

———. 1993b. "Strangers in a strange land: Ethnic cemeteries in America." In Meyer, ed. *Ethnicity and the American Cemetery*, 1–13. Bowling Green: Bowling Green State University Popular Press.

———. 1993c. "The literature of necroethnicity in America: An annotated bibliography." In Meyer, ed., *Ethnicity and the American Cemetery*, 222–237.

Miller, Kerby A. 1990. "Class, culture, and immigrant group identity in the United States: The case of Irish-American identity." In Virginia

Yans-McLaughlin, ed. *Immigration Reconsidered: History, Sociology, and Politics*, 96–129. New York: Oxford University Press.

* Millman, Joel. 1997. *The Other Americans: How Immigrants Renew Our Country, Our Economy, and Our Values*. New York: Viking.

Milspaw, Yvonne J. 1980. "Segregation in life, segregation in death: Landscape of an ethnic cemetery." *Pennsylvania Folklife* 30, 1:36–40.

Min, Pyong Gap. 1988. *Ethnic Business Enterprise. Korean Small Business in Atlanta*. New York: Center for Migration Studies.

———. 1992. "The structure and social functions of Korean immigrant churches in the United States." *International Migration Review* 26: 1370–1394.

———. 1993. "Korean immigrants in Los Angeles." In Ivan Light and Parminder Bhachu, eds. *Immigration and Entrepreneurship: Culture, Capital, and Ethnic Networks*, 185–204. New Brunswick, N.J.: Transaction.

Mitchell, Tony. 1996. *Popular Music and Local Identity: Rock, Pop and Rap in Europe and Oceania*. London: Leicester University Press.

Mitchell, William E. 1978. *Mishpokhe: A Study of New York City Jewish Family Clubs*. The Hague: Mouton.

Mittelberg, David, and Mary C. Waters. 1992. "The process of ethnogenesis among Haitian and Israeli immigrants in the United States." *Ethnic and Racial Studies* 15:412–435.

Miyares, Ines. 1995. "Changing perceptions of space and place as measures of Hmong acculturation." Paper presented at the annual meeting of the Association of American Geographers, Chicago, April 1995.

Modarres, Ali. 1992. "Ethnic community development: A spatial examination." *Journal of Urban Affairs* 14, 2:97–107.

Mohr, Eugene V. 1982. *The Nuyorican Experience: Literature of the Puerto Rican Minority*. Westport, Conn.: Greenwood.

Mollenkopf, John H. 1993. *New York in the 1980s: A Social, Economic and Political Atlas*. New York: Simon & Schuster.

Morawska, Eva. 1990. "The sociology and historiography of immigration." In Virginia Yans-McLaughlin, ed. *Immigration Reconsidered: History, Sociology, and Politics*, 187–238. New York: Oxford University Press.

Morley, David, and Kevin Robbins. 1995. *Spaces of Identity: Global Media, Electronic Landscapes and Cultural Boundaries*. London: Routledge.

Morrill, Richard. 1995. "Racial segregation and class in a liberal metropolis." *Geographical Analysis* 27, 1:22–41.

Mountz, Alison, and Richard A. Wright. 1996. "Daily life in the transnational migrant community of San Augustin, Oaxaca, and Poughkeepsie, New York." *Diaspora* 5, 3:403–427.

Mufwene, Salikoko S., John R. Rickford, Guy Bailey, and John Baugh.

1998. *African-American English: Structure, History, and Use*. London & New York: Routledge.

Mugiraneza, Juvenal. 1988. *The Origins of the Ethnic Problem in Burundi*. Bujumbara, Burundi: N. p.

Muller, Thomas. 1993. *Immigrants and the American City*. New York: New York University Press.

Murdock, Stephen H., and David R. Ellis. 1991. *Patterns of Ethnic Change 1980 to 1990*. 2 vols. 1990 Census Series no. 2, Departmental Technical Report 91-2. College Station: Texas A&M University & Texas Agricultural Experiment Station.

Myers, Ernest R. 1994. "Korean American marketing in the African-American community: An exploratory study in the nation's capital." In Myers, ed. *Challenges of a Changing America: Perspectives on Immigration and Multiculturalism in the United States*, 175–213. San Francisco: Austin & Winfield.

Myers, Steven Lee. 1993. "Bazaar with the feel of Bombay, right in Queens." *New York Times*, 4 January, B1, B10.

Myrdal, Gunnar. 1944. *An American Dilemma*. New York: Harper.

———. 1974. "The case against romantic ethnicity." *Center Magazine*, July/August: 26–30.

Naficy, Hamid. 1993. *The Making of Exile Cultures: Iranian Television in Los Angeles*. Minneapolis: University of Minnesota Press.

Nagel, Joane. 1994. "Constructing ethnicity: Creating and recreating ethnic identity and culture." *Social Problems* 41:152–176.

———. 1996. *American Indian Ethnic Renewal: Red Power and the Resurgence of Identity and Culture*. New York: Oxford University Press.

Nagengast, Carol, and Michael Kearney. 1990. "Mixtec ethnicity: Social identity, political consciousness, and political activism." *Latin American Research Review* 25:61–91.

Nakashima, Cynthia L. 1992. "An invisible monster: The creation and denial of mixed-race people in America." In Maria P. P. Root, ed. *Racially Mixed People in America*, 162–178. Newbury Park, Calif.: Sage.

*Nash, Manning. 1989. *The Cauldron of Ethnicity in the Modern World*. Chicago: University of Chicago Press.

Nelli, Humbert S. 1970. *The Italians in Chicago, 1880–1930*. New York: Oxford University Press.

Nelson, Candace, and Marta Tienda. 1985. "The structuring of Hispanic ethnicity: Historical and contemporary perspectives." In Richard D. Alba, ed. *Ethnicity and Race in the U.S.A.: Toward the Twenty-First Century*, 49–74. London: Routledge & Kegan Paul.

Nelson, Pamela B. 1990. *Ethnic Images in Toys and Games*. Philadelphia: Balch Institute for Ethnic Studies.

Newbold, K. Bruce. 1999. "Evolutionary immigrant settlement patterns: Concepts and evidence." In Kavita Pandit and Suzanne Davies Withers, eds. *Migration and Restructuring in the United States: A Geographic Perspective*, 250–270. Lanham, Md.: Rowman & Littlefield.

Newfield, Christopher, and Avery F. Gordon. 1996. "Multiculturalism's unfinished business." In Gordon and Newfield, eds. *Mapping Multiculturalism*, 76–115. Minneapolis: University of Minnesota Press.

Newman, William M. 1973. *American Pluralism: A Study of Minority Groups and Social Theory*. New York: Harper & Row.

Nielsen, François. 1985. "Toward a theory of ethnic solidarity in modern societies." *American Sociological Review* 50 : 133–149.

Niemonen, Jack. 1993. "Some observations on the problem of paradigms in recent racial and ethnic relations texts." *Teaching Sociology* 21, 3 : 271–286.

Noble, Allen G., ed. 1992. *To Build in a New Land: Ethnic Landscapes in North America*. Baltimore: Johns Hopkins University Press.

Noriega, Chon A., and Ana M. López, eds. 1996. *The Ethnic Eye: Latino Media Arts*. Minneapolis: University of Minnesota Press.

Novak, Michael. 1972. *The Rise of the Unmeltable Ethnics: Politics and Culture in the Seventies*. New York: Macmillan.

———. 1974. "The new ethnicity." *Center Magazine*, July/August: 18–25.

Nye, Russel Blaine. 1966. *This Almost Chosen People: Essays in the History of American Ideas*. East Lansing: Michigan State University Press.

Oakes, Timothy S. 1997a. "Ethnic tourism in rural Guizhou: Sense of place and the commerce of authenticity." In M. Picard and R. Woods, eds. *Tourism, Ethnicity, and the State in Asian and Pacific Societies*, 35–70. Honolulu: University of Hawaii Press.

———. 1997b. Personal communication, October 21.

O'Grady, Ingrid P. 1981. "Shared meaning and choice as components of Armenian immigrant adaptation." *Anthropological Quarterly* 5, 2 : 76–81.

O'Hare, William. 1998. "Managing multiple-race data." *American Demographics* 20, 4 : 42–44.

O'Hare, William, William H. Frey, and Dan Fost. 1994. "Asians in the suburbs." *American Demographics* 16, 5 : 32–38.

Ojito, Mirta. 1996. "A house of worship, a sign of permanence." *New York Times*, 12 August, B1, B4.

Okamura, Jonathan Y. 1981. "Situational ethnicity." *Ethnic and Racial Studies* 4 : 452–465.

Olson, Kristen. N.d. Ethnicity in the landscape: The case of Mexican

Americans in Pilsen and Little Village. Unpublished paper, University of Chicago, Department of Sociology.

Omi, Michael, and Howard Winant. 1986. *Racial Formation in the United States from the 1960s to the 1980s*. New York and London: Routledge & Kegan Paul.

Ong, Qihwa. 1992. "Limits to cultural accumulation: Chinese capitalists on the American Pacific Rim." In Nina Glick Schiller, Linda Basch, and Cristina Blanc Szanton, eds. *Towards a Transnational Perspective on Migration*, 125–143. [*Annals of the New York Academy of Sciences* 645, July 6].

Orfalea, Gregory, and Sharif Elmusa. 1988. *Grape Leaves: A Century of Arab American Poetry*. Salt Lake City: University of Utah Press.

Orleck, Annelise. 1987. "The Soviet Jews: Life in Brighton Beach, Brooklyn." In Nancy Foner, ed. *New Immigrants in New York*, 273–304. New York: Columbia University Press.

Osako, Masako. 1995. "Japanese Americans: Melting into the All-American melting pot." In Melvin G. Holli and Peter d'A. Jones, eds. *Ethnic Chicago: A Multicultural Portrait*, 409–437. 4th ed. Grand Rapids, Mich.: William B. Eerdmans.

Ostergren, Robert C. 1981."The immigrant church as a symbol of community and place in the Upper Midwest." *Great Plains Quarterly* (Fall): 225–238.

"Overseas Filipinos: A new breed of professionals." 1974. *Archipelago*, June: 10–15.

Pacyga, Dominic A., and Ellen Skerrett. 1986. *Chicago: City of Neighborhoods*. Chicago: Loyola University Press.

Padgett, Deborah. 1980. "Symbolic ethnicity and patterns of ethnic identity assertion in American-born Serbs." *Ethnic Groups* 3:55–77.
———. 1981. "An adaptive approach to the study of ethnicity: Serbian-Americans in Milwaukee, Wisconsin." *Nationalities Papers* 9:117–130.

Padilla, Felix M. 1985. *Latino Ethnic Consciousness: The Case of Mexican Americans and Puerto Ricans in Chicago*. Notre Dame: University of Notre Dame Press.

Park, Siyoung. 1994. "Suburbanization of Korean immigrants in Chicago." Paper presented at the annual meeting of the Association of American Geographers, San Francisco, April 1994.

Patterson, Orlando. 1987. "The emerging West Atlantic System: Migration, culture, and underdevelopment in the United States and the Circum-Caribbean region." In W. Alonso, ed. *Population in an Interacting World*, 227–260. Cambridge: Harvard University Press.

Pavalko, Ronald M. 1980. "Racism and the new immigration: A

reinterpretation of assimilation of white ethnics in American society." *Sociology and Social Research* 65:56–77.

Peach, Ceri. 1980. "Ethnic segregation and intermarriage." *Annals of the Association of American Geographers* 70:371–381.

———. 1983. "Ethnicity." In Michael Pacione, ed. *Progress in Urban Geography*, 103–127. London: Croom Helm.

———. 1997. "Pluralist and assimilationist models of ethnic settlement in London 1991." *Tijdschrift voor Eeconomische en Sociale Geografie* 88, 2:120–134.

Pearlstone, Zena. 1990. *Ethnic L.A.* Beverly Hills: Hillcrest Press.

Pedraza-Bailey, Silvia. 1990. "Immigration research: A conceptual map." *Social Science History* 14, 1:43–67.

Penninx, Rinus. 1996. "Immigration, minorities policy and multiculturalism in Dutch society since 1960." In Rainer Bauböck, Agnes Heller, Aristide R. Zolberg, eds. *The Challenge of Diversity: Integration and Pluralism in Societies of Immigration*, 187–206. Aldershot, U.K.: Avebury.

Petersen, William. 1980. "Concepts of ethnicity." In S. Thernstrom, ed. *Harvard Encyclopedia of American Ethnic Groups*, 234–242. Cambridge: Harvard University Press.

———. 1997. *Ethnicity Counts*. New Brunswick, N.J.: Transaction.

Pido, Antonio J. A. 1986. *The Pilipinos in America: Macro/Micro Dimensions of Immigration and Integration*. Staten Island: Center for Migration Studies.

Piersen, William D. 1993. *Black Legacy: America's Hidden Heritage*. Amherst: University of Massachusetts Press.

Pileggi, Nicholas. 1979. "Risorgimento: The red, white, and greening of New York." In David R. Colburn and George E. Pozzetta, eds. *America and the New Ethnicity*, 117–132. Port Washington, N.Y.: Kennikat Press.

Pillsbury, Richard. 1998. *No Foreign Food: The American Diet in Time and Place*. Boulder: Westview.

Pillsbury, Richard, Arthur D. Murphy, and Deborah Duchon. 1993. "The new Southerners." In Sanford H. Bederman, ed. *Alligators, Souseholes, and a Trek down Peachtree Street: A Guide to Field Excursions*, 30–33 [for the 1993 annual meeting of the Association of American Geographers]. Washington: Association of American Geographers.

Pincus, Fred L., and Howard J. Ehrlich. 1994. "The study of race and ethnic relations." In Pincus and Ehrlich, eds. *Race and Ethnic Conflict: Contending Views on Prejudice, Discrimination and Ethnoviolence*, 3–10. Boulder: Westview Press.

Pocock, Philip. 1980. *The Obvious Illusion: Murals from the Lower East Side*. New York: George Braziller.

Porter, Philip W., and Fred E. Lukermann. 1976. "The geography of utopia." In David Lowenthal and Martyn J. Bowden, eds. *Geographies of the Mind: Essays in Honor of John K. Wright*, 197–223. New York: Oxford University Press.

Portes, Alejandro. 1987. "One field, many views: Competing theories of international migration." In James T. Fawcett and Benjamin V. Cariño, eds. *Pacific Bridges: The New Immigration from Asia and the Pacific Islands*, 53–70. Staten Island: Center for Migration Studies.

———. 1995a. "Children of immigrants: Segmented assimilation and its determinants." In Portes, ed. *The Economic Sociology of Immigration: Essays on Networks, Ethnicity, and Entrepreneurship*, 248–279. New York: Russell Sage Foundation.

*———. 1995b "Transnational communities: Their emergence and significance in the contemporary world system." Paper presented at the Nineteenth Annual Conference on the Political Economy of the World System, University of Miami, April.

Portes, Alejandro, and Jozsef Böröcz. 1989. "Contemporary immigration: Theoretical perspectives on its determinants and modes of incorporation." *International Migration Review* 23 : 606–630.

Portes, Alejandro, and Leif Jensen. 1987. "What's an ethnic enclave? The case of conceptual clarity." *American Sociological Review* 52 : 768–771.

Portes, Alejandro, and Robert D. Manning. 1991. "The immigrant enclave: Theory and empirical examples." In N. Yetman, ed. *Majority and Minority: The Dynamics of Race and Ethnicity in American Life*, 319–332. 5th ed. Boston: Allyn and Bacon.

*Portes, Alejandro, and Ruben G. Rumbaut. 1990. *Immigrant America: A Portrait*. 2d. ed. Berkeley: University of California Press.

Portes, Alejandro, and Richard Schauffler. 1996. "Language acquisition and loss among children of immigrants." In Silvia Pedraza and Ruben G. Rumbaut, eds. *Origins and Destinies: Immigration, Race, and Ethnicity in America*, 432–443. Belmont, Calif.: Wadsworth.

Portes, Alejandro, and Alex Stepick. 1993. *City on the Edge: The Transformation of Miami*. Berkeley: University of California Press.

Posadas, Barbara M. 1981. "Crossed boundaries in interracial Chicago: Filipino American families since 1925." *Amerasia Journal* 8 : 3–52.

Pratt, Mary Louise. 1992. *Imperial Eyes: Travel Writing and Transculturation*. London: Routledge.

Price, Marie D. 1996. Personal communication, December 31.

Prorok, Carolyn V. 1994. "Hindu temples in the Western world: A study in social space and ethnic identity." *Geographia Religionum* 8 : 95–108.

Quinn, William W., Jr. 1990. "The Southeast Syndrome: Notes on Indian descendant recruitment organizations and their perceptions of Native American culture." *American Indian Quarterly* 14 : 147–154.

Raghavan, Sudarsan. 1998. "Ethnic communities are planting roots in cyberspace." *Philadelphia Inquirer*, 26 August, A1, A10.

Raitz, Karl B. 1978. "Ethnic maps of North America." *Geographical Review* 68 : 335–350.

———. 1979. "Themes in the cultural geography of European ethnic groups in the United States." *Geographical Review* 69 : 77–94.

Rangaswamy, Padma. 1995. "Asian Indians in Chicago: Growth and change in a model minority." In Melvin G. Holli and Peter d'A. Jones, eds. *Ethnic Chicago: A Multicultural Portrait*, 438–462. 4th ed. Grand Rapids, Mich.: William B. Eerdmans.

Rao, N. Madhusadana. 1994. "Ethnogenesis of a 'visible minority': Asian Indians in the U.S." *Population Review* 38 : 46–60.

Ratner, Sidney. 1987. "Horace M. Kallen and cultural pluralism." In Milton R. Konvitz, ed. *The Legacy of Horace M. Kallen*, 48–63. Cranbury, N.J.: Associated University Press.

Ravitch, Diane. 1990. "Multiculturalism: E pluribus plures." *American Scholar* 59 : 337–354.

Ray, Dorothy Jean. 1977. *Eskimo Art: Tradition and Innovation in North Alaska*. Seattle: University of Washington Press.

Regis, Humphrey A., and Leroy L. Lashley. 1992. "The editorial dimensions of the connection of Caribbean immigrants to their referents." *Journal of Black Studies* 22 : 380–391.

Reimers, David M. 1992. *Still the Golden Door: The Third World Comes to America*. 2d ed. New York: Columbia University Press.

Relph, Edward C. 1984. *Place and Placelessness*. 2d ed. London: Pion.

Richardson, Milda B. 1995. "Lithuanian cemetery art." *Newsletter of the Association for Gravestone Studies* 19, 4 : 4–6.

Richman, Karen Ellen. 1992. They will remember me in the house: The *pwen* of Haitian transnational migration. Ph.D. dissertation, University of Virginia.

Riesman, David. 1953. *The Lonely Crowd: A Study of the Changing American Character*. Garden City, N.Y.: Doubleday.

Riess, Steven A. 1992. "Sport, race, and ethnicity in the American city, 1870–1950." In Michael D'Innocenzo and Josef P. Sirefman, eds. *Immigration and Ethnicity: American Society — "Melting Pot" or "Salad Bowl*," 191–220. Westport, Conn.: Greenwood Press.

———. 1995. "Ethnic sports." In Melvin G. Holli and Peter d'A. Jones, eds. *Ethnic Chicago: A Multicultural Portrait*, 529–556. 4th ed. Grand Rapids, Mich.: William B. Eerdmans.

Robertson, Roland. 1992. *Globalization: Social Theory and Global Culture*. London: Sage.

Robertson, Roland, and JoAnn Chirico. 1985. "Humanity, globalization and worldwide religious resurgence: A theoretical perspective." *Sociological Analysis* 46:219–242.

Robinson, Deanna Campbell, Elizabeth B. Buck, and Marlene Cuthbert. 1991. *Music at the Margins: Popular Music and Global Cultural Diversity*. Newbury Park, Calif.: Sage.

Roche, John Patrick. 1982. "Suburban ethnicity: Ethnic attitudes and behavior among Italian Americans in two suburban communities." *Social Science Quarterly* 63:145–163.

Rodriguez, Richard. 1989. "An American writer." In Werner Sollors, ed. *The Invention of Ethnicity*, 3–13. New York: Oxford University Press.

Rooks, Noliwe M. 1996. *Hair Raising: Beauty, Culture, and African American Women*. New Brunswick, N.J.: Rutgers University Press.

Roosens, Eugene E. 1989. *Creating Ethnicity: The Process of Ethnogenesis*. Newbury Park, Calif.: Sage.

*Root, Maria P. P., ed. 1992. *Racially Mixed People in America*. Newbury Park, Calif.: Sage.

Rose, Nikolas. 1996. "Authority and the genealogy of subjectivity." In Paul Heelas, Scott Lash, and Paul Morris, eds. *Detraditionalization: Critical Reflections on Authority and Identity*, 294–327. Oxford: Blackwell.

Rose, Peter I. 1985. "Asian Americans: From pariahs to paragons." In Nathan Glazer, ed. *Clamor at the Gates: The New American Immigration*, 181–212. San Francisco: Institute for Contemporary Studies.

Royce, Anya Peterson. 1982. *Ethnic Identity: Strategies of Diversity*. Bloomington: Indiana University Press.

Rubinstein, Ruth P. 1995. *Dress Codes: Meanings and Messages in American Culture*. Boulder: Westview Press.

Rumbaut, Ruben G. 1991. "Passages to Americas: Perspectives on the new immigration." In Alan Wolfe, ed. *America at Century's End*, 208–244. Berkeley: University of California Press.

———. 1994. "Origins and destinies: Immigration to the United States since World War II." *Sociological Forum* 9:583–621.

———. 1995. "Ties that bind: Immigration and immigrant families in the United States." Paper presented at the National Symposium on International Migration and Family Change, Pennsylvania State University, November 1995.

Runblom, Harald. 1994. "Swedish multiculturalism in a comparative European context." *Sociological Forum* 9:623–640.

Said, Edward W. 1978. *Orientalism*. New York: Pantheon.

*———. 1993. *Culture and Imperialism*. New York: Knopf.

Sakong, Myungduk C. 1990. Rethinking the impact of the enclave: A comparative analysis of Korean-Americans' economic and residential adaptation. Ph.D. dissertation, State University of New York–Albany.

Salvo, Joseph J., and Ronald J. Ortiz. 1992. *The Newest New Yorkers: An Analysis of Immigration into New York City during the 1980s*. New York: Department of City Planning.

Sandefur, Gary D., and Trudy McKinnell. 1986. "American Indian intermarriage." *Social Science Research* 15:347–371.

Sandór, Gabrielle. 1994. "The other Americans." *American Demographics* 16, 6:36–42.

* San Juan, E., Jr. 1992. *Racial Formations/Critical Transformations: Articulations of Power in Ethnic and Racial Studies in the United States*. Atlantic Highlands, N.J.: Humanities Press.

Saran, Paratma. 1985. *The Asian Indian Experience in the United States*. Cambridge, Mass.: Schenkman.

Sarna, Jonathan D. 1978. "From immigrants to ethnics: Toward a new theory of 'ethnicization.'" *Ethnicity* 5:370–378.

Sassen-Koob, Saskia. 1987. "Formal and informal associations: Dominicans and Colombians in New York." In Constance R. Sutton and Elsa M. Chaney, eds. *Caribbean Life in New York City: Sociocultural Dimensions*, 278–296. Staten Island: Center for Migration Studies of New York.

Schlesinger, Arthur M., Jr. 1992. *The Disuniting of America*. New York: W. W. Norton.

Schmidt, Ronald J. 1993. "Language policy conflict in the United States." In Crawford Young, ed. *The Rising Tide of Cultural Pluralism: The Nation-State at Bay?*, 73–92. Madison: University of Wisconsin Press.

Schneider, Jo Anne. 1990. "Defining boundaries, creating contacts: Puerto Rican and Polish presentation of group identity through ethnic parades." *Journal of Ethnic Studies* 18, 1:33–57.

Schrag, Peter. 1971. *The Decline of the WASP*. New York: Simon & Schuster.

Schuchat, Molly G. 1981. "Hungarian Americans in the nation's capital." *Anthropological Quarterly* 5:89–93.

Schultz, April R. 1994. *Ethnicity on Parade: Inventing the Norwegian American through Celebration*. Amherst: University of Massachusetts Press.

Schwarz, Benjamin. 1995 "The diversity myth: America's leading export." *Atlantic Monthly* 275, 5:57–67.

Sclair, Helen A. 1995. "Ethnic cemeteries: Underground rites." In Melvin G. Holli and Peter d'A. Jones, eds. *Ethnic Chicago*, 618–639. 4th ed. Grand Rapids, Mich.: William B. Eerdmans.

Scott, George M., Jr. 1990. "A resynthesis of the primordial and circumstantial approaches to ethnic group solidarity: Towards an explanatory model." *Ethnic and Racial Studies* 13, 2:147–171.

See, Katherine O'Sullivan, and William J. Wilson. 1988. "Race and ethnicity." In Neil Smelser, ed. *Handbook of Sociology*, 223–242. Beverly Hills: Sage.

Selassie, Bereket H. 1996."Washington's new African immigrants." In Francine Curro Cary, ed. *Urban Odyssey: A Multicultural History of Washington, D.C.*, 264–275 Washington: Smithsonian Press.

Seligman, Edwin R. A., and Alvin Johnson, eds. 1930–34. *Encyclopedia of the Social Sciences*. 15 vols. New York: Macmillan.

Seller, Maxine Schwartz, ed. 1983. *Ethnic Theatre in the United States*, Westport, Conn., Greenwood Press.

Shatzky, Joel, and Michael Taub, eds. 1997. *Contemporary Jewish-American Novelists: A Bio-Critical Sourcebook*. Westport, Conn.: Greenwood Press.

Shear, Walter. 1986. "Saroyan's study of ethnicity." *MELUS* 13, 2:45–55.

Sherman, William C. 1983. *Prairie Mosaic: An Ethnic Atlas of Rural North Dakota*. Fargo: North Dakota Institute for Regional Studies.

Sheth, Manju. 1995. "Asian Indian Americans." In Pyong Gap Min, ed. *Asian Americans: Contemporary Issues and Trends*, 169–198. Thousand Oaks, Calif.: Sage.

Shinagawa, Larry. 1993. "The Asian and Pacific Islander multicultural phenomenon in the United States." In United States Bureau of the Census. *Research Conference on Undercounted Ethnic Populations: Abstract*, 5–6. Washington, D.C.

Shinagawa, Larry, and Gin Yong Pang. 1988. "Intraethnic, interethnic, and interracial marriages among Asian Americans in California." *Berkeley Journal of Sociology* 13:95–114.

Shipler, David K. 1997. *A Country of Strangers: Blacks and Whites in America*. New York: Knopf.

Shipman, Pat. 1994. *The Evolution of Racism: Human Differences and the Use and Abuse of Science*. New York: Simon & Schuster.

* Shohat, Ella, and Robert Stam. 1994. *Unthinking Eurocentrism: Multiculturalism and the Media*. New York: Routledge, 1994.

Shokeid, Moshe. 1988. *Children of Circumstances: Israeli Emigrants in New York*. Ithaca: Cornell University Press.

Shortridge, Barbara G., and James R. Shortridge. 1998. *The Taste of American Place: A Reader on Regional and Ethnic Foods*. Lanham, Md.: Rowman & Littlefield.

Showstack, Gerald L. 1990. "Perspectives in the study of American Jewish ethnicity." *Contemporary Jewry* 11, 1:77–89.

Sills, David L., ed. 1968–70. *International Encyclopedia of the Social Sciences*. 19 vols. New York: Macmillan and Free Press.

Silverman, Carol. 1991. "Strategies of ethnic adaptation: The case of Gypsies in the United States." In Stephen Stern and John Allan Cicala, eds. *Creative Ethnicity: Symbols and Strategies of Contemporary Ethnic Life*, 107–121. Logan: Utah State University Press.

Silverman, Deborah Anders. 1997. "Dyngus Day in Polish American communities." In Tad Tuleja, ed. *Usable Pasts: Traditions and Group Expressions in North America*, 68–95. Logan: Utah State University Press.

Sinke, Suzanne. 1992. "Tulips are blooming in Holland, Michigan: Analysis of a Dutch-American festival." In Michael D'Innocenzo and Josef P. Sireman, eds. *Immigration and Ethnicity: American Society — "Melting Pot" or "Salad Bowl"?*, 3–14. Westport, Conn.: Greenwood Press.

Skeldon, Ronald. 1997. *Migration and Development: A Global Perspective*. Harlow, U.K.: Longman.

Small, Cathy A. 1997. *Voyages: From Tongan Villages to American Suburbs*. Ithaca: Cornell University Press.

Smith, Anthony D. 1981. *The Ethnic Revival*. Cambridge: Cambridge University Press.

———. 1987. *The Ethnic Origins of Nations*. New York: Blackwell.

Smith, Christopher J. 1995. "Asian New York: The geography and politics of diversity." *International Migration Review* 29, 1:59–84.

Smith, Robert. 1993. *"Los Ausentes Siempre Presentes": The Imagining, Making and Politics of a Transnational Community between New York City and Ticuani, Puebla*. Institute of Latin American and Iberian Studies, Papers on Latin America no. 27. New York: Columbia University.

Smith, Tom W. 1980. "Ethnic measurement and identification." *Ethnicity* 7:78–95.

Smolicz, J. J. 1997. "Australia: From migrant country to multicultural nation." *International Migration Review* 31,1:171–186.

Snipp, C. Matthew. 1986. "Who are American Indians? Some observations about the perils and pitfalls of data for race and ethnicity." *Population Research and Policy Review* 5:237–257.

Sollors, Werner. 1980. "Literature and ethnicity." In Stephan Thernstrom, ed., *Harvard Encyclopedia of American Ethnic Groups*, 647–665. Cambridge: Harvard University Press.

———. 1986. *Beyond Ethnicity: Consent and Descent in American Culture*. New York: Oxford University Press.

*————. 1989. "Introduction: The invention of ethnicity." In Sollors, ed. *The Invention of Ethnicity*, viii–xx. New York: Oxford University Press.

Sontag, Deborah. 1998. "A Mexican town that transcends all borders." *New York Times*, 21 July, A1, A16–17.

Sontag, Deborah, and Celia W. Dugger. 1998. "The new immigrant tide: A shuttle between worlds." *New York Times*, 19 July, A1, A28–30.

* Spickard, Paul R. 1989. *Mixed Blood: Intermarriage and Ethnic Identity in Twentieth-Century America*. Madison: University of Wisconsin Press.

Spoonley, Paul. 1988. *Racism and Ethnicity*. Auckland: Oxford University Press.

Sreenivasan, Sreenath. 1996. "As mainstream papers struggle, the ethnic press is thriving." *New York Times*, 22 July, D-7.

Stafford, Susan Buchanan. 1987. "The Haitians: The cultural meaning race and ethnicity." In Nancy Foner, ed. *New Immigrants in New York*, 131–158. New York: Columbia University Press.

Stansfield, Charles A. 1996. "Heritage tourism: The role of epitome districts." Paper presented at the annual meeting of the Association of American Geographers, Charlotte, April 1996.

Stathakis, Paula M. 1996. "Locational analysis of Greek-owned restaurants in Charlotte, N.C., and Columbia, S.C." In D. Gordon Bennett, ed. *Snapshots of the Carolinas: Landscapes and Cultures*, 37–42. Washington: Association of American Geographers.

Staub, Shalom. 1989. *Yemenis in New York City: The Folklore of Ethnicity*. Philadelphia: Balch Institute Press.

Steele, C. Hoy. 1982. "The acculturation/assimilation model in urban Indian studies: A critique." In Norman R. Yetman and Steele, eds. *Majority and Minority: The Dynamics of Race and Ethnicity in American Life*, 282–289. 3rd ed. Boston: Allyn & Bacon.

Stein, Howard F., and Robert F. Hill. 1977. *The Ethnic Imperative: Examining the New White Ethnic Movement*. University Park: Pennsylvania State University Press.

Steinberg, Stephen. 1989. *The Ethnic Myth: Race, Ethnicity, and Class in America*. Rev. ed. Boston: Beacon Press.

Stephan, Cookie White, and Walter G. Stephan. 1989. "After intermarriage: Ethnic identity among mixed-heritage Japanese-Americans and Hispanics." *Journal of Marriage and the Family* 51:507–519.

Stephen, Lynn. 1993. "Weaving in the fast lane: Class, ethnicity, and gender in Zapotec craft commercialization." In June Nash, ed. *Crafts in the World Market: The Impact of Global Exchange on Middle American Artisans*, 25–57. Albany: SUNY Press.

Stern, Gail F., ed. 1984. *Ethnic Images in Advertising*. Philadelphia: Balch Institute for Ethnic Studies.

Stokes, Martin. 1994. "Introduction: Ethnicity, identity and music." In Stokes, ed. *Ethnicity, Identity and Music: The Musical Construction of Place*, 1–27. Oxford: Berg.

Sung, Betty Lee. 1990. "Chinese American intermarriage." *Journal of Comparative Family Studies* 21: 337–352.

Suro, Robert. 1993. "'At home' in two cultures." *Washington Post*, 6 June, A1, 26, 27.

Suttles, Gerald D. 1968. *The Social Order of the Slum: Ethnicity and Territory in the Inner City*. Chicago: University of Chicago Press.

Sutton, Constance R. 1987. "The Caribbeanization of New York City and the emergence of a transnational socio-cultural system." In Sutton and Elsa M. Chaney, eds. *Caribbean Life in New York City: Sociocultural Dimensions*, 15–30. Staten Island: Center for Migration Studies of New York.

*————. 1992. "Transnational identities and cultures: Caribbean immigrants in the United States." In Michael D'Innocenzo and Josef P. Sirelman, eds. *Immigration and Ethnicity: American Society — "Melting Pot" or "Salad Bowl"?*, 231–241. Westport, Conn.: Greenwood Press.

Sutton, Constance R, and Susan R. Makiesky-Barrow. 1987. "Migration and West Indian racial and ethnic consciousness." *Caribbean Life in New York City: Sociocultural Dimensions*. Staten Island: Center for Migration Studies of New York.

Sutton, Gordon F., Ronald Chilton, and Kathryn Tingos. 1993. "Minority counts and minority preferences." In David C. Whitford, comp. *1993 Research Conference on Undercounted Ethnic Population. Proceedings*, 313–343. Washington: United States Bureau of the Census.

Swearingen, Christine M., and James M. Perrin. 1977. "Foreign medical graduates in rural primary care: The case of western New York State." *Medical Care* 15, 4: 331–337.

Takaki, Ronald. 1989. *Strangers from a Different Shore: A History of Asian Americans*. Boston: Little, Brown.

Taylor, Charles. 1989. *Sources of the Self: The Making of the Modern Identity*. Cambridge: Harvard University Press.

Taylor, D. Garth, Paul B. Sheatsley, and Andrew M. Greeley. 1978. "Attitudes toward racial integration." *Scientific American* 238, 6: 42–49.

Taylor, Timothy D. 1997. *Global Pop: World Music, World Markets*. New York: Routledge.

TeSelle, Sallie, ed. 1974. *The Rediscovery of Ethnicity*. New York: Harper & Row.

*Thernstrom, Stephan, ed. 1980. *Harvard Encyclopedia of American Ethnic Groups*. Cambridge: Harvard University Press.

*Thompson, Richard H. 1989. *Theories of Ethnicity: A Critical Appraisal*. Westport, Conn.: Greenwood Press.

Tindall, George Brown. 1967. *The Ethnic Southerners*. Baton Rouge: Louisiana State University Press.

Tinker, John N. 1973. "Intermarriage and ethnic boundaries." *Journal of Social Issues* 29:49–66.

Toll, William. 1991. "Jewish intermarriage and the urban West: A religious context for cultural change." In *Women, Men and Ethnicity: Essays on the Structure and Thought of American Jewry*, 150–162. Lanham, Md.: University Press of America.

Tricarico, Donald. 1984. "The 'new' Italian-American ethnicity." *Journal of Ethnic Studies* 12:75–93.

Trotter, Richard W. 1981. "Charters of panethnic identity: Indigenous American Indians and immigrant Asian Americans." In C. F. Keyes, ed. *Ethnic Change*, 271–305. Seattle: University of Washington Press.

Tsai, Yung-mei, and Lee Sigelman. 1982. "The community question: A perspective from national survey data — the case of the USA." *British Journal of Sociology* 33:579–588.

Tseng, Yen-Fen. 1995. "Beyond 'Little Taipei': The development of Taiwanese immigrant businesses in Los Angeles." *International Migration Review* 29, 1:33–58.

Tuan, Yi-Fu. 1996. "Home and world, cosmopolitanism and ethnicity: Key concepts in contemporary human geography." In Ian Douglas, Richard Hugget, and Mike Robinson, eds. *Companion Encyclopedia of Geography*, 939–951. New York: Routledge.

Ungar, Sanford J. 1995. *Fresh Blood: The New American Immigrants*. New York: Simon & Schuster.

United States Department of Labor. 1991. *A Report on the Glass Ceiling Initiative*. Washington, D.C.: Government Printing Office.

United States Immigration and Naturalization Service. 1993. *1992 Statistical Yearbook of the Immigration and Naturalization Service*. Washington, D.C.: Government Printing Office.

Upton, Dell. 1996."Ethnicity, authenticity, and invented tradition." *Historical Archaeology* 30:1–7.

*Van den Berghe, Pierre. 1984. "Ethnic cuisine: Culture in nature." *Ethnic and Racial Studies* 7:387–397.

Van Esterik, Penny. 1982. "Celebrating ethnicity: Ethnic flavor in an urban festival." *Ethnic Groups* 4:207–228.

Van Reenan, Antanas J. 1990. *Lithuanian Diaspora: Königsberg to Chicago*. Lanham, Md.: University Press of America.

Vecoli, Rudolph J. 1970. "Ethnicity: A neglected dimension of American history." In Herbert J. Bass, ed. *The State of American History*, 70–88. Chicago: Quadrangle Books.

———. 1985. "Return to the melting pot: Ethnicity in the United States in the Eighties." *Journal of American Ethnic History* 5,1 : 8–20.

Velikonja, Joseph. 1993. "Ethnicity, geography and communication." Paper presented at the IGU Symposium on Ethnicity and Geography, Ljubljana, September 1993.

Veysey, Laurence. 1979. "The autonomy of American history reconsidered." *American Quarterly* 31 : 455–477.

Vigilante, Joseph. 1972. "Ethnic affiliation, or, kiss me, I'm Italian." *Social Work* 17 : 10–20.

Vinitzky-Seroussi, Vered. 1998. *After Pomp and Circumstance: High School Reunion as an Autobiographical Occasion*. Chicago: University of Chicago Press.

Vlach, John M. 1976. "The shotgun house: An African architectural legacy." *Pioneer America* 8 : 47–56; 57–70.

Wacquant, Loïc J. D. 1994. "The new urban color line: The state and fate of the ghetto in post-Fordist America." In Craig Calhoun, ed. *Social Theory and the Politics of Identity*, 231–276. Oxford: Blackwell.

Waksberg, Joseph, and Gary A. Tobin. 1984. *A Demographic Study of the Jewish Community of Greater Washington 1983*. Bethesda, Md.: United Jewish Appeal Federation of Greater Washington, D.C.

Waldinger, Roger. 1987. "Beyond nostalgia: The old neighborhood revisited." *New York Affairs* 10, 1 : 1–12.

*———. 1989. "Immigration and urban change." *Annual Review of Sociology* 15 : 211–232.

———. 1996. *Still the Promised City? African-Americans and New Immigrants in a Postindustrial New York*. Cambridge: Harvard University Press.

Waldinger, Roger, and Howard Aldrich. 1990. "Trends in ethnic businesses in the United States." In Waldinger, Aldrich, and Robin Ward. *Ethnic Entrepreneurs: Immigrant Business in Industrial Societies*, 49–78. Newbury Park, Calif.: Sage.

Waldinger, Roger, and Mehdi Bozorgmehr. 1996. "The making of a multicultural metropolis." In Waldinger and Bozorgmehr, eds. *Ethnic Los Angeles*, 3–37. New York: Russell Sage Foundation.

Waldinger, Roger, and Michael Lichter. 1996. "Anglos: Beyond ethnicity?" In Waldinger and Mehdi Bozorgmehr, eds. *Ethnic Los Angeles*, 413–441. New York: Russell Sage Foundation.

Waldinger, Roger, David McEvoy, and Howard Aldrich. 1990. "Spatial dimensions of opportunity structures." In Waldinger, Aldrich, and Robin Ward. *Ethnic Entrepreneurs: Immigrant Business in Industrial Societies*, 106–130. Newbury Park, Calif.: Sage.

Waldinger, Roger, and Yenfen Tseng. 1992. "Divergent diasporas: The Chinese communities of New York and Los Angeles compared." *Revue Européenne des Migrations Internationales* 8, 3 : 91–104.

Waldrop, Judith. 1993. "The newest Southerners." *American Demographics* 15, 10 : 38–43.

Walko, M. Ann. 1989. *Rejecting the Second Generation Hypothesis: Maintaining Estonian Ethnicity in Lakewood, New Jersey*. New York: AMS Press.

Wallerstein, Immanuel. 1991. "The national and the universal: Can there be such a thing as world culture?" In Anthony D. King, ed. *Culture, Globalization and the World-System: Contemporary Conditions for the Representation of Identity*, 91–105. Binghamton: SUNY–Binghamton.

Walzer, Michael. 1980. "Pluralism: A political perspective." In Stephan Thernstrom, ed. *Harvard Encyclopedia of American Ethnic Groups*, 781–787. Cambridge: Harvard University Press.

Ward, David. 1989. *Poverty, Ethnicity, and the American City, 1840–1925: Changing Conceptions of the Slum and Ghetto*. Cambridge: Cambridge University Press.

Ware, Caroline F. 1931."Ethnic communities." In Edwin R. A. Seligman, ed. *Encyclopedia of the Social Sciences*, vol. 5, 607–613. New York: Macmillan.

Warner, R. Stephen. 1998. "Immigration and religious communities in the United States." In Warner and Judith G. Wittner, eds. *Gatherings in Diaspora: Religious Communities and the New Immigration*, 3–34. Philadelphia: Temple University Press.

* Warner, W. Lloyd, and Leo Srole. 1945. *The Social Systems of American Ethnic Groups*. New Haven: Yale University Press.

Warren, Robert, and Ellen Percey Kraly. 1985. *The Elusive Exodus: Emigration from the United States*. Washington: Population Reference Bureau.

* Waters, Mary C. 1990. *Ethnic Options: Choosing Identities in America*. Berkeley: University of California Press.

———. 1994. "Ethnic and racial identities of second-generation black immigrants in New York City." *International Migration Review* 28 : 795–819.

———. 1996. "Optional ethnicities: For whites only?" In Silvia Pedraza and Ruben C. Rumbaut, eds. *Origins and Destinies: Immigration, Race, and Ethnicity in America*, 444–454. Belmont, Calif.: Wadsworth.

Webber, M. M. 1964. "Order in diversity: Community without propinquity." In L. Wingo, Jr., ed. *Cities and Space: The Future Use of Urban Land*, 23–54. Baltimore: Johns Hopkins University Press.

Weed, Perry L. 1973. *The White Ethnic Movement and Ethnic Politics*. New York: Praeger.

Wei, William. 1993. *The Asian American Movement*. Philadelphia: Temple University Press.

Weibel-Orlando, Joan. 1991. *Indian Country, L.A.: Maintaining Ethnic Community in Complex Society*. Urbana: University of Illinois Press.

Weiss, Richard. 1979. "Ethnicity and reform: Minorities and the ambience of the depression years." *Journal of American History* 66:566–585.

Western, John. 1992. *A Passage to England: Barbadian Londoners Speak of Home*. Minneapolis: University of Minnesota Press.

White, Michael J. 1987. *American Neighborhoods and Residential Differentiation*. New York: Russell Sage Foundation.

White, Michael J., Ann E. Biddlecom, and Shenyang Guo. 1993. "Immigration, naturalization, and residential assimilation among Asian Americans in 1980." *Social Forces* 72, 1:93–117.

White, Otis. 1993. "This could end the rural doctor shortage." *Medical Economics* 70, 23:42–44, 47–49.

Whitford, David C., comp. 1993. *1993 Research Conference on Undercounted Ethnic Populations. Proceedings*. Washington: United States Bureau of the Census.

Wilkie, Richard W., and Jack Trager, 1991. *Historical Atlas of Massachusetts*. Amherst: University of Massachusetts Press.

Williams, Brett. 1988. *Upscaling Downtown: Stalled Gentrification in Washington, D.C.* Ithaca: Cornell University Press.

Williams, Jerry R. 1982. *And Yet They Come: Portuguese Immigration from the Azores to the United States*. Staten Island: Center for Migration Studies.

Williams, John Alexander. 1989. "Italian-American identity, old and new: Stereotypes, fashion, and ethnic revival." *Folklife Center News* 11:4–7.

Williams, Raymond. 1983. *Keywords: A Vocabulary of Culture and Society*. Rev. ed. New York: Oxford University Press.

Williams, Raymond Brady. 1988. *Religions of Immigrants from India and Pakistan: New Threads in the American Tapestry*. Cambridge: Cambridge University Press.

Wilson, Clint C., II, and Félix Gutiérrez. 1995. *Race, Multiculturalism, and the Media: From Mass to Class Communication*. Thousand Oaks, Calif.: Sage.

Winant, Howard. 1995. "Dictatorship, democracy, and difference: The historical construction of racial identity." In Michael Peter Smith and

Joe R. Feagin, eds. *The Bubbling Cauldron: Race, Ethnicity, and the Urban Crisis*, 31–49. Minneapolis: University of Minnesota Press.

*Winnick, Louis. 1990. *New People in Old Neighborhoods: The Role of New Immigrants in Rejuvenating New York's Communities*. New York: Russell Sage Foundation.

Woldemikael, Tekle Mariam. 1989. *Becoming Black American: Haitians and American Institutions in Evanston, Illinois*. New York: AMS Press.

Woll, Allen L., and Randall M. Miller. 1987. *Ethnic and Racial Images in American Film and Television: Historical Essays and Bibliography*. New York: Garland.

Wong, Bernard. 1992. "Chinese-Americans." In John D. Buenker and Lorman A. Ratner, eds. *Multiculturalism in the United States: A Comparative Guide to Acculturation and Ethnicity*, 193–214. Westport, Conn.: Greenwood Press.

Wong, David W. S. 1998a. "Spatial patterns of ethnic integration in the United States." *Professional Geographer* 50 : 13–30.

———. 1998b. "A geographical analysis of multiethnic households in the United States." Paper submitted to the *International Journal of Population Geography*.

Wong, Morrison G. 1989. "A look at intermarriage among the Chinese in the United States in 1980." *Sociological Perspectives* 32 : 87–107.

Wong, Sau-ling Cynthia. 1993. *Reading Asian American Literature: From Necessity to Extravagance*. Princeton: Princeton University Press.

Wood, Joseph. 1997. "Vietnamese American place making in Northern Virginia." *Geographical Review* 87 : 58–72.

Wright, Lawrence. 1994. "One drop of blood." *New Yorker*, 25 July, 46–55.

Wu, William F. 1982. *The Yellow Peril: Chinese Americans in American Fiction 1850–1940*. Hamden, Conn.: Archon.

Wynar, Lubomyr R. 1975. *Encyclopedic Directory of Ethnic Organizations in the United States*. Littleton, Colo.: Libraries Unlimited.

———. 1988. *Guide to the American Ethnic Press: Slavic and East European Newspapers and Periodicals*. Kent: Kent State University, School of Library Science.

Wynar, Lubomyr R., and Lois Buttlar. 1978. *Guide to Ethnic Museums, Libraries and Archives in the United States*. Kent: Kent State University, School of Library Science.

Wynar, Lubomyr R., and Anna T. Wynar. 1976. *Encyclopedic Directory of Ethnic Newspapers and Periodicals in the United States*. 2d ed. Littleton, Colo.: Libraries Unlimited.

Yancey, William L., Eugene P. Erickson, and Richard N. Juliani. 1976. "Emergent ethnicity: A review and reformulation." *American Sociological Review* 41 : 391–403.

Yang, Jeff, Dina Can, and Terry Hong. 1997. *Eastern Standard Time: A Guide to Asian Influence on American Culture from Astro Boy to Zen Buddhism*. New York: Houghton Mifflin.

* Yinger, J. Milton. 1981. "Toward a theory of assimilation and dissimilation." *Ethnic and Racial Studies* 4 : 249–264.

———. 1985. "Ethnicity." *Annual Review of Sociology* 11 : 151–180.

Young, Crawford. 1993. "The dialectics of cultural pluralism: Concept and reality." In Young, ed. *The Rising Tide of Cultural Pluralism: The Nation-State at Bay?*, 3–35. Madison: University of Wisconsin Press.

Younis, Adele L. 1995. *The Coming of the Arabic-Speaking People to the United States*. Edited by Philip M. Kayal. Staten Island: Center for Migration Studies.

Zack, Naomi, ed. 1995. *American Mixed Race: The Culture of Microdiversity*. Lanham, Md.: Rowman & Littlefield.

Zangwill, Israel. 1911. *The Melting-Pot: Drama in Four Acts*. New York: Macmillan.

Zaniewski, Kazimierz J., and Carol J. Rosen. 1998. *The Atlas of Ethnic Diversity in Wisconsin*. Madison: University of Wisconsin Press.

Zelinsky, Wilbur. 1961. "An approach to the religious geography of the United States: Patterns of church membership in 1952." *Annals of the Association of American Geographers* 51 : 139–193.

———. 1974. "Selfward bound? Personal preference patterns and the changing map of American society." *Economic Geography* 50 : 144–179.

———. 1985. "The roving palate: North America's ethnic restaurant cuisines." *Geoforum* 16 : 51–72.

*———. 1988a. *Nation into State: The Shifting Symbolic Foundations of American Nationalism*. Chapel Hill: University of North Carolina Press.

———. 1988b. "Where every town is above average: Welcoming signs along America's highways." *Landscape* 30 : 1–10.

———. 1990. "Seeing beyond the dominant culture." *Places* 7 : 32–35.

———. 1992. *The Cultural Geography of the United States*. Rev. ed. Englewood Cliffs, N.J.: Prentice-Hall.

Zhou, Min. 1992. *Chinatown: The Socioeconomic Potential of an Urban Enclave*. Philadelphia: Temple University Press.

Zhou, Min, and John R. Logan. 1991. "In and out of Chinatown: Residential mobility and segregation of New York City's Chinese." *Social Forces* 70 : 387–407.

Zunz, Olivier. 1988. "The genesis of American pluralism." *Tocqueville Review* 9 : 201–219.

Zwerin, Michael. 1976. *A Case for the Balkanization of Practically Everyone: The New Nationalism*. London: Wildwood House.

INDEX